The War Inside

The War Inside is a groundbreaking history of the contribution of British psychoanalysis to the making of social democracy, childhood, and the family during World War II and the postwar reconstruction. Psychoanalysts informed understandings not only of individuals, but also of broader political questions. By asserting a link between a real "war outside" and an emotional "war inside," psychoanalysts contributed to an increased state responsibility for citizens' mental health. They made understanding children and the mother–child relationship key to the successful creation of a democratic citizenry. Using rich archival sources, the book revises the common view of psychoanalysis as an elite discipline by taking it out of the clinic and into the war nursery, the juvenile court, the state welfare committee, and the children's hospital. It traces the work of the second generation of psychoanalysts after Freud in response to total war and explores its broad postwar effects on British society.

MICHAL SHAPIRA is Assistant Professor of History and Gender Studies at Tel Aviv University. Her research deals with the domestic, sociocultural, crossnational and imperial legacies of World War II in Britain and beyond.

Studies in the Social and Cultural History of Modern Warfare

General Editor
Jay Winter, *Yale University*

Advisory Editors
David Blight, *Yale University*
Richard Bosworth, *University of Western Australia*
Peter Fritzsche, *University of Illinois, Urbana-Champaign*
Carol Gluck, *Columbia University*
Benedict Kiernan, *Yale University*
Antoine Prost, *Université de Paris-Sorbonne*
Robert Wohl, *University of California, Los Angeles*

In recent years the field of modern history has been enriched by the exploration of two parallel histories. These are the social and cultural history of armed conflict, and the impact of military events on social and cultural history.

Studies in the Social and Cultural History of Modern Warfare presents the fruits of this growing area of research, reflecting both the colonization of military history by cultural historians and the reciprocal interest of military historians in social and cultural history, to the benefit of both. The series offers the latest scholarship in European and non-European events from the 1850s to the present day.

A full list of titles in the series can be found at:
www.cambridge.org/modernwarfare

The War Inside

Psychoanalysis, Total War, and the Making of the Democratic Self in Postwar Britain

Michal Shapira

CAMBRIDGE UNIVERSITY PRESS

CAMBRIDGE
UNIVERSITY PRESS

University Printing House, Cambridge CB2 8BS, United Kingdom

Published in the United States of America by Cambridge University Press, New York

Cambridge University Press is part of the University of Cambridge.

It furthers the University's mission by disseminating knowledge in the pursuit of education, learning, and research at the highest international levels of excellence.

www.cambridge.org
Information on this title: www.cambridge.org/9781107035133

First published 2013

Printing in the United Kingdom by T J International Ltd. Padstow Cornwall

A catalogue record for this publication is available from the British Library.

Library of Congress Cataloguing in Publication data
Shapira, Michal, 1975–
The war inside : psychoanalysis, total war, and the making of the democratic self in postwar Britain / Michal Shapira.
    pages   cm. – (Studies in the social and cultural history of modern warfare)
ISBN 978-1-107-03513-3 (hardback)
1. Psychology – History – Great Britain.   2. Psychoanalysis –
History.   3. Great Britain – History – 20th century.   4. Civilians in war – Trauma –
Great Britain.   5. War victims – Mental health – Great Britain.   6. World War,
1939–1945 – Children – Great Britain.   7. World War, 1914–1918 – Social
and Cultural Aspects – Great Britain.   8. World War, 1939–1945 – Social
and Cultural Aspects – Great Britain.   9. Popular Culture – Great
Britain – History – 20th century.   10. Childhood – History – Great Britain.
I. Title.
RC552.P67S424   2013
616.85'212–dc23

                                                                2013000172

ISBN 978-1-107-03513-3 Hardback

In memory of my relatives who were murdered by the Nazis in 1941–1942 in the area of Eastern Europe where the family had lived for centuries: my great-grandparents, Zelda Fenster (Sussman) (b. 1890, homemaker and farmer), Mayer Yacob Sussman (b. 1877 or 1880, merchant and farmer), and Faiga-Tzipora Just (b. 1871, homemaker); and my great-aunts, Toba (b. 1908, tailor), Eta (b. 1916 [or 1922], tailor), and Rachel Fenster (Sussman) (b. 1923), and Temma Tanenbaum (and her family) (b. 1896, homemaker).

Contents

Illustrations

Acknowledgments

This book was conceived, researched, and written in New York, London, and Tel Aviv and I feel deeply grateful to have the support of my family, friends, colleagues, and mentors as well as the funding of a number of institutions. My first thanks are to my professors in Israel, where I had many fine teachers. Throughout the years, I particularly enjoyed the kind support of Billie Melman, a truly committed British historian and dedicated mentor, as well as that of Moshe Sluhovsky and Igal Halfin. At Rutgers University, my sincere gratitude goes to my dissertation advisor Bonnie G. Smith for her scholarly rigor, continuous and level-headed moral support, and the widest academic horizons. For me, she is the intellectual model of a historian. I also thank John R. Gillis, Joan W. Scott, Seth Koven, Temma Kaplan (the first to talk with me about Anna Freud), Donald R. Kelley, and Keith Wailoo, and truly everyone else in the history department. Special thanks go to Elizabeth Grosz for her intellectual guidance and real kindness. I thank everyone at Amherst College for my first full-time assistant professorship and for their collegiality, intellectual support, and assistance, especially Catharine Epstein, Margaret Hunt, and Bob Bezucha. At Barnard College and Columbia University, I was fortunate to have the best colleagues, mentors, and friends, and I am particularly indebted to Lisa Tiersten, Deborah Valenze, Samuel Moyn, Mark Mazower, Joel Kaye, Carl Wennerlind, Deborah Coen, Nara Milanich, Tarik Amar, Celia Naylor, Herb Sloane, and Gergely Baics. Each and every one of them has been so helpful at many different levels, and I have the deepest gratitude to all. I wholeheartedly thank Susan Pedersen for her generosity and ongoing support, her meticulous approach to the study of history, and our conversations on British studies and beyond.

I am grateful for the financial support of the history departments and graduate schools at Rutgers, Tel Aviv, Cambridge, Princeton, and Cornell Universities. I also thank the Andrew W. Mellon Foundation (for a travel fellowship and a British history seminar fellowship at

Columbia University) and the American Psychoanalytic Association (for the Fund for Psychoanalytic Research and for their general Fellowship Program). The completion of this book was also assisted by an ACLS New Faculty Fellow award with support of the Andrew W. Mellon Foundation, and by the Thomas Arthur Arnold Fund, Tel Aviv University, and AFTAU. Thanks to all my co-fellows of the Mellon seminar of British history at Columbia University run by Susan Pedersen, the fellows of the American Psychoanalytic Association, the organizers of and participants in the Kandersteg Seminar of NYU's Remarque Center, and those of the School of Criticism and Theory at Cornell. Thanks also to the organizers of various seminars and conferences who invited me to present my work and to my students throughout the years. Chapter 1 was published as "The Psychological Study of Anxiety in the Era of the Second World War," *Twentieth Century British History* (January 25, 2012) and is here reproduced with changes with the journal's permission. Chapter 4 was published in a different format as "Psychoanalysts on the Radio: Domestic Citizenship and Motherhood in Postwar Britain," in Joanna Regulska and Bonnie G. Smith (eds.), *Women and Gender in Postwar Europe: From Cold War to European Union* (New York: Routledge, 2012), pp. 71–86, and appears here with Routledge's permission.

Different scholars and individuals helped me in a variety of ways throughout my work on this book. I apologize for any accidental omissions from this list. I thank Daniel Pick, James Vernon, Peter Mandler, Michael Roper, Atina Grossmann, Chris Otter, Chris Waters, the late Elisabeth Young-Bruehl, Dagmar Herzog, Guy Ortolano, Veronika Fuechtner, Dror Wahrman, Nikolas Rose, Denise Riley, Barbara Taylor, Sally Alexander, Matt ffytche, Lewis Aron, George Makari, Lesley Cladwell, Deborah Thom, Lisa Appignanesi, John Forrester, Jay Winter, Dori Laub, the late Tony Judt, Katherine Fleming, Élisabeth Roudinesco, Deborah Cohen, Alison Winter, Dominick LaCapra, Omer Bartov, Tara Zahra, Eileen Gillooly, Emma Winter, Robert Mills, Paddy Scannell, Jean Seaton, David Hendy, Siân Nicholas, Kristin Skoog, Suzanne Franks, Kate Murphy, Stephen Frosh, Alan Bass, Eduardo Duniec, Nellie Thompson, José Brunner, Amalia Ziv, Orly Lubin, Susan Grayzel, Rebecca Scales, Katherine McGilly, Judith Surkis, Teresa Delcorso, Dawn Ruskai, Rhea Cabin, Sully Rios, Eran Rolnik, Lawrence Black, Stephen Brooke, and Laura Lee Downs. Thanks to Yael Lev for help with the bibliography. Special thanks to everyone at Cambridge University Press, especially editor Michael Watson, Karen Anderson Howes, Chloe Dawson, Beata Mako, and to the readers of the typescript for their suggestions.

The staff at the Rutgers, Barnard, Columbia, and Amherst libraries, New York Public Library, NYU's Bobst and Law Libraries, the British National Archives at Kew, and the British Library was of great help. I am also grateful to the teams at the archives of the British Institute of Psychoanalysis, the Wellcome Institute, the Tavistock Institute, the Centre for Crime and Justice Studies, the Freud Museum, the Wiener Library, the BBC Written Archives Centre (Trish Hayes in particular), the Institute of Education at the University of London, and the Kluge Research Fellowship staff at the Library of Congress. Analyst Elizabeth Spillius, Honorary Archivist of the Melanie Klein Collection, provided crucial help.

My love and thanks to my longtime friends with whom I just could not do without and to whom I owe so much: Eyal Shpringer, Keren Cohen, Daniela Hochbaum, Roy Flechner, Daniel Ussishkin, and Nir Cohen. Efrat Ginot, On Barak, Yofi Tirosh, Jill Payne, Sheli Landau, Tariq Jaffer, Smadar Zilber, Ilana Szobel, Einav Zilber, Ifat Shpringer, Nomi Borenstein, Jonathan Shulman, Ronnie Regev, Anat Elberg, Rotem Tashach, Miri Rozmarin, Gary Ross, Richard Stuart Perkins, Jonathan Cohen, Rona Yona, Ilana Nesher, Michael Weinman, Samara Heifetz, Zohar Kfir, Boaz Neumann, Jennifer Manion, Carla MacDougall, Sandrine Sanos, Charles Upchurch, Alla Gaydukova, Carolyn Weiss, Yuval Shaul, Marc Matera, Ellen Boucher, Dina Fainberg, Anna Fishzon, Odelia Silver, Meredith TenHoor, Ben Kafka, Shirli Sela-Levavi, Penny Sinanoglou, Tal Zalmanovich, Yaelle Kayam, and Assaf Snir provided fine friendship as well.

The book is dedicated to my family – old and new. It was written in an indirect dialogue with my extended Shapira, Just, Fenster, and Falkon family's twentieth-century Jewish history in Europe, Canada, and Israel. My love and thanks to all family members. My special gratitude and love to my parents, Tzippi and Gadi, and my sister Mor Shapira for giving me unconditional support, and to my niece Maya for bringing much joy and laughter to life. I also thank with love Ely, Shoshana, and Nat Levin. In April 2002, I was extraordinarily lucky to meet Jessica Levin on a New York subway platform. Since then, she has shared everything with me, traveled with me between London, New York, and Tel Aviv, and has been constantly patient, calm, and supportive. She has always been the first to listen to my ideas and I am fortunate to have had her read and comment on my drafts. I could not have done anything without her love, encouragement, companionship, and humor (as well as movie viewing and occasional pop music appreciation). She makes life so much brighter and good in ways more than words here can express.

Introduction: the war inside

During World War II and the brutal experience of German attacks against civilians on the home front, Britain underwent a consequential, yet unstudied, development. This total war elevated British psychoanalysis to a role not enjoyed anywhere else in the world. Under the shock of bombing and evacuation, exiled continental analysts such as Anna Freud (Sigmund Freud's daughter) and Melanie Klein and native analysts such as John Bowlby (the "British Dr. Spock") and Donald Winnicott were called upon to treat a diverse group of men, women, and children. Children occupied a privileged position in this expert work. They came to be seen, on the one hand, as vulnerable and in need of protection; on the other hand, as anxious, aggressive subjects requiring control. The war proved a decisive moment for the history of psychoanalysis, and, in turn, its evolving theories and practices helped produce new expectations for selfhood, citizenship, mental health, and the emergent social democracy. While scholars of World War I have highlighted the effects of shellshock on culture and society, we have yet to understand how the brutalities of World War II, and the theories of selfhood developed under its guise, reshaped postwar Britain. By examining together both the ideas and practices of child psychoanalysts and their wide impact on public opinion and social policy, *The War Inside* reconstructs this essential social and cultural legacy of World War II. While looking at analyst–patient interactions in the clinic, significantly, this book takes the history of psychoanalysis beyond the couch. It follows psychoanalytic practice in a variety of social and institutional settings such as the war nursery, the juvenile court, the state committee, the radio, and the hospital. Spanning the periods before, during, and after the war, it reveals how psychoanalysis became important for much public and welfare-state thinking about democracy, mental health, childhood, and the family.

Psychoanalytic experts made the understanding of children and the mother–child relationship key to the successful creation of social democracy in two ways. First, by asserting a link between a real "war outside" and an emotional "war inside" individuals, analysts helped make the state increasingly responsible for the mental health and family life of citizens. Second, rather than being an elite science confined to the private clinic (as the discipline has been characteristically described by many historians), psychoanalysis informed new and changing understandings not only of individuals and their health, but also of broader political questions in the age of mass violence and mass anxiety. Psychoanalysts sought to understand the underlying emotional mechanisms that led to violence, so as to advance human well-being in ways that could secure the future of democracy. They targeted the child's psyche as a site for expert knowledge and mediated ideas regarding citizenship, democracy, and the family that influenced both citizens and welfare legislation. They contributed in important ways to the reshaping of modern British society.

The War Inside is located at the intersection of history and psychoanalysis while placing the relationship between self and expert culture in a historical frame. Historians have rarely looked at psychoanalysts other than Sigmund Freud as social actors in their cultures, leaving the histories of psychoanalytic movements' influence on their European societies still largely uncharted.[1] Even psychoanalysts who have studied the theoretical ideas of their predecessors have seldom situated them historically or explored their social impact using archival sources.[2] Unlike previous histories of psychoanalysis, this book approaches the second generation of psychoanalysts after Sigmund Freud as actors in specific political and social circumstances. While Bowlby, Winnicott, Klein, and Anna Freud were prominent then and today, this group also included psychoanalysts who are now long forgotten such as Edward Glover, Melitta Schmideberg (Klein's daughter), and Kate Friedlander. These psychoanalysts all provided an important secular account of inner life, and they described a world much wider than that of privileged patients lying on the couch. Integrally tied to the tumultuous history of war and violence in the twentieth century, this generation of analysts forged a new project of thinking about the place of aggression in democratic societies.

---

[1] See Élisabeth Roudinesco, *Jacques Lacan & Co.: A History of Psychoanalysis in France, 1925–1985* (University of Chicago Press, 1990).

[2] This is also true for the biographies that are available on these experts. For example, see Suzan van Dijken, *John Bowlby: His Early Life, A Biographical Journey into the Roots of Attachment Theory* (New York: Free Association Books, 1998); Raymond Dyer, *Her Father's Daughter: The Work of Anna Freud* (New York: J. Aronson, 1983); Brett Kahr, *D. W. Winnicott: A Biographical Portrait* (London: Karnac, 1996); Elisabeth Young-Bruehl, *Anna Freud: A Biography* (New York: Summit, 1988).

During the 1930s, Britain became home both to native psychoanalysts and to many Jewish refugees fleeing the Nazis and continental anti-Semitism. Out of the once-flourishing psychoanalytic societies in Europe, only London remained as a real hub and a center for a unique intellectual diaspora.[3] Yet Britain was no safe haven. The anticipated attacks on and the actual ruthless bombardment of British civilians during World War II made it a unique setting for this generation of psychoanalysts to explore the experiences of violence, especially upon children. The cataclysm of the war and the projected and real human suffering allowed experts in the psychological science of anxiety, trauma, and aggression to step forward with solutions and address some of the main dilemmas of the time. They offered new ways of looking at psychological trauma and the self. They provided novel interpretations of the civilian condition under shelling, and of human relations more broadly.

For Anna Freud and her staff in London's Hampstead War Nurseries, for example, the war brought work with a large number of dislocated children, or "infants without families."[4] Among these young war victims were children whose homes had been destroyed, children who were sent back from evacuation, and "Tube Sleepers," i.e., children who had been taken to Underground shelters at night and lost their ability to sleep. Anna Freud and her staff aimed to repair the perceived mental damage already caused to the children, to prevent what was seen as possible future disorder due to mother–child separation, and to conduct research on the psychological conditions deemed necessary for the normal development of the child. During wartime, Anna Freud's skills as an organizer as well as a theorist were deployed. She and her staff ran several houses in London and its vicinity. The detailed reports that she wrote during the nights of air raids provide a rich testimony of the work of psychoanalysts with children under fire. The war allowed her not only to develop her theories, but also to put them into practice and to reevaluate them for dissemination in peacetime. Along with the ideas of other psychoanalysts, such work shaped a generation of parents and policymakers.

The War Inside explores the contribution of British psychoanalysis to a certain psychologization of the self and the child as these two separate but

---

[3] See Gregorio Kohon (ed.), *The British School of Psychoanalysis: The Independent Tradition* (New Haven: Yale University Press, 1986), pp. 24–50; Riccardo Steiner, "It Is a New Kind of Diaspora," *Int. R. Psycho-Anal.* Vol. 16 (1989), pp. 35–72.

[4] Anna Freud and Dorothy Burlingham, *Infants without Families: Reports of the Hampstead Nurseries, 1939–1945*, vol. III of *The Writings of Anna Freud*, 8 vols. (New York: International Universities Press, 1967–1981).

interconnected phenomena developed during the mid twentieth century.[5] Following the evolving ideas of psychoanalysts and their actual work, it looks at the world that made psychoanalysts, and how they in return shaped it as well.[6] Collaborating with other experts, state officials, and citizens, analysts became involved in the war effort and in the postwar development of the welfare state, influencing social policy, law, popular culture, and public opinion. What kind of understanding of childhood and of the self emerged from the intensity of a total war experience? How did experts comprehend emotions of fear and anxiety and conceptualize outbreaks of violence? What were the long-term consequences of home-front brutality on postwar society? The book engages with these broad questions and adds to the still-underdeveloped literature on the larger and long-lasting sociocultural effects of World War II as a total war that killed more civilians than soldiers worldwide.[7]

The War Inside provides examples of a tighter interaction between psychoanalysis and politics than scholars have previously offered.[8]

---

[5] Indeed, general studies of the history of psychology in twentieth-century Britain are strikingly scarce. Mathew Thomson recently provided the main exception, yet his study deliberately looks beyond the particular history and influence of psychoanalysis. It is important to note, however, that when discussing mid-century developments Thomson uses the writings of many analysts without emphasizing this as such. And indeed analysts themselves did not always emphasize their distinctiveness but rather identified as psychologists, experts, or psychiatrists. It is important then to follow their work beyond obvious locales such as the British Psycho-Analytical Society (though this location was important as well), and to see how they participated in larger debates on crime, evacuation, and wartime anxiety etc. in order to show their broad impact. The history told here is therefore not limited to psychoanalytic institutions or high-minded debates, but looks at the deep impact of a set of psychoanalytic discourses on different realms of British society in ways and degrees that have remained unrecognized by scholars. See Mathew Thomson, *Psychological Subjects: Identity, Culture, and Health in Twentieth-Century Britain* (Oxford University Press, 2006). See also Leslie S. Hearnshaw, *A Short History of British Psychology, 1840–1940* (London: Methuen & Co., 1964).

[6] See George Makari, *Revolution in Mind: The Creation of Psychoanalysis* (New York: HarperCollins, 2008), p. 2. Broad intellectual histories of the Western self rarely look at it in detailed context. For example: see Jerrold Seigel, *The Idea of the Self: Thought and Experience in Western Europe since the Seventeenth Century* (Cambridge University Press, 2005); and Charles Taylor, *Sources of the Self: The Making of the Modern Identity* (Cambridge University Press, 1989). See also the more detailed studies of Dror Wahrman, *The Making of the Modern Self: Identity and Culture in Eighteenth-Century England* (New Haven: Yale University Press, 2004); and James Hinton, *Nine Wartime Lives: Mass Observation and the Making of the Modern Self* (Oxford University Press, 2010).

[7] The chief exceptions are Sonya Rose, *Which People's War?: National Identity and Citizenship in Britain, 1939–1945* (Oxford University Press, 2003); Susan Grayzel, *At Home and Under Fire* (Cambridge University Press, 2012); and Tara Zahra, *The Lost Children: Reconstructing Europe's Families after World War II* (Cambridge, MA: Harvard University Press, 2011). Cf. the American context: William M. Tuttle, *"Daddy's Gone to War": The Second World War in the Lives of America's Children* (Oxford University Press, 1995).

[8] Cf. Denise Riley, *War in the Nursery: Theories of the Child and Mother* (London: Virago, 1983). Though I see my study as complementary to Riley's superb work, her views about

Psychoanalysis was not only high theory; it also had very real implications for public debate and social policy. It should be looked at as knowledge and practice operating in relation to particular sociocultural settings and, in this sense, one could say that each country has "its own psychoanalysis."[9] Like historians of revolutionary Russia and the Soviet Union who study Marxism as a lived civilization, I make psychoanalysis here the object rather than the subject of study, that is, psychoanalysis is not a theory that I use in my investigation, but an intellectual constellation that I examine.[10] Indeed, British psychoanalysis was bound to the rationale of a specific understanding of social democracy in a period of war and peace. Through the focus on different versions of separation theories, stressing the need for a constant bond between children and their caretakers, psychoanalysis offered influential answers to questions regarding the possibility of harmonious and cooperative human relations in the

psychoanalysis and its lack of impact on the question of daytime war nurseries for working mothers could not be extended to other realms, for example, to that of child hospitalization. Furthermore, scholars such as Carl Schorske and William McGrath believed that, in fin-de-siècle Vienna, the analytic turn to the inner world of the psyche was a sign of political disillusionment or was counterpolitical. I show how in twentieth-century Britain the analytic focus on "the war inside" was profoundly political. For a survey of literature on this topic, see Joy Damousi and Mariano Ben Plotkin (eds.), *Psychoanalysis and Politics: Histories of Psychoanalysis under Conditions of Restricted Political Freedom* (Oxford University Press, 2012), pp. xi–xvi.

[9] As suggested by Edith Kurzweil, *The Freudians: A Comparative Perspective* (New Haven: Yale University Press, 1989). See also Damousi and Ben Plotkin (eds.), *Psychoanalysis and Politics*. Damousi and Ben Plotkin make the argument that psychoanalysis is able to flourish under forms of political authoritarianism. They argue against those who believe that a certain level of political and social freedom is a precondition for a successful implantation of psychoanalysis. In non-European countries, for example, in Latin American cases of restricted political freedom in the 1930s to the 1970s, psychoanalytic practice did flourish. Damousi and Ben Plotkin notice that in Europe, in the conditions that emerged in fascist Italy, Nazi Germany, Franco's Spain, and the Soviet Union, psychoanalysis almost ceased to exist. But they argue that the situation was more nuanced and that, curiously, the practice did survive even in Europe, with much compromise to accommodate the new regimes and with the removal of the Jewish analysts. They therefore offer to eradicate the distinction between "real" and "false" psychoanalysis, and to look instead at psychoanalysis as it "really existed" in different contexts. I believe that whether or not a modified and racist form of psychoanalysis could still be called "psychoanalysis" is an open question. My goal here, however, is to map the encounter of psychoanalysis with British democracy, emphasizing that even the working of the discipline under favorable conditions of social freedom took specific forms.

[10] Igal Halfin, *From Darkness to Light: Class, Consciousness, and Salvation in Revolutionary Russia* (University of Pittsburgh Press, 2000); Jochen Hellbeck, *Revolution on my Mind: Writing a Diary under Stalin* (Cambridge, MA: Harvard University Press, 2009). For historians who employ psychoanalytic theory, see Peter Gay, *The Bourgeois Experience: From Victoria to Freud*, 5 vols. (New York: W. W. Norton, 1999); Lyndal Roper, *Oedipus and the Devil: Witchcraft, Sexuality and Religion in Early Modern Europe* (London: Routledge, 1994); Dominick LaCapra, *Representing the Holocaust: History, Theory, Trauma* (Ithaca: Cornell University Press, 1994); Lynn Hunt, *The Family Romance of the French Revolution* (Berkeley: University of California Press, 1992).

twentieth century. Psychoanalysis helped make the modern democratic self in Britain.

Analysts operated within a historically specific configuration of childhood which they in turn helped to shape. Some background on the history of childhood and the early development of psychoanalysis as well as child psychoanalysis in Britain in the time leading up to our period is therefore essential. Indeed, as Philippe Ariès long ago established, childhood has a history.[11] In Britain, the modern concept of the child evolved mainly during the eighteenth and nineteenth centuries. Industrialization and urbanization, a new emphasis on the domestic sphere, and debates about compulsory schooling and child labor all contributed to a new awareness of childhood as a period detached from the world of adults. In contrast with previous eras, childhood was seen (at least in theory) as a period of education, and less of labor, and the child was often perceived as innocent and dependent. By the later nineteenth and early twentieth centuries, as the health of children was gradually seen as vital to the future of the nation and empire, their bodies were increasingly subject to state intervention.[12] Child psychology, too, became a distinct area of study in the late decades of the nineteenth century and since then the child has also been increasingly made an object of scientific research and psychological inquiry.[13] After World War I in particular, a time when psychology and psychoanalysis developed as disciplines, the mental health and psychology of children gradually became the focus of expert discussion.[14] While psychoanalysis contributed to that shift "from bodies to minds," its key role came right before, during and after World War II as it reified the child's psyche and parental relationships as central to the normal development of the future adult citizen.[15]

---

[11] Philippe Ariès, *Centuries of Childhood: A Social History of Family Life* (New York: Vintage, 1962).
[12] Harry Hendrick, *Child Welfare: Historical Dimensions, Contemporary Debate* (Bristol: Policy Press, 2003); Hugh Cunningham, *Children and Childhood in Western Society since 1500* (New York: Longman, 1995); Jane Lewis, *The Politics of Motherhood: Child and Maternal Welfare in England, 1900–1939* (London: Croom Helm, 1980).
[13] See Riley, *War in the Nursery*, pp. 42–79.
[14] Hendrick, *Child Welfare: Historical*, pp. 149–176.
[15] Cathy Urwin and Elaine Sharland, "From Bodies to Minds in Childcare Literature: Advice to Parents in Inter-War Britain," in Roger Cooter (ed.), *In the Name of the Child: Health and Welfare in England, 1880–1940* (New York: Routledge, 1992), pp. 174–199; Nikolas Rose, *The Psychological Complex: Psychology, Politics and Society in England, 1869–1939* (London: Routledge and Kegan Paul, 1985); Nikolas Rose, *Governing the Soul: The Shaping of the Private Self* (London: Routledge, 1999, 2nd edn.). The literature on the history of the child in twentieth-century Britain is still a limited one, and scholars have concentrated their investigations on the period before World War II. See Jane Lewis, *The Politics of Motherhood*; Deborah Dwork, *War Is Good for Babies and Other Young*

It was between the 1930s and 1960s that psychoanalysis actually attained a significant social role in the specific historical making of a desired, functioning, "healthy" democratic individual self.[16]

Psychoanalysis was first introduced in Britain in the 1890s through the work of F. W. H. Myers, the founder of the British Society for Psychical Research, and through the writing of physician Mitchell Clarke and the psychologist-sexologist Havelock Ellis. Psychoanalysis had already attracted wide interest among medical professionals, anthropologists, and artists before World War I, but it increased greatly during the war and its aftermath, partially in relation to the phenomenon of shellshocked soldiers.[17] The 1910s and 1920s were years of growth for British psychoanalysis mobilized in part by the enthusiasm of Ernest Jones (1879–1958), a Welsh neurologist and psychiatrist who started practicing psychoanalysis as early as 1905.[18] Together with David Eder, a Jewish physician, early Zionist, and socialist,[19] Jones founded the London Psycho-Analytical Society on October 30, 1913; it became the British Psycho-Analytical Society (BPAS) on February 20, 1919, after Jones dissolved the original Society. The International Psycho-Analytical Press and the *International Journal of Psycho-Analysis* were established in 1920. The London Clinic of Psycho-Analysis was founded in 1924 and the Institute of Psycho-Analysis was set up in the same year.[20] By 1925,

---

Children: A History of the Infant and Child Welfare Movement in England, 1898–1918 (New York: Tavistock Publications, 1987); Carolyn Steedman, *Strange Dislocations: Childhood and the Idea of Human Interiority, 1780–1930* (Cambridge, MA: Harvard University Press, 1995); Ellen Ross, *Love and Toil: Motherhood in Outcast London, 1870–1918* (Oxford University Press, 1993). The literature on the child in the period of the 1930s–1960s is minimal. It is discussed in a survey by Harry Hendrick and more extensively in Denise Riley's book on psychological theories of mother and child: Hendrick, *Child Welfare: Historical*; Riley, *War in the Nursery*, pp. 42–80. See also Harry Hendrick, *Child Welfare: England 1872–1989* (New York: Routledge, 1994), pp. 149–176.

[16] See Nikolas Rose, *The Psychological Complex*, p. 190. My book therefore concentrates on these years and covers the period just before World War II and the years immediately following it, bridging existing historical scholarship that studies the war and postwar periods as separate eras.

[17] After the Great War, an interest in the occult and psychoanalysis often went hand in hand. See Alex Owen, *The Place of Enchantment: British Occultism and the Culture of the Modern* (University of Chicago Press, 2004), p. 231.

[18] Ernest Jones, "Reminiscent Notes on the Early History of Psychoanalysis in English Speaking Countries," *Int. J. Psycho-Anal.* Vol. 26 (1945), pp. 8–9.

[19] Edward Glover, "Eder as a Psychoanalyst," in Joseph Burton Hobman (ed.), *David Eder: Memoirs of a Modern Pioneer* (London: Victor Gollancz, 1945), pp. 88–116.

[20] The Society, Clinic, and the Institute were in the same house at 96 Gloucester Place, London, until 1950, when the Institute moved to Mansfield House, New Cavendish Street in London. During the first fifty years of its existence about 3,090 patients had been psychoanalyzed for little or no fee under the auspices of the Clinic. See Pearl King, "Background and Development of the Freud–Klein Controversies in the British Psycho-Analytical Society," in Pearl King and Riccardo Steiner (eds.), *The Freud–Klein*

there were fifty-four members in the Society from diverse professional disciplines – a characteristic of the British branch of psychoanalysis ever since. The press challenged the Society's legitimacy at that time because it included both medical and lay colleagues, but Jones was instrumental in securing its professional status.[21] In the interwar years, shellshock doctors, such as W. H. R. Rivers, used Freud's theories very selectively, yet helped nevertheless with their dissemination.[22] Oxford and Cambridge were centers of informal cultural interest in Freud.[23] In addition, the Bloomsbury Group, despite its complex relationship with psychoanalysis, contributed too to its spread during those years. From the Bloomsbury Group, James and Alix Strachey became psychoanalysts at the BPAS, as did Adrian Stephen, the younger brother of Virginia Woolf, and his wife Karin, a niece of Bertrand Russell. The first collected works of Freud were produced by Leonard and Virginia Woolf's Hogarth Press. After World War II they were published as the Standard Edition, the official English translation edited by James Strachey.[24]

Sigmund Freud himself did not directly treat child patients.[25] However, it was among psychoanalysts, and those in Britain in particular,

Controversies, 1941–1945 (New York: Routledge, 1991), pp. 10–11; Riccardo Steiner, "Jones, Ernest (1879–1958)," in *International Dictionary of Psychoanalysis* (Detroit: Macmillan Reference Books, 2005).

[21] With his help, the British Medical Association recognized in 1929 that psychoanalysts are legitimate, special, and separate kinds of practitioners. See King, "Background," pp. 12–13; "Report of Psycho-Analysis Committee," *Supplement to the British Medical Journal* (29 Jun. 1929), pp. 262–270.

[22] For example, W. H. R. Rivers, "Freud's Psychology of the Unconscious," *Lancet* Vol. 189 (16 Jun. 1917), pp. 912–914. The psychiatrist Henry Butter Stoddart also had a role in spreading psychoanalysis through his textbook *Mind and its Disorders: A Text-Book for Students and Practitioners*, as did Bernard Hart in his popular textbook *The Psychology of Insanity*.

[23] See Laura Cameron and John Forrester, "Tansley's Psychoanalytic Network: An Episode out of the Early History of Psychoanalysis in England," *Psychoanalysis & History* Vol. 2 (2000), pp. 189–256. John Maynard Keynes was also exposed to psychoanalysis at Cambridge and through the Bloomsbury Group: see Edward Winslow, "Keynes and Freud: Psychoanalysis and Keynes' Account of the 'Animal Spirits of Capitalism,'" *Social Research* Vol. 53 (1986), pp. 549–578.

[24] Kohon (ed.), *The British School*, pp. 24–50; Sally Alexander, "Psychoanalysis in Britain in the Early Twentieth Century: An Introductory Note," *History Workshop Journal* Vol. 45 (Spring 1998), pp. 135–143; Perry Meisel and Walter Kendrick (eds.), *Bloomsbury/Freud: The Letters of James and Alix Strachey, 1924–1925* (New York: Basic Books, 1985); King, "Background"; Pearl King, "Biographical Notes on the Main Participants in the Freud–Klein Controversies in the British Psycho-Analytical Society, 1941–1945," in King and Steiner (eds.), *The Freud–Klein Controversies*, pp. ix–xxv; Barbara Caine, "The Stracheys and Psychoanalysis," *History Workshop Journal* Vol. 45 (1998), pp. 145–169.

[25] The exception is the indirect analysis of "Little Hans" conducted by the boy's father with Freud's help: see Sigmund Freud, "Analysis of a Phobia in a Five-Year-Old Boy [1909]," SE/PEP Vol. X, pp. 3–149.

that the most innovative and influential theories of child psychology were developed.[26] The 1920s and 1930s were major decades for interest in child psychoanalysis and in new theories of the mother–child relationship. Work done by child-study pioneers Melanie Klein in Berlin and Anna Freud in Vienna contributed to the growing attention paid to psychoanalytic theories. Both women ended up in London; while Klein moved there in 1926 under more favorable political conditions, Anna Freud, along with her father and some of her extended family, fled there as Jewish refugees in 1938. Early theoretical disputes between Anna Freud and Klein began during the interwar period and would reach a climax during World War II in what became known as "the Controversial Discussions" in the BPAS. During the 1920s and 1930s, native British psychoanalysts such as Jones, Susan Isaacs, Joan Riviere, and others showed early interest in child psychoanalysis (and Klein's ideas in particular), thus shaping the BPAS to have a particular interest in childhood. No isolated elitists, psychoanalysts were instrumental in popularizing psychoanalysis and helped raising public interest in it among teachers and parents.[27] Barbara Low, for example, a teacher and founding member of the BPAS, wrote a psychoanalytic book for mass consumption that ran into several editions starting in 1920. Low's many public lectures appealed equally to a wide circle of educators.[28] Isaacs, an educational psychologist and psychoanalyst, also known by her pseudonym "Ursula Wise," introduced psychoanalytic ideas in her popular columns for parents published in the journals *Nursery World* and *Home and School* between 1929 and 1940 and in additional widely circulated books on childcare.[29]

Indeed, during the interwar years "Psycho-Analysis became a craze as well as a serious study."[30] It was widely discussed among the general educated public in a wave of popular books that enjoyed considerable

---

[26] Riley, *War in the Nursery*, p. 72.

[27] Cf. Kurzweil, *The Freudians*, p. 31. Sigmund Freud's own writings began appearing in English in 1909 (New York) and 1913 (Britain), with different translations spanning several editions. The Controversial Discussions are examined in Ch. 3.

[28] Barbara Low, *Psycho-Analysis: A Brief Account of the Freudian Theory* (London: Allen & Unwin, 1920).

[29] See press clippings of the DC/SI Papers of Susan Isaacs Collection at the Archives of the Institute of Education, London. The most popular texts were Susan Isaacs, *The Nursery Years: The Mind of the Child from Birth to Six Years* (London: Routledge, 1929); Susan Isaacs, *Intellectual Growth of Young Children* (London: Routledge, 1930); Susan Isaacs, *Social Development in Young Children* (London: Routledge, 1933).

[30] Charles Mowat, *Britain between the Wars 1918–1940* (London: University of Chicago Press, 1955), p. 214. See also R. D. Hinshelwood, "Psychoanalysis in Britain: Points of Cultural Access, 1893–1918," *Int. J. Psycho-Anal.* Vol. 76 (1995), pp. 135–151.

success, and in magazines and novels.[31] Journalists in the national press started using psychoanalytic vocabulary about inner life, regression, and emotional conflicts.[32] At the end of 1922, the *Daily News* wrote, "We are all psycho-analysts now, and know that apparently innocent dreams are the infallible signs of the most horrible neurosis; and so we suppress our nightly divagations as feverishly as a murderer tries to remove blood from his shirt-front."[33] In 1923, the *New Statesman* used very similar words: "We are all psychoanalysts now. That is to say that it is as difficult for an educated person to neglect the theories of Freud and his rivals as it would have been for his father to ignore the equally disconcerting discoveries of Darwin."[34] In addition to pursuing psychoanalytic treatment of individuals, during the interwar years, analysts offered popular public lectures and study groups to medical and psychology students, social workers, teachers, parents, and those interested in party politics.[35] Among fiction writers and dramatists, some knowledge of psychoanalysis became essential.[36] Despite the existence of opposition to the new discipline from the church, the medical establishment, and some members of the public, by 1939, W. H. Auden was able to publish a memorial poem for Sigmund Freud saying, "if often he was wrong and, at times, absurd, to us he is no more a person now but a whole climate of opinion."[37] Thus, even before World War II, psychoanalysis in various guises had a

[31] For accounts focused on the popularization of psychoanalysis in Britain during World War I and the interwar period, see Sandra Ellesley, "Psychoanalysis in the Early Twentieth Century: A Study in the Popularisation of Ideas" (unpublished Ph.D. thesis, University of Essex, 1995); Dean Rapp, "The Reception of Freud by the British Press: General Interest and Literary Magazines, 1920–1925," *Journal of the History of the Behavioral Sciences* Vol. 24 (1988), pp. 191–201; Dean Rapp, "The Early Discovery of Freud by the British General Educated Public, 1912–1919," *Social History of Medicine* Vol. 3, No. 2 (1990), pp. 217–243; Graham Richards, "Britain on the Couch: The Popularization of Psychoanalysis in Britain, 1918–1940," *Science in Context* Vol. 13 (2000), pp. 183–230.
[32] Ted Bogacz, "War Neurosis and Cultural Change in England 1914–1922: The Work of the War Office Committee of Enquiry into 'Shell-Shock,'" *Journal of Contemporary History* Vol. 24 (1989), p. 234.
[33] Quoted in Robert Graves and Alan Hodge, *The Long Weekend: A Social History of Great Britain 1918–1939* (London: Faber & Faber, 1940), p. 103.
[34] Quoted in Samuel Hynes, *A War Imagined: The First World War and English Culture* (New York: Atheneum, 1991), p. 366.
[35] Archives of the British Psycho-Analytical Society (hereafter ABPAS): Annual Reports for 1933, 1934, and 1935; and Decennial Report, May 1926–May 1936, pp. 20–21. Analysts wrote and lectured on issues as diverse as psychoanalysis and education, childrearing, fashion, design, nursing, birth control, sterilization, war, art, film, crime, masculinity and femininity, and theatre.
[36] On Graham Greene's psychoanalytic treatment, see Norman Sherry, *The Life of Graham Greene*, Vol. I, *1904–1939* (New York: Penguin, 1989), pp. 92–116.
[37] W. H. Auden, "In Memoriam Sigmund Freud," *Another Time: Poems* (London: Faber & Faber, 1940), p. 118.

stronghold in British society, one that would strengthen during the war and as psychoanalysts contributed considerably to discussions on anxiety and fear among civilians. Psychoanalytic terminology became commonplace. More importantly, it opened up novel possibilities for diagnosing new kinds of personal and sociopolitical issues.[38] When Sigmund Freud was asked in 1923 whether he would like to "psycho-analyze Europe in the hope of finding a cure for her ills," he replied, "I never take a patient to whom I can offer no hope."[39] But as the twentieth century progressed, Freud himself and his followers in Britain developed ideas that engaged directly and indirectly with the political questions of the time.

Indeed, to understand the development of the BPAS during the mid twentieth century, it is also necessary to position it against the background of international dynamics and the ascent of Nazism. Hitler's rise to power in 1933 and the Nazi occupations of neighboring states threatened not only the lives of Jewish psychoanalysts but also the continuation of psychoanalysis in Europe. Anti-Semitic Nazi policies and legal restrictions put the predominantly Jewish psychoanalytic societies in Berlin, Munich, Frankfurt, Budapest, Prague, and Vienna in the greatest danger. A complex, internationally collaborative rescue operation between psychoanalytic societies developed during the 1930s in order to help their members flee the continent. The number of psychoanalysts forced to migrate and those who came to their assistance reached about seven hundred. Most of those seeking safety migrated to London and New York, while others went to Palestine, South Africa, South America, and Australia. Thus the mid twentieth century saw the creation of an intellectual diaspora that placed psychoanalysts in high concentration at one side of the prospective fighting forces of World War II.[40] The first wave of refugee analysts to Britain came primarily from Berlin early in the 1930s. The second wave hailed mostly from Vienna toward the end of the decade.[41]

While still in Vienna, Sigmund Freud's family was spared direct violence, but it was soon obvious that psychoanalysis in this city had no

[38] Richards, "Britain on the Couch," p. 201. Richards claims (pp. 204–205) that, while in the early 1920s psychoanalysis made some serious inroads into the mainstream, during the 1930s this trend petered out and the BPAS became more insular and less utopian in its vision. I will show evidence to the contrary.
[39] Quoted in Nathan G. Hale, *Freud and the Americans*, Vol. II, *The Rise and Crisis of Psychoanalysis in the United States, 1917–1985* (New York: Oxford University Press, 1995), p. 78.
[40] Steiner, "It Is a New Kind of Diaspora," p. 38. See also Adam Limentani, "The Psychoanalytic Movement during the Years of the War (1939–1945) According to the Archives of the IPA," *Int. R. Psycho-Anal.* Vol. 16 (1989), pp. 3–13.
[41] Steiner, "It Is a New Kind of Diaspora"; Peter Gay, *Freud: A Life for our Time* (New York: Norton, 1988), pp. 611–651.

future under Nazi rule. The Nazis did, however, pay visits to Freud's home, and the Gestapo arrested Anna Freud for interrogation. The threat was immense. Anna and her brother, Martin Freud, had even contemplated the possibility of taking poison were they to be tortured. The Nazis associated international organizations with international communism and, after a long day at the Gestapo headquarters, Anna managed to persuade her interrogators that the International Psychoanalytical Association – the organization that Sigmund Freud founded in 1910 – was a purely scientific body, not a political one. The incident, however, convinced the Freud family of the necessity to leave Austria despite Sigmund Freud's old age (he was 82) and bad health. Unlike some of the non-Jewish members of the Psychoanalytic Society in Berlin who decided to collaborate with the Nazis, most members of the Vienna Psychoanalytic Society decided to migrate with Freud.[42] An intense international diplomatic effort to move the Freud family to London took place. Anna Freud's communication with Ernest Jones in London was instrumental to the cause. Together they arranged for immigration documents. Interestingly, in January 1938, the British government circulated a confidential report on leading personalities in Austria. This report mentioned that two years earlier the government had sent a letter of congratulations to Sigmund Freud for his birthday, yet at the same time had ensured that no mention of this letter should appear in the press.[43] Jones, however, described how when he approached Samuel Hoare, then the home secretary, Hoare was very sympathetic to the idea that a refuge in Britain would be offered to Freud, his family, and a number of colleagues.[44] By June 6, 1938, Sigmund Freud's closest family landed in their new homeland. Once in London, the Freud family was warmly accepted as psychoanalysis was already a contested yet thriving, recognized field.[45] It is important, however, to note that due to Nazi regulations and immigration policies in Britain, not all of Sigmund Freud's extended family could leave with him. He was forced to leave behind his four elderly sisters in Vienna, believing that no one would hurt

[42] Gay, *Freud*, pp. 611–651. See also Geoffrey Cocks, *Psychotherapy in the Third Reich: The Goering Institute* (Oxford University Press, 1985).

[43] National Archives (hereafter NA)/FO/371/22320. See also NA/FO/371/22321.

[44] Cf. Ernest Jones, "Sigmund Freud 1865–1939," *Int. J. Psycho-Anal.* Vol. 21 (1940), p. 3; Anna Freud, "Personal Memories of Ernest Jones [1979]," in *Writings of Anna Freud*, Vol. VIII, pp. 346–353.

[45] For example, the *British Medical Journal* wrote, "The medical profession of Great Britain will feel proud that their country has offered an asylum to Professor Freud, and that he has chosen it as his new home": quoted in Ernest Jones, *Sigmund Freud: Life and Work*, 3 vols., vol. III, *1919–1939* (New York: Basic Books, 1957), p. 229; ABPAS: Annual Reports for 1937 and 1938.

women in their seventies and eighties who had no political affiliation. After the war, however, a letter from the Red Cross informed Anna Freud that the sisters had all been deported by the Nazis out of Vienna and murdered.[46]

Other Jewish psychoanalysts beyond Freud's family had to overcome immigration difficulties because as liberal professionals and as doctors they needed to demonstrate an economic necessity for their work in Britain.[47] While Jones was helpful in the rescue of refugees and used his contacts with all the various embassies, the Home Office, and the Foreign Office, he also made decisions that were based on his preference for specific analysts. Wilhelm Reich, for example, who mixed psychoanalysis with Marxism and with radical sexual theories in ways that were deemed to dangerously politicize psychoanalysis, was regarded as a *persona non grata*.[48] Nevertheless, Britain was more welcoming to lay analysts without medical backgrounds than was the United States. According to Jones, the Home Office approved all his requests for entry for lay analysts.[49] The active BPAS, made up of native analysts such as Ernest Jones, Edward Glover, Susan Isaacs, Barbara Low, Sylvia Payne, John Rickman, Joan Riviere, John Bowlby, Donald Winnicott, and Ella Freeman Sharpe, was then joined in the 1930s by exiled analysts such as Paula Heimann, Kate Friedlander, and Eva Rosenfeld from Berlin and Anna Freud, Wilhelm and Hedwig Hoffer, Klara Frank, Karl Weiss, Edward and Grete Bibring, Robert and Jenny Wälder, Otto and Salomea Isakower, and Ernst and Marianne Kris from Vienna.[50] Hans Foulkes escaped from Frankfurt, where during the 1930s psychoanalysts had had a fruitful exchange with sociologists in the Marxist-oriented Institute for Social Research. After Melanie Klein moved to London, she was followed by her daughter, Melitta Schmideberg, with her husband Walter – both also psychoanalysts.[51] Indeed, the immigration

---

[46] Young-Bruehl, *Anna Freud*, pp. 279–280. Others tied to the analytic world also suffered under the Nazis. German-Jewish analyst Edith Jacobson, for example, was imprisoned by the Gestapo after she refused to denounce a former patient of hers. She later managed to escape.

[47] See Louise London, *Whitehall and the Jews, 1933–1948: British Immigration Policy, Jewish Refugees and the Holocaust* (Cambridge University Press, 2003).

[48] Steiner, "It Is a New Kind of Diaspora."

[49] Eran Rolnik, *Osei Nefashot: Im Freud le'Eretz Yisrael 1918–1948* (Tel Aviv: Am Oved, 2007 [in Hebrew]), pp. 150–158.

[50] The final three couples in this list left during the war for the USA. While in Britain, Ernst Kris worked with the BBC on analyzing Nazi propaganda. Wilhelm Stekel fled from Vienna to Britain in 1938 but committed suicide in 1940.

[51] ABPAS: Annual Reports, Vols. I–III; Ministry of Heath – Neurosis Survey Questionnaire, ABPAS/G10/BD/F02/10. Michael Balint and Barbara Lantos escaped from Budapest while Hilde Maas and Hans Thorner came from Munich. I concentrate on analysts working out of London, especially as the city was the center for those

influx profoundly changed the BPAS. Unlike the psychoanalytic societies on the continent that were predominantly Jewish, the British Society had mainly comprised middle-class Christian professionals prior to the refugees' arrival. By 1939, the number of continental analysts in the British Society totaled thirty-nine, a third of all members in the British group that year.[52] The war years brought great creativity to many psychoanalysts as they provoked many to respond in practice and in theory to the extreme political developments.[53]

Sigmund Freud's death in London on September 23, 1939, at the outbreak of World War II, symbolizes a new chapter in the history of British psychoanalysis, one of new opportunities, debates, and political-social commitments to be continued in the postwar period. At the beginning of World War II, most second-generation analysts were still in the early to middle stages of their careers. The bombing of cities and the experience of evacuation offered them an abundance of work with civilians and caused a shift in the nature of their profession that crystallized earlier interwar developments.[54] Before the war began, British analysts had already

interested in child psychoanalysis. Others worked outside London. Ronald Fairburn, for example, worked in isolation in Edinburgh, while S. H. Foulkes worked in Exeter, and Balint worked from Manchester (and later London).

[52] Rolnik, *Osei Nefashot*, pp. 150–158. During the 1920s, many British analysts and trainees visited the continent and formed connections with the analysts there.

[53] The predominance of Jews in early continental psychoanalytic circles and the Jewish connections of psychoanalysis were a source of mixed feelings for analysts, ranging from pride to discomfort about the label "Jewish science" for psychoanalysis as whole. Alongside ongoing concern for securing psychoanalysis's claim to objectivity and universality, with the rise of Nazism and anti-Semitism, there was growing anxiety among both Jewish and non-Jewish analysts about maintaining the non-ideological nature of psychoanalysis. Interestingly, throughout the history of psychoanalysis (even until today), with few exceptions, psychoanalysts have rarely analyzed the phenomena of anti-Semitism. But it is especially curious to note that even in the hybrid analytic Society in London, made of intellectual, medical, and literary non-Jews joined by Jewish refugees, there was silence about anti-Semitism. While analysts discussed the volatility of democracy in relation to the fragility of selfhood, they very seldom referred to anti-Semitism. This is a striking omission given the facts that many of the Jewish analysts knew of those in danger and that the non-Jewish analysts were directly involved in the rescue of Jewish analysts. Even when news about the murder of Jews on the continent reached them, they chose not to discuss anti-Semitism as a phenomenon, siding perhaps with the desire to keep psychoanalysis "neutral." The fear for the professional status of this discipline and the desire to maintain distance from Jewishness continued, it seems, even after the war. See Ernest Jones, "The Psychology of the Jewish Question," in Ernest Jones, *Essays in Applied Psycho-Analysis* (London: Hogarth Press, 1951). On psychoanalysis, Jewishness, and anti-Semitism more generally, see Stephen Frosh, *Hate and the "Jewish Science": Anti-Semitism, Nazism, and Psychoanalysis* (London: Palgrave, 2005).

[54] The perceived psychological effects of World War II in general, and on the home front in particular, are understudied when compared to that of World War I. Furthermore, as Sonya Rose notes, despite the central place that evacuation took in the popular memory of

begun to examine how they could contribute as individuals to society and help in dealing with panic and mental breakdown caused by air raids on the civilian population.[55] However, the chief contribution of psychoanalysts during the war beyond their general conceptualization of anxiety and aggression was the work they did with children – the home front's most visible victims.[56]

Like Anna Freud in her War Nurseries, other psychoanalysts – many of whom gradually became famous – joined the war effort in a time of emergency and high concern for the future of democracy. Donald Winnicott also dealt with large numbers of displaced children during the war.[57] He was a consultant psychiatrist for the Government Evacuation Scheme in Oxfordshire and took care of evacuated children, setting up evacuation hostels for them run by psychological "mother" and "father" figures, who disciplined delinquent behavior.[58] This work gave him unique practical experience and the chance to learn not only about treatment but also about residential care and management. Working with child war victims, who experienced what he saw as strong emotional disruptions and displayed delinquent behavior, was a clinical departure for Winnicott, who had limited previous exposure to child delinquency.[59]

John Bowlby's life and career changed as well due to the war. Before the war, he had already been involved with Labour politicians in thinking about the connections between war, aggression, and democracy. He discussed the least harmful way to conduct the evacuation of children and warned against the separation of young children from their mothers. During the war, Bowlby served as an army psychiatrist in a War Neurosis Centre. He later moved to work with children in Cambridge, a town that hosted 6,700 evacuees, and he was involved with Winnicott and Melanie

the war, it is still not extensively analyzed: Sonya Rose, *Which People's War?*, p. 57 n. 124. The best existing studies are: John Welshman, *Churchill's Children: The Evacuee Experience in Wartime Britain* (Oxford University Press, 2010); Richard Titmuss, *Problems of Social Policy* (London: HMSO, 1950); and Angus Calder, *The People's War: Britain, 1939–1945* (New York: Pantheon Books, 1969), pp. 35–50.

[55] Pearl King, "Activities of British Psychoanalysts during the Second World War and the Influence of their Inter-Disciplinary Collaboration on the Development of Psychoanalysis in Great Britain," *Int. J. Psycho-Anal.* Vol. 16 (1989), pp. 15–32.

[56] On analysts' work in the British military, see Tom Harrison, *Bion, Rickman, Foulkes and the Northfield Experiments: Advancing on a Different Front* (London: Jessica Kingsley, 2000).

[57] Together with his future wife, the social worker Clare Britton: Joel Kanter (ed.), *Face to Face with Children: The Life and Work of Clare Winnicott* (London: Karnac, 2004).

[58] King, "Background," p. 29.

[59] Kahr, *D. W. Winnicott*, pp. 83–85; Robert Rodman, *Winnicott: Life and Work* (Cambridge, MA: Da Capo Press, 2003), pp. 89–105; A. T. Alcock, "War Strain in Children," *BMJ* Vol. 1 (25 Jan. 1941), p. 124.

Klein in *The Cambridge Evacuation Survey*, edited by Susan Isaacs.[60] Klein
herself continued to see adult and child patients throughout the war. She
analyzed their interest in current events as a psychological preoccupation
with their private "Hitler inside." Anna Freud and her staff's many
war-related tasks also involved the treatment of young orphans from a
Nazi concentration camp in a shelter arranged at Bulldogs Bank, south of
London. This humanitarian project served as an unusual experiment for
psychoanalysts in trying to instill democratic values in children after a
period that was murderous without precedent.[61]

Building on the war's increased opportunities for community involvement, child psychoanalysts in Britain continued to combine practical and
theoretical work with public commitment during the postwar period.
They used radio, popular magazines, and other forums to disseminate
their ideas throughout society. Anna Freud and her circle continued to
work at the new Hampstead Clinic serving the local community.
Winnicott became one of the great popularizers of child psychoanalysis
through nearly sixty BBC Radio broadcasts with advice to parents that
aired from 1939 to 1962, reaching millions of Britons; other analysts were
also invited to broadcast on the BBC regularly. Winnicott continued his
work at Paddington Green Children's Hospital where he had been
involved in some 60,000 mother–child consultations since 1923. In the
postwar period, under the presidency of Edward Glover, psychoanalysts
from the Institute for the Scientific Treatment of Delinquency (ISTD)
claimed to be able to account for "asocial abnormal elements" in the
nation and to help to promote good citizenship and harmonious democratic society. They contributed to the discussion of what was seen as a
wave of juvenile delinquency due to the upheaval of war and the breakup
of families. The ISTD attained a strong position of influence, reaching a
high case-load of patients, delivering popular public lectures, and giving
expert testimony to numerous government committees.[62] Working
during postwar reconstruction at the Tavistock Clinic, Bowlby there
wrote his famous work on the effects of mother and child separation.[63]
He also conducted experiments and film work in the Separation Research
Unit, together with James Robertson, a social worker and a student of
Anna Freud's War Nurseries. These psychoanalysts, and many others, all

[60] Van Dijken, *John Bowlby*, pp. 103–128; Susan Isaacs (ed.), *The Cambridge Evacuation Survey: A Wartime Study in Social Welfare and Education* (London: Methuen, 1941).
[61] Anna Freud and Sophie Dann, "An Experiment in Group Upbringing," in Anna Freud, *Writings*, vol. IV, pp. 163–229.
[62] Edward Glover, "The Roots of Crime," in Edward Glover, *The Roots of Crime* (New York: International Universities Press, 1960), p. 21, n. 1.
[63] Van Dijken, *John Bowlby*, pp. 129–152.

helped establish the importance of children's mental welfare to democracy. Their psychoanalytic work had practical effects on society, significantly changing procedures for child hospitalization and juvenile delinquency, the gendered roles of parents, and the general perception of the child in welfare legislation.

The war and the development of the welfare state posed moral, theoretical, and practical questions for psychoanalysts that reshaped their discipline. As with other human sciences, the evolution of psychoanalysis in Britain did not happen within the walls of academia or among the intellectual elite. It developed as it addressed social problems. Psychoanalysis posited itself as a science of normal mental health, aiming to maximize the abilities of individuals and to minimize their debilitating troubles. It also claimed to be able to solve the problems of the abnormal child, which posed a potential threat to the community.[64]

Psychoanalysts were crucial to describing the kind of selfhood required of democratic citizens during and after the war (and when their writings are read today this fact is rarely remembered). Indeed, we know more about the Soviet, Nazi and fascist selves than we do about the democratic self.[65] Nowadays democracy is often thought of as an abstract political model (one that could be implemented, for example, in different societies emerging out of non-democratic regimes), rather than as a system that changes in relation to specific historical experiences. Our basic notions of a normal self in a democratic society are taken for granted and seen as ahistorical, while in fact they developed in an intense historical period. Indeed, the idea that democracy requires maturity and a certain level of mental stability stemming out of healthy childhood developed in fact in the mid twentieth century, and in Britain in particular. *The War Inside* demonstrates how ideas of childhood, family, and democratic selfhood changed in reaction to the Blitz, the evacuation process, and the experiences of total war in Britain. This is the period in which the question of whether a certain form of government required a specific form of subjectivity (often called "human nature" or "individuality" in the language of the time) was articulated. Thus the search for a stable democracy was tied to discussions about what would be the kind of selfhood suitable for such a regime. From the 1930s, Nazism, fascism, and communism catalyzed a rethinking of democracy as being about more than the liberal

---

[64] These ideas are taken from Nikolas Rose, *The Psychological Complex*, pp. 1–10.

[65] See Igal Halfin, *Terror in My Soul: Communist Autobiographies on Trial* (Cambridge, MA: Harvard University Press, 2003); Hellbeck, *Revolution on my Mind*; Mabel Berezin, *Making the Fascist Self: The Political Culture of Interwar Italy* (Ithaca: Cornell University Press, 2007); Claudia Koonz, *The Nazi Conscience* (Cambridge, MA: Harvard University Press, 2003).

rights of the individual.[66] Further accelerated by the experience of war, by the 1940s, these competing ideologies with their new visions on life, government, society, and selfhood, placed British policymakers under pressure to reshape their vision of democracy.[67] Psychoanalytic experts were part of this process as they called for new socially democratic forms of welfare. Among other channels, it was through psychoanalysis that the ideals of government developed in this time no longer emphasized human rationality, reason, and levelheaded choice. The question instead was how to produce a person fit for democracy, who is able to "stand with civilization and fight against barbarism," and whose base instincts are in check. Addressing the problem of human aggression and anxiety, psychoanalysts hoped, would enable individuals to maintain the right to live and work freely in ways that would propagate a just, peaceful, and democratic society. Psychoanalysts sought to produce new types of democratic selves able to cooperate with one another and repress what analysts saw as their natural aggression and anxiety that had been so foregrounded by the experience of war. The answer to such a challenge, analysts believed, was tied to loving family relations and a healthy childhood. New plans and social policies for a better world, analysts argued, had to take the understanding of the family and of the psychological relations between external and internal aggressive realities seriously, in order to guarantee reconstruction and the maintenance of peace. Thus, while historians often emphasize social and economic principles as the basis of the welfare state, *The War Inside* stresses how contemporary thinking about the welfare state was also mobilized by psychological principles. At the foundation of British social democracy were psychological ideas about who constitutes the healthy individual capable of being a good citizen.[68]

The family and the gendered roles of parents (both the real figures and those imagined by the child) were therefore central to psychoanalysis.[69] The family – and its ability to provide emotional care for children – was seen as essential to secure future social stability. Psychoanalysts contributed to the gendered and heterosexual perception of "motherhood" and "fatherhood." In a period of increased employment for women, they

---

[66] This process had also started earlier.

[67] Mark Mazower, *Dark Continent: Europe's Twentieth Century* (New York: Vintage, 1998).

[68] When looking at expert discussions, the idea here is to place what happened in Britain and the support for the welfare state and social democracy more in conversation with a threatening European context. For a historical scope focusing almost entirely on Britain, see Ross McKibbin, *Parties and People: England, 1914–1951* (Oxford University Press, 2010), Ch. 4 and its bibliography.

[69] See Jane Lewis, *Women in Britain since 1945: Women, Family, Work and the State in the Post-War Years* (Oxford: Blackwell, 1992).

emphasized the idea of full-time motherhood and endless psychological care as important to the development of a normal child, and claimed that maternal deprivation might cause delinquency and social disorder. Fathers, on the other hand, were envisioned as breadwinner companions, ensuring discipline and responsibly cooperating with the state after the disruption of family life during the war.[70] And yet we must look beyond later feminist debates that simply labeled analysts such as Bowlby and Winnicott as anti-feminists, by situating them instead within the prevailing understanding of gender and sexuality at the time.[71]

Without doubt, this generation of psychoanalysts constituted a diverse group whose divisions were reflected in the Controversial Discussions between Anna Freud and Melanie Klein (of less importance to us here as they had limited public significance at the time) as well as between those who saw their practice as a hermeneutic art and those who saw it as science.[72] There were also gender divisions between the male and female analysts in the BPAS; some male analysts with medical degrees stressed the need to conduct research with more scientific methods, thereby criticizing the lay analysts in the society, particularly women (who were, unusually, welcomed into the analytic profession). Yet, taken together, psychoanalytic discourse was remarkably unified and characterized by "forgotten solidarities," as Michel Foucault called them.[73] Its image of the child emphasized his or her vulnerability and the importance of the relationship with the mother, whether real or imaginary. The child was uniformly seen as dependent and in need of care, yet controlled by aggressive urges and acute anxieties that called for direction and restraint. Drawing connections between experiences of early life and the fragility of mental stability and social relations, psychoanalysts collectively helped to create a place for social intervention.

Rather than trying to decide whether psychoanalysts were "right" or "wrong" in their explanations, the present study follows the configuration of notions of the child, the self, and mental health through psychoanalysis and historical events. It explores what emotions, behaviors, and views were highlighted via psychoanalysis, and how this interpretive knowledge

[70] *Ibid.*, pp. 1–26.
[71] Cf. Juliet Mitchell, *Psychoanalysis and Feminism* (New York: Basic Books, 2000 [1974]).
[72] See Ch. 3.
[73] Instead of examining psychoanalytic statements according to their author's identity, it is therefore important to look at them in terms of "what they have in common … their repetition in time and place, the channels by which they are diffused, the groups in which they circulate; the general horizon that they outline for men's thought, the limits that they impose on it": Michel Foucault, *The Archeology of Knowledge* (New York: Routledge, 1972), pp. 141–142; Halfin, *From Darkness*, p. 7.

of the self led people to describe their past, present, and future anew. My interest is in the links that psychoanalytic discourse helped to create between the personal lives of citizens and social democratic order.[74]

The historiography of psychoanalysis in Britain, especially when compared to that of the United States, has remained fragmented and largely unwritten.[75] Historians often see psychoanalysis in Britain as confined within the walls of the BPAS, with its meticulous theoretical debates, or limited to the work of Ernest Jones.[76] Jones was indeed an important actor, yet the development of British psychoanalysis was limited neither to his work nor to that of the BPAS. Rather it included other figures, to be explored here, who operated both inside and, more importantly, outside the BPAS, in their efforts to reach out to other professionals, officials, and the general public.[77] Historians have long assumed that the British were reluctant to accept Freud's radical "continental" theories, foreign to the local mores and empirical traditions.[78] And early twentieth-century British psychoanalysts liked to portray themselves as an attacked minority.[79] However, the little existing revisionist historiography on the interwar period demonstrates that, far from receiving only hostile reactions, psychoanalysis had in fact been discussed considerably in different forums in Britain since the early twentieth century, often in a partially favorable manner.[80] Such revisionist accounts suggest that, although it was smaller in scale, the popularization of psychoanalysis in Britain did not lag behind the United States chronologically or in the quantity of published material,

---

[74] Ian Hacking, *Rewriting the Soul: Multiple Personality and the Sciences of Memory* (Princeton University Press, 1995), pp. 16, 67–68; Peter Miller and Nikolas Rose, "The Tavistock Programme: The Government of Subjectivity and Social Life," *Sociology* Vol. 22, No. 2 (May 1988), p. 176.

[75] See n. 31; Hale, *Freud and the Americans*, Vol. II, and Vol. I, *The Beginnings of Psychoanalysis in the United States, 1876–1917* (New York: Oxford University Press, 1971). See also Peter Mandler, *Return from the Natives: How Margaret Mead Won the Second World War and Lost the Cold War* (New Haven: Yale University Press, 2013).

[76] Jones himself helped establish this idea by providing what was for many years the main reference in the history of psychoanalysis in Britain: Ernest Jones, *Free Associations: Memories of a Psycho-analyst* (New York: Basic Books, 1959). Daniel Pick has now supplied an account on analytic clinical encounters with leading Nazis and psychoanalysts' interpretation of Nazism: Daniel Pick, *The Pursuit of the Nazi Mind: Hitler, Hess, and the Analysts* (Oxford University Press, 2012).

[77] See also Suzanne Raitt, "Early British Psychoanalysis and the Medico-Psychological Clinic," *History Workshop Journal* Vol. 58 (2004), p. 63.

[78] For example, M. J. Clark, "The Rejection of Psychological Approaches to Mental Disorder in Late Nineteenth-Century British Psychiatry," in Andrew Scull (ed.), *Madhouses, Mad-Doctors, and Madmen: The Social History of Psychiatry in the Victorian Era* (Philadelphia: University of Pennsylvania Press, 1981), pp. 271–312.

[79] Glover, "Eder as a Psychoanalyst," p. 93.   [80] See n. 31.

as was previously assumed.[81] Reception grew more widespread in the war's aftermath.

Offering the first broad, interdisciplinary history of British psychoanalysis and its wide social and cultural impact, *The War Inside* draws on published materials alongside a wide range of unexplored archival material and clinical records of psychoanalysts, nurseries, clinics, women's groups, courts, government committees, and the BBC. These were collected from the British Psycho-Analytical Society, the National Archives, the Wellcome Institute, the Tavistock Clinic, the BBC Written Archives, the Wiener Library, King's College, London, the Archives of the Institute of Education at the University of London, the Freud Museum in London, and other locations. The story told here is part of the history of the cultural and social effects of total war and the development of expert culture in the twentieth century.

Chapter 1 draws much needed connections between World War I and World War II, characterizing the entire period as one animated by anxiety. If public focus in the World War I era was on the emotional instability of soldiers and the study of shellshock, during World War II, national interest concentrated on the mental health of civilians and children under aerial bombardment. This chapter contextualizes psychoanalysis alongside the work of medical and lay literature. It shows how civilian fear became an accepted reaction to total war and how expertise shaped the notions of anxiety and human fragility.

Chapter 2 demonstrates how child psychoanalysts contributed considerably to the making of a new understanding of anxiety that called for expert knowledge and care. The chapter portrays the actual work of psychoanalysts before and during the war, especially during child evacuation. It scrutinizes the work both of the BPAS and of individual analysts, and then concentrates on that of Anna Freud and her colleagues' work with London's evacuated children and with Jewish orphans from Europe. Chapter 3 studies the war as it was experienced in the clinic of Melanie Klein, using her extensive and never-before-explored archival clinical records of patients' dreams and thoughts of the Nazis and Hitler. While other psychoanalysts worked in public forums during the war, Klein's efforts were mostly confined to her consulting room, where she developed her influential theories about the child and the relationship between the "war outside" and the "war inside." The claims of psychoanalysts that all modern selves have destructive drives that should be studied and controlled became increasingly widespread in circles of official planners

---

[81] Rapp, "The Early," p. 242.

and the public. Planners started to realize the need to understand the mechanism of mental health and the dynamism of early childhood relationships, in order to prevent a turn to submission to an authoritarian leader.[82]

Chapter 4 shows that their wartime work gave child psychoanalysts a growing public role after the war and that their theories became a dominant way in which individuals made sense of themselves. Concentrating on Winnicott's BBC broadcasts, this chapter examines the relationship between psychoanalysts and the mass media and the popularization of their ideas on the child, the self, a gendered concept of parenting, and democracy.

Chapter 5 investigates the role of psychoanalysts in changing common views and social regulations in relation to delinquency through the influential psychoanalytic ISTD. Going back to the interwar period, and mapping the general history of the ISTD while offering a biographical sketch of its leading luminaries, the chapter tells the story of this important institution for the first time. It demonstrates how psychoanalysis gradually became a leading language of criminology in the mid century, and had far-reaching effects on the lives of law-breakers, the legal and probation systems, the police, and governmental offices. Chapter 6 explores how ISTD psychoanalysts advocated in postwar government committees, such as those on capital punishment or homosexuality and prostitution, that crime should be treated psychologically rather than penalized. These two chapters stress the influence of psychological arguments on welfare legislation, an issue rarely emphasized in the literature on the development of the welfare state.

Chapter 7 studies analytic experiments and films involving hospitalized children. It scrutinizes how Bowlby and his staff at the Separation Research Unit popularized the idea of the importance of the mother–child relationship. Any separation from the mother, they claimed, might harm the mental health of the child. Their scientific films were immensely influential and revolutionized hospital regulations that, early in the century, prohibited or only allowed limited visits to children who might be hospitalized for months without seeing their parents. The chapter explores the long-term effects of the war and the influence of psychoanalysis on social policy, creating a new relationship between the state, the family, and the child.

---

[82] Mathew Thomson, "Before Anti-Psychiatry: 'Mental Health' in Wartime Britain," in Marijke Gijswijt-Hofstra and Roy Porter (eds.), *Cultures of Psychiatry and Mental Health Care in Postwar Britain and the Netherlands* (Amsterdam: Rodopi, 1998), pp. 43–59.

The War Inside locates psychoanalysis within the context of broader debates about the meaning of democracy and the need to deal with aggression in the age of catastrophe and total war. It aims to rehabilitate the place of psychoanalysis in the shift from a democracy based on rights to one which, to a greater extent, penetrated social and familial life. It examines ideas on the self in their historical contexts and looks at expert practice alongside its social and political effects. The work of the second generation of psychoanalysts after Freud, I argue, was one of the key, if overlooked, avenues through which World War II and its traumas were processed and transformed into new understandings as intimate as selfhood and child–parent relations, and as public as democracy and the welfare state in Britain.

1   The psychological study of anxiety: from World War I to World War II

Atrocities against civilians were at the center of World War II. The war made civilians a legitimate target for violence and turned modern cities into battlefields.[1] In Britain, Nazi aerial bombing subjected millions of people to terror, destruction, and loss. These attacks brought mass evacuation from cities, affecting almost a third of the country's population. During the first month of the Blitz, September 1940, as many as 5,730 civilians were killed and 10,000 seriously injured.[2] On the whole, more than 43,000 civilians lost their lives to bombs, and some 17,000 died in the remaining years of the war; 86,000 civilians were seriously injured and 150,000 were slightly injured. Almost 4 million houses were damaged or destroyed.[3] London suffered more than half of the total damage in Britain, with fifty-seven consecutive nights of bombing at the beginning of the Blitz. Indeed, the war transformed the material realities of daily life for large numbers of civilians in ways no less dramatic, and at times more so, than for those serving in the military.[4]

However, despite the significant toll of casualties and massive rupture of social life, the impact of the war on the British home front was far less extensive than had been projected before hostilities actually began. Throughout the interwar period, British government administrators, journalists, novelists, social scientists, and psychological experts had predicted tens of thousands of casualties, as well as millions of cases of civilians suffering from mass panic, fear, and anxiety in the event of Nazi air attacks on the home front. During the 1930s, the possibility of a new

---

[1]   Causing unprecedented devastation, the conflict took the lives of more civilians worldwide than soldiers. In Britain, "not until two years of war had passed did the number of civilians killed fall below the total of fatalities among soldiers and airmen": Richard Titmuss, *Problems of Social Policy* (London: HMSO, 1950), pp. 335–336.

[2]   Juliet Gardiner, *Wartime: Britain 1939–1945* (London: Headline, 2004), p. 294.

[3]   Titmuss, *Problems*, pp. 330–331, 335, 343; Angus Calder, *The People's War: Britain 1939–1945* (New York: Pantheon Books, 1969), pp. 35, 223–227.

[4]   As Jose Harris observed in "War and Social Change: Britain and the Home Front during the Second World War," *Contemporary European History*, Vol. 1, No. 1 (Mar. 1992), p. 22.

world war raised none of the thrill witnessed before World War I. World War II had long been dreaded by many as a war that would bring an end to civilization.[5] Yet once the bombing had started, it became clear that the real toll of violence was only a small fraction of the nightmarish prewar prophecies.

Since World War II, scholars have been engaged in an ongoing debate about the extent of the effects of war and aerial bombardment on civilian behavior and emotions. In 1950, social researcher Richard Titmuss first provided the standard interpretation that no events of mass panic occurred during the war on the home front.[6] Historian Arthur Marwick and others supported his claim.[7] Challenging these optimistic accounts, revisionist historians, such as Angus Calder, questioned the "myth of the Blitz" and demonstrated that behind an image of national unity existed limited incidents of fear and defeatism, as well as black market-eering, looting, and juvenile delinquency.[8] Recently, however, a number of historians have returned to a view closer to the earlier optimistic accounts. Robert Mackay, for example, determines that, despite the presence of such incidents shown by the revisionists, as a whole civilians did, to a remarkable degree, demonstrate resilience to the hardships of war.[9]

While these various scholars offer divergent historical interpretations as to what happened on the British home front, it is important to recognize the similarities in their methodology. First, while the issue of state propaganda and the work of popular culture in constructing reality have not gone unnoticed in their accounts, common to all of them is still an attempt to establish the "true facts" about civilian emotions, and to distin-guish between "myths" and "realities." All of them wish to assess whether anxiety on the home front was, in effect, "high" or "low." Second, these different scholars often resort to reading primary governmental and medical

---

[5] Titmuss, *Problems*, p. 21. Pacifists in particular protested against the possibility of another war. The British peace movement was the most influential of any major country in the interwar period and enjoyed a relative legitimacy due to the long-established heritage of pacifist thought in Britain. By the end of the 1930s, pacifism's popularity was decreasing: see Martin Ceadel, *Pacifism in Britain 1914–1945: The Defining of a Fight* (New York: Oxford University Press, 1980).

[6] Titmuss, *Problems*, pp. 337–355.

[7] Arthur Marwick, *The Home Front: The British and the Second World War* (London: Thames and Hudson, 1976), pp. 68–71; Philip Ziegler, *London at War 1939–1945* (New York: Knopf, 1995).

[8] Angus Calder, *The People's War* and his later, more controversial book, Angus Calder, *The Myth of the Blitz* (London: Pimlico, 1991); Clive Ponting, *1940: Myth and Reality* (Chicago: I. R. Dee, 1991); Donald Thomas, *The Enemy Within: Hucksters, Racketeers, Deserters, and Civilians during the Second World War* (New York University Press, 2003).

[9] Robert Mackay, *Halt the Battle: Civilian Morale in Britain during the Second World War* (Manchester University Press, 2002).

documents on civilian emotions as accurate testimony to the actualities of war. Consequently, they frequently pay little attention to the psychological discourse through which experiences and emotions were formulated, and the narratives of human psychology that came into being in connection with aggression and destruction in the mid twentieth century.[10]

Rather than charting which sentiments could fall under the categories of "low" or "high" anxiety, or comparing "myth" with "reality," I offer an examination of how these emotions were conceptualized and shaped by psychological experts.[11] My focus is, therefore, not on the social history of how people felt or behaved on the home front. Instead, I follow the rising problematization of anxiety and fear as new concepts calling for expert knowledge and management, a process that emerged in connection to new discussions about civilians in general and children in particular.[12]

Fear and anxiety seemed to many contemporaries to be at the center of World War II. Despite the fact that most citizens were not actually hurt by the bombing, the war forced the majority of them to face dreadful new realities on an everyday basis. As Titmuss noted, "all the time there were threats; of bombs, of gas, of sabotage, of invasion and, at the end, of new and unsuspected horrors."[13] On average, Londoners were threatened once every thirty-six hours for more than five years, with sirens heard on 1,224 occasions. Civilians were exposed to the sight of dead and injured bodies and were under threat of becoming part of the statistics according

---

[10] For example, a recent article tries to reexamine all governmental and medical records and to establish the true facts about civilian emotions during the war. However, not once are these sources discussed as reflecting a specific mode of thought, rather than an empirical reality. See Edgar Jones *et al.*, "Civilian Morale during the Second World War: Responses to Air Raids Re-examined," *Social History of Medicine* Vol. 17, No. 3 (2004), pp. 463–479. The question of the emotions of citizens is perhaps an impossible one to answer. Existing reports written by the Ministry of Information or by Mass Observation rely on diverse research methods and definitions. The government's official "Neurosis Survey" by C. P. Blacker, which aimed to investigate the extent of neurosis, could not even define what neurosis was or measure its incidence. See Ben Shephard, *A War of Nerves: Soldiers and Psychiatrists in the Twentieth Century* (Cambridge, MA: Harvard University Press, 2001), p. 179; C. P. Blacker, *Neurosis and the Mental Health Services* (London: Oxford University Press, 1946).

[11] In psychoanalytic theory, anxiety is at times distinguished from fear. In the historical debates that follow these concepts were intertwined. While moving toward a cultural analysis of fear, Amy Bell too tries at times to evaluate how common was this feeling among civilians: Amy Bell, "Landscapes of Fear: Wartime London, 1939–1945," *Journal of British Studies* Vol. 48 (2009), 153–175. For a discussion of other methodological problems, see Joanna Bourke, "Fear and Anxiety: Writing about Emotion in Modern History," *History Workshop Journal* Vol. 55 (2003), pp. 111–133.

[12] This is not to say that fear and anxiety were not real. The goal here is to analyze the ways in which these wartime emotions incited discussion and debate.

[13] Titmuss, *Problems*, p. 324.

to which, for every civilian killed, thirty-five civilians suffered damage to their homes.[14]

Indeed, as mentioned, scholars studying World War I have showed the effects of shellshock and the impact that knowledge of mental health had on British culture,[15] but World War II has not engendered similarly elaborate types of investigation. This chapter explores the work of diverse medical professionals studying anxiety (dividing them by "analytic" and "functional" methodologies) before and during World War II. The following chapters will focus on practicing psychoanalysts and their crucial role in the formation of this discourse of wartime emotionality.

From the mid 1930s, when the threat of a new war became real, attention gradually shifted from the problem of "shellshocked" soldiers to that of civilians panicking at the prospect of enemy aerial attack.[16] This change was generated through intense public debate in which hypothetical civilian psychiatric casualties and the emotions of fear and anxiety were imagined through specific narratives, images, metaphors, threats, and dangers. As Britons began speculating about "the shape of things to come," drawing from military theory on aerial bombing, as well as the experiences of World War I and the Spanish Civil War, fear and anxiety were increasingly seen as the normal reactions to total war.[17] During World War I and its immediate aftermath a display of fear among male soldiers was still stigmatized and seen as a symptom of cowardice. Throughout the 1930s, and as the psychological heritage of World War I continued to reverberate, this stigma faded, especially as a new world war loomed toward a civilian population that included women, old people, and children. While state officials at times believed that the war at home would be won by a resilient civilian population and a stiff-upper-lip attitude in the face of attack, fear and anxiety were simultaneously becoming accepted reactions to modern warfare among psychological professionals and beyond.[18]

---

[14] *Ibid.*, pp. 324, 329.

[15] See, for example, Peter Leese, *Shell Shock: Traumatic Neurosis and the British Soldiers of the First World War* (New York: Palgrave, 2002); Samuel Hynes, *A War Imagined: The First World War and English Culture* (New York: Atheneum, 1991).

[16] The existing historiography concentrates on World War I combat shellshock and post-Vietnam post-traumatic stress disorder (PTSD). The subject of military mental casualties of World War II has remained little studied: Ben Shephard, "'Pitiless Psychology': The Role of Prevention in British Military Psychiatry in the Second World War," *History of Psychiatry* Vol. 10 (1999), pp. 491–524.

[17] *The Shape of Things to Come* is the title of the 1933 novel by H. G. Wells which contributed to a vision of an approaching catastrophe.

[18] This development was a slower one where soldiers rather than civilians were concerned. See Joanna Bourke, "Disciplining the Emotions: Fear, Psychiatry and the Second World War," in Roger Cooter, Mark Harrison, and Steve Sturdy (eds.) *War, Medicine and Modernity* (Stroud: Sutton Publishing, 1998), pp. 225–238.

From World War I to World War II: gradual change in attitudes toward fear

Prior to 1914, mental problems were often stigmatized as moral failures of character, duty, and patriotism.[19] Significant change, however, came with World War I. The Great War generated a critical discussion of whether or not shellshocked male soldiers should be dealt with as cowards or as ill and needing care. The phenomenon of shellshock contributed to the spread of psychological and psychoanalytically oriented medicine over an organic one. This was a partial and evolutionary development and one that, to an extent, had pre-1914 roots, yet its importance should not be understated.[20]

Before World War I, some British doctors were already using psychological methods to treat mental disorders, among them Hugh Crichton-Miller, members of the Medico-Psychological Clinic of London set up in 1913, and David Eder, Ernest Jones, David Forsyth, and others who belonged to the newly established (also 1913) London Psycho-Analytical Society. Despite criticism, by 1914 psychoanalysis had established a toehold in Britain, and it enjoyed the support of several respectable medical figures such as Wilfred Trotter, Bernard Hart, and C. Stanford Read.[21] Other doctors were willing to think in psychological ways, albeit partly within a somatic framework of the nerves.[22] The prevailing medical thought, however, was in the tradition of pragmatic physicalist empiricism. Preference was given to the use of rest, baths, massage, and "commonsense" positive attitude and encouragement, rather than hypnosis or psychoanalysis.[23] Many military officials treated

---

[19] Leese, *Shell Shock*, pp. 17–19. For the early history of traumatic neurosis, see Wolfgang Schivelbusch, *The Railway Journey: The Industrialization of Time and Space in the Nineteenth Century* (Berkeley: University of California Press, 1986); Anson Rabinbach, *The Human Motor: Energy, Fatigue and the Origins of Modernity* (New York: Basic Books, 1990); and M. S. Micale, *Approaching Hysteria: Disease and its Interpretations* (Princeton University Press, 1995).

[20] As emphasized by Mathew Thomson, *Psychological Subjects: Identity, Culture, and Health in Twentieth-Century Britain* (Oxford University Press, 2006), pp. 182–186. Thomson calls for a more nuanced narrative of change and views World War I as less of a rupture point in the history of psychology than other historians. He too, though, admits that the shellshock phenomenon encouraged an important change.

[21] Martin Stone, "Shellshock and the Psychologists," in W. F. Bynum, Roy Porter and Michael Shepherd (eds.), *The Anatomy of Madness*, Vol. II (London: Tavistock Publications, 1985), pp. 242–248; Janet Oppenheim, *"Shattered Nerves": Doctors, Patients and Depression in Victorian England* (New York: Oxford University Press, 1991), pp. 303–318.

[22] Thomson, *Psychological Subjects*, p. 182. Cf. Peter Barham, *Forgotten Lunatics of the Great War* (New Haven: Yale University Press, 2004).

[23] Leese, *Shell Shock*, pp. 71–73.

shellshock as a disciplinary problem rather than a medical one. Yet despite the fact that organically oriented research and the disciplinary attitude continued during and after the war, the phenomenon of shellshock also helped to develop attitudes toward mental disorders in more psychological directions; barriers between sanity and insanity lowered, the stigma of mental illness relaxed, treatment in outpatient clinics rose, and medical students began to receive some kind of psychological training.[24] By the end of the Great War, psychotherapy was used in some military hospitals, and in the early 1920s many doctors who had previously treated shellshock cases published an extensive number of books and articles on psychotherapy and psychopathology. Several neurology textbooks were revised, with references to psychoanalysis added.

Furthermore, a number of doctors, such W. H. R. Rivers, William MacDougall, William Brown, and C. S. Myers, advanced their careers while studying shellshock using "potted versions of Freud's theories."[25] Rivers was perhaps the most famous of them, associated with quasi-psychoanalytic methods of dream analysis and the talking cure and with the conviction that regression and unconscious conflicts between duty and self-preservation were at the core of war neurosis. His "watered-down" version of psychoanalysis – characteristic of the period – emphasized the need to focus on real battlefield experience, rather than the more classic Freudian concentration on emotional conflict of childhood sexuality.[26] It was in this moderate form that such shellshock doctors helped popularize psychoanalytic techniques amid substantial opposition to their work in army hospitals.[27] Yet, by 1916, there were quite a few doctors using different methods of psychotherapy. Many of them discussed Freud's work and found much of value in it, although they rarely accepted it wholesale. Many who supported psychotherapeutic methods other than Freud's still drew heavily on his ideas. British psychoanalysts themselves presented earlier versions of the inventive idea – to be later modified in relation to World War II – that the Great War had brought back to life repressed sexual, sadistic, and

---

[24] The war served as a catalyst to these developments: Thomson, *Psychological Subjects*, p. 185.

[25] Martin Stone, "Shellshock"; Graham Richards, "Britain on the Couch: The Popularization of Psychoanalysis in Britain, 1918–1940," *Science in Context* Vol. 13 (2000), pp. 196–197.

[26] On differences between Rivers' earlier and later thought, see Shephard, *A War of Nerves*, pp. 83–89, 120–121.

[27] Since 1920, one version of psychoanalysis was also discussed at the newly established Tavistock Square Clinic.

violent impulses and the soldier's own "inner war" with his family members in early childhood.[28]

In ways that influenced discussions of fear and anxiety, psychoanalysis reflected a break from an older mainstream positivist psychology that was interested in the conscious mind.[29] Thus, already before the Great War, Sigmund Freud contributed to the idea that individuals are not rational but are governed by conflicted unconscious instincts, wishes, and anxieties. Yet it was through the discussion of war neurosis that Freud arrived at a more distrustful view of human psychology as both irrational and potentially destructive.[30] Freud influentially suggested in 1920 that in the mind there was not just a simple effort to seek pleasure and avoid displeasure, but a conflict between life and death instincts. Through this idea, and especially his notion of the "death drive," it was easier to understand the human attraction to violence.[31] Psychoanalysts would develop these ideas during the interwar years and apply them to contemporary tensions. But even those ambivalent about psychoanalysis often had to engage with the implications of its dark view of human psychology as anxious, fearful, irrational, aggressive, and fragile. Despite opposition to psychoanalysis, it was substantially discussed in different circles.[32] This feeling that psychoanalysis was precisely attuned to the age in which it emerged had to do with a widespread sense of crisis of civilization in the cultural world of interwar Britain. As the science of the irrational, psychoanalysis was especially attractive to a wide public eager to learn more about psychology after the Great War, a time when the ideas of neurosis and anxiety became widely accepted as modern realities. The belief that

[28] Martin Stone, "Shellshock," pp. 254–255; Richards, "Britain on the Couch," pp. 196–197; Ernest Jones, "War Shock and Freud's Theory of the Neuroses [1918]," in Sándor Ferenczi et al. (eds.), Psychoanalysis and the War Neuroses (London: International Psychoanalytic Library, 1921), pp. 44–59. Cf. Paul Lerner, Hysterical Men: War, Psychiatry, and the Politics of Trauma in Germany, 1890–1930 (Ithaca: Cornell University Press, 2003), pp. 163–189.
[29] Richard Overy, The Morbid Age: Britain between the Wars (London: Penguin, 2009), p. 145.
[30] Lerner, Hysterical Men, pp. 163–189.
[31] Sigmund Freud, "Beyond the Pleasure Principle [1920]," SE/PEP Vol. XVIII, pp. 1–64. He later developed this idea to a political level when he pessimistically argued that, because civilization restricted sexual and aggressive impulses in individuals, it was inevitable that social life was fraught with frustration that governed relationships between human beings and created the hostility that individuals felt toward civilization. See Sigmund Freud, "Civilization and its Discontents [1930]," SE/PEP Vol. XXI, pp. 57–146.
[32] Dean Rapp, "The Early Discovery of Freud by the British General Educated Public, 1912–1919," Social History of Medicine Vol. 3, No. 2 (1990), pp. 235–236; Dean Rapp, "The Reception of Freud by the British Press: General Interest and Literary Magazines, 1920–1925," Journal of the History of the Behavioral Sciences Vol. 24 (1988), pp. 191–201.

humans are dangerously irrational caught attention and helped focus more medical emphasis on the problem of anxiety.[33]

Official and public debate on mental combat casualties and fear during the early interwar years was partly influenced by psychoanalysis. In 1922, the government's War Office Committee of Enquiry into "Shellshock" held traditional ideas regarding mental illness that viewed it as organic illness or as cowardice. Yet the report that it produced was an ambiguous document that vacillated between a "modern" psychological notion of shellshock (influenced by modified psychoanalysis) and "traditional" ideas of character and biology. The Committee's investigation was itself a reflection of and a contribution to increased public awareness in the 1920s of the idea of mental illness and of theories such as psychoanalysis. While they repudiated Freud, the writers of the report still employed elements of his theories and used his vocabulary, demonstrating overall how impossible it had become in this period to speak of mental illness without some recourse to his ideas. The connection between shellshock and cowardice was not completely debunked by the Committee yet, representing the shifting of thought occurring during the interwar period, it acknowledged that responsible men could "break" during modern warfare.[34] With help from the writings of Freud, World War I officers such as Siegfried Sassoon, Wilfred Owen, and others, the war was increasingly seen as irrational and wasteful by the early 1930s, and male war trauma as a reality to be addressed.[35]

Indeed, the debates on shellshock, fear, and cowardice were closely connected to contemporary views of masculinity.[36] Historian Michael Roper has convincingly shown how a change in growing reflexivity on the codes of masculinity emerged in this period (at least among the British middle classes). Despite the diffuse and eclectic nature of psychoanalysis at the time, psychoanalytic ideas were central in the new concepts of masculinity that emerged after the war, their main contribution being an

---

[33] Overy, *The Morbid Age*, pp. 136–218.

[34] Ted Bogacz, "War Neurosis and Cultural Change in England 1914–1922: The Work of the War Office Committee of Enquiry into 'Shell-Shock,'" *Journal of Contemporary History* Vol. 24 (1989), p. 250.

[35] Hynes, *A War Imagined*. For a discussion that goes beyond the influence of the literary world of officers, see Barham, *Forgotten Lunatics*.

[36] See the different accounts of Elaine Showalter, *The Female Malady: Women, Madness and English Culture, 1830–1980* (London: Virago, 1987), and Joanna Bourke, *Dismembering the Male: Men's Bodies, Britain, and the Great War* (University of Chicago Press, 1996). On the effect of gender on wartime Britain more generally, see Nicoletta Gullace, *"The Blood of Our Sons": Men, Women and the Renegotiation of British Citizenship during the Great War* (New York: Palgrave, 2002); Susan Grayzel, *Women's Identities at War: Gender, Motherhood, and Politics in Britain and France during the First World War* (Chapel Hill: University of North Carolina Press, 1999).

emphasis on the deep instability of subjectivity, a perception of childhood development as an unstable process, and a discussion of the unconscious, repression, and irrationality. More to the point in terms of our discussion, fear slowly became a universal, even "natural" reaction to war during this time.[37] While the process of development of a more fragile, reflexive self emerged in the interwar period, it reached maturation only during World War II and especially through the work of psychoanalysts. Taking into account the two world wars together, and placing the move toward acceptance of fear in the context of discussions about the approaching new conflict, it becomes clear that this process, at first only partially manifest, was only deepening.

Attacks on all senses: medical experts on the problem of anxiety

The expectation of a future war dominated by new technologies of destruction raised deep concern in Britain.[38] The war was frequently described in a narrative of impending apocalypse. One prime common statistical reference used to predict casualties that circulated during the interwar period was the 1917–1918 German Zeppelin air raids on Britain, which caused 4,820 casualties. Relying on these figures, different officials tried to estimate the casualty ratio of the future war, while envisioning an attack on a much bigger scale.[39] The public imagination during the 1930s was preoccupied with these horrific speculations. Stanley Baldwin added to this alarmed atmosphere with a statement at the House of Commons saying, "the bomber will always get through . . . I think it is well also for the man in the street to realize that there is no power on earth that can protect him from being bombed."[40] His words expressed the sentiment that, in

---

[37] As argued by Michael Roper, "Between Manliness and Masculinity: The 'War Generation' and the Psychology of Fear in Britain, 1914–1950," *Journal of British Studies* Vol. 44 (Apr. 2005), pp. 343–362. Roper uses the label "psychology" to refer to what is mostly psychoanalysis.

[38] See also Barry D. Powers, *Strategy without Slide-Rule: British Air Strategy, 1914–1939* (London: Croom Helm, 1976); Richard Overy, *The Air War: 1939–1945* (London: Potomac, 1980). During the interwar period, Britain and the USA were the only major powers convinced that aerial bombing could be part of a successful military strategy. Germany did not develop air power as extensively as the British; however, once the war began it was the Germans who first conducted aerial attacks against civilians. It was after the bombing of London that the British decided to retaliate in kind. See Robert G. Moeller, "On the History of Man-Made Destruction: Loss, Death, Memory, and Germany in the Bombing War," *History Workshop Journal* Vol. 61 (2006), pp. 103–134. See also David E. Omissi, *Air Power and Colonial Control: The Royal Air Force 1919–1929* (Manchester University Press, 1990).

[39] Titmuss, *Problems*, p. 4.   [40] Quoted *ibid.*, p. 9.

aerial war, no one is protected. One contemporary account estimated that in the next war there would be "200 bombs per day, each carrying 1½ tons of bombs, in 10 days. In congested districts such raiding might cause at least 200,000 casualties."[41] Winston Churchill described London as "the greatest target in the world, a kind of tremendous, fat, valuable cow, tied up to attract beasts of prey." Others believed that bombs "might jeopardize the whole future of Western civilization."[42] Officials and medical authorities anticipated unprecedented calamity, one in which the democratic state might fail to defend helpless citizens. The projected consequences of the coming war included physical casualties and material damage, yet the costs of war dreaded most were social distress and mass mental disorder. While medical debates began during the 1920s and 1930s, they intensified greatly in the late 1930s. In 1938, for example, eighteen eminent psychiatrists warned the Ministry of Health to set up services to cope with civilian mental casualties. They predicted that psychiatric casualties might exceed physical casualties by three to one, and foresaw some 3–4 million cases of acute panic, hysteria, and other neurotic conditions during the first six months of air attack.[43] The most frightening image of the impending disaster was that of a civilian population losing emotional control. Indeed, the government's plans for evacuating civilians out of danger zones were affected by such psychological worries.[44]

The Spanish Civil War of 1936–1939 was another reference point for the calculation of mental casualties and instances of anxiety and fear. Despite the positive report from Barcelona by psychiatrist Emilio Mira that there were no signs of mass hysteria during the civil war, others in Britain remained concerned.[45] The Spanish experience of air raids seemed to many Britons to be a preview of what would happen in their country once a war with Germany broke out.

Advised by psychoanalyst John Rickman, journalist John Langdon-Davies wrote in 1938 a typical, alarmist report on the war in Spain and its implication for Britain, which medical men then frequently utilized in their discussions about anxiety. The psychoanalytic element in his work lay in the pessimistic emphasis on irrationality. After witnessing the bombardment of Barcelona, Langdon-Davies believed anxiety and mass

---

[41] *Ibid.*, Ch. 1, n. 12.
[42] Tom Harrisson, *Living through the Blitz* (New York: Schocken Books, 1976), p. 22.
[43] *Ibid.*, p. 41; Titmuss, *Problems*, p. 20.
[44] John Welshman, "Evacuation and Social Policy during the Second World War: Myth and Reality," *Twentieth Century British History* Vol. 9, No. 1 (1998), pp. 28–53.
[45] Emilio Mira, "Psychiatric Experience in the Spanish War," *BMJ* Vol. 1 (7 June 1939), pp. 1217–1220.

panic should be treated as a grave problem. In language characteristic of this period, he talked about the danger created by "bombs" – rather than by the people dropping them – and envisioned these weapons as almost anonymously "falling from the skies." Langdon-Davies claimed that a level of panic was reached only after recurring bombing. Demonstrating that panic was now less connected to character failure and cowardice than was dominantly thought during the World War I era, he further argued that by the end he "was unable to find anyone who did not frankly admit that he was reduced to a state of impotent terror."[46] Indeed, air raids were attacks on all senses. The new air warfare, he believed, was directed "against the nerves of the people." Since a modern state at war depends on a productive population at the rear toiling rationally, frequent bombing could cause civilians to "regress to a condition of meaningless, useless and therefore dangerous action."[47] Langdon-Davies proposed engaging people in rational work activity.[48] Influenced by Rickman's psychoanalytic ideas that drew on Freud, Langdon-Davies concluded, "the air raid stuns the man's power of conscious thought, but not his body's power of action, nor his unconscious need tying him to his fellows."[49] In this new form of warfare, writers like him suggested, psychology was central. Total war induced an irrationality that should be combated by taking into account the perceived limitations of individual and group psychology. Mass fear and anxiety demanded a widening sphere of action and responsibility for the state.

Medical professionals in particular had an important role in warning the public and the government about the need to treat the psychological aspects of civilian warfare as issues of first priority. Their debates intensified, especially after the Munich Crisis, when war seemed almost imminent after Hitler had demanded control over the Sudetenland in Czechoslovakia, but was temporarily appeased.[50] These experts' descriptions and conceptualizations of expected and real-time war emotions transformed anxiety and fear into problems requiring professional

---

[46] John Langdon-Davies, *Air Raid* (London: Routledge, 1938), p. 15.   [47] *Ibid.*, p. 88.

[48] *Ibid.*, p. 138. This concern about crowds had a class element to it as well, as many believed that the working classes (and, at times, minorities such as Jews) were more likely than others to show emotion. Mass Observation researcher Tom Harrisson described how before the war a belief prevailed that "the proletariat were bound to crack, run, panic, even go mad, lacking the courage and self-discipline of their masters or those regimented in the forces": Harrisson, *Living through the Blitz*, p. 22. See also Sonya Rose, *Which People's War?: National Identity and Citizenship in Britain, 1939–1945* (Oxford University Press, 2003).

[49] Langdon-Davies, *Air-Raid*, p. 138. For Rickman, see Ch. 2.

[50] Until after the Munich Crisis, the government kept most of the information about its wartime measures non-disclosed and censored within Whitehall: Titmuss, *Problems*, p. 9.

attention and diverse solutions. Sigmund Freud's influence on main-stream medicine was "complicated and patchy." Yet psychoanalysis provided many of the interpretive foundations on which the ideas of others would rest, and it cast a wide shadow on the ways in which human psychology was conceived.[51] Other medical conceptualizations beyond psychoanalysis emphasized the ephemerality of feelings and the ability to alter them without in-depth treatment. Yet even experts who emphasized simple, instrumental, and "functional" treatment of fearful civilians nevertheless accepted the idea that anxiety and irrationality were part of the psychological response to total war. This was also the assumption of the analytically influenced doctors who were ready for more lengthy investigations of emotions.

In the military, in contrast to civilian life, some moral judgment toward anxiety and fear remained throughout World War II. However, there was less intolerance of fear, with the death penalty for cowardice abolished. Historian Ben Shephard has argued that, despite innovations,[52] there were elements of continuity in military psychiatry between the world wars of both the disapproving "disciplinary" approach to fear and the "analytic" quasi-Freudian one. Overall, the lesson of the Great War in military psychiatry was to implant a hard-line attitude toward soldiers suffering mentally during World War II. Shephard briefly implies that civilians were treated roughly as well during World War II.[53]

Yet the medical discussions about civilians also reveal a picture of gradual change too, rather than just continuity during the war. As in the military, one can see traces of both the "disciplinary" and the "analytic" approaches in the new debates about civilians. But discussions about anxiety softened, with the old "disciplinary" approach losing its moral edge and now chiefly entailing short treatment and a "functional" attitude (henceforward, I therefore use the term "functional" rather than "disci-plinary," while "analytic" will refer to doctors influenced by psychoanal-ysis who are not practicing psychoanalysts). Discussions became more fragmented and pragmatic, with no new theoretical orthodoxy developing except in the branch of psychoanalysis. Most importantly, both "func-tional" treatment advocates and "analytic" ones did not condemn fear among civilians as cowardice or lack of character. The diverse medical discussions of the time show that a growing recognition of fear and anxiety as normal reactions to warfare became characteristic of this period.

---

[51] Shephard, *A War of Nerves*, pp. 163–164.
[52] In the areas of human-resource selection, drugs, and group psychotherapy; see John R. Rees, *The Shaping of Psychiatry by War* (New York: Norton, 1945).
[53] Shephard, "'Pitiless,'" p. 493.

By 1939, the medical consensus was that war neuroses were psychological rather than physical in origin. The government hoped to treat these neuroses quickly. A memorandum for the medical profession by the Ministry of Health (advised by World War I doctors Gordon Holmes and Bernard Hart) recommended that, in the new war, terms such as "shellshock" should be avoided. Patients should be convinced that their symptoms indicate no serious injury and would soon disappear. Hysterical symptoms should be treated by showing the patient that a powerless limb is not paralyzed or by making a speechless patient utter a sound. While the recommendation was for a firm but sympathetic attitude, importantly there was no condemnation of the expression of fear, but rather an overall acceptance that anxiety cases would be common and deserved early, if brief treatment.[54] Official policy, then, determined by veteran World War I doctors, remained somewhat stiff, but a new generation of medical men was increasingly willing to study anxiety uncritically in the era of World War II.[55]

Medical professionals often connected the experiences of World War I with those of the coming war in novel ways, aiming to draw new conclusions from its perceived psychological lessons. Writing on January 29, 1939, the "functional" Dr. Louis Minski argued, "the civilian population in future wars would be subjected to as much stress and strain as the result of air raids as the combatants on the front line."[56] While he reported from Epsom and London on only a small number of casualties, amounting to nine cases of nervous breakdowns in female patients, this was seen as a sign for worry given the fact that hostilities in Britain had not yet begun. Minski speculated that the number of civilian breakdowns would be extremely high, since the younger members of the population had no previous experience of warfare. He connected the problems of his patients to "realistic worries," such as concern for their children's gas masks but, like the analytically inspired Langdon-Davies, Minski too saw human psychology as easily influenced by the expectation of violence.[57] The "analytic" Dr. Hugh Crichton-Miller of the Tavistock Clinic also emphasized that lack of real experience with mass violence could influence the reaction of civilians, and he therefore expected the worst psychological results after the first air bombardment. Yet rather than "realistic worries," he stressed that civilians' particular emotional development in childhood

---

[54] "Neuroses in War Time: Memorandum for the Medical Profession," *BMJ* Vol. 2 (16 Dec. 1939), p. 1201.
[55] Shephard, *A War of Nerves*, pp. 161, 165.
[56] Louis Minski, "Mental Disorder associated with the Recent Crisis," *BMJ* Vol. 2 (29 Jan. 1939), p. 163.
[57] *Ibid.*, pp. 163–164.

would influence their reactions to air attack as well. He proposed with approval that a free expression of fear and anxiety and "talking it out" would be of great help to neurotic and timid patients.[58] Thus, by early 1939, the pattern of not judging fear and accepting human vulnerability was established among both "functional" and "analytic" doctors.

In the World War II era, fear and anxiety became more gender-neutral, and were viewed as affecting women and men alike in a manner that did not connote disgrace. Writing on September 9, 1939, just after the war broke out, yet before major aerial attacks had begun, the "analytic" psychiatrist Maurice B. Wright also warned that the present conflict posed a psychological difficulty to all men and women. "It is a problem that everyone . . . is having to face . . . shall I break down; shall I keep sane or normal under the conditions I may have to endure? . . . many, perhaps most, of us cannot feel quite sure of the answer." Fear – no longer stigmatized – would affect all since "war directed against a civilian population exempts no one, excludes no one."[59] Wright's solution to this problem was radical. He suggested that civilians should be treated as if they were combat troops and kept under personally known authority.[60] At the same time, he was determined to study emotions beyond this practical solution.

Anxiety and fear, for Wright and other medical men, were seen as posing a real social threat, requiring categorization and close study. Wright classified these emotions using psychoanalytic vocabulary.[61] One type of fear was "simple terror," i.e. a short-lived biological reaction. Another, more pathological response was "anxiety hysteria," described as influenced by "internal conflicts."[62] The symptoms that accompany this fear "are so intense that no amount of reassurance, or removal to a place of safety, no appeal to any ego ideal of courage, elicits any response." A more severe reaction was that of "hysterical stupor" which could induce violent attacks during recovery.[63] While these were extreme reactions, when discussing the treatment of "simple terror," Wright recommended that patients be told that their fear was only "natural," demonstrating again the increased tolerance of this sentiment.[64]

Medical professionals as a whole believed they had a "big responsibility" in the time of war when "psychological principles" were being challenged.[65]

---

[58] "Neuroses in War Time," pp. 169–170.
[59] Maurice B. Wright, "Psychological Emergencies in War Time," *BMJ* Vol. 2 (9 Sep. 1939), p. 576.
[60] *Ibid.*
[61] Wright was a member of the original 1913 London Psycho-Analytical Society.
[62] *Ibid.*   [63] *Ibid.*   [64] *Ibid.*, p. 616.   [65] Rees, *The Shaping*, pp. 13, 10.

Alarmed by the troubles to come, "analytic" psychotherapist A. C. D. Telfer[66] called for the establishment of treatment centers and rallied his colleagues: "*Now* is the time to enlist your services for defence of the nation's nerves."[67] Indeed, during the first weeks of war, the "functional" psychiatrist George Pegge recorded new mental cases. Pegge suggested that the Britons especially susceptible to mental casualties were those with a "less strongly established sense of social responsibility and usually less education," and those who were highly intelligent and conducted war work. For the non-analytic Pegge, anxiety had less to do with inner conflicts or childhood experiences and more to do with fatigue or hunger. He hoped that, in light of the rapid recovery of some patients with simple rest, the adoption of long-term methods would be delayed. Notably, he too claimed no negative opinion of the patients who did become afraid.[68]

While the consensus among medical professionals held that anxiety casualties would be prevalent, already by December 1939, doubts were raised as to how widespread the phenomenon would be.[69] In the months that passed after the war broke out, during the "Phony War," when no major military actions had yet occurred, new worries emerged regarding the psychological effects of boredom among Air Raid Precautions workers on the home front who at this point had little work to do.[70]

Nevertheless, medical interest in anxiety continued, with different ideas about its causes. In June 1940, Dr. Harry Stalker reported from Jordanburn Nerve Hospital that breakdowns were uncommon and occurred only in predisposed persons who had suffered emotional instability before the war. Stalker, influenced by psychoanalysis, believed that anxiety was related to mental history. He described, for example, a man who became acutely anxious after bombing. While this man intended to bicycle to work, he instead found himself cycling miles away for three days. Stalker linked this incident to the fact that as a child this man had been afraid of strangers, the dark, and blood and had had relatives who were in mental hospitals. This man also participated in the Great War and had suffered from "neurotic symptoms." When World War II broke out,

---

[66] For his unique methods, see A. C. D. Telfer, "Group Psychology," *BMJ* Vol. 1 (28 Feb. 1942), pp. 309–310.

[67] A. C. D. Telfer, "Psychological Treatment Centres," *BMJ* Vol. 2 (7 Oct. 1939), p. 744.

[68] George Pegge, "Notes on Psychiatric Casualties of the First Days of War," *BMJ* Vol. 2 (14 Oct. 1939), p. 765.

[69] "Treatment of Neurosis in the Emergency Medical Service," *BMJ* Vol. 2 (3 Dec. 1939), p. 1242.

[70] W. Greenwood, "Panic in Wartime," *BMJ* Vol. 1 (16 Mar. 1940), p. 448; A. J. Brock, "Boredom on the Home Front," *BMJ* Vol. 1 (30 Mar. 1940), p. 547.

he admitted to having "spent his free time gazing eastwards and wondering when the Germans would come."[71] Stalker did indeed believe that his patients had "abnormal" personalities, yet he did not equate their anxieties with cowardice. Once the Blitz finally began, both "functional" and "analytic" doctors continued suspending moral judgment about fear.

The experience of real violence did not stop expert speculation, but rather increased discussions of anxiety with language that remained sympathetic and refrained from judgment even when describing the loss of emotional control by civilians of both genders. After September 7, 1940, when the air raids had intensified, accounts of anxious civilians who had been in danger appeared. On October 26, "functional" Pegge reported twenty-nine cases brought to London Hospital. Many of his cases were exposed to bomb scenes and were described as suffering from "uncontrolled emotional behaviour and weeping – in men as well as women."[72] Among the typical cases was that of a woman who had lost a sister-in-law in the bombings and was now "incapable of dealing reasonably with her fear."[73] Another case involved a male air-raid warden who "was shivering violently ... [and] sobbed uncontrollably at times." Pegge's recommendation was for early therapy and reassurance.[74] While other medical experts had more patience for lengthy treatments, Pegge aimed for efficiency. Though he was not a Freudian, he too subscribed to the largely analytic conclusion that there was no absolute binary between "neurotic" and "non-neurotic" citizens, thereby demonstrating how psychoanalysis could have indirect influence on "functional" doctors as well in this period.

Even in the most technical of treatments offered at the time, emotions were treated in an impartial manner. The question of treatment for fear and anxiety rose in the discussion of a unique "sound therapy" offered by "functional" F. L. McLaughlin and W. M. Millar working in a military hospital. McLaughlin and Millar developed a peculiar technique for overcoming fear to be used with soldiers who had been exposed to noises such as gunfire, bombing, and sirens, and had become hypersensitive to the sounds of warfare. With the help of the BBC, the treatment these doctors offered was to recondition and desensitize the soldiers by exposing them

[71] Harry Stalker, "Panic States in Civilians," *BMJ* Vol. 1 (1 Jun. 1940), p. 888. Others were less tolerant than Stalker of such anxiety cases, yet they continued to argue about their meaning and their treatment. See *BMJ* Vol. 2 (24 Aug. 1940), p. 257.
[72] George Pegge, "Psychiatric Casualties in London, September 1940," *BMJ* Vol. 2 (26 Oct. 1940), p. 553.
[73] *Ibid.*, pp. 553–554.
[74] Cf. "Problems of War Casualties," *BMJ* Vol. 1 (29 Mar. 1941), p. 490.

to gramophone recordings of warfare.[75] Applying their knowledge to the issue of air raids against citizens, McLaughlin and Millar insisted: "fear, which is simply a normal protective instinct, can be countered by enlightenment, and aerial bombardment is unlikely to achieve its demoralizing object if the experience is not a complete surprise."[76] If fear and anxiety were the most dreaded natural wartime emotions, then civilians could be trained by experts to control their feelings, they implied.

At the core of debates on anxiety stood the question of what should be done about wartime emotions and who should be responsible not only for civilians' bodies and material needs, but also for their psyches. Therefore, "sound therapy" raised a number of responses in which anxiety was tied to extended notions of democracy and citizenship. Critiquing this method and calling for a more thorough "analytic" therapy, Dr. J. C. Mackwood protested a policy movement afoot to deny the reality of psychoneurotic conditions. The civilian, "who has been praised for his courage on the 'front line,'" was overlooked by professionals and was denied the right to a diagnosis of psychoneurotic conditions, he argued. Mackwood then linked the right to psychological treatment to a comprehensive notion of citizenship that included the right to mental health care. He added, "it would be a catastrophe if we regressed to an orientation to neurosis that prevailed during the last war, and the treatment of anxiety states were held to be only a reconditioning process."[77] Similarly, other responses implied that untreated mental cases posed a threat to good citizenship and to the relationships between citizens.[78] Dr. Arthur Hurst, however, took Mackwood's comments on the methods employed in the last war as an insult. Hurst (previously more receptive to psychoanalysis) insisted that the simple rapid methods of persuasion and reeducation were the best treatments.[79]

Yet most mental-health professionals now pushed to extend the therapeutic responsibility of the state to its citizens. Demanding extended

---

[75] F. L. McLaughlin and W. M. Millar, "Employment of Air-Raid Noises in Psychotherapy," *BMJ* Vol. 2 (2 Aug. 1941), p. 157.

[76] *Ibid.* Similarly, Dr. A. E. Carver suggested that if civilians could condition themselves against the fear of noise, air raids would lose their fear value. Cows, he pointed out, when placed in a field alongside a railway are at first uncomfortable, yet eventually they get used to the noise and are able to ignore it. He recommended that civil-defense workers would attend "blitz-concerts." See A. E. Carver, "Conditioned to Bangs," *Lancet* (14 Mar. 1942), pp. 330–331.

[77] J. C. Mackwood, "Air-Raid Noises in Psychotherapy," *BMJ* Vol. 2 (23 Aug. 1941), pp. 279–280.

[78] Tom Harrisson, "Obscure Nervous Effects of Air Raids," *BMJ* Vol. 1 (12 Apr. 1941), pp. 573–574. For other reactions, see *BMJ* Vol. 1 (26 Apr., 10 and 25 May, 14 Jun. 1941).

[79] Arthur Hurst, "Air-Raid Noises in Psychotherapy," *BMJ* Vol. 2 (6 Sep. 1941), p. 354.

government accountability, Dr. Felix Brown from Guy's Hospital, a young "analytic" psychiatrist,[80] criticized other prevalent claims about civilian mental casualties. Writing in May 1941, he attacked Ministry of Health instructions to simply persuade hysterical patients that what they thought of as a powerless limb was not in fact paralyzed. Instead of these minimal means, Brown suggested the usage of a combination of "functional" and "analytic" treatments.[81] Brown stressed that anyone who had been near a bombed building could suffer from "acute emotional shock," fear, anxiety, sensitivity to noise, and restlessness. He offered treatments such as reassurance, rest, occupational therapy, and drugs, yet he also used a Freudian framework when connecting war neurosis and sexual history or when he talked about the need to restore lost memory through dream analysis.[82]

While medical men had already gained experience dealing with combat soldiers under military discipline during World War I, handling civilians in a democratic context posed a new set of questions. Like others of his time, Brown was interested in comparing the experiences of soldiers to those of civilians. Civilian psychological reactions, he argued, overall resemble those of soldiers. Yet, unlike the army, a civilian population includes the old and the young, men and women, the mentally sound and the emotionally unstable – none of whom was under military discipline. Nevertheless, Brown optimistically believed that, as civilians are not members of any conscript body from which they wish to escape, they would have no motive for continuation of symptoms any longer than necessary. This probably accounts, he argued, for the fact that "the average previously healthy civilian has proved remarkably adjustable."[83]

In contrast, in March 1942, the "functional" practitioner Henry Wilson reported a relatively high number of 134 civilians who suffered from fright and anxiety in London Hospital. Yet what is important for our investigation is not whether these emotions were prevalent or not, but that his account further demonstrates the acceptance of the expression of these feelings in this period and how, in contrast to Edwardian views of the self, it was now more widely believed that fear and anxiety were universal reactions to war. Wilson's patients were told that their reaction was due to fear, that fear was a common reaction, and that they should resist temptation to exaggerate their war experiences. Thus, even when treated

[80] Brown had formally worked with Adolf Meyer.
[81] Felix Brown, "Civilian Psychiatric Air-Raid Casualties," *Lancet* (31 May 1941), p. 687.
[82] Brown, influenced by Freud, also remarked on the surprisingly positive reactions of some well-established psychoneurotics to the bombing; he conceptualized this in ways similar to those of some psychoanalysts that will be discussed below.
[83] *Ibid.*

hurriedly at London Hospital, and in a manner similar to that recommended by the Ministry of Health, fear was not regarded as shameful. Wilson reported that a common reaction to the air raids was: "Anyone saying he's not nervous is a liar. Kid other people, never kid yourself."[84] Wilson classified as "normal" those who admitted to being afraid of the bombs and expressed statements such as "I tremble a bit" or "I get excited and pass a lot of water." The "abnormal" were those who denied the fear completely and those who developed shelter phobia and claustrophobia during bombardment. He believed that the admission of fear was a safeguard against breakdown in conditions of stress.[85] Similarly to Wilson, the "functional" Aubrey Lewis of Maudsley Hospital[86] provided vast statistics on civilian mental casualties from across England and claimed that anxiety was a much more widespread and universal reaction to the war than commonly perceived by others. Significantly, the staff of the Bristol Child Guidance Clinic reporting to him mentioned without judgment that a generalized fear of air raids was so universal that they omitted it for the purposes of the investigation.[87]

In sum, while doctors did label some reactions to total war as abnormal, overall, both "functional" and "analytic" medical men accepted that anxiety and fear were normal reactions in general in the era of World War II. Indeed, the assumption that human psychology is fragile, anxious, and prone to irrationality traveled after World War I well beyond those referring to Freud.

Lay views on anxiety

The preoccupation with feelings of anxiety and fear was common in this period beyond circles of medical experts. As a short digression, it is worth mentioning the ways in which attention to the emotions, informed by professional focus, appeared in contemporary writings and diaries. For example, George Orwell, who participated in the Spanish Civil War and was hardly an ordinary citizen, still represented in his Blitz diaries common feelings of the time in his introspective writing about a gamut of emotions – from fear to denial and boredom. On June 25, 1940, he

---

[84] Henry Wilson, "Mental Reactions to Air-Raids," *Lancet* (7 Mar. 1942), p. 284.

[85] *Ibid.*, p. 287.

[86] Lewis was not impressed by either psychological or physical approaches to mental illness. In his relation to wartime anxiety he could be labeled a "functional" doctor recommending simple treatment. See Edgar Jones, "Aubrey Lewis, Edward Mapother and the Maudsley," *Medical Journal* Vol. 22 (2003), pp. 3–38.

[87] Aubrey Lewis, "Incidence of Neurosis in England under War Conditions," *Lancet* (15 Aug. 1942), pp. 176–178.

described how he and his wife denied the danger after hearing an air-raid warning at night: "We got up and dressed, but did not go to the shelter. This is what everyone did, i.e., got up and then simply stood about talking, which seems very foolish. But it seems natural to get up when one hears the siren, and then in the absence of gunfire or other excitement one is ashamed to go to the shelter."[88] On the night of August 29, 1940, after air-raid alarms prevented Londoners from sleeping, Orwell still believed that the raids did not worry him at all. In the morning, however, after putting in a couple of hours' sleep, he admitted: "I had a very disagreeable dream of a bomb dropping near me and frightening me out of my wits."[89] However, by August 31, 1940, the air-raid warning had become a "great bore."[90] Orwell described how, "of the people strolling in Regent's Park, I should say at least half pay no attention to a raid warning."[91]

After bombing intensified in London on September 17, 1940, Orwell enumerated the psychological reactions of two young men and a woman he met as showing both fear and curiosity: "They were quite openly and unashamedly frightened, talking about how their knees were knocking together, etc. and yet at the same time excited and interested, dodging out of doors between bombs to see what was happening and pick up shrapnel splinters."[92] By March 1941, Orwell noted that his friends who "only came up to London a few weeks ago and have seen nothing of the blitz, say that they find Londoners very much changed, everyone very hysterical, talking in much louder tones, etc. etc. If this is so, it is something that happens gradually and that one does not notice when in the middle of it, as with the growth of a child."[93]

But Orwell, like other contemporaries, was also interested in the atmosphere of routine and adjustment which developed during the German attacks. On May 6, 1941, he wrote: "astonishing sights in the Tube stations when one goes through late at night. What is most striking is the cleanly, normal, domesticated air that everything has. Especially the young married couples ... tucked up together under pink counterpanes. And the large families one sees here and there, father, mother, and several children all laid out in a row like rabbits on the slab."[94] Some of Orwell's descriptions then use the increasingly common idea that "London can

[88] George Orwell, "War-Time Diary 28 May 1940–28 August 1941," in *The Collected Essays, Journalism and Letters of George Orwell*, Vol. II, *My Country Right or Left 1940–1943* (Boston: Nonpareil Books, 2000), p. 356.
[89] *Ibid.*, p. 369.
[90] Journalist and author Ritchie Calder (see n. 110) claimed that "Bomb-talk became boring and 'bad taste'": Ritchie Calder, *The Lesson of London* (Plymouth: Mayflower Press, 1941), p. 64.
[91] Orwell, "War-Time," p. 369.   [92] *Ibid.*, p. 373.   [93] *Ibid.*, p. 384.   [94] *Ibid.*, p. 399.

take it!" – a notion also prescribed in state propaganda advocating that, despite the bombings, Britons could withstand the violence.[95] Yet later in the war, on March 15, 1942, Orwell described fear again mixed with denial: "Short air-raid alert about 11:30 this morning . . . Inwardly rather frightened, and everyone else evidently the same, though studiously taking no notice and indeed not referring to the fact of there being a raid on until the All Clear had sounded."[96]

The diaries and accounts of volunteer reporters for the unique Mass Observation social research project recording everyday life in Britain provide further examples of the heightened attention to civilian emotional response among non-medical contemporaries. Once the first siren was heard in London, one man reported to feel "a nasty inward fear when the warning went." He tried to hide his emotions from his wife despite his trembling. Later that night, he was pleased when a second alert caused him "no fear."[97] In contrast, one lawyer described how, in reaction to "the wailing of hundreds of sirens like souls in torment," he "was filled with an ecstasy of *exquisite and thrilling panic*."[98] Once the first bombs fell, another woman wrote that the atmosphere was "one of excitement, and interest. People looked cheerful, and though they *talked* about nerves and shock, they showed no signs of either."[99] In one public shelter, however, one woman was reported to be screaming "they're coming! They'll bomb us! I can't stand it! Oh God I can't stand it!"[100] Another young woman said, "this war's killing me."[101]

In the Mass Observation reports, more incidents of horror, crying, fear, and anxiety appeared after September 1940 and the start of the Blitz, as well as an overall desire to control excited emotions and fear; a phase of toughening up was reported to follow the initial stage of panic. After a raid on September 18, 1940 that left child victims' limbs hanging from the bricks, one woman chronicled the reactions of her friends: "Everyone was frightened, but they controlled themselves. Hetty cried, but she cried quietly, and no one saw her. Gertie fainted but she fainted at the back and didn't make a fuss."[102] Reporting from Hampstead, London, on September 9, another woman described contradictory emotions of fear and happiness, a pattern that appeared in other Blitz accounts. She humorously complained how "one trouble about the raids [was that] people do nothing but make tea and expect you to drink it." Yet she

---

[95] This was the title of Humphrey Jennings' and Harry Watt's 1940 film for the Ministry of Information in which Londoners were depicted as stoical and fearless: *London Can Take It!* (dir. Humphrey Jennings and Harry Watt, 1940).
[96] Orwell, "War-Time," p. 412.   [97] Harrisson, *Living through the Blitz*, p. 44.
[98] *Ibid.*, p. 48.   [99] *Ibid.*, p. 55.   [100] *Ibid.*, p. 56.   [101] *Ibid.*, p. 57.   [102] *Ibid.*, p. 66.

admitted that during the raids she "felt all swollen up with irritation, a bloated sort of feeling, but actually it was fear … A horrid, sick sort of fear, it's quite different from worry, much more physical."[103] Later she described the special feeling of being happy and triumphant after being bombed: "It seems a terrible thing to say, when many people must have been killed and injured last night; but never in my whole life had I ever experienced such *pure and flawless happiness*."[104]

As in medical reports, a few Mass Observation diarists portrayed cases of overwhelming fear and anxiety without attaching shame to their expression. On September 17, one woman reportedly cried, "I can't bear it, I can't *bear* it! If them sirens go again tonight, I shall die!"[105] Another person complained: "It's my nerves, they're all used up, there's nothing left of me strength like I had at the start." A 60-year-old working-class grandmother complained, "It's the dread, I can't tell you the dread, every night it's worse," and a middle-aged construction worker cried, "It's getting more than flesh and blood can stand – it just can't be endured, night after night like this." Another woman protested, "Anything like this shouldn't be allowed."[106] One housewife felt that the Germans were after her personally and stated, "I like to go shopping *when it's busy*, so they won't notice me along the street."[107]

Experts' interest in dreams induced Mass Observation diarists to record these as well as the emotions and thoughts that accompanied them. A young civil servant in the Midlands, for example, dreamed of an argument with Hitler, ending with a long harangue on the rights and wrongs of total war. Hitler, he found, "was fairly humble but obviously unconvinced." Another woman dreamed that she was in bed with Hitler who had his boots on. A man from Ipswich dreamed that Hitler came for tea. He wondered whether Hitler would understand him if he asked for his autograph.[108] Respect toward Hitler was common in these nocturnal relationships, as with a dream by an Essex widow, aged 69, who was anxiously trying to tidy up a room because she felt Hitler might be coming. A retired schoolmistress in London found herself in Germany – as many war dreamers did – so close to the Führer that she was suddenly kneeling "and looking up into his face with a feeling of devotion."[109]

Journalist Ritchie Calder's description of anxiety and fear in London provides another typical example of the new focus on, as well as acceptance of, these feelings among non-medical experts. Writing in 1941, Calder also claimed that fear soon became something natural. "All of us learned quickly that fear was nothing of which to be ashamed and that bravado was not

---

[103] *Ibid.*, p. 78.   [104] *Ibid.*, p. 81.   [105] *Ibid.*, p. 95.   [106] *Ibid.*   [107] *Ibid.*, p. 113.
[108] *Ibid.*, p. 320.   [109] *Ibid.*

bravery. Fear, we found, was rather like being sea-sick; once you had 'got it over' and, better still, frankly acknowledged it, you felt fit to carry on indefinitely." Like a few medical experts, Calder mentioned the curious phenomenon in which "often it was the normally excitable individual who panicked in peace-time about missing trains, and who now acted with unexpected pluck and resource."[110] Claims such as these would be explored in systematic depth by psychoanalysts, to whom the next chapter turns.

A close examination of the discourse on wartime civilian emotionality reveals a picture of gradual – yet decisive – change between the two world wars. When we draw connections between the two wars (and address this gap in the historiography) it becomes apparent that an important emotional resonance flowed from World War I. The shift in discourse about mental health that began during World War I grew deeper during World War II. World War I attracted attention to soldiers in the battlefields who suffered from mental breakdown, still connected to the stigma of cowardice and a crisis of masculinity. Yet before and during World War II, the debates on mental health extended from combat to the civilian population on the home front, and thus the moralization connected to the expression of fear decreased (though less so in the military context). Since the projected Nazi air-raid attacks were seen to be aimed against a civilian population that included women and children, the stigma around fear, anxiety, and panic decreased. A growing perception that every person could be affected by a feeling of terror related to bombing contributed to a more widespread acceptance of the idea of the inherent fragility of subjectivity in the age of total war waged against civilians as much as soldiers.

Apart from the differences in opinion regarding the extent of emotional stability and social unity in wartime Britain, both orthodox and revisionist historians are in agreement that widespread hysteria and major public psychological breakdown *did not* occur during the war. Looking beyond the question of whether or not mass panic materialized on the home front, and instead turning our gaze to the problematization of wartime emotions, it is now clear that what *did* emerge during World War II was a new social concept of anxiety.

As anxiety and fear became feelings from which no one was seen to be immune in a new war against civilians, it was now clear that scientific knowledge of emotions was critical to the war effort.[111] Anxiety turned into a topic of discussion during the 1930s in connection to aerial warfare.

---

[110] Ritchie Calder was a socialist and pacifist journalist and a member of the Labour Party: Ritchie Calder, *The Lesson*, p. 65.
[111] Bourke, "Disciplining," pp. 225–226.

For both "functional" and "analytically influenced" doctors, anxiety became something to understand and manage during this period when psychological explanations for what were seen as uncontrolled feelings became more accepted. The mid twentieth century was "a new age of anxiety" that saw a new problematization of this emotion. Yet the real innovations, we shall see next, were to emerge in the field of psychoanalysis itself.

As is already evident with the quotes above from the more psychoanalytically minded doctors, psychoanalysis made a central contribution to the discussion of anxiety and fear. Through their work with adult citizens and children, psychoanalysts were the ones who offered the most wide-ranging, "in-depth" political explanation to the problem of anxiety, linking "the war inside" to the "war outside." Via the process of evacuation in particular, psychoanalysts offered influential ways to bring into being and make sense of these mid-century predicaments of the self. The focus was now on childhood, the unconscious, and aggression. The more crude speculation on mental health prior to World War II would mature, as we will see, into greater refinement during the war through a psychoanalytic crafting of a new typology of emotions and inner life.

2 Under fire: children and psychoanalysts in total war

In the development of the mid-century problematization of anxiety as a concept calling for expert and government intervention, psychoanalysis became central. Among other experts, psychoanalysis developed an important role in contemporary thinking about fear and violence, connecting the real "war outside" to an emotional "war inside." The war on the home front, and more specifically the evacuation of children from cities, provided analysts with the opportunity to spread their views on anxiety and the vulnerability of the self, and to extend their mandate from treating those diagnosed as mentally disordered to treating the general population. The British Psycho-Analytical Society (BPAS) as a whole, now comprising both native professionals and a rising number of exiled analysts, sought new ways to contribute to the war effort and to discussion about anxiety. Individual child psychoanalysts, such as Anna Freud and her staff of Jewish refugees, also invested in societal efforts during times of evacuation as hostilities began. Their theories and practices developed in relation to the experiences of total war.[1]

British psychoanalysis in this period became a discipline committed to particular visions of social change, working with citizens of diverse backgrounds, and advancing new concepts of self and mental health. To be a British psychoanalyst meant having a social commitment to reducing human suffering and to understanding the emotional structures that led to violence and misery. It meant making sense of modern warfare and calling for a new notion of social welfare. Psychoanalysts added to the 1940s discourse that demanded a redefinition of democracy and an enlargement of the scope of state involvement in mental-health protection. Whereas the role of psychoanalysis during World War I had been limited to influencing ways of dealing with the problems of the combat population and shellshock,

---

[1] While scholars have examined the social aspect of child evacuations, what was said to be the "psychological" side of this process is understudied. See Travis L. Crosby, *The Impact of Civilian Evacuation in the Second World War* (London: Croom Helm, 1986); Ruth Inglis, *The Children's War: Evacuation, 1939–1945* (London: Collins, 1989).

World War II and the experience of evacuation of children in particular transformed psychoanalysis from being an emerging field into being an influential and popular political force with a chief social role in conceptualizing the child and general welfare. Psychoanalysts helped shift attention from the care of children's bodies to care of their psyches.

Psychoanalytic ideas about anxiety and aggression and the "death drive" were already developed before the war, yet the threat of militarism and the rise of totalitarian regimes during the 1930s foregrounded the need to explain violence. Total war, the aerial bombing of civilians, the evacuation of children from cities, and family separation focused attention on the relationship between culture, society, and mental health. Psychoanalysts provided a framework for a new understanding of anxiety that was attached to a complex notion of modern selfhood. They positioned themselves as bearers of the knowledge necessary to develop and maintain a healthy democratic society of mentally fit citizens, able to withstand the dramatic upheavals of the mid twentieth century.

Psychoanalysts proposed a crucial intervention and an increasingly popular explanation of the problem of anxiety – one that emphasized the importance of the unconscious and early childhood, looked "inwardly" and linked an internal turmoil with the actual war.[2] Not everything that psychoanalysts said about anxiety and fear was new and unique, yet they helped refine this discourse and offered a more radical vision than any others. For analysts, as for others, anxiety was a medical problem and an issue for the state to address. Yet analysts transcended these definitions and argued that the problem of anxiety required a reconsideration of the nature of violence and of the very possibility of democracy. Psychoanalysts emphasized the need to understand the "war inside," i.e., what they saw as the aggression, sadism, and anxiety that in part constitute every subjectivity. Analysts made early-life family dynamics important in understanding the behavior of citizens and the working of democracy. Through their writings, experts became more necessary than ever to secure a stable regime. In this period of national worry over the stability of family as central to reconstructing society, psychoanalysis received wider recognition and became socially engaged in the government of citizens and of children as potential citizens.

Psychoanalysis before and during the war

Working in part from the BPAS, native and refugee analysts, like others in Britain explored in Chapter 1, utilized insights from World War I to warn

---

[2] Most analysts now discussed sexuality in public to a much lesser extent than they did early in the century.

against the possibility of mass mental breakdown due to air raids. Throughout the 1930s, the BPAS discussed the question of wartime emotion and violence while offering its services to the state and the public. In 1934, for example, the Society offered a popular public course on "The Psychology of Social Violence" with lectures on "War and the Aggressive Impulse" and on "Can Wars be Averted?"[3] During 1938, three symposia were held at the Society: one with D. Emilio Mira, who spoke about civilians' reaction to the Spanish Civil War, and two others on "Psychoanalytic Aspects of the War Crisis" and "Mental Casualties in Wartime."[4] Arising out of the discussion on "War Time Casualties," a sub-committee presented a report on the treatment of acute anxiety states.[5] The London Clinic of Psycho-Analysis organized a Temporary Psychological Aid Centre in collaboration with the official scheme for the Organization of Mental Casualties for Wartime London. And regular activities at the Society continued during the international crisis.[6]

Indeed, psychoanalysts in the BPAS felt that they held special knowledge on anxiety and aggression as experts on inner emotional dynamics. "A Memorandum on War Research" envisioned a team of psychoanalytically oriented experts across fields working together to research how outbreaks of war could be traced to "deeper dynamic factors present in man himself" and to "fear and persecutory feelings."[7] Political and violent realities were regularly viewed as tied to private internal experiences to be decoded by experts. A letter sent to the government on April 21, 1939, by Edward Glover, the director of the London Clinic of Psycho-Analysis and Ernest Jones' second-in-command, emphasized the special expertise of psychoanalysts in the study of fear, anxiety, and violence and offered the services of the Clinic in dealing with war neurosis.[8] While the Clinic did not play a leading role in the Government Emergency Scheme, it did participate

[3] The Archives of the British Psycho-Analytical Society (hereafter ABPAS): Institute of Psycho-Analysis, Annual Report for 1935.
[4] Pearl King, "Activities of British Psychoanalysts during the Second World War and the Influence of their Inter-Disciplinary Collaboration on the Development of Psychoanalysis in Great Britain," *Int. J. Psycho-Anal.* Vol. 16 (1989), p. 16.
[5] ABPAS/G01/BB/F02/03.   [6] King, "Activities," p. 17.
[7] Memorandum (apparently written by Edward Glover), ABPAS/G06/BA/F04/04, pp. 2 and 4.
[8] ABPAS/G03/BA/F01/14, p. 1. Edward Glover (1888–1972) was one of the leading psychoanalysts of the time, though he is now nearly forgotten. He became an associate member of the BPAS in 1921. He had a degree in medicine and had work experience in Scotland's hospitals. Initially, Glover was a supporter of Melanie Klein's work but later he became critical of it and perceived it as unscientific and incompatible with Sigmund Freud's theories. He resigned from the Society in 1944, joining the Swiss Psychoanalytic Society instead. See Pearl King, "Biographical Notes on the Main Participants in the Freud–Klein Controversies in the British Psycho-Analytical Society, 1941–1945," in

in what was known as the Neurosis Survey, supplying information to the government on the condition of patients during the war.[9] Glover also sent the Ministry of Information a memorandum with his opinion on its work on preventing public anxiety.[10] In addition, as it had been decided to keep the Clinic open during the war,[11] interest in its work came from the Mental Health Emergency Committee of the National Council for Mental Hygiene.[12] Despite blackouts and bombings, the understaffed Clinic (many of the members were evacuated out of London or were called into National Service) remained in high demand throughout the war, with a waiting list of patients seeking help.[13]

Throughout the war, the London Clinic of Psycho-Analysis, then, was a relative success. The economic classes from which its patients were drawn were extremely varied.[14] In 1939–1940, the Clinic conducted eighty-one consultations, some of them at the Temporary Psychological Aid Centre. Despite the war conditions, there were eighty-seven patients on the waiting list. Glover believed that the patients' disorders did not differ much from those in peacetime and had no obvious war correlation, yet he held that the war stimulus produced more and more personal and infantile responses the deeper it probed into "the layers of the mind."[15] During the second year of war, and as the Blitz began, a decrease in the number of consultations at the Clinic took place, reaching a total of sixty-three. The number of people on the waiting list was only twenty-nine and the Children Department in particular suffered due to the Blitz.[16] In 1941–1942, the Clinic conducted more consultations, amounting to ninety-six cases. This increase in attendance was due to the comparative stabilization of war on the home front. In spite of blackouts and traffic difficulties in the winter, patients under

Pearl King and Riccardo Steiner (eds.), *The Freud–Klein Controversies, 1941–1945* (New York: Routledge, 1991), p. xiii. For Glover's leading role in the Institute for the Scientific Treatment of Delinquency, see Chs. 5–6.

[9] Ministry of Heath – Neurosis Survey Questionnaire, ABPAS/G10/BD/F02/10; C. P. Blacker, *Neurosis and the Mental Health Services* (London: Oxford University Press, 1946).

[10] National Archives (hereafter NA)/INF/1/318: Edward Glover, "Memorandum on the Functions of the Ministry of Information" (19 Nov. 1940); see also Edward Glover, "The Birth of Social Psychiatry," *Lancet* (24 Aug. 1940), p. 239, which was also submitted to the government. Glover became chairman of the Home Morale Advisory Committee, yet eventually fell out of favor among civil servants. See Mathew Thomson, *Psychological Subjects: Identity, Culture, and Health in Twentieth-Century Britain* (Oxford University Press, 2006), pp. 229–231.

[11] ABPAS/G03/BA/F01/11, p. 1.

[12] ABPAS/G03/BA/F01/17 and 19; G01/BB/F02/08, 04, 06.

[13] ABPAS/G03/BA/F01/20, p. 1. Many of the patients had already sought help before the war.

[14] Ministry of Heath – Neurosis Survey Questionnaire, ABPAS/G10/BD/F02/10.

[15] ABPAS/G03/BA/F01/22, pp. 1–2; Edward Glover, *War, Sadism and Pacifism* (London: Allen & Unwin, 1946 [1933]), p. 106.

[16] ABPAS/G01/BB/F05/12, pp. 1–3.

treatment attended regularly.[17] The year 1942–1943 saw a rise in the number of Clinic consultations, amounting to 150 patients. Not only did the number of consultations rise in comparison with the previous war years, but they were also higher than any peacetime year. An increase was also noted in the number of patients sent to the Clinic by private doctors, hospitals, and emergency hospitals. Due to wartime conditions, it was necessary to start treatment as early as 7 a.m and to extend it past 7 p.m to accommodate patients conducting war work.[18] The following year, 1943–1944, saw another increase in consultations, reaching a total of 176. Patients were sent from private doctors, hospitals, military or emergency hospitals, the Tavistock Clinic, and private psychotherapists.[19] That year, a case of an ex-serviceman patient led the Ministry of Pensions to give the Clinic official recognition and financial support for the treatment of ex-service pensioners. Cases had to be officially approved by the Ministry, which reserved the right to periodically review the need for treatment.[20] During the last year of the war, there was a reduction in the number of consultations in the Clinic, to 125, due to the Clinic's own policy of selecting and restricting treatment.[21] The Clinic's work was significant considering the fact that many psychiatrists had joined the military and that few other treatment centers were operating (among them were the Tavistock Clinic, specialized hospitals with psychiatric staff, and War Neurosis Centres based in the vicinity of London) and serving hardly any patients seeking help.[22] The Clinic operated under the assumption that "there is no adult neurosis without an infantile neurosis." Writing to the Ministry of Health, psychoanalysts' recommendation for the future was: "the more extensive facilities for child observations and treatment, the more effective will measures of prevention become." Analysts called for the government to develop adequate mental-health services and advocated the urgent extension of specialist training.[23] Thus, during the war, psycho-analysts offered practical treatment to numerous patients seeking their support. Ideas regarding anxiety and the relationship between "a war inside" and "a war outside," which analysts discussed in professional, official, and public circles, were found compelling to those patients who continued to come in greater numbers for consultations.

[17] ABPAS/G03/BA/F01/29, pp. 1–3.   [18] ABPAS/G03/BA/F01/30, p. 1.
[19] ABPAS/G03/BA/F01/35, p. 1.   [20] *Ibid.*   [21] ABPAS/G03/BA/F01/36, p. 1.
[22] The Tavistock was prepared to receive a large number of neurotic air-raid casualties before the war, but during the "Phony War" it continued to see "ordinary neurotic" ones at the War Neurosis Centres. See H. V. Dicks, *Fifty Years of the Tavistock Clinic* (London: Routledge & Kegan Paul, 1970), pp. 94–120; Emanuel Miller (ed.), *The Neuroses in War* (New York: Macmillan, 1940), pp. 226–227.
[23] Ministry of Heath – Neurosis Survey Questionnaire, ABPAS/G10/BD/F02/10.

Yet the work of psychoanalysts was not confined to treatment alone. Psychoanalysts looked to provide a broader explanation of violence and anxiety as they tied political and perilous realities to private internal experiences. Already in the early 1930s, Glover had linked anxiety to aggression in order to explain the causes of war and the best ways to prevent it. In a set of lectures linking psychoanalysis to politics given before various League of Nations Societies and published in different editions from 1933, Glover proposed the provocative thesis that some of the psychological impulses to promote peace were similar to those giving rise to war. Behind even pacifist thinking lay aggressive origins, he argued. Pacifists, he believed, ignored the complex psychological dynamics that led to war and were therefore offering a simplistic solution to the problem of aggression. They were dangerously ignoring their own aggression and the aggression of others. For Glover, the phenomenon of war could not be understood until the unconscious forces of sadism that existed inside every individual were taken into account. It was only if this common, repressed inner aggression were to be made conscious and be recognized that society would be safe. An unsuccessful repression of sadism could lead to a dangerous inner feeling of anxiety. Anxiety, for Glover, was a treacherous feeling as it bred hatred and hostility to the nearest available object. In wartime, an "inner hatred enemy" stemming from the feeling of anxiety is projected onto an "outer enemy" in "an attempt to convert an inner (psychic) stimulus into an outer (reality) stimulus."[24] War then was a problem tied to selfhood and its aggression. Peacetime, like wartime, demanded the constant management of personal aggression. In order to save democracy and peace, then, Glover advised: "Know thine own (unconscious) sadism."[25] According to this formulation, the psychoanalyst was a privileged student of war and peace familiar with the power of these inner forces and the dangers of anxiety.

Communicating such ideas in public forums, psychoanalyst John Rickman – later famous for his war work with soldiers – was especially instrumental in reaching out to professionals from different fields.[26] He

[24] Glover, *War, Sadism, and Pacifism*, p. 19. [25] *Ibid.*, p. 32.
[26] John Rickman (1880–1951) joined the BPAS in 1920. Earlier, in 1916, he worked for the Quaker War Victims Relief Unit in Russia. He was interested in the work of Klein, with whom he had analysis in the 1930s, but he later became part of the "middle group" standing between Klein and Anna Freud. Before World War II, Rickman worked with members of the Medical Peace Campaign and the Quaker Medical Society and worked with the All London Aid Spain Council, concerned with getting food to Spanish war child victims. During World War II, Rickman served as an army psychiatrist. The involvement of Rickman, Wilfred Bion, and others in the treatment of soldiers has been relatively well researched; I will not repeat it here in an investigation that concentrates on civilians. See King, "Biographical," p. xviii; Ben Shephard, *A War of Nerves: Soldiers and Psychiatrists in*

was invited to write many of the leading *Lancet* articles on the international political crisis and was often quoted in newspapers, having a considerable influence on contemporary medical and lay opinion.[27] In a key June 1938 article, Rickman educated medical readers of various backgrounds about Sigmund Freud's definitions of fear, anxiety, and panic.[28] Fear, Rickman quoted Freud, required a definite object of which one was afraid. Anxiety, on the other hand, lacked an object and was undefined. Panic could appear as an individual generalized dread or as a collective dread accompanied by a loss of self-control.[29] Air raids, Rickman argued, were likely to produce mental strain arising from two sources: "external danger" and "internal danger." While "external" air raids could induce fear among civilians, the critical cause rose from "internal dangers," that is, unconscious infantile impulses and anxieties, or internal wars. Rickman believed that civilians have all struggled with internal dangers as children and that with age they managed to partially overcome these fears. He therefore argued optimistically that while air raids might be new to most of the population, the internal dangers the attacks might have induced were not new at all. Civilians, in this conceptualization, were already at war (with their own selves) before the outbreak of war. With this psychoanalytic insight in mind, Rickman turned to giving the government practical advice about the prevention of panic. He believed that the government could help civilians master their air-raid anxiety by encouraging them to work on behalf of others. The supply of food, for Rickman, was of great psychological importance as it provided "internal support" to civilians; its constant supply would create a solid group spirit and good relationship with the government. Rickman also believed that good leadership would create stability among civilians and prevent panic.[30] World War II, he implied, was to be understood in direct connection to the irrational and aggressive psychology of civilians. And war itself was a familiar mental predicament. Such ideas cast a wider influence than is often recognized and were absorbed by "functional" and "analytic" experts and in different governmental, medical, and popular venues.[31]

    the Twentieth Century (Cambridge, MA: Harvard University Press, 2001), pp. 187–197; Tom Harrison, *Bion, Rickman, Foulkes and the Northfield Experiments: Advancing on a Different Front* (London: Jessica Kingsley, 2000).

[27] King, "Activities"; John Rickman, "Panic and Air Raid Precautions," *Lancet* (4 Jun. 1938), pp. 1291–1295. Cf. W. R. Bion, "The 'War of Nerves': Civilian Reaction, Morale and Prophylaxis," in Miller (ed.), *The Neuroses in War*, pp. 180–200.

[28] Sigmund Freud had, in fact, several different conceptualizations of anxiety. But what is important here are the ways in which a certain concept of anxiety was used in public. For Freud's evolving ideas, see Jean Laplanche and J.-B. Pontalis, *The Language of Psycho-Analysis* (New York: Norton, 1974), pp. 48, 184, 379, 422, 37–40 and Ch. 7.

[29] Rickman, "Panic," p. 1291.   [30] *Ibid.*, pp. 1293–1295.

[31] Shephard, *A War of Nerves*, p. 164.

Indeed, psychoanalysts aimed to research emotions in earnest. Right after the Munich Crisis in 1938, when the possibility of a new world war loomed closer, the Institute of Psycho-Analysis circulated questionnaires among analysts in order to study the psychology of civilians in relation to war. Notes were taken by twenty analysts on the reactions of a hundred patients at both the London Clinic and the Emergency Clinic that the Institute established in order to provide short-term treatment.[32] Most analysts agreed that the majority of patients were upset and reacted with various degrees of anxiety. Yet nearly all practicing analysts believed that the nature and intensity of patients' reactions were explainable by "infantile and for the most part unconscious patterns and conflicts," rather than the international tensions – an idea that, we have seen, spread beyond them to other "analytical" doctors influenced by their work.[33] Most analysts also agreed that patients reacted to the Crisis and its leading personalities, such as Hitler, Chamberlain, and Churchill, as if they were "family imagoes," for example, their good, bad, or indifferent father.[34] On November 29, 1938, for instance, John Bowlby reported on one patient, an anxious woman suffering from an "Anxiety State with much depression," who "felt very bitterly about the dismemberment of Czecho-Slovakia and felt utterly ashamed of our [Britain's] acquiescence."[35] Yet Bowlby connected her attitude to the threat of war to her own private history and her guilt feelings about miscarriages that her mother had had when the woman was a child.[36] Bowlby analyzed the patient's condition, then, by connecting inner conflicts, childhood, and world tensions. Despite infamous theoretical differences between psychoanalysts working at the time, this view (with variations) was common to all of them.[37] Calling for greater responsibility for psychoanalytic experts and emphasizing their social importance, Glover argued that "the reactions

---

[32] Edward Glover, "Notes on the Psychological Effects of War Conditions on the Civilian Population," *Int. J. Psycho-Anal.* Vol. 22 (1941), pp. 132–146.

[33] *Ibid.*, p. 139. Despite the fact that they did offer a variety of opinions on the importance of internal reality and its relation to endopsychic and environmental factors.

[34] *Ibid.*, p. 140.

[35] John Bowlby's Collection at the Archives and Manuscripts Collection, the Wellcome Library (hereafter WAMC)/PP/BOW/G.1/2: "Answer to the Questionnaire regarding the War Crisis," p. 1. John Bowlby (1907–1990) studied medicine in Cambridge and qualified as an associate member of the BPAS in 1937. Even before the war broke out, he worked with children at the London Child Guidance Clinic and had special interest in delinquent children and in researching mother–child separation, something that he would develop during the war and in its aftermath. He was initially a supporter of Klein but gradually developed a more independent position. King, "Biographical," pp. ix–xx. See Ch. 7.

[36] WAMC/PP/BOW/G.1/2.

[37] See Jacqueline Rose, *Why War?: Psychoanalysis, Politics, and the Return to Melanie Klein* (Cambridge, MA: Blackwell, 1993).

observed in pathological groups enable one to forecast, however tentatively, the reactions of more 'normal' groups."[38]

While most patients of the BPAS's study reported anxiety and distress, some showed signs of improvement during the Munich Crisis. The causes for that were again said to stem from "internal dynamics." For example, analyst Hedwig Hoffer, who moved from Vienna to London in 1938, reported on one patient suffering from hysteria who "felt relieved because people were too busy to pay attention to her."[39] A minority of patients had little or no reaction to the Crisis. Glover reported on such a patient and quoted her as saying that "she would not care two pence if her husband were killed; she cannot understand why people get so excited about it." Glover interpreted the apparent indifference to the Crisis as actually an inner "restraint of sadistic enjoyment."[40] When Glover was invited to speak on the popular BBC Radio Home Service in February and July 1940, he further popularized this analytic angle on fear and anxiety, which stressed the importance of mental processes, in contrast to other professionals who supported a more functional, straightforward approach.[41]

In contrast with many, though not all, contemporary reports stating that incidents of bomb anxiety neurosis were uncommon, once the Blitz and the actual bombing of Britain had begun, analysts argued that the majority of cases bypassed experts' examination.[42] Glover warned that while the prewar "Mass-Neurosis Myth" was unfounded, a new inaccurate "No Neurosis Myth" was now in formation. Most analysts, however, believed that once the Blitz had started the majority of patients were "surprisingly uninfluenced by the stimulus."[43]

Melitta Schmideberg, the daughter of Melanie Klein and an important and understudied analyst at the BPAS, argued, however, that "the fact that only comparatively few people broke down does not prove that the stimulus was negligible but that powerful psychological factors were working in favour of mental stability."[44] Throughout her account of civilian anxiety, Schmideberg emphasized the importance of childhood memory

[38] Glover, "Notes" (1941), p. 141.   [39] *Ibid.*, p. 137.   [40] *Ibid.*

[41] BBC Written Archives Centre (hereafter BBC WAC): Microfilm T659/183. A popular 1940 Penguin Special book included a modified version of some of Glover's talks: Edward Glover, *The Psychology of Fear and Courage* (Harmondsworth: Penguin, 1940).

[42] Edward Glover, "Notes on the Psychological Effects of War Conditions on the Civilian Population," *Int. J. Psycho-Anal.* Vol. 23 (1942), pp. 17–37.

[43] *Ibid.*, pp. 30, 36.

[44] Melitta Schmideberg, "Some Observations on Individual Reactions to Air Raids," *Int. J. Psycho-Anal.* Vol. 23 (1942), p. 150. Melitta Schmideberg (1904–1983) received a medical degree and joined the Berlin Psychoanalytic Society after her husband, Walter

and "inner reality" – seen by her as by many analysts to be also aggressive and sadistic – in the perception of violent reality. For example, the fact that many people were afraid of being alone during a raid was interpreted as "largely influenced by some infantile fear of being left alone or shut in." Anxiety that arose due to evacuation was seen as connected to unconscious conflicts. This way "a husband's guilt over his unconscious satisfaction at getting rid of his wife and the desire to take advantage of her absence might make him feel unable to get on without her."[45] Psychological experience here dictated thoughts and actions during the Blitz.

Like other analysts, Schmideberg stressed the importance of human psychology (as she, and they, saw it) to comprehending industrial warfare. Sirens and bombs, according to Schmideberg, held very personal meanings to anxious patients. She described how for many of them the sirens symbolized scolding voices of their parents, and the raids represented the physical punishment that followed. One patient, for example, obeyed the sirens slowly, in a disgruntled manner, precisely as he once answered the summons from his parents. In contrast, another patient felt that he ought not to run away from the raids but "face up to them." His wish was connected with his childhood experience of waiting for his parents to quarrel, an experience he wished for and dreaded simultaneously, and that gratified his hostility. Another patient, diagnosed as "schizophrenic depressive," was reported to have said that "she would mind them [the raids] if she were well, but that she was too preoccupied with her personal problems to have time for 'normal anxieties.'" Like Glover, Schmideberg interpreted that this patient was actually not indifferent, but derived pleasure from the bombs as she even once complained of feeling so bad that she "couldn't even enjoy the raids."[46] To other patients, the bombs brought a feeling of tranquility. One man, Schmideberg reported, who had been an officer during the previous war, experienced "a deep sense of peace of mind" during the night raids. He felt happy, she claimed, because the situation reminded him of the Great War, when he had been young and dashing.[47] The war,

---

Schmideberg. Due to growing anti-Semitism, the Schmidebergs moved to London and joined the BPAS. Initially, Melitta made frequent use of her mother's ideas. Later, and as she went to analysis with Glover, her criticism of Klein grew. She withdrew from active participation in the BPAS in 1944. Nowadays, Melitta Schmideberg is unjustly remembered in a negative light due to her quarrels with her mother and her relationship with Glover. Nevertheless, she formulated many astute and influential ideas, some of which I represent here and in the following chapters as a corrective to her one-dimensional reputation. See King, "Biographical," p. xix. For more on her important work with delinquents, see Chs. 5 and 6.

[45] Schmideberg, "Some," pp. 151–152.   [46] *Ibid.*, p. 159.   [47] *Ibid.*, p. 157.

Schmideberg insisted, had private, coded meanings related to specific mental perception and past experiences.

Violence, Schmideberg claimed, liberated existing sadistic and libidinal impulses in the self. "The fact that there is more outlet for these impulses under war conditions ... is one reason why certain neurotics improve," she believed.[48] While non-psychotic patients rarely expressed a wish that somebody should be killed, during the war "they often admitted that 'they wouldn't mind' if a bomb fell rather near certain persons, especially if these had been pompous and patronizing."[49] Similarly, Schmideberg saw the blackout as representing a "sadistic intercourse between the parents." In addition, destruction of places of entertainment, such as the Café de Paris, was interpreted as a punishment for enjoyment of sexual life.[50]

Anxiety was an essential concept to the understanding of the hidden dynamics of total war. Schmideberg described how some anxious citizens treated going to the shelter like going to church, hoping that in reward for their obedient behavior they would be protected. Again, psychological reality was believed to determine wartime conduct. In this manner, "four old ladies went conscientiously to the shelter every night, except on Saturdays. Having done their duty, they presumably felt that they deserved a nice long sleep in bed on Sunday. On a Sunday morning they were killed." Other people dealt with danger and fear through acute denial. One woman "went on with her life as usual. She made a point of not allowing her habits to be interfered with by the raids. Though she suffered from severe insomnia in peace-time, she slept through almost all the raids."[51] Anxiety, then, was articulated in innovative, creative, and gradually influential ways by psychoanalysts. The evacuation process was instrumental in this development.

Psychoanalysis and the evacuation process

Evacuation from cities and the war at large were seen by many Britons to create a "family crisis." Not only were a large number of children evacuated away from their homes to reception areas, but military service also produced long separations. By 1945, there were around 5 million men and women in the armed forces. Around 30 percent of all men of working age were in service (and over half of the servicemen were married) and many of them had been continuously abroad from two to even five or more years. Women were recruited to essential war services and

---

[48] *Ibid.*, p. 159.   [49] *Ibid.*, p. 157.   [50] *Ibid.*, pp. 159, 157, 153.

[51] *Ibid.*, pp. 163–164. Schmideberg cautiously concluded, however, that it was not always possible to establish a definite correlation between realistic and unrealistic anxieties.

industries. Altogether 7.75 million women were in paid employment by 1943 (of whom 43 percent were married as compared to only 16 percent in 1931). The state itself intervened in family life in new ways and the boundaries between public and private, and between state and society, had been redrawn during the war.[52] Indeed, much was made of family separation during the war when Britons became preoccupied with the family unit and children to an unprecedented degree. Importantly, these debates were constructed with psychological language and vocabulary to which psychoanalysis was a main contributor.

The evacuation experience, seen in the work of one commentator as "a cruel psychological experiment on a large scale,"[53] produced extensive (psychoanalytic and non-psychoanalytic) literature on the effects of the process on children. Differences of class, geography, religion, and upbringing, and the contrast between city and country life, all contributed to reported difficulties between children and their foster parents.[54] Writers talked about different problems of evacuation, yet at the top of the list were enuresis (bedwetting) and anxiety. Common to different non-analytic writers was the straightforward, descriptive tone that they took. By contrast, psychoanalysts offered a most thoroughgoing, theoretically "deep" portrayal of inner life, and provided new and increasingly popular ways of conceptualizing the dynamics of aggression, fear, and anxiety among children separated from their families, while describing the threat those children could pose to democratic society.[55]

The first wave of evacuation occurred around the time that war was declared in September 1939 when about 3.5 million civilians fled to safer areas in England and Wales; 2 million of them evacuated privately. However, around 1.5 million evacuees used the official government scheme, the majority of whom were schoolchildren or mothers with young children who were also disproportionately from impoverished families. By early 1940, due to the quiet phase of no major hostilities of the "Phony War," many evacuees returned to their homes. A second, smaller wave of evacuation of about 1.5 million people occurred in the spring and fall of 1940 after the fall of France and once the Blitz started.

---

[52] Geoffrey Field, "Perspectives on the Working-Class Family in Wartime Britain, 1939–1945," *International Labor and Working-Class History* Vol. 38 (1990), pp. 3–7.

[53] Katharine M. Wolf, "Evacuation of Children in Wartime," *Psychoanal. St. Child* Vol. 1 (1945), p. 389. See also Arthur T. Jersild, "Mental Health of Children and Families in Wartime," *Review of Educational Research* Vol. 13, No. 5 (Dec. 1943), pp. 468–477.

[54] See Sonya Rose, *Which People's War?: National Identity and Citizenship in Britain, 1939–1945* (Oxford University Press, 2003), pp. 56–62, 206–214.

[55] See Nikolas Rose, *Governing the Soul: The Shaping of the Private Self* (London: Routledge, 1999, 2nd edn.).

The third and last evacuation of about 1 million people took place in the summer of 1944 due to the flying bomb attacks.

Evacuation, especially its first wave, incited a debate about the successes and failures of existing health and welfare services. It increased expectations for better services for everyone and more state involvement in the future.[56] For example, while some still blamed parents and the home as the source of hygiene problems, others – including psychoanalysts – started calling for an enlargement of state responsibility for the welfare of the population and for the betterment of health services.[57] In areas of care for the physical needs of children, the war created a change that had roots in earlier, 1930s developments. But in the case of child mental health, I argue, the war brought perhaps more innovation than in other areas. The war helped focus attention on existing psychological and psychoanalytic ideas but it also served as an arena for their theoretical development in inventive ways. The war produced a greater willingness among officials and others to think in a psychological manner rather than mostly along the class-biased lines about the "bad habits" of the urban working classes. While evacuation contributed to a classist discussion of juvenile delinquency and of theories on the "problem family," it also helped encourage a growth in child mental-health debates. The use of evacuation hostels and nurseries, some of which were run by psychoanalysts, spurred the development of more progressive institutions for the elderly and mentally ill, and anticipated postwar innovations in "community care."[58]

Paying attention to mental health and its outcomes, analysts John Bowlby and Donald Winnicott together with Emanuel Miller had already published a letter in December 1939 warning the public against the dangers of evacuation. Prolonged separation of a small child from the mother, the letter claimed, could cause persistent delinquency, mild behavior disorder, anxiety, and a tendency to vague physical illness. The writers concluded by saying that the evacuation of small children without their mothers "can lead to a big increase in juvenile delinquency in the next decade."[59] In another published letter, Rickman wrote, "Even a

---

[56] Richard Titmuss, *Problems of Social Policy* (London: HMSO, 1950), pp. 100–110, 355–370; Angus Calder, *The People's War: Britain 1939–1945* (New York: Pantheon Books, 1969), pp. 35–50; Sonya Rose, *Which People's War?*; John Macnicol, "The Evacuation of Schoolchildren," in H. L. Smith (ed.), *War and Social Change: British Society in the Second World War* (Manchester University Press, 1986), pp. 3–31.

[57] John Welshman, "Evacuation and Social Policy during the Second World War: Myth and Reality," *Twentieth Century British History* Vol. 9, No. 1 (1998), pp. 28–53.

[58] *Ibid.*

[59] John Bowlby, Emanuel Miller, and D. W. Winnicott, "Evacuation of Small Children," *BMJ* (16 Dec. 1939), pp. 1202–1203.

situation of emergency should not be allowed to divert our attention for the basic needs of the mental and social development of our future fellow citizens."[60] In contrast, other contemporaries writing on juvenile delinquency later tied it to poor living conditions and the low standards of parental discipline rather than to psychological difficulty or the failure of mothers to be present for children during the war.[61]

In March 1940 the journal the *New Era in Home and School* dedicated a whole issue to the evacuation process. Psychoanalysts wrote half of the articles in this issue and emphasized the importance of stable family ties and of prevention of anxiety to the mental health of the child as a future member of democratic society. Susan Isaacs, for example, characterized the child as having a limited understanding, and being dependent, in need of affection, and prone to anxiety.[62] Anxiety, for her, was an important concept that operated in different ways. Many young children had shown anxiety, and feared that their homes and their parents might be bombed. This fear, Isaacs thought, was very acute and, especially if it was unconscious, had a good deal to do with many of the evacuated children's difficulties. Suffering a separation from their familiar environment, some anxious children chose a selective perception of reality. Instead of feeling open dread for the safety of their parents and homes, these children clung to the belief that the war and the blackout were only reality in the place to which they were evacuated.

Isaacs claimed that children who were billeted to families of different social and economic standards faced more problems adapting to new food, clothes, and accents. Yet, besides these concerns, Isaacs focused her attention on their internal realities, believing that parting from parents stirred up in the child intense early conflicts and anxieties. Here, the outside reality of war was connected to the way in which Isaacs psychoanalytically saw the development of children. She explained in theoretical depth that every child has conflicted feelings of love toward the parents, but also impulses of greed, jealousy, and defiance. The

[60] John Rickman, "Letter: Evacuation and the Child's Mind," *Lancet* (2 Dec. 1939), p. 1192.

[61] Women's Group on Public Welfare, *Our Town: A Close Up* (Oxford: Oxford University Press, 1943), quoted in Welshman, "Evacuation and Social Policy," p. 49; Sonya Rose, *Which People's War?*, pp. 56–62.

[62] Susan Isaacs, "The Uprooted Child," *New Era in Home and School* Vol. 21, No. 3 (Mar. 1940), p. 54. Susan Isaacs (1885–1948) became an associate member of the BPAS in 1921. Working as the principal of the Malting House School, Cambridge, from 1924 to 1927, Isaacs did her pioneering research in child development. From 1933, Isaacs served as the head of the new Department of Child Development at the Institute of Education, University of London, where she continued to practice analytic ideas. See King, "Biographical," p. xv; ABPAS: Annual Report for 1935.

children might feel as if they had been sent away from home because they were bad or due to their feelings of hatred and jealousy. The children might also believe that the parents might get hurt as a result of these feelings.[63] Attention to human psychology could also have life-and-death implications, as many of the evacuees began drifting back from the countryside to the cities by the beginning of 1940. If the authorities, Isaacs argued, had planned for the problems of evacuation "with a tithe of the labour and intelligence which we put into questions of transport, if human nature had been taken into equal account with geography and railway timetables, there would in all likelihood not have been so serious a drift back to the danger areas."[64]

Bowlby, who served as an army psychiatrist in a War Neurosis Centre during the war and who helped Isaacs in her evacuation report, also contributed to the special issue of the *New Era*, reiterating the same logic of his earlier public letter with Winnicott and Miller.[65] He believed that a child separated from the mother could "grow up [to be] a discontented and difficult adolescent and … a chronic social misfit in later life."[66] Bowlby's main practical advice was that mothers should be evacuated with their children. Babies less than two years old should not be evacuated to the care of strangers, and efforts should be made for them to be evacuated to friends or relatives, he thought. He also argued that children should be visited frequently.[67] Bowlby saw bedwetting as a specific nervous psychological symptom of the child being alone in an unfamiliar environment.[68] This was in contrast with other observers, such as the Women's Group on Public Welfare writers of the *Our Towns* report, who argued that bedwetting was not due to the upheaval of war but was rather a lazy habit of "a certain social strata" living in poor housing conditions in the London slums.[69]

---

[63] Isaacs, "The Uprooted Child," p. 57. Isaacs was influenced by Klein here.

[64] Susan Isaacs (ed.) *The Cambridge Evacuation Survey: A Wartime Study in Social Welfare and Education* (London: Methuen, 1941), p. 4.

[65] Suzan van Dijken, *John Bowlby: His Early Life, A Biographical Journey into the Roots of Attachment Theory* (New York: Free Association Books, 1998), pp. 103–128. On Bowlby's work with soldiers, see Shephard, *A War of Nerves*, pp. 171–172.

[66] John Bowlby, "The Problem of the Young Child," *New Era in Home and School* Vol. 21, No. 3 (Mar. 1940), pp. 59–60.

[67] *Ibid.*

[68] WAMC/PP/BOW/C.5/4/1: "Bed-Wetting." See also Robert Hutchison and Donald Winnicott, "Enuresis," *Public Health* Vol. 51 (Oct. 1937–Sep. 1938), pp. 340–341.

[69] Quoted in Welshman, "Evacuation," p. 49. However, Bowlby and other analysts had their own class-biased agenda as they emphasized the importance of round-the-clock motherhood during a time when many working-class and also middle-class women were part of the work force.

Winnicott chose to concentrate in his *New Era* article on the anxieties of mothers, and what he termed the "Deprived Mother," rather than those of children. The process of a mother separating from her children, Winnicott emphasized, has a fantastic element related to her anxieties and guilt. For example, a mother could say to herself, "Yes, of course, take them [the children] away, I was never worthy of them; air raids are not the only danger, it is my own self that fails to provide them with the home they ought to have."[70] When the children were back, the mother needed again to "reorganize" her inner thoughts and anxieties alongside other practical arrangements, he believed.

During the war, Winnicott had plenty of opportunities to spread analytic ideas on anxiety. He gave numerous public lectures to doctors, teachers, educational psychologists, and psychiatric social workers, and consulted different public bodies about child analysis.[71] He was a consultant psychiatrist for the Government Evacuation Scheme in Oxfordshire and worked in the Oxfordshire Evacuation Hostel Scheme. There, with his future wife, the analytic social worker Clare Britton, he helped set up evacuation hostels to care for around 300 "difficult children" who could be "too anxious" to adapt to their foster parents.[72] In all these forums, the discussion of anxiety was central.

In Winnicott's and Britton's wartime hostels, the concern was two-fold: for the anxious children and for the future stability of the democratic regime. The goal of the hostels was to supply a replacement for the family so that the children's anxiety could be alleviated and they could find "social adjustment." In a mass pamphlet on "Children's Communities: Experiments in Democratic Living," Winnicott and Britton expressed concern about the institutional child who "tends to lack something not only in personal happiness, but also in the development of character and in the qualities of citizenship."[73] In the hostels where they worked together in different roles, Winnicott and Britton hoped to remedy this

---

[70] D. W. Winnicott, "The Deprived Mother," *New Era in Home and School* Vol. 21, No. 3 (Mar. 1940), p. 64. The article was based on a BBC broadcast Winnicott gave in 1939. D. W. Winnicott (1896–1971), one of the greatest popularizers of psychoanalysis, studied medicine at Cambridge and in 1923 started working at Paddington Green Children's Hospital in London. In the same year, he also started undergoing psychoanalytic treatment. In 1927, Winnicott began training with the British Psycho-Analytical Society, qualifying as an adult analyst in 1934 and as a child analyst in 1935. See also Ch. 4.

[71] ABPAS/G03/BA/F01/28, p. 1.

[72] Brett Kahr, *D. W. Winnicott: A Biographical Portrait* (London: Karnac, 1996), pp. 83–85. During the war, the government had to open special hostels for children who were unbilletable: Harry Hendrick, *Child Welfare: Historical Dimensions, Contemporary Debate* (Bristol: Policy, 2003), p. 109.

[73] D. W. Winnicott and Clare Britton, "The Problem of Homeless Children," in *Children's Communities: Experiments in Democratic Living* (London: NEF Monograph, 1944).

problem by ensuring the well-balanced life of these future members of democratic society. Every child that is neglected, they stressed, "becomes a burden on society, hardening into an anti-social character, or developing some other sort of mental illness."[74] Winnicott and Britton defined "a good home" as one in which "father and mother live together in a stable relationship into which the child can be accepted and welcomed."[75] In order to provide at least a substitute home for the children, it was recommended that a man and a woman should be appointed as joint wardens and that the hostels should be supervised by a psychiatrist and a psychiatric social worker. Thus Winnicott and Britton envisioned the heterosexual family with traditional roles for men and women as the healthy environment for children and as the right ideal and normal home. They tried to recreate this in the hostels.

Winnicott and Britton emphasized, however, that when children are anti-social, their care "cannot avoid being dictatorial." Children "must gradually be brought up against the consequences of their own destructive actions."[76] In these wartime analytic evacuation hostels, the worry about the aggressivity of evacuated children was pronounced and was tied to a perceived need of constant attention and home life. The future of democracy and of the possibility of cooperation among citizens rested on such values of care. Emotions were therefore seen as a problem for democracy. The war only aggravated these concerns and posed new challenges. Significantly, their pamphlet describing the hostels' work was also submitted at the end of the war as evidence to the Government's Care of Children Committee (known as the Curtis Committee).[77]

This new psychoanalytic emphasis on children's emotions and the dangers they embody is counterposed to the dominant interwar hygienist and behaviorist literature on childrearing. Hygienist and behaviorist models concentrated not on children's feelings but on children's bodies and practical routines. In the writings of hygienist authors, the emphasis was not on maternal love but on forming habits regarding toilet training, fresh air, and cold baths in order to prevent disease and bad moral character in adults. In behaviorist writings, tenderness was taboo and too much cuddling was seen to create potential invalidism, nest habits, or a "mother's boy syndrome." Mothers were even encouraged to leave their children for a large part of each day. For some behaviorists, the institution, rather than

---

[74] *Ibid.*, p. 2.   [75] *Ibid.*, p. 4.
[76] *Ibid.*, p. 6. See also A. T. Alcock, "War Strain in Children," *BMJ* Vol. 1 (25 Jan. 1941), p. 124. Winnicott worked closely with the child guidance officer, Alcock, who claimed that, while the physical conditions of children might improve in the country, their mental strain was great and due to their separation from their home and from their mother.
[77] See NA/MH/102/1451/B.

the family, was an ideal environment for rearing children in a scientific manner.[78] Thus, psychoanalysis with its emphasis on continuous maternal love and childhood emotion was a direct challenge to hygienist and behaviorist writings. After the carnage of World War I, it was what was then called the New Psychology – incorporating different psychoanalytic ideas – that opened the possibility that children could be in conflict with their environment and that emotions are not to be conditioned, but are rather part of an individual psychology. While the immediate effects of the Great War had been to promote behaviorist childrearing based on control and routine, the war experience also catalyzed trends of thought, such as psychoanalysis, that emphasized children's emotions, motivations, and resistances. Susan Isaacs, as mentioned, was the most influential figure to promote a psychodynamic approach to parenting in the 1920s and 1930s. She approached upbringing through an understanding of children's emotions and the child's point of view. By the 1930s, many leading childcare books had been influenced by the New Psychology and by Isaacs' ideas. The publication of *On the Bringing Up of Children*, edited by John Rickman in 1936, further helped shifting the focus from habits to emotions and the broadening of parenthood as now responsible for the promotion of emotional stability.[79] In the stormy interwar period, the search for ways in which to cultivate emotional stability in children made psychoanalysis, with its emphasis not only on mother love but also on the meaning of aggression of young children, more relevant than behaviorism. Especially important was the psychoanalytic idea that "the problem of war will not be solved until individuals recognize their own aggressive impulses," as Ella Freeman Sharpe put it.[80] Against the background of the rise of Nazism and fascism, historians Cathy Urwin and Elaine Sharland argued, the issue was "not simply the nature of human aggression and human love but social and political implications of how these emotions were handled in child-reading practices."[81] Behaviorism with its strong emphasis on rigid habits was now identified with "Prussianism," and the ideal of the institution was equated with the totalitarian state. Attentive parent–child relationships were to be seen instead as tied to democracy.[82]

---

[78] Cathy Urwin and Elaine Sharland, "From Bodies to Minds in Childcare Literature: Advice to Parents in Inter-War Britain," in Roger Cooter (ed.), *In the Name of the Child: Health and Welfare, 1880–1940* (New York: Routledge, 1992), pp. 174–199.

[79] The years of economic depression were also the years of growth for the child guidance movement, which in its turn helped the expansion of more psychological child psychiatry. Cf. Deborah Thom, "Wishes, Anxieties, Play, and Gestures: Child Guidance in Inter-War England," in Cooter (ed.), *In the Name of the Child*, pp. 200–219.

[80] Analyst Ella Freeman Sharpe, quoted in Urwin and Sharland, "From Bodies to Minds," p. 191.

[81] *Ibid.*   [82] *Ibid.*, pp. 191–195. See also Ch. 4.

World War II drew further attention to the links between the family and democracy, as psychoanalysts now emphasized more than before that motherhood was central to the production of healthy maturity. While different psychoanalysts stressed the importance of experiences of early childhood already in the 1930s, World War II, family separation, and the perceived dangers of evacuation to children's psyches helped further this process and focus more attention on motherhood as mitigating inner aggressiveness and anxiety. The goal now was to understand the war upheaval from the point of view of the child (the foundation of the self) and his or her inner battles. Such a psychological emphasis was used to criticize the government and its way of handling the evacuation process and to call for a change in the reach of local and state services – all for the purpose of securing the future of democracy.

Indeed, the evacuation process was not a smooth one. For different reasons, such as illness, the young age of the child, or the mere wishes of working parents to keep their children close to them during the war, numerous children were not evacuated and were in need of a nursery in cities (Illus. 1). Psychoanalysts Anna Freud, her friend and colleague Dorothy Burlingham,[83] and their staff – many of them Jewish refugees from the continent – offered unique care for these children in their Hampstead War Nurseries in London. No other account of the connections between anxiety, aggression, war, and the child – besides the one offered by Melanie Klein to be discussed in Chapter 3 – could compete in its thoroughness with the one of Anna Freud describing the work of the Nurseries under fire. Anxiety, in specific, was a crucial emotion to be explored from the point of view of the child's inner battles.

Total war: Anna Freud's Hampstead War Nurseries, London

Starting in October 1940, Anna Freud (1895–1982) and her staff opened the first two houses of the Nurseries in Hampstead, London, within walking distance of 20 Maresfield Gardens, where the Freud family resided.[84] Grants from different sources, including the American Foster

---

[83] Dorothy Burlingham (1891–1979) was an American who became a member of the Vienna Society and a close friend of Anna Freud. She joined the Freud family in London and became a member of the BPAS. See King, "Biographical," pp. x–xii.

[84] During the early months of World War II, the non-Kleinian group of analysts consisting of the Viennese refugees held discussion meetings in Anna Freud's house. They met regularly on Wednesdays "bombs or no bombs," as Eva Rosenfeld, one of the attendants, described. Other group members attending included Barbara Low, Wilhelm and Hedwig Hoffer, Elizabeth R. Zerzel, Dorothy Burlingham, Barbara Lanton, and Kate

Parents' Plan for War Children in New York, made it possible to also open a country house in Essex for the purpose of evacuation.[85] The declared goal of the Nurseries was to provide wartime homes for children "whose family life has been broken up" owing to war conditions. The staff tried to reestablish for the children what they were said to have lost, that is, "the security of a stable home with its opportunities for individual development."[86] Interestingly, however, unlike in the hostels of Winnicott–Britton modeled on heterosexual family units of substitute mothers and fathers, in Anna Freud's Nurseries the emphasis was on substitute mothering in particular.

By the time the Nurseries opened, Anna Freud, Sigmund Freud's youngest daughter, was already recognized as a pioneer of child psychoanalysis. Anna Freud's endeavors in Vienna were a forerunner to her work in Britain. During World War I, for example, she worked as a teacher in Vienna and later gave lectures on psychoanalytic pedagogy to teachers and social workers. Her colleagues with left-leaning affiliations shared her interest in child psychoanalysis and education and contributed to her ideas of community work.[87] She worked in a day-care center for working-class children, and volunteered helping Jewish children orphaned or made homeless by the war. With others, she started in 1937 the experimental Jackson Nursery for poor young children until the Nazis closed it down in 1938.[88] Her experiences with their social vision fueled her work at the Hampstead Nurseries in Britain during World War II.[89] From February 1941 to December 1945, Anna Freud submitted monthly reports to the Foster Parents' Plan for War Children

Friedlander. During the Blitz, Anna Freud also conducted a research seminar for the BPAS. See Raymond Dyer, *Her Father's Daughter: The Work of Anna Freud* (New York: J. Aronson, 1983), pp. 146–147.

[85] Anna Freud and Dorothy Burlingham, *Infants without Families and Reports of the Hampstead Nurseries 1939–1945* (New York: International Universities Press, 1973), vol. III of *The Writings of Anna Freud*, 8 vols. (New York: International Universities Press, 1967–1981) (hereafter *RHN*), pp. xxiii–xxiv.

[86] *RHN*, p. xxv.

[87] Anna Freud herself was not a socialist: Elisabeth Young-Bruehl, *Anna Freud: A Biography* (New York: Norton, 1988), pp. 99–102, 158–159. Anna Freud became a member of the Vienna Society in 1922. After she moved to Britain with her father in 1938, she was immediately elected a member and a training analyst of the BPAS: King, "Biographical," pp. xi–xii.

[88] Like her predecessor, the Viennese psychoanalyst Hermine Hug-Hellmuth, Anna Freud believed that psychoanalysts needed to study children through observation and first-hand empirical exploration rather than by gathering information from the treatment of adults: Young-Bruehl, *Anna Freud*, pp. 218–219; George Makari, *Revolution in Mind: The Creation of Psychoanalysis* (New York: HarperCollins, 2008), pp. 420–425.

[89] Sigmund Freud himself believed that psychoanalysts should extend the reach of therapy beyond the confines of the upper classes and into "the wider social strata." He hoped for a time when society would see that the poor had a right to assistance for their minds. He

where she described the work of the Nurseries.[90] The war allowed her both to develop her theories and to put them into practice.[91]

Yet the Nurseries were not only a laboratory for ideas. The kinds of help and relief the psychoanalytically trained staff hoped to provide to children under their care offered a revitalized view of psychoanalysis as a socially engaged discipline (according to a particular set of ideas, undoubtedly). Starting in February 1941, one of the Nurseries' houses in Hampstead was reorganized and included a nursery school, a toddlers' room, a large room suitable as a dressing room or a room for afternoon naps, a babies' room, a doctor's office, a hospital room, a parents' clubroom, a work room for the staff, and four staff bedrooms. The basement had a kitchen, dining room, and two shelters. These shelters were supposed to provide protection from bombs and blasts but not from a direct hit.[92] The initial staff included: Josephine Stross as a pediatrician; Hedwig Schwarz as a head nursery-school teacher, with two assistants, two trainees, and a baby nurse; Sofie Wutsch as a cook; James Robertson (later known for his films with psychoanalyst John Bowlby) as a social worker; Jula Weiss as a bookkeeper; and further help for laundry and cleaning.[93] All but Robertson were Jewish refugees. Voluntary fire-service men guarded the children (some were their fathers), and gas masks and boxes were placed in the shelters.[94] Later on, this staff grew. Schwarz directed a team of young nursery assistants, most of them again Jewish refugees from the continent. Anna Freud admitted young women as staff in training. The team also included Ilse Hellman, a Jewish refugee who had fled from Vienna and was employed by the Home Office to work with evacuees and later became a recognized analyst.[95] The Jewish refugee Alice Goldberger, who had fled from Berlin, also joined the staff and became the superintendent of the country house, as did the sisters Sophie and Gertrud Dann, refugees from Augsburg. Sophie was appointed the head

believed that "the neuroses threaten public health no less than tuberculosis, and can be left as little as the latter to the impotent care of individual members of the community" (quoted in Young-Bruehl, *Anna Freud*, p. 81).

[90] The findings were available to contemporaries in two major publications: Dorothy Burlingham and Anna Freud, *Young Children in War Time in a Residential War Nursery* (London: Allen & Unwin, 1942), and Anna Freud and Dorothy Burlingham, *Infants without Families* (London: Allen & Unwin, 1943).

[91] The reports are therefore unique documents that have hardly been explored as historical sources representing a certain wartime theoretical view in the making.

[92] *RHN*, pp. 3–4.   [93] *Ibid.*, pp. 4–5.   [94] *Ibid.*, pp. 8–9.

[95] See Ilse Hellman, *From War Babies to Grandmothers: Forty-Eight Years in Psychoanalysis* (London: Karnac, 1990). See also her report on what happened to the children when they became adults: ABPAS/G03/BB/F06/16: Ilse Hellman, "Hampstead Nursery Follow-Up Study" (7 Nov. 1966); Ilse Hellman, "Work in the Hampstead War Nurseries," *Int. J. Psycho-Anal.* Vol. 64 (1983), pp. 435–439.

of the babies' room, mothers' room, milk kitchen, and later the sickroom, while Gertrud was in charge of the junior toddlers' room.[96]

Some background on the Dann sisters illuminates the situation of forced migration of Jewish women working for Anna Freud and the hardships that they faced in their new country. Sophie and Gertrud Dann were born to a well-established family.[97] Both of them were trained nurses. When the Nazis came to power and began persecuting Jews, Sophie started to look after the 1,200 members of Augsburg's Jewish Congregation. After the war, only six Jews from their congregation – those who were in mixed marriages – had survived, while all the others were murdered. Gertrud worked from 1937 in the Jewish Children's Home in Munich. When the sisters' father, Albert Dann, was imprisoned in November 1938, they started to think about leaving Germany. The sisters eventually escaped Germany on April 4, 1939, after they were able to secure work for themselves in London as domestic servants. This job was well below their previous economic class and a common choice imposed on female refugees by the Home Office wishing to make sure that newcomers be able to support themselves. Forced to leave one job after another as foreigners in their new country, Sophie was eventually referred by an agency to work as a private nurse to Anna Freud's aunt, Sigmund Freud's sister-in-law, Minna Bernays. In December 1940, Anna Freud asked the two sisters to work in her War Nurseries and offered them the relatively high pay of £2 10s a week. The sisters finally arrived in June 1941 at the Nurseries. Sophie wrote in her unpublished memoir, "It was an ideal job; nursing, training our young students, and having time for writing and thinking out new charts.[98] Of course there were also air raids, many of them … There was a room for about 50 children, but the new-born babies were only carried down in emergencies. All bigger children were taken down every evening; they slept in bunks protected by strong nets, all made by Anna Freud" (Illus. 2–4).[99]

[96] Wiener Library Archives, London, Dann Family Papers (hereafter WLA/DFP): Personal Papers (hereafter PP) of Gertrud Dann, "Gertrud Dann," 1070/2/1–6.
[97] WLA/DFP: PP of Sophie Dann, "Sophie Dann," 1070/3/1–20; WLA/DFP: PP of Sophie Dann, "A Jewish Family in Augsburg, Bavaria," 1070/3/1–20; and WLA/Bio Index G15: (Press cutting) "The Danns' Desperate Flight to Freedom."
[98] During her work Sophie developed a number of study charts, such as a sleeping chart for baby twins and a chart that showed the number and duration of day and night air raids for one month: WLA/DFP: PP of Gertrud Dann, "Gertrud Dann," 1070/2/1–6.
[99] WLA/DFP: PP of Sophie Dann, "Sophie Dann," 1070/3/1–20. The sisters later worked in Bulldogs Bank, another of Anna Freud's war-related projects that provided help for orphaned Jewish children from a Nazi concentration camp and will be explored later. See Dyer, *Her Father's Daughter*, pp. 148–151.

Different official and voluntary authorities, such as the Hampstead Billeting Authorities, hospitals from the poorer parts of London, and psychiatric social workers from the East End Rest Centres, sent the children who came to the Hampstead War Nurseries. The reasons for admission were diverse. Some children came from bombed houses. Others had been taken to Tube shelters where they had to sleep on the platform alongside running trains; there they lost their ability to sleep and cried continually. Infants sent back from evacuation comprised another group at the Nurseries. Other admitted children suffered from shelter bronchitis or were recovering from infectious diseases. The breakup of families due to the father's service in the armed forces and the mother's work was also among the reasons listed for entering the Nurseries.[100]

The Hampstead War Nurseries were located in an upper-middle-class part of London, yet many of the children came from the poor East End and from humble backgrounds. Noting these class differences, Anna Freud's reports mentioned that the staff had been warned that London parents of the poorer classes would be unappreciative, critical, and "only too glad to dump their children on us and forget all about them and their further obligations." Yet she stressed that what the staff experienced was exactly the opposite and that they ended up admiring the efforts that the parents made for their children under the worst possible conditions, their attempts to cooperate with the staff, and their real delight about every opportunity offered to their children. She also mentioned that, although the Nurseries did not require payment, several of the parents insisted on paying.[101] The war conditions were, ironically, advantageous to some children coming from poor families, Freud noted. During the war, these children were reported to be better fed than ever before. Despite the fact that food was rationed, the change was gradual and allowed enough time to adjust. The government's preferential treatment of children under five, and the favoring of children in institutions over those in private homes, made it possible for the staff to provide a healthy diet. For children who came from families where the food budget was tight, "war and peace conditions are reversed ... They have lived under serious food restrictions at a time when there was plenty to be had, and they have entered into a world full of food for them at a time when the world around them had less than it has had before."[102]

These points about class made by Freud and her staff were written as political statements in opposition to those contemporaries who used the condemning rhetoric – popular from the Victorian era onward – that linked the urban poor to social disorder. Indeed, the evacuation focused

---

[100] *RHN*, pp. 5–7.   [101] *Ibid.*, p. 9.   [102] *Ibid.*, pp. 151–152.

a national spotlight on the lives of city children and their mothers, but perhaps more broadly on the question of poverty and social class. Public debates were characterized by mixed language which condemned poor parents (especially mothers) for their behavior while expressing shock at their living conditions. The position of Freud and her staff was on one end of the scale, in contrast with the common class-biased concern about "problem families" and "irresponsible mothers."[103] Instead, Freud and her staff stressed the parents' limited social resources and the absurdities of state neglect that made war a better time for the urban poor. Instead of stressing morality, Freud and her staff focused on bad conditions and the struggles of the poor. In a political manner, they made a positive claim for the parents and for their family dynamics (although Freud and her staff did also emphasize that poor mothers handled their children is ways that were rougher than expected). Their emphasis on the universal psychological problems of children from different parts of the population, and from the urban poor in particular, could be seen as part of the rhetoric of democratic citizenship and of social justice that developed in the 1940s; they participated in the shift in discussion of the scope of state responsibility for civilian well-being. They, along with other analysts, contributed to the critique of existing health services. They were also conceptualizing the predicaments of poor children with greater sympathy than other contemporaries. Analysts tried to sidestep the condemnatory, class-biased discourse used about poor mothers, which viewed them as the source of their children's bad manners and bad hygiene practices.[104] Yet at the same time one should note that analysts made all mothers, including those who worked or wanted to work to contribute to their family economy, responsible full-time for educating their children's emotions of anxiety and aggression.[105]

The annual report submitted at the end of 1941 offers a nuanced glimpse into conditions on the home front in wartime London that enabled the further development of psychoanalytic ideas on anxiety.[106] By that time, the Nurseries consisted of 103 children of ages ranging from several weeks to 10 years old. The family situation of these children varied. The fathers of thirty-six children and the mothers of two were serving in the armed forces. The fathers of twenty-five children and the mothers of

---

[103] Sonya Rose, *Which People's War?*, pp. 56–62. See also Ina Zweiniger-Bargielowska, *Austerity in Britain: Rationing, Controls, and Consumption, 1939–1955* (Oxford University Press, 2000), pp. 128–150.

[104] Field, "Perspectives"; Welshman, "Evacuation and Social Policy."

[105] See also Ch. 7.

[106] The report was also published in popular format in the journal *New Era in Home and School*.

twenty-seven were engaged in war work, while thirty-one children still had parents in civilian occupations. Six mothers had worked in the Nurseries themselves and were able to care for their own babies if they wished. Seven children had lost their fathers due to the bombings, and one father had committed suicide during the war.[107]

All of the children went through complex war experiences. First and foremost, all children over 16 months who were alive during the Blitz and in earlier months had been exposed to numerous air raids. The houses of fifteen children had been destroyed or badly damaged. Shelter sleeping was an experience common to the children. Thirty-five children were regular shelter sleepers in big Tube stations before joining the Nurseries. All other children slept in their homes, "either in Anderson shelters, on ground floors, in basements, or under the stairs."[108] In addition, twenty-six children had been evacuated beforehand, but had had to return to London for various reasons, such as the illness of a father and the wish of a mother to attend to him, the mother's need to search for war work in London, or an intolerable situation at the billet.[109]

In these conditions, Anna Freud and her staff offered a unique way of looking at the mid-century self by offering new links between childhood, anxiety, inner aggression, and real violence. Childhood, embodying the origin of selfhood, was not foreign to violence, but rather deeply immersed in it, according to Anna Freud and her staff. Curiously, it is Anna Freud's opponent, Melanie Klein (whose work will be discussed in Chapter 3), who is usually remembered for her emphasis on the place of violence and aggression in the individual. Theoretical differences between the two women had reached a climax during the Controversial Discussions, a set of nuanced theoretical debates at the BPAS. Yet in their war writings, it is in fact the similarities between Anna Freud and Klein that are more apparent.[110] In passages that sound as if they were taken from Klein's articles, the Hampstead War Nurseries' reports repeatedly emphasized aggression in children.[111]

In contrast to the common view of the child as innocent and gentle, Anna Freud and her staff offered two quite different conclusions: the first suggested that children were not traumatized by exposure to violence and

---

[107] *RHN*, p. 143.   [108] *Ibid.*, p. 145.   [109] *Ibid.*, p. 347.

[110] See Ch. 3 for more on the Controversial Discussions. See also Jacqueline Rose, *Why War?*; Lyndsey Stonebridge, "Anxiety at a Time of Crisis," *History Workshop Journal* Vol. 45 (1998), pp. 171–182; Adam Phillips, "Bombs Away," *History Workshop Journal* Vol. 45 (1998), pp. 183–198.

[111] Anna Freud never directly used her father's term "death drive," but she did talk about aggression in general. In the Nurseries' reports, she comes very close to supporting it. See Young-Bruehl, *Anna Freud*, p. 162.

bombs themselves; the second was that violence is actually natural to children and the real problem was how to educate them against it. "General sympathy," they said, "has been aroused by the idea that little children, all innocently, should thus come into close contact with the horrors of war. It is this situation which led many people to expect that children would receive traumatic shocks from air raids and would develop abnormal reactions very similar to the traumatic or war neuroses of soldiers in the last war."[112] From the staff observations, however, no signs of "traumatic shock" appeared in these children. Instead, their reports argued that trauma and anxiety in children were chiefly dependent on the anxiety demonstrated by their parents, and on whether the children suffered separation from them. Violence and destruction in and of themselves were not foreign or harmful to the children. On the contrary, the reports argued that children at the age of one or two are actually very aggressive, when put together "they will bite each other, pull each other's hair, and steal each other's toys without regard for the other child's happiness." The staff was often saying half-jokingly that "there is continual war raging in a nursery." The reason for that, it was argued, was that children were passing through a stage of development in which destruction and aggression played leading parts; in adults, these impulses occur when they are let loose for the purposes of war. Freud and her staff reiterated a particular psychoanalytic logic about the problem of violence:

The real danger is not that the child, caught up all innocently in the whirlpool of war, will be shocked into illness. The danger lies in the fact that the destruction raging in the outer world may meet the very real aggressiveness which rages in the inside of the child ... Children have to be safeguarded against the primitive horrors of the war not because horrors and atrocities are so strange to them, but because we want them at this decisive stage of their development to overcome and estrange themselves from the primitive atrocious wishes of their own infantile nature.[113]

As violence was seen as part of the self from early life, the danger was then that inner and outer reality would be seen as inseparable. Violence outside was repeatedly tied to violence inside.

Indeed, by September 1942, after three years of war, the idea of fighting, killing, and bombing was now accepted by most children as "an essential part of their picture of the world."[114] Violence, the reports

---

[112] *RHN*, p. 160.   [113] *Ibid.*, p. 163.

[114] *Ibid.*, p. 277. By June 1944, a month of heavy air raids in London, the Nurseries' reports claimed that the children had become indifferent to violence. Once in the shelter, nearly all the children were remarkably unaffected by the noise of the raids. Babies looked "bored and fretful" when a day went by without sirens: *RHN*, pp. 410–411. See also WLA/DFP: PP of Sophie Dann, "Sophie Dann," 1070/3/1–20, WLA/DFP: PP of Sophie Dann, "Two Refugee Sisters in England," 1070/3/1–20.

from the Nurseries argued, had become part of these children's already aggressive selves. Children interpreted war experiences in a very personal way. For Janet, a 5-year-old, a bomb that dropped near the nursery was a "punishment because the children were too noisy." She was reported to have said that it was a kind German bomber since it did not drop the bomb on the Nursery itself. To her, Freud and her staff claimed, "the German bombers had . . . behaved as she had often known her parents to behave: he had threatened punishment, had frightened her, but had in the end not carried out the threat."[115] Again, we see the perception of outside reality mingled with the violence inside.

Anna Freud and her staff suggested that, while some children displayed anxiety, its cause was not necessarily the bombs and air raids themselves. Five types of air-raid anxiety were outlined. The first type of anxiety was connected to a fear of real bombs, but reality was said to only play part of it and the children were quick to ignore or forget the danger. The second type of anxiety appeared in the child who was said to have recently succeeded in overcoming "inner aggression." When faced with aggression in reality this child feared that his or her aggressiveness would come to life again. The third kind of anxiety was connected to the general infantile fear of threatening imagined objects. The children "are afraid of sirens and of bombs as they are afraid of thunder and lightning. Hitler and German planes take the place of the devil, of the lions and the tigers." Infectious anxiety was the fourth type of discomfort. Here children were said to be most influenced by the anxious reaction of their mothers to the air raids. The fifth type of anxiety was shown in children who lost their fathers in the bombing. Every bomb appeared to these children to be the one that had killed the father. The reaction of these children was therefore to the death of their father and not an anxiety strictly connected to the air raids.[116] Anxiety deserved its own nomenclature and the war was never simply its sole cause. External dangers, analysts seemed to argue, were more easily endured than internal ones. The outside reality of war was never experienced as purely external. War brought together the internal and external and was, more than anything, an internal problem and an issue experienced psychologically.[117]

Indeed, the psychoanalytic records of children's anxieties at the Nurseries contributed to the debate about the effects of evacuation. Air raids were believed to be, once again, secondary in creating "traumatic psychological effects." The reports argued: "The war acquires

[115] *RHN*, p. 279.   [116] *Ibid.*, pp. 163–172.
[117] Cf. Melanie Klein, "Envy and Gratitude [1975]," in Melanie Klein, *Envy and Gratitude and Other Works, 1946–1963* (New York: Free Press, 1975), pp. 176–235.

comparatively little significance for children so long as it only threatens their lives, disturbs their material comfort, or cuts their food rations. It becomes enormously significant the moment it breaks up family life and uproots the first emotional attachments of the child within the family group. London children, therefore, were on the whole much less upset by bombing than by evacuation to the country as a protection against it."[118] For Anna Freud and her staff, as for other analysts, most dangerous to the child in times of war was separation from the mother. Due to the "shock of separation," they argued, children fell ill and developed violent reactions. Privileging the importance of the mother, the reports said that separation from the fathers, with whom contact was fragmented to begin with in most families, was experienced as less traumatic.[119]

The Nurseries' reports compared the evacuated children to children whose parents had actually been killed as result of enemy action. Due to the evacuation, "thousands of artificial war orphans will be added to the smaller number of children who are really orphaned by the war. It is true that these children's loss is only one of feeling and attachment. But so far as their inner stability and their further psychological development are concerned, the consequences may be just as harmful."[120] Freud and her staff recommended, then, that the child be made familiar with a substitute mother, and that the biological mother should visit frequently in order to prevent the likelihood of anxiety, shock, and trauma. For children younger than 5 years old, only nurses known to the children ahead of time should accompany them to the countryside, or their mothers could offer to join as paid domestic staff.[121] The children's needs and emotions, conceived as requiring full-time care, were the first priority.

Interestingly, before the start of the war, psychological warnings fueled the radical decision of the government to lead massive civilian evacuation out of cities. Fearing the danger of mass mental casualties due to aerial bombing, it seemed wiser for officials to mobilize the population in an unprecedented exodus out of danger zones. Yet here we are faced with the flip side of this psychological logic, as nothing for analysts, not even bombings, was seen to be as dangerous as placing the mother–child bond – at the core of emotional and social development – at risk. Placing evacuees out of harm's way did not protect them from all the war's dangers, now seen as internal as well as physical. Such a psychological emphasis was used to criticize the government and its way of handling the evacuation and to call for a change in the reach of local and state services.

---

[118] *RHN*, pp. 172–173.   [119] *Ibid.*, p. 185.   [120] *Ibid.*, p. 211.   [121] *Ibid.*, pp. 208–211.

Anna Freud and her staff believed that the most important help they provided was in the form of the "right emotional support" according to psychoanalytic child upbringing. By this they hoped to serve people of diverse social backgrounds beyond the private setting of a clinic and to ensure the development of future "normal" functioning citizens in postwar society. For example, in order to limit the harm of separation, the staff developed "artificial families" in the Nurseries; specific workers were assigned to specific children and formed units of approximately four children each so that the children could form a "substitute attachment" to the female workers at the Nurseries.[122] Unlike in other nurseries, parental visits were allowed at any time of the day, and the mothers of newborn babies were admitted with them.[123] Some mothers were able to work at the Nurseries so that they could both have a job and be close to their children. This efficient scheme solved the problem of domestic help that other nurseries had suffered from during the war.[124] Indeed, the social scope that Anna Freud and her staff set out for themselves for psychoanalytic care of children was wide. "Our aim is to educate the children toward a mastery of their drives, not based on repression ... but based on a very gradual transformation and redirection of instinctual forces."[125] The functionality of future democratic citizenry depended on this.

Besides the psychological nursing of the children, the staff was remarkably resourceful during the war in taking care of material and physical needs. For example, since vegetables and fruits were hard to obtain during the war, the staff managed to grow and produce a substantial amount in their garden.[126] They made new toys and repaired the existing equipment.[127] Furthermore, the Nurseries were a three-year analytic training school for young nurses who later contributed to other institutions in Britain and around the world. The Nurseries trained sixty-six students, and in addition were a center for training of welfare workers and of personnel from voluntary services in Britain and the continent.[128]

Without referring to the question of whether or not the claims Freud and her personnel produced are true or false, it is clear that the reports of the Nurseries offered a unique conceptualization of the problems of children in total war and an advanced problematization of the notion of anxiety as well as of aggression and war. They further linked a "war

---

[122] *Ibid.*, pp. 219–222.

[123] *Ibid.*, pp. 535–536. James Robertson was responsible for maintaining a close connection with the parents, a task that also helped in the children's return to their homes at the end of the war.

[124] *Ibid.* The total number of mothers working at the Nurseries was twenty-one.

[125] *Ibid.*, p. 479.   [126] *Ibid.*, p. 277.   [127] *Ibid.*, pp. 285–286.   [128] *Ibid.*, pp. 537–538.

inside" and a "war outside," hoping to show the extent to which they were intertwined. Indeed, the Hampstead War Nurseries can be seen as a milestone in the development of child psychoanalysis in the mid twentieth century. The Nurseries were a place for combining practice, theory, and training and served as a hothouse for producing psycho-analytic ideas whose conclusions were distinctive for the time. The Nurseries served as a bridge between aid for the community beyond the private consulting room and provided what the staff believed to be systematic investigation in psychoanalytic pedagogy. Their reports also illuminate an important chapter in the study of the ways in which war influenced the development of psychoanalysis as a socially engaged discipline in a specific democratic national context that made the question of raising anxious children into non-aggressive "normal" adults an acute one.

The Bulldogs Bank project: an experiment in group upbringing of concentration-camp survivor children, 1945–1946

Anna Freud and the refugees working for her were also involved in providing help to six Jewish orphans who came to Britain after they survived the Nazi transit concentration camp of Terezin. The accounts of the work with the child Holocaust survivors were also concerned with the problems of anxiety, aggression, and the possibility of human relation-ships after the war.[129] If World War II destroyed the structure of the family and Nazism distorted intimate relationships, the way back to civilized democratic life required the rehabilitation of such relationships, or rather a "psychological Marshall Plan." Reeducation for democracy required a transformation of individual psychology as Freud and her personnel attempted here.[130]

---

[129] First published as Anna Freud and Sophie Dann, "An Experiment in Group Upbringing," *Psychoanal. St. Child* Vol. 6 (1951), pp. 127–168. I am using the version published in Anna Freud, *Writings*, Vol. IV, pp. 163–229.

[130] The seemingly universal psychoanalytic emphasis on the family and proper parenthood as preventing children's anxiety and other psychological problems, though, had specific meanings in different national and ethnic contexts and among diverse actors. For United Nations relief workers in postwar continental Europe who embraced psychoanalysis and Anna Freud's ideas in particular, for example, rehabilitation depended on healthy family life, while this same idea was a complex issue for the Jewish children who survived the Holocaust and had no family to return to. See Tara Zahra, "Lost Children: Displacement, Family, and Nation in Postwar Europe," *Journal of Modern History* Vol. 81 (March 2009), pp. 45–86.

The six orphans spent two to three years as inmates of the "Ward for Motherless Children" in Terezin. Soon after their births, these children's parents had been deported to Poland and murdered by the Nazis. The survival of these children is miraculous given the fact that the murder of Jewish children in Europe during that time was almost total. As the war ended, around 500 children were found in Terezin, among them these six.[131] The children were flown to England with other child survivors who were the first of 1,000 children for whom the British Home Office had granted permits of entry (Illus. 5).[132] They arrived in August 1945 at a reception camp in Windermere, in the north of England, which was organized by the psychoanalyst Oscar Friedmann[133] and Alice Goldberger, the former superintendent in the Hampstead War Nurseries.[134] Together with the Foster Parents' Plan for War Children, Betty Clarke, wife of major landowner and Conservative MP Ralph Clarke, helped establish for the six children a country house called "Bulldogs Bank" in West Hoathly, Sussex. This house was to provide the children with the opportunity to psychologically adjust to a new life. The house was staffed by the sisters Sophie and Gertrud Dann, who had previously worked in the Hampstead War Nurseries, and by two other assistants. Anna Freud later provided theoretical analytical oversight.

Sophie Dann described in her unpublished memoir how Bulldogs Bank came to life. During the war, Anna Freud invited Betty Clarke, who had provided financial support to the Hampstead War Nurseries, to the Nurseries' lectures. When the war was over, the Dann sisters were to lose their jobs at the Nurseries. Not knowing what their future as refugees would be, Clarke kindly invited them to her own house in West Hoathly. She offered to buy a nearby house so that the sisters could run it as a nursery. Gertrud Dann mentioned to Clarke the orphans, who had just been rescued from concentration camps and who were staying in a Reception Centre. In

---

[131] Only 11 percent of Jewish children who were alive in 1939 survived the war. In all, around 1.5 million Jewish children and adolescents were murdered during the Holocaust: Deborah Dwork, *Children with a Star* (New Haven: Yale University Press, 1991); Nicholas Stargardt, *Witnesses of War: Children's Lives under the Nazis* (London: Jonathan Cape, 2005).

[132] See Martin Gilbert, *The Boys: The Story of 732 Young Concentration Camp Survivors* (London: Holt, 1998).

[133] Friedmann was a German teacher and social worker who fled to Britain.

[134] Goldberger was the matron of a home for children who survived concentration camps where Gertrud Dann, after the Bulldogs Bank project was closed, later worked for nine years. On Goldberger's activities, see Gilbert, *The Boys*. Before the war, Goldberger was in charge of a center in Berlin for families suffering from the economic depression. See press cuttings of Goldberger at WLA: Bio Index G15 and WLA/DFP: PP of Gertrud Dann, "Gertrud Dann," 1070/2/1–6.

response, Clarke offered the Bulldogs Bank house rent-free for the youngest of the rescued victims on condition that the Dann sisters run it.[135]

The child survivors, born in Berlin and Vienna, arrived at Terezin when they were less than 1 year old, and reached Bulldogs Bank when they were around the age of 3. They were named by the staff John, Ruth, Leah, Paul, Miriam, and Peter.[136] Because their parents had been murdered, none of the children, as Anna Freud and Sophie Dann described, had known any other life circumstances than those of group settings. They also had no experience of life outside a camp or a large institution.[137]

When the children arrived at Bulldogs Bank their behavior toward adults was described by Sophie Dann and Anna Freud as follows:

They showed no pleasure in the arrangements which had been made for them and behaved in a wild, restless, and uncontrollably noisy manner . . . they destroyed all the toys and damaged much of the furniture. Toward the staff they behaved either with cold indifference or with active hostility . . . They would turn to an adult when in some immediate need, but treat the same person as nonexistent once more when the need was fulfilled. In anger, they would hit the adults, bite, or spit. Above all, they would shout, scream, and use bad language.[138]

In contrast to their hostility toward adults, the children's positive feelings were said to be centered exclusively within their own group. They had no wish other than to be together and became upset when they were separated from each other, even for short moments. When they were together, they acted as "a closely knit group of members with equal status, no child assuming leadership for any length of time, but each one exerting a strong influence on the others by virtue of individual qualities, peculiarities, or by mere fact of belonging."[139] Their unusual emotional dependence on each other was also demonstrated by the almost complete absence of jealousy, rivalry, and competition, which, according to Sophie Dann and Anna Freud, usually developed between brothers and sisters from "normal families." The children were described to share their possessions with pleasure, take care and help one another, and act with extreme sensitivity and consideration for each other's attitudes and

---

[135] WLA/DFP: PP of Sophie Dann, "Sophie Dann," 1070/3/1–20; WLA/DFP: PP of Gertrud Dann, "Gertrud Dann," 1070/2/1–6.

[136] Ruth, for example, was born in Vienna in 1942. Her parents and her brother and sister were murdered when Ruth was a few months old. She was cared for in a Jewish nursery and was sent to Terezin with this nursery. Peter's parents, on the other hand, were deported and murdered in 1942 when he was only a few days old. He was found abandoned in a public park, cared for first by a convent and when he was found to be Jewish, was taken to the Jewish hospital in Berlin and then brought to Terezin: Dann and Freud, "An Experiment."

[137] Ibid., pp. 166–167.   [138] Ibid., pp. 168–169.   [139] Ibid., p. 171.

feelings, and, "since adults played no part in their emotional lives at the time, they did not compete with each other for favors or for recognition."[140] For example, in November 1945, John cried when there was no cake left for a second helping for him. Ruth and Miriam offered him what was left of their portions. While John ate their pieces of cake, they petted him, and commented contentedly on what they had given him.[141] The only child whose behavior differed somewhat from that of the rest of the group was Ruth. According to Dann and Freud, this was because she was the only child with a recorded history of "passionate attachment to a mother substitute." Unlike the other children, she was reported to have some feelings of envy, jealousy, and competition.[142]

When they arrived, the children were said to behave with strong and uncontrolled aggression toward adults. As they spent time in Bulldogs Bank, however, these "infantile modes of aggression gave way to the usual verbal aggression used by children between three and four years."[143] The children also started to form their first positive relations with adults and showed consideration, helpfulness, and identification with them. Later, the children also developed first signs of "individual personal attachments" to adults and displayed "resentment of separations" from their caregivers. Gertrud Dann described how "at first it [the work with the children] looked almost hopeless but after a while we began to make progress with them and they learned to trust us."[144] War, in this conceptualization, was breaking and disturbing human relationships and the very ability to form relationships. The road to democratic maturity included a formation of healthy relationships with others in positions of authority while moderating – yet not completely overcoming – inner aggression.

In addition to various "disturbances" such as problems with food and toilet habits, problems coping with the unfamiliar world around them, and language difficulties, the children were also said to suffer from fear and anxiety – of interest to us here. Anxiety and fear, Sophie Dann and Anna Freud argued, were only partly due to the fact that the children had grown up in an atmosphere laden with terror at Terezin, a camp with a large death toll and from which many people were also deported to death camps and others experienced family loss. Although the Bulldogs Bank children had no conscious memories of these matters, some of their attitudes seemed to bear witness to the impressions made on them at that time. Yet, alongside these "fears based on memories," Dann and Freud claimed that unexpectedly the children showed only the usual variety of

---

[140] *Ibid.*, p. 174.   [141] *Ibid.*, p. 175.   [142] *Ibid.*, pp. 181–182.   [143] *Ibid.*, p. 186.
[144] WLA/Bio Index G15: (Press cutting) "The Danns' Desperate Flight to Freedom."

"transient individual anxieties which are the manifest expression of the underlying conflicts and difficulties normal for their ages." They argued, "Surprisingly enough, these common forms of anxiety were not more noticeable and widespread than with children who grow up under normal conditions; they were, if anything, less in evidence."[145] Since Dann and Freud believed that children were deeply affected by their mothers' conscious and unconscious fears and anxieties, their explanation for this "normal level of anxiety" was that the surviving infants, though they lived in closest proximity with their adult guardians, did not have the intimate emotional contact with them which provides the path for the contagion of feeling between mother and child. Dann and Freud added that perhaps the fact that the children had never known peaceful surroundings rendered them more indifferent to the horrors happening around them or that possibly the children possessed "strong defenses against anxiety" in their close relationship to each other which acted as reassurance and protection. Indeed, the children were reported to be insecure and anxious as soon as they were separated from each other.[146]

The exploration of family dynamics and emotions went further. Dann and Freud's founding assumption was that, in "normal families," the child's relationship to brothers and sisters is a function of his or her relationship to the parents. For example, feelings such as aggression or sexual wishes, which are inhibited toward the parents, could be expressed through the siblings. The underlying relationship with a sibling is a negative one with an overlay of positive feelings when siblings are used for the discharge of libidinal trends deflected from the parents. When the relations of the children in the family become positive, they do so because of their common identification with the parents. In contrast, the relations of the children at Bulldogs Bank to each other were totally different from "ordinary siblings' attitudes." Freud and Dann claimed that the children were not merely orphaned at the time of observation, but most of them had no early mother or father image in their unconscious minds to which their earliest libidinal strivings might have been attached. As a result, "their companions of the same age were their real love objects and their libidinal relations with them [were] of a direct nature, not merely the products of laborious reaction formation and defenses against hostility. This explains why the feelings of the six children toward each other show a warmth and spontaneity which is unheard of in ordinary relations between young contemporaries."[147] Overall, the Bulldogs Bank children were said to be more "disturbed" than the Hampstead War Nurseries children.

---

[145] Dann and Freud, "An Experiment," p. 218.   [146] *Ibid.*, p. 219.   [147] *Ibid.*, p. 226.

The former were "hypersensitive, restless, aggressive, difficult to handle." But Dann and Freud also wanted to stress that, in contrast to other analysts who claimed that every disturbance of the maternal relations during early life would cause severe consequences, this was not the case for the Bulldogs Bank children. Despite the fact that the children had no mothers, "they had found an alternative placement for their libido and, on the strength of this, had mastered some of their anxieties, and developed social attitudes."[148] What is important in the two quite different accounts from the War Nurseries and from Bulldogs Bank is that in both the issues of anxiety and mental health were seen as central and urgent. The ability to master anxiety and aggression in the correct manner and via attachment to the parents or to substitute-parent figures was pivotal to the capacity to become a functional adult in democratic society.

Before concluding this chapter and as a short excursus from its discussion of the concept of anxiety in different psychoanalytic writings and endeavors, it is interesting to note that as Jewish refugees the Dann sisters had a complex and somewhat ambivalent relationship with Anna Freud, on whom they were partly dependent for their employment. Sophie, for example, had to nurse and attend to Anna Freud and to people related to her. In January 1946, Anna Freud suffered from pneumonia and Sophie had to reluctantly leave the Bulldogs Bank children for 10 weeks and look after her. Sophie also had to attend Dorothy Burlingham and her grandchildren after the war, a task she seemed to resent.[149] In 1950, Sophie described how she either was looking after Burlingham, nursing Anna Freud, or nursing the Clarke family.[150] In between, she had to sort out thousands of Hampstead Nurseries Observation Cards and to write cross-reference cards to most of them.[151] When restitution money from Germany finally arrived, the Dann family's life became much easier. Yet Betty Clarke continued to generously help the family.[152] In 1948, Gertrud joined the large group of older children rescued from concentration camps and looked after them with Alice Goldberger until 1957. After that, Gertrud became the librarian of the Hampstead Child Therapy Clinic in London while Sophie typed for the Clinic's library.[153] The Dann sisters also helped with the indexing of Sigmund Freud's library. Gertrud described how, "It was most interesting to handle all

---

[148] *Ibid.*, p. 229.
[149] As well as the fiancée of Clarke's son, WLA/DFP: PP of Sophie Dann, "Sophie Dann," 1070/3/1–20.
[150] She also took care of her refugee parents.
[151] WLA/DFP: PP of Sophie Dann, "Sophie Dann," 1070/3/1–20.
[152] WLA/DFP: PP of Sophie Dann, "Lady Clarke of Brook House," 1070/3/1–20.
[153] WLA/DFP: PP of Sophie Dann, "Two Refugee Sisters in England," 1070/3/1–20.

those beautiful precious books – but I did not like it a bit. There were all those art treasures standing around. One day I was just about to come down from the ladder when I realised that one of the Egyptian gods had stuck his outstretched hand into my cardigan pocket – with the next movement the whole lot of statuettes would have fallen down. I was greatly relieved when the work was finished without any mishaps."[154] This work ended when Sophie needed to attend Anna Freud again in her final illness. When the Freud Museum opened in London in 1986, Sophie was pleased to see these books in perfect condition and all the antique gods that had made work difficult for the sisters and all the famous treasures in place. Yet she added, "it was with very mixed feelings to be again in No. 20 [Maresfield Gardens, Freud's house-now-museum] where I had been working on and off for 40 years."[155] As for the Bulldogs Bank children, after 10 months they joined a group of other rescued children at Weir Courtney in Lingfield, Surrey. From there, they were separated and different families adopted some of them.[156]

The mid twentieth century, the previous two chapters have suggested, was "a new age of anxiety" that saw a new problematization of this emotion. Total war, waged against civilians as much as soldiers, incited advanced discussions about emotional and mental well-being. During this time, "all 'human science' disciplines – psychology, politics, economics, sociology – had to reorient themselves to acknowledge the power of unconscious drives."[157] Psychoanalysts played a leading part in this development. The emphasis on unconscious processes – itself originally not unique to psychoanalysis (that had nevertheless given it a particular edge) – became increasingly identified in the war period with psychoanalysis. Psychoanalysis offered ideas with broad implications for understanding not only of mental illness, but also of human relations in general, culture, and politics.[158] Psychoanalysts' experimentation in clinics, nurseries, residential houses, and hostels for children during the war produced a dominant conceptualization of the emotions and of family life. The

---

[154] WLA/DFP: PP of Gertrud Dann, "Gertrud Dann," 1070/2/1–6.
[155] WLA/DFP: PP of Sophie Dann, "Sophie Dann," 1070/3/1–20.
[156] WLA/DFP: PP of Gertrud Dann, "A Very Late Thank You," 1070/2/1–6. For interviews with the Bulldogs Bank children when they were adults, see Sarah Moskovitz, *Love despite Hate: Child Survivors of the Holocaust and their Adult Lives* (New York: Schocken Books, 1983).
[157] Mathew Thomson, "Before Anti-Psychiatry: 'Mental Health' in Wartime Britain," in Marijke Gijswijt-Hofstra and Roy Porter (eds.), *Cultures of Psychiatry and Mental Health Care in Postwar Britain and the Netherlands* (Amsterdam: Rodopi, 1998), p. 44.
[158] Graham Richards, "Britain on the Couch: The Popularization of Psychoanalysis in Britain, 1918–1940," *Science in Context* Vol. 13 (2000), p. 194.

exploration of anxiety in the context of total war was tied to the need to explain the emergence of murderous regimes, the eruption of war, and the possibility of maintaining democracy and containing human aggression. Understanding urges, instincts, and fantasies was believed to be essential to the keeping of the peace and of democracy. Healthy family dynamics during childhood and, more importantly, the formation of a good bond between mother and child were to safeguard British society from barbarism and disintegration.

The ideas advocated by psychoanalysts became fundamental to the thinking about the child and the self during the time of war, and were to turn into convention in the postwar era. The understanding of children and the procedures for ensuring stable early development became essential to the success of a democratic society in the mid century. The mental health of the individual, seen as determined in childhood, became important, more so than ever before, to the well-being of this regime.

Evacuation itself, designed by the government to prevent mass casualties and mass mental breakdowns, was described in psychoanalytic language in different forums before and during the war as a mistake. Consequently, by 1950, an edition of the standard British psychiatric textbook was already declaring, "the effects of separation from parents are much more pernicious than the effects of exposure to danger."[159] Psychoanalysts can be seen as contributing to the making of policy that redefined the reciprocal obligations of parents and the state and reflected "a new 'social democratic' conception of the family as the basic unit of society and the chief incubator of citizenship and community values."[160]

The concentration on the psychology of the child allowed psychoanalysts to emphasize the vulnerability of subjectivity and to create a link between what they believed to be the unconscious life in adulthood and the emotions and anxieties of childhood. Psychoanalytic conceptualization of the child's troubles and "psychological depths" contributed to a remaking of concepts of selfhood in the mid century, connecting it now to experiences of early life, aggression, and fears. Their discussion of selfhood was no longer only centered on the individual, but also on the fragility of relationships between individuals and on the self in relation to others – the paradigmatic case being the mother and the child. Psychoanalysts were at the forefront of a contemporary literature that had implications for the newly formed connections between the psychology of individuals and

---

[159] K. D. Henderson and R. D. Gillespie, *Textbook of Psychiatry*, 7th edn. (Oxford University Press, 1950), quoted in Shephard, *A War of Nerves*, p. 175.

[160] Field, "Perspectives," p. 3.

groups and moral and political choice, and investigated the relationship between culture, politics, and mental health.[161]

Indeed, psychoanalysis had flirted with politics since its early days. Despite Sigmund Freud, Ernest Jones, and other psychoanalysts' attempts to "keep it scientific," and dissociate the discipline from politics, since at least the 1920s, psychoanalysis had often been linked with different trends, from Marxism to Zionism to liberalism. After World War I, psychoanalysis in Germany and Austria was tied to social reformist movements. Once analysts left the European continent for Britain, they tied their future and faith to social democracy and joined the efforts of their native colleagues in fighting against fascism.[162]

Chapter 3 will explore the war work of Anna Freud's opponent, Melanie Klein, and her suggestions to look at the "Hitler inside" rather than the real figure in the outside world. Both Klein and Anna Freud emerged as theorists at the same time, yet Klein advanced Sigmund Freud's theory of the "death drive" to a new level. Once she moved to Britain, Klein's ideas, developed in Central Europe, had a new and more unique edge to them. The fact that these ideas were developed in the interwar period and during World War II should not be forgotten.

That psychoanalysts had something to say about war neurosis and anxiety does not come as a surprise. Indeed, they were not the only ones discussing these ideas. After the experience of World War I, mental-health experts were mobilizing to take the psychological effects of total war more seriously. They were in part responsible for the development of more government attentiveness to this issue and to the overall nervousness about the possible outcomes of the aerial war and about the question of sustaining continuous support for democracy during the conflict itself.

---

[161] Work that used psychoanalysis to connect psychology and ethics before and during the war included: Glover, *War, Sadism and Pacifism*; William Brown, *War and Peace: Essay in Psychological Analysis* (London: A. & C. Black, 1939); Roger Money-Kyrle, "Towards a Common Aim: Psychoanalytic Contribution to Ethics," *British Journal of Medical Psychology*, Vol. 20 (1944), pp. 105–117; Roger Money-Kyrle, *Psychoanalysis and Politics: A Contribution to the Psychology of Politics and Morals* (London: Duckworth, 1951). A discussion of psychology, the unconscious, and the importance of the mother–child bond to the later development of democratic citizenship also appeared in the influential book by Evan Durbin, *The Politics of Democratic Socialism* (London: Routledge, 1940). See also John Carl Fluger, *Man, Morals and Society: A Psycho-Analytical Study* (New York: International Universities Press, 1945); D. W. Winnicott, "Some Thoughts on the Meaning of the Word Democracy," *Human Relations* Vol. 3 (1950), pp. 175–186; Wilfred R. Bion, "Psychiatry at a Time of Crisis," *British Journal of Medical Psychology* Vol. 21 (1948), pp. 281–289; H. V. Dicks, "In Search of our Proper Ethics," *British Journal of Medical Psychology* Vol. 21 (1948), pp. 1–14; Ernest Jones, "The Psychology of Quislingism," *Int. J. Psychoanal.* Vol. 22 (1941), pp. 1–12; Ernest Jones, "How Can Civilization Be Saved?" *Int. J. Psychoanal.* Vol. 24 (1942), pp. 1–7.

[162] Makari, *Revolution in Mind*, p. 404.

Yet among psychiatrists and psychologists, psychoanalysts were on the radical side of the spectrum of ideas as they argued that deeper, inner emotional processes were operating during the time of war – as well as peace. War, in specific, was seen as posing a stimulus that required a renewed internal negotiation with the outside world. What was central during war was internal dynamics themselves.

The discussion of the "war inside" and the new attention to aggression was a trend that developed among native British psychoanalysts before World War II. As mentioned, Jones, Eder, Glover, and others were already writing about these themes early in the interwar period. The Jewish refugee analysts who joined them brought traditions of commitment to social issues and social reform. The more radical, socialist tone of such ideas lost its edge when they moved to Britain. Yet they still retained a unique call for mental health and social welfare. They now emphasized aggression and anxiety as tied to a concern for the preservation of democratic values of cooperation and harmony in relationships. Due to Nazism, psychoanalysis in continental Europe was wrecked during the 1940s. Analytic societies were either shattered or operating under Nazi rule. The European center of psychoanalysis moved to London. Now, in new ways, analytic theories of childhood were tied to the politics of the time.[163] Starting after World War I, the process by which psychoanalysis became a more socially engaged discipline was developed further during World War II.

---

[163] *Ibid.*

3   The Hitler inside: Klein and her patients

In looking at World War II and the development of the self, the figure of controversial psychoanalyst Melanie Klein emerges at the heart of this project. The writings of Anna Freud and her colleagues – refugees displaced by war and anti-Semitism, and working during the Blitz – distinctly conceptualized extreme violence as a perilous internal reality. Klein similarly advanced her ideas in the age of total war. Anti-Semitism and professional marginalization had already displaced Klein from the continent to Britain in the mid 1920s. Unlike Anna Freud, who endured the Blitz's bombs in London, Klein spent part of the war evacuated to rural Scotland. Yet Klein's writing during this time also placed aggression and anxiety at the center of modern selfhood and its predicaments. While other British analysts wrote for wide consumption during the interwar period and worked during the war in nurseries and hostels serving hundreds of children, Klein mainly worked in private practice with a few patients. Her views, however, tremendously influenced many of her British colleagues[1] who used versions of her work in public forums. In this way, unusual ideas developed in Klein's clinic were to reach a vast audience. Klein's immense and uncharted archival records allow examination of her work as a kind of laboratory that developed a language on violence. Total war was to inflect her words and metaphors with imagery and descriptions full of brutality and mêlée. The analysis in this chapter places her writing on the self within the context of the mid-century crisis.[2]

---

[1] Some of them later repudiated her work.

[2] Klein's archive at the Archives and Manuscript Collection, the Wellcome Library (hereafter WAMC) contains twenty-nine boxes, twelve of which are of clinical notes; the vast majority of them remained unexplored. See Elizabeth Spillius, "Melanie Klein Revisited: Her Unpublished Thoughts on Technique," in Elizabeth Spillius, *Encounters with Melanie Klein: Selected Papers of Elizabeth Spillius* (New York: Routledge, 2007), pp. 67–86. The notes are exceptionally rich and are often challenging to decipher, especially as they do not follow Standard English. Since these notes have never been published, I hope that I am successful in presenting their main ideas. This chapter could not have been written without the kind and generous help of Elizabeth Spillius.

Dislocated in a new country before World War II, Klein was quickly successful in gaining professional status as a foreign laywoman at the British Psycho-Analytical Society (BPAS). However, she soon needed to defend her theoretical ideas against internal criticism. During the years leading to the war, the psychoanalytical community became deeply divided between her followers and adherents of Anna Freud's ideas – chiefly, we shall see, over differences regarding child psychoanalysis. The Controversial Discussions in the BPAS (discussed below), where these ideas were debated in the early 1940s, were "a war within a war," and indeed others have commented that it would have taken "more than a World War to stop analysts from fighting each other."[3]

Nevertheless, the prewar and war periods were productive times for Klein. She inventively conceptualized the different reactions of her patients both to the Nazi invasion of Austria and to the Munich Crisis of 1938, as she followed their ideas and dreams about Hitler and the possibility of war.[4] She also undertook extensive wartime clinical notes on a boy she named "Patient A." Klein had treated Patient A in Pitlochry, Scotland, while evacuated there in July 1940. In September 1941, she returned to London where the analysis of Patient A resumed.[5] Klein analyzed another child evacuee in Scotland named "Richard" whose case was published at length.[6] In contrast, the archival notes on the war work with Patient A, which consist of more than 300 pages, remained unknown.[7] Klein discussed only a small segment from the analysis of Patient A in an article published in 1930, where she named him

---

[3] Adam Limentani, "The Psychoanalytic Movement during the Years of the War (1939–1945) According to the Archives of the IPA," *Int. R. Psycho-Anal.* Vol. 16 (1989), p. 6.

[4] WAMC/PP/KLE/B.84: Patients' Material, "Crisis I, Reactions of Patients to Events in Austria," and WAMC/PP/KLE/B.85: Patients' Material, "Crisis II: Before and After the Crisis" (hereafter Crisis I or II).

[5] Phyllis Grosskurth suggested that Klein had deserted him when she came back to London, until she resumed the analysis in 1943. However, the archival notes show that Klein continued her analysis of him immediately right after she got back to London. See Phyllis Grosskurth, *Melanie Klein: Her World and her Work* (New York: Knopf, 1986), p. 269, n*.

[6] Melanie Klein, *Narrative of a Child Analysis: The Conduct of the Psycho-Analysis of Children as Seen in the Treatment of a Ten-Year-Old Boy* (New York: Free Press, 1961) (*The Writings of Melanie Klein*, vol. IV); Melanie Klein, "The Oedipus Complex in the Light of Early Anxieties [1942]," in Melanie Klein, *Love, Guilt, and Reparation and Other Works 1921–1945* (New York: Free Press, 1975) (*The Writings of Melanie Klein*, vol. I), pp. 370–419.

[7] The existence of these notes is not mentioned in any of the literature on Klein: WAMC/PP/KLE/B.48: Child Patients, "'Patient A' I: Nov.–Dec. 1941," and WAMC/PP/KLE/B.49: Child Patients, "'Patient A' II: Dec. 1941–July 1942, 1943, 1945" (hereafter Patient A I or II). Almost all the notes are from 1941 and 1942.

"Dick."[8] During the war, Patient A followed world events closely and discussion of them appeared often in his sessions. Klein's archival notes show her theoretical work-in-progress as she developed and reworked her ideas on anxiety and aggression in close relation to practice and to the world conflict.[9] Yet her important archival documents from 1938 and those on Patient A have never before been explored. In her wartime practice, Klein formed connections between war, the self, and psychoanalysis that were unique, yet akin in many ways to those of other psychoanalysts. Psychoanalytic scholars often concentrate on the theoretical differences between Anna Freud and Klein before and during the war. Yet a historical reading of these two women's archival and published war work reveals that they were more similar than they first appeared. They both emphasized anxiety, aggression, and the fragility of selfhood, and the social as well as personal need to acknowledge and work through such emotions.

Different scholars have shown that human beings, their emotions, and notions of inner life, should not be seen as self-explanatory facts, but rather as historically made phenomena.[10] Inspired by the work of Michel Foucault, Nikolas Rose argues that in modern Western societies "human beings have come to understand and relate to themselves as 'psychological' beings, to interrogate and narrate themselves in terms of a psychological 'inner life' that holds the secrets of their identity, which they are to discover and fulfill, which is the standard against which the living of an 'authentic' life is to be judged."[11] This chapter adds a more historically specific dimension to Rose's claims by looking at Klein's contribution to the remaking of the mid-century self. A pioneer of child psychoanalysis, Klein saw the key to understanding the self as lying in early-life anxieties and conflicts. It is important to look, then, at records on the sessions of both adults and children, since Klein came back to childhood experiences in adult treatments as well.

---

[8] Patient A is "Dick," personal communication with Elizabeth Spillius, Feb. 2006. See Melanie Klein, "The Importance of Symbol-Formation in the Development of the Ego [1930]," in Klein, *Love, Guilt, and Reparation and Other Works*, pp. 219–232.

[9] Cf. Jacqueline Rose, *Why War?: Psychoanalysis, Politics, and the Return to Melanie Klein* (Cambridge, MA: Blackwell, 1993), pp. 138–139. Indeed, as had already been observed in the early 1930s, "Freud made sex respectable, and Klein made aggression respectable" (quoted in Grosskurth, *Melanie Klein*, p. 189). Klein believed that anxiety originated from the presence and danger of the death instinct within the self: *ibid.*, p. 191; Melanie Klein, *The Psycho-Analysis of Children* [1932] (New York: Free Press, 1982) (*The Writings of Melanie Klein*, vol. II).

[10] The classic text is Norbert Elias, *The Civilizing Process*, Vol. I, *The History of Manners* (Oxford: Blackwell, 1978 [1939]).

[11] Nikolas Rose, *Inventing our Selves: Psychology, Power, and Personality* (Cambridge University Press, 1998), p. 22.

Klein, her notes reveal, had a complex way of dealing with the war. On the one hand, she was personally influenced by its experience as she needed to evacuate to the countryside and was in the midst of a professional conflict.[12] On the other hand, she theoretically emphasized a partial view of her present time that mainly looked at the violence "inside individuals" and not in the "outside world." Klein looked to the war only to look away from it and into the self. She partly ignored real warfare only to invoke an alternate narrative that, as we shall see, was no less violent. War was something she both recognized and denied; she incorporated violence into her work while mostly disavowing the reality of aerial bombardment.[13] It was the war inside that was of interest to her. Her ideas stressed depth instead of surface; truth about violence could be found inside her patients, not in the newspaper reports on the war which they tried to read to her.

Born in Vienna in 1882 to a traditional Jewish family, Melanie Klein aspired in her youth to be a doctor. She never had the opportunity to pursue academic education, but she read widely on her own. She encountered psychoanalysis around 1914 while living in Budapest, where she first read Sigmund Freud. Early in World War I, already unhappily married with children, Klein sought treatment with Hungarian analyst Sándor Ferenczi who encouraged her to analyze children in her work as an emerging psychoanalyst. Heeding his advice, Klein analyzed her own children. Klein moved to Berlin in 1922 due to anti-Semitism and political upheaval in Budapest, and continued her analysis with Karl Abraham who became her mentor at the Berlin Psychoanalytic Society. There, Klein's ideas about treating children's play within psychoanalytic sessions like adult free association, and her willingness to analyze and verbalize harsh feelings of anxiety and aggression in her young patients, were criticized. Luckily for her, in 1925 Klein was invited to lecture on child analysis at the BPAS in London, which she did successfully.[14] Ernest Jones even reported to Sigmund Freud that Klein "made an extraordinary deep impression on all of us and won the highest praise both by her personality and her work."[15] After Karl Abraham died in December 1925, Klein's ideas were criticized more intensely than ever and, amid a

---

[12] Klein's imaginative concentration on practice and everyday anecdotes was increasingly seen as "unscientific," especially by male medical colleagues. See Ch. 7 for Bowlby's critique.

[13] Psychoanalysts could claim that war was Klein's fetish.

[14] Pearl King, "The Life and Work of Melanie Klein in the British Psycho-Analytical Society," *Int. J. Psycho-Anal.* Vol. 64 (1983), pp. 251–260.

[15] R. Andrew Paskauskas (ed.), *The Complete Correspondence of Sigmund Freud and Ernest Jones, 1908–1939* (Cambridge, MA: Harvard University Press, 1993), p. 577.

climate of growing anti-Semitism, she decided to leave Berlin. She relocated to London in September 1926. While her migration was only partly voluntary, this decision would spare Klein from the terror that awaited other European psychoanalysts several years later, in the 1930s, when they became refugees (Illus. 6).[16]

Klein's move to Britain marked the formation of a Kleinian center in London that would stand against Anna Freud's ideas on child psychoanalysis, which were supported by analysts in Vienna. Before Anna Freud and her supporters fled to British soil, Klein's position in London was relatively secure. Klein then had the support of most of the members of the BPAS, and it was at that time that she published her article on the child "Dick."[17] The seeds of conflict between Anna Freud and Melanie Klein were sown in 1927 as Anna Freud attacked in print Klein's work, and Klein and other British analysts published a series of responses.[18] Yet, for a period of time, Klein enjoyed the support of Jones, who defended her work in his letters to the skeptical, and at times antagonistic, Sigmund Freud. Freud felt that the British had launched a Kleinian campaign against the work of his daughter Anna. In response, Jones described in 1927 the BPAS's impression of Klein again in positive terms:

There is general confidence in her method and results ... and she makes the general impression of a sane, well-balanced person ... we have come to regard her extension of psycho-analysis into this new field [child psychoanalysis] not only a valuable addition to our powers, but as opening up the most promising avenue to direct investigation of the earliest and deepest problems.[19]

The loyalties to and affiliations with these two women would soon be tested once Anna and Sigmund Freud moved, along with several colleagues, to London in 1938. A state of discord soon developed between the "Kleinian school" and the "Anna Freudian school," with analysts from the two groups now based in Britain itself. The schism was already

---

[16] Ernest Jones heard about Klein from Alix and James Strachey. Jones had an intellectual and personal interest in child psychoanalysis. Besides sharing her knowledge of children with the BPAS, part of the arrangements made for Klein's arrival was that she would analyze Jones' wife and children. See Perry Meisel and Walter Kendrick (eds.), *Bloomsbury/Freud: The Letters of James and Alix Strachey, 1924–1925* (New York: Basic Books, 1985), pp. 145–146; Grosskurth, *Melanie Klein*, pp. 154–162; Paskauskas (ed.), *The Complete Correspondence*, p. 617.

[17] Grosskurth, *Melanie Klein*, p. 183.

[18] Anna Freud, "Four Lectures on Child Analysis (1927) [1926]," in Anna Freud, *The Writings of Anna Freud*, vol. I (New York: International Universities Press, 1974), pp. 3–69, esp. 36–49; cf. Melanie Klein, Joan Riviere, M. N. Searl, Ella F. Sharpe, Edward Glover, and Ernest Jones, "Symposium on Child-Analysis," *Int. J. Psycho-Anal.* Vol. 8 (1927), pp. 339–391.

[19] Paskauskas (ed.), *The Complete Correspondence*, p. 628.

underway as psychoanalysts from the continent started arriving in Britain from 1933 onward. Indeed, by 1938 a third of the psychoanalysts in the BPAS were from the continent and the atmosphere in the Society was altered. Fearing loss of support for her work, Klein wrote to Donald Winnicott at the time, "It will never be the same again. This is a disaster." For their part, the German-speaking analysts believed that what they found, professionally, in London upon their arrival was "war, absolute war," with regard to the direction of psychoanalysis developing in Britain.[20] It is thus interesting to note that Klein's archival notes on the reactions of patients to the Nazi invasion were taken in London before the Freuds arrived there on June 6, 1938, while her observations on the Munich Crisis were written once the Freuds were already in Britain.

Patients' reactions to the Nazi invasion of Austria, 1938

Recording the reactions of patients to the Nazi invasion of Austria in her unpublished notes, Klein came closer than in any of her published writings to dealing with the connection between political questions and the self. Explaining her reasons for making these unusual records, she said, "The phenomenon of whole nations submitting to dictators and being kept under by them seems to be much more interesting even than the psychology of dictators ... We get to understand this better if we study the reactions of people who are not directly implied, but stirred in their feelings by happenings like the overrunning of Austria."[21] Klein thought that her location in Britain put her at an advantage for understanding the feelings and mental attitudes that enabled support for a violent dictator and for war.

Before we explore how Klein viewed her patients' reactions to world events, it is important to understand how in these notes she mapped childhood experiences and their importance to the emerging self. Klein believed that every child experiences different emotional situations that are "intimately bound up with the individual's own phantasy[22] attacks against his parents, brothers and sisters, and so on." "Normally," the child has a split identification with conflicting internal images of a good and a

---

[20] Grosskurth, *Melanie Klein*, pp. 241, 243.   [21] Crisis I, p. 1.

[22] The word "phantasy" in Kleinian psychoanalysis refers to the mental representation of an instinct; it is also the basic stuff of all mental processes. See Elizabeth Bott Spillius, "Developments in Kleinian Thought: Overview and Personal View," *Psychoanalytic Inquiry* Vol. 14 (1994), pp. 324–364. For a detailed analysis of Klein's theories more generally, see Hanna Segal, *Introduction to the Work of Melanie Klein* (New York: Basic Books, 1980 [1964]); Meira Likierman, *Melanie Klein: Her Work in Context* (London: Continuum, 2002).

bad father and a good and a bad mother. Goodness is identified with love while badness is identified with hatred. The child also experiences an imagined notion of "good parents" united with each other and providing a sense of security and harmony, and "bad parents" united against the child yet also dangerous to each other and to the child.[23]

Klein believed that the ability to cope well with these early harsh unconscious inner representations is crucial to a future ability to develop moral and social capacities. The ways in which the child deals with the early hatred against internal "bad father" and "bad mother" is of fundamental importance to the later development of a sense of right and wrong and moral courage in the individual, she argued. For Klein, hatred is ultimately hatred of one's own "bad" and violent tendencies. If this hatred were to be bound up with love for the imagoes of "good mother and father" which are to be protected against "bad aggressors" (ultimately against oneself), the foundation would be laid for a moral attitude in which the hatred would be turned against what is felt to be unfair, wrong, and violent, not only to oneself, but also to people and things one loves and who need protection.[24]

Klein presented a glimpse into what would later be called object relations theory. For Klein, the mind is referring to people or "objects" in complex and changing ways. Other people or "objects" are first experienced in a partial manner in the child's mind and are split into "good" and "bad" objects. The mother, in particular, as the main object for the infant, is split into partial objects of a good nurturing breast and a bad depriving breast. With age, the child begins recognizing that these two emotionally split objects are actually part of one whole object – the mother. This realization raises guilt, deep regret, and depression as the child feels sorry for the previous imaginary attacks on the mother. Yet Klein emphasized that these two states – an earlier "paranoid position" where objects are split and a later "depressive position" where objects are whole – are not phases to be completed. The feelings and defense mechanisms associated with both positions continue to exist in the mind throughout life.[25]

Based on these assumptions, Klein explained that the "deeper reasons" for submitting to a dictator, who mentally represented an image of a sadistic father, had to do with a wish to deny one's own hatred of him in order to escape from internal early conflicts.[26] With these ideas in mind, Klein listened in her London clinic to the changing attitudes of patients to

---

[23] Crisis II, p. 61.   [24] *Ibid.*, pp. 62–63.

[25] Melanie Klein, "A Contribution to the Psychogenesis of Manic-Depressive States," in Klein, *Love, Guilt and Reparation and Other Works*, pp. 262–289.

[26] Crisis II, pp. 63, 66.

the international tensions. Klein saw the child's mind as a battlefield set for fighting anxiety which arose from aggression. Her therapeutic goal was to bring this anxiety to the surface through "deep interpretations" of "internal struggles." Her notes on patients' reactions first to the Nazi invasion of Austria, and second to the Munich Crisis, reveal how the political events of the time offered Klein new clinical and theoretical opportunities. While others in this period were busy finding ways to prevent a real war, Klein believed it was also crucial to map the internal war of modern selves.

One of Klein's adult male patients, for example, expressed a complex attitude toward the Nazi invasion of Austria.[27] At a session right after the invasion took place, this patient criticized the British government and expressed his sympathy with Austria, with Jews, and with Sigmund Freud, who was still trapped in Vienna. Knowing that Klein was originally Austrian, the patient also showed sympathy for her. In the following session, however, the patient's feelings completely reversed. He now criticized psychoanalytic writings and revealed, according to Klein, that behind his feelings of sympathy he found a sadistic satisfaction in the difficult situation of psychoanalysts in Vienna as well as hatred toward Klein, whom he wanted to see humiliated. Klein linked the reactions of this patient to the external circumstances of violent militarism to aggression and sadism residing in his own mind. She said, "It now became clear that Austria and myself were standing for the mother who [in his mind] had been raped, injured and humiliated, and that sadistic phantasies of this kind had been strongly aroused in the patient through this [real] event."[28] The patient confessed that he was not aware of these sadistic wishes, yet leaving the session, according to Klein, he revealingly said with relief, "I feel as if I had had an undeserved holiday."[29] In the subsequent session, this patient came filled with guilt due to the fact he felt that he had, in his mind, "deserted" and "injured" Klein, here as a representation of a "good mother." Klein noted that he also had homosexual phantasies directed toward Hitler due to what she believed was his growing fear and identification with an internal and external aggressive father.[30] For Klein, the patient's contradictory feelings were indeed triggered by world events. Yet where she directed her sole attention was to the patient's supposed "reality inside" as it was connected to the various infant's imagoes of parents.

---

[27] Klein named this patient "Patient A." To avoid confusion with the boy who was also called Patient A, whom I analyze later, I omit this fact from the body of the text.
[28] Crisis I, p. 3.   [29] Ibid., pp. 3–4.   [30] Ibid., pp. 4–5.

"Patient B," another adult male patient, came to his session after the invasion of Austria, hopeless about his own analysis. Klein suggested to him that these feelings were connected with the invasion and that, because he felt that Austria and Klein had been "injured," he therefore believed that no help could be expected from Klein as an analyst.[31] In a later session, Patient B reported a fear for his wife in future air raids, but Klein interpreted this as his own anxiety of air raids and of an imagined "terrifying father." She believed that B felt an inability to protect his wife from an internal bad father, and that he had lost faith in the goodness in himself and in the analysis. According to Klein, Patient B was anxious because of his worry for an internal injured mother and his incapacity to emotionally protect and save her.[32] Thus, while Patient B was talking about fear of real bombs, for Klein this was just the surface of meaning.

Klein's notes on both of these patients reveal how the German invasion of Austria for her took on meaning personalized by patients' family dramas. Invaded Austria became a symbol for an "injured" analyst and a mother under attack, while Hitler became a symbol for a hostile father. The inability to save the injured mother/Austria/Klein led to guilt and depression. Klein saw these feelings as connected more to early life than to the invasion itself, and therefore insisted that the understanding of politics was masked by an individual perception.

To give another example, after the invasion an adult woman named "Patient C" experienced contradictory feelings of anxiety and pleasure, and fear and attraction to what Klein called the "bad Nazi father." Patient C dreamed that she was in Germany talking to the Nazi leader Hermann Göring. She wanted to shoot him, but she did not know how to use a pistol. In the dream, Göring remained friendly and explained to her how to use it, and she could not help feeling a certain attraction for Göring.[33] Klein interpreted this to mean that the patient felt that she could not adequately fight back against "the dangerous father," simultaneously an object of attraction that C wanted to please and take away from her mother or kill out of fear and jealousy.[34] Curiously, Klein's interpretation did not include any reference to the real Göring or to Patient C's possible desire to kill a real future enemy. Her focus remained on the "inner world."

Klein then saw the invasion of Austria as stirring anxieties in her patients that had to do with their personal experiences. In her clinical notes on the Munich Crisis, she further conceptualized the ways in which individuals made sense of violent conflicts. The Nazis' aggressive moves toward Austria and Czechoslovakia allowed Klein an atypical occasion

[31] *Ibid.*, p. 6.   [32] *Ibid.*, pp. 8–11.   [33] *Ibid.*, p. 12.   [34] *Ibid.*, pp. 12–14.

to advance her theories. In essence, Klein utilized some theoretical vocabulary pre-dating 1938, yet she used the unfolding international developments as a laboratory for developing her ideas on modern selves. The Munich Crisis provided a perfect setting for experimentation.

Notes on the Munich Crisis

In September 1938, citizens all over Britain held their breath during the Munich Crisis when Prime Minister Neville Chamberlain tried to appease Hitler in an effort to prevent an outbreak of war. For Klein as an analyst this was also a fruitful time to explore inner crises and to decipher the psychological dynamics leading to violence. Klein distinguished between three stages of emotional reaction to the Munich Crisis. She connected the counterintuitive changes in attitude of her patients to "deeper layers of the mind."[35] The first stage took place over the days prior to the Munich Crisis, when war seemed probable. The international situation at this stage activated in most patients deep anxieties about the actual external dangers. Their analytic treatment at this time, however, concentrated on the interpretation of internal anxieties. According to Klein, "the anxieties are so much intensified ... because the fight with an internal father is so overwhelmingly dangerous – much more than any fight with the external father-figure could be."[36] For Klein, Hitler's real militant demands were seen to pose less dread in her patients than the aggression of their internalized father. Once those inner anxieties were analyzed, the patients were more capable of dealing with the external international situation and with making practical decisions.[37]

The second stage of patients' reaction to the Crisis happened during the days immediately preceding the diplomatic meetings in Munich, when war seemed definite. In those days, Klein noticed, there was a striking, seemingly irrational change in the attitude of most patients. Rather than becoming more anxious about the possible outbreak of war, most patients surprisingly expressed relief. Klein believed that this was due to their feeling of indignation about Hitler's violent attitude, which seemed to leave no doubt that Britain had to defend itself, and freedom in general, against him.[38] Yet for Klein, the true reason for relief was the patients' ability to identify with a "good father" (symbolized by Chamberlain) against a "bad father" (represented by Hitler) and their wish to protect "the mother." Patients were now able to express their hatred of the "bad Hitler father," and their love for the "good father and mother" that had

[35] Crisis II, p. 72.   [36] Ibid., p. 68.   [37] Ibid., p. 56.   [38] Ibid., p. 57.

earlier been repressed. Thus, the relief from anxiety really came from externalization of an internal conflict, a process made possible once the war became more definite. Anxiety was further relieved by the feeling that reparation in the outside world would also repair the inner world.[39] Patients' attitudes were again connected to childhood experiences rather than to the international emergency. The real players in the political drama, i.e., Hitler and Chamberlain, were seen as symbols of an internal unconscious world.

The third stage of reaction followed the Munich Agreement and was characterized by another illogical change of attitude among the patients. Despite the fact that war seemed to be avoided (at least for the time being), many patients became depressed.[40] What could account for the fact that the patients were demoralized, rather than relieved, by the fact that war seemed to have been prevented? According to Klein, despite the immediate relief from the acute danger of war, most patients "felt dissatisfaction and shame because of the feeling that Czecho-Slovakia had been betrayed and the feeling that Britain had bowed to the bad father – Hitler – , distrust in him and in future peace and freedom disturbed the relief experienced from the point of self-preservation."[41] A form of readjustment to the new reality of external loss and the expected persecution of the helpless people of Czechoslovakia was therefore needed. In some patients, the relief from fear of the dangers of war caused a feeling of guilt and loss of faith in the goodness in themselves along with a feeling that bad and destructive parts inside themselves had gained power. It led to despair of "goodness surviving in the external and internal world."[42] Klein reciprocally connected destructive aggression in the outside world to destructiveness in the self. A growing identification with the bad father – now represented by Hitler or Chamberlain or both – and a feeling that the "good objects" inside the self were not saved, was part of the depression in stage three.

In fairness to Klein, it is important to mention that in these notes she did not wish to consider external circumstances, but was instead concerned "with internal situations which arose out of a multitude of factors."[43] However, the notes show that Klein seemed to have no actual theory of reality itself. Outside reality was marginally interesting for her in comparison to the inner realities of her patients. Harsh inner realities were worsened or mitigated by external events, but patients' reactions to outside reality served mostly as indications of early-life anxiety and aggression.

---

[39] *Ibid.*, pp. 69–70.   [40] *Ibid.*, p. 71.   [41] *Ibid.*, p. 72.   [42] *Ibid.*, p. 76.   [43] *Ibid.*, p. 60.

For example, in his session on September 19, 1938, during the phase "before the crisis" according to Klein's periodization, adult male "Patient M" felt anxious about his son's violent behavior and expressed feelings of despair. M did not say a word about the international situation, however. Klein interpreted this to mean that his actual fear was that his own uncontrollable violence would be stirred by the external circumstances and that he was also afraid of "the violent father." Thus, she linked fear of violence in reference to the world to the individual's aggression. Two days later, M said to Klein that she looked well and shared his fantasy of having sexual relations with her. Klein interpreted these comments on her looks as Patient M's desire to show that "I [Klein] am not injured within or can stand the strain of the dangerous Hitler inside me."[44] M, she believed, wanted the sexual act as a reassurance that Klein was all right inside and so was he. M's anxiety for his son, who was being difficult, stood for fear of Hitler and for fear for M and Klein's "internal disaster." The real "Hitler outside" for Klein then was connected to a "Hitler inside" and to Patient M's very personal perception.

In response to her, Patient M confessed his wish to yell in the room so that Klein would stop analyzing. For M, Klein believed, she herself contained the Hitler-father, and analysis felt like an attack on him.[45] According to Klein, M avoided recognizing his despair about the international situation. This was because of his anxieties about a dangerous external and internal father, his fear of his internal parents allied against him, and his feeling that the mother was being destroyed were all "too strongly stirred by the actual situation."[46] She formed, then, a hyperbolic cyclical process: the realities of the international situation evoked old anxieties and mental occupations that in turn twisted the perception of the world. In Patient M's case, Hitler became a personal, adaptable symbol of other fears. Hence, despite the fact that Klein was reported to be personally worried during the Munich Crisis and was "in a state of agitation about the threat of invasion," the focus of her work was removed from the external situation.[47] Whenever Patient M brought up material related to the upcoming war, Klein saw this as externalization of inner wars.[48]

"Patient T" began his session on September 20, 1938, the phase "before the crisis" when war seemed probable but not evident, by expressing despair about the international situation and telling Klein of "the awful conflict that one is relieved about avoiding war, but horrified about what is ahead of one." His horrible feeling of uncertainty and dread felt to him like the danger of "falling into an abyss." Klein, in return, referring to

---

[44] Ibid., pp. 37–38.   [45] Ibid., p. 39.   [46] Ibid., p. 40.
[47] Quoted in Grosskurth, Melanie Klein, p. 240 n.   [48] Crisis II, p. 44.

the patient's previously expressed fears of a woman's bodily insides, interpreted this to mean that "the fear of the actual situation seems to be represented by the fear of the dangerous and unknown inside and genitals of the woman."[49] War or otherwise – fears of the unknown were tied to the patient's personal dreads.

Klein also took notes on the sessions of a "Patient A" – most likely the same boy discussed in detail in the next section. On the most critical day of the Munich Crisis, Patient A was anxious and spoke about gas masks and Hitler bombing London. He lay down on the couch and complained that his appendix hurt him. His appendix had been removed some years earlier and thus Klein interpreted this as the appendix hurting him again because he was being attacked "by Hitler inside."[50] Due to this interpretation, Klein reported, A felt much better and was able to consider what needed to be done during the war. The real Hitler would indeed bomb Britain as the war began, yet to think of the place of the Hitler inside seemed to Klein to be more urgent in the analysis of Patient A during this time.

Violence, aggression, anxiety, and the analysis of "Patient A"

As enemy aliens in Britain, Austrian psychoanalysts such as Anna Freud were not allowed to leave London once World War II started. Klein, on the other hand, who had been a British subject since 1934, had moved to Cambridge, where she had joined forces with her ally, the psychoanalyst Susan Isaacs. Klein saw patients in Cambridge and advised Isaacs on the evacuation report she edited.[51] In Cambridge, Klein confessed, "Anything I could write seemed so utterly unimportant in comparison with world happenings."[52] Yet Klein was able to write something substantial during the war, and in 1945 she published an article in which she discussed some of her war work with the boy "Richard" in Scotland.[53] As mentioned, another significant unknown manuscript from the war period came in the form of her archival notes on Patient A.

A short, unpublished essay that Klein wrote around June 1940 clarifies some of the ideas she had in mind when she wrote her notes on Patient A's

---

[49] *Ibid.*   [50] *Ibid.*, p. 134.
[51] Susan Isaacs (ed.), *The Cambridge Evacuation Survey: A Wartime Study in Social Welfare and Education* (London: Methuen, 1941). See Ch. 2.
[52] Quoted in Grosskurth, *Melanie Klein*, p. 249.
[53] Klein, "The Oedipus Complex." She also published a groundbreaking article: Melanie Klein, "Mourning and its Relation to Manic-Depressive States [1940]," in Klein, *Love, Guilt and Reparation and Other Works*, pp. 344–369.

wartime analysis.[54] In this essay, Klein claimed that if during the war the individual experiences too much internal terror – related to one's own destructiveness and "nervous-murderousness" and an inability to distinguish between love and hate – this might have a paralyzing effect in relation to external dangers. Klein concluded that an important step in human development is the capacity to split imagoes into good and bad ones. This capacity goes hand in hand with the individual ability to trust one's constructive tendencies and feelings of love. Only then is it "possible to hate with full strength what is felt to be evil in the external world – to attack and destroy at the same time protecting oneself with one's good internal object as well as external loved objects, country, etc. against the bad things."[55]

The ways in which the individual is fighting the internal war are crucial to the fighting of the outside war. Klein believed that, if the balance between internal and external situations was weak, the individual might feel overwhelmed by a real war situation. If such an individual feels that the external war is really going on inside and "that an internal Hitler is fought inside," then the individual would feel that it is impossible to fight the war. If, on the other hand, there is a better balance between internal and external happenings and "the war inside is not predominating, then one can turn with strength and determination against the external enemy."[56]

Klein saw the wartime analytic sessions as confirming her principle that reassurance of the patient was of little value and that the continual analysis of aggression and guilt was the most helpful way forward. She wished patients would not regress to their internal "good objects" so that they could act courageously and fight against external evil. She also said that, in analyzing patients during the war, psychoanalysts must "remain aware of the constant interplay [between the] present and [the] external situation, with internal [sic] and with the past, as well as past experiences."[57] Throughout the analysis of Patient A, such ideas were further refined.

Dick/Patient A

During the Battle of Britain, the parents of Patient A – the boy earlier named by Klein "Dick" – became worried about his safety and decided to move him to Pitlochry, Scotland. Klein joined them in July 1940, in what

---

[54] Joan Riviere's letter reacting to this essay is dated 3 June 1940.
[55] WAMC/PP/KLE/C.95: Unpublished paper, Melanie Klein, "What Does Death Represent to the Individual," p. 2.
[56] *Ibid.*   [57] *Ibid.*

she saw as an opportunity to rest and work during the war. Klein wrote to Winnicott on July 2 once she arrived there and described her enjoyment of Scotland. She told him how she was reading Churchill's *Great Contemporaries* with admiration and confessed her feeling of reassurance that such a statesman was in charge "of our so terribly difficult position."[58] Indeed, in October 1940 as the Blitz went on, Klein's London house too was hit by a bomb and partially damaged. Another reason that kept Klein in Pitlochry was the news coming from London that there was little work available and no financial security for psychoanalysts there during the war. In contrast, in Pitlochry, Klein received patients' fees for seeing Dr. Jack Fieldman; Richard; Patient A and his brother; and Dr. David Matthew. She wrote, "This time in Pitlochry has not been lost. Solitude & great leisure have done quite a lot for me – I have been *taking in* in various ways (how I enjoy now reading history!) and I have been *thinking* a lot. I am sure I have progressed and done better work with myself."[59]

At the same time, however, Klein was eager to return to London where her friends and patients were. Klein also worried about the growing opposition to her work by those analysts who remained in London, chiefly from the ex-Viennese Anna Freudians. Klein wrote to Winnicott worrying about what she saw as a struggle to preserve the essence of psychoanalytic science. She commented, "Does it sounds funny that I compare this great struggle we are in for the preservation of freedom in the *world* with such a small thing as the goings on in our [psychoanalytic] Society?"[60] Due to these concerns, Klein decided to return to London in September 1941. Her wartime analysis with Patient A resumed there in November 1941.

The first account we have of Patient A's early history is through the paper Klein published in 1930 where she called him Dick. In this article Patient A/Dick was a four-year-old boy. Klein portrayed him as an extremely unusual child.[61] Dick, Klein described, was largely devoid of affect, and was indifferent to the presence or absence of caregivers. He had only rarely displayed anxiety and had almost no interests, did not play, and had no contact with his environment.[62] Dick was antagonistic to his mother, displayed insensitivity to pain, and had no wish to be comforted or touched. Klein believed that he grew up in an environment unusually deprived of love, and suggested that he was unable to tolerate and deal with his own anxiety, destruction, and aggression. She reported that she was able to activate in Dick the development of interest and anxiety and a

---

[58] Quoted in Grosskurth, *Melanie Klein*, p. 254.   [59] Quoted *ibid.*, p. 60.
[60] Quoted *ibid.*, p. 260. These paragraphs are entirely based on pp. 245–261.
[61] In the analytic community today, Dick is usually considered to be autistic.
[62] Klein, "The Importance of Symbol-Formation," pp. 26–27.

better relationship with the outside world. During her continuous analysis of Patient A over the course of the war, Klein's disagreements with Anna Freud would erupt in the form of the Controversial Discussions that took place in the BPAS and centered, among other issues, primarily on childhood.[63]

The Freud–Klein Controversies

As German bombs fell on London during World War II, the differences between Klein and Anna Freud were intensely disputed at the BPAS. So heated were the arguments that, during one incident of aerial attack while these Controversial Discussions carried on, Winnicott was even reported to have raised a timid hand and, when finally given the right to speak, he suggested that the attending members would postpone whatever urgent theoretical issue they were debating in order to take shelter.[64] Other psychoanalytic scholars have investigated the Freud–Klein Controversies and their theoretical exploration are beyond the scope of this book, especially as they had little public significance at the time (even students at the Society seem to be unaware of them).[65] It is important, however, to examine the differences between Anna Freud and Klein in order to note hidden similarities between the work of the two women (Illus. 7).[66]

Between Anna Freud and Klein lay a number of points of difference. While Klein believed that psychoanalysis was of great benefit to every normal child – and not just the abnormal ones – Anna Freud discarded such an idea. Anna Freud acknowledged the value of Klein's play technique as a key method in child analysis and recognized its value as a tool for observing the child. However, she believed that Klein went too far both in seeing child's play as serving the same function as adult free association and in her wish to find complex symbolic meaning behind any of the child's play gestures. Indeed, Klein is famous for attaching sexual and aggressive interpretations to the most innocent of games. Unlike Klein, Anna Freud did not think that the child went through a real "transference neurosis" (an unconscious direction of feelings which in fact originated in childhood) to the analyst because she believed that the child was not yet

---

[63] See Pearl King and Riccardo Steiner (eds.), *The Freud–Klein Controversies 1941–1945* (New York: Routledge, 1991). The main discussions took place between January 1943 and May 1944.

[64] Dominique Scarfone, "'Controversial Discussions': The Issue of Differences in Method," *Int. J. Psycho-Anal.* Vol. 83 (2002), p. 453.

[65] Daniel Pick and Jane Milton, "Interview with Betty Joseph," www.melanie-klein-trust.org.uk/downloads.

[66] See King and Steiner (eds.), *The Freud–Klein Controversies*.

ready to produce a new edition of his or her love relationship in place of the one with the real parents. Since the child, according to Anna Freud, did not yet have a strong super-ego, the analyst must also educate the young patient and not give free rein to all his drives at a young and fragile age, both of which were practices Klein strongly objected to. Anna Freud believed that child psychoanalysis could not be conducted in the same way adult analysis is carried out. Unlike adults, children are usually not conscious of their disorder or need for help. The young child cannot lie on a couch and free associate, and does not develop the same strong relationship to the analyst as adults. For Klein, in contrast, child's play is something to be thoroughly analyzed in order to discover unconscious conflicts and the most hostile of feelings, which are to be communicated to the child. Unlike Anna Freud, Klein believed that the child established strong transference to the analyst and she did not hesitate to meticulously interpret negative transference as well. Klein did not believe that the real parents prevented transference, since the child brings into treatment the internal phantasized parental figures. The educational methods that Anna Freud suggested were, for Klein, interference with real treatment, as Klein believed in the existence of a developed super-ego in young children. Klein also dated the Oedipus complex to a much younger age than did Sigmund Freud.[67]

Anna Freud and Klein developed their ideas from different backgrounds and political commitments. Like many other analysts in Vienna, Anna Freud mostly identified the sources of the child's suffering as stemming from a deprived environment that was unable to meet the infant's emotional needs. The Viennese child treatments were mixing psychoanalysis with corrective pedagogy. Unlike Anna Freud, who was a committed teacher associating with different socially conscious analysts, Melanie Klein was neither a teacher nor a social reformer. Klein's ideas developed mostly out of her engagement with psychoanalytic theory. She rejected the emphasis on education for social norms, and as time went on she paid increasingly less attention to an unloving or cruel environment and more to the child's own psychological makeup, his or her inner fears and anxieties. Children, for her, were terrorized by their own inner "death drive," which when projected outward, manifested itself in human aggression.[68]

[67] Claudine Geissmann and Pierre Geissmann, *A History of Child Psychoanalysis* (New York: Routledge, 1998), pp. 102–108, 122–125; King and Steiner (eds.), *The Freud–Klein Controversies*; Anna Freud, "Four Lectures"; Klein, *The Psycho-Analysis of Children*.

[68] George Makari, *Revolution in Mind: The Creation of Psychanalysis* (New York: Harper Collins, 2008), pp. 427–431.

The differences between Anna Freud and Klein were debated in a set of scientific debates with members of the BPAS representing the two groups offering papers and questions for discussion. At the core of the debates was the question of theoretical leadership of the psychoanalytic movement after Sigmund Freud. Among Klein's supporters at the time of the Controversial Discussions were Jones, Paula Heimann, Joan Riviere, the Stracheys, and Susan Isaacs. Edward Glover, first a supporter of Klein, was now fiercely against her, and so were her own daughter and son-in-law, Melitta and Walter Schmideberg.[69] Kate Friedlander and the Hoffers supported Anna Freud. John Bowlby and Donald Winnicott were early followers of Klein, yet they grew more independent of her ideas; however, during the time of the debates, Winnicott was still considered a Kleinian. These bitter theoretical discussions in the BPAS eventually concluded with a creative solution that secured the existence of the Society with all its different theoretical threads. In 1944, a revised training scheme was created to offer two parallel training courses for candidates who supported Klein (A group) and those who supported Anna Freud (B group). Those who did not strictly follow the theories of these two women and remained "independent psychoanalysts" formed what was called the "middle group."[70]

The point most important to our discussion, however, is that, despite these theoretical differences between Klein and Anna Freud, during World War II there were also concealed similarities, or "forgotten solidarities," as Foucault called them,[71] between them. During the world conflict, they both saw connections (of various degrees) between psychological and external realities and linked the "war inside" with the "war outside." Both saw the child as being in need of care, yet at the same time full (to different extents) of anxiety and aggression. As Chapter 2 showed, during the war, Anna Freud paid more attention to internal dynamics, yet she still emphasized the importance of the real relationship with the mother. Klein's analysis of Patient A was conducted in ways very different from those of Anna Freud, yet the similarities mentioned could be traced throughout her notes which, at times, with their greater internal outlook, resembled those of Anna Freud and her colleagues at the Hampstead War Nurseries.

Patient A during the war

At the time of his war analysis Patient A dealt with, among other problems, his feeling that he was not capable of doing any good. He was childish and

---

[69] Klein and her daughter never reconciled.
[70] King and Steiner (eds.), *The Freud–Klein Controversies*.
[71] See Introduction for this suggestion.

dependent on his parents. Patient A's father was a psychoanalyst training with Klein in London, and who at one point during the war worked in Edinburgh, where the family moved after staying in Pitlochry.[72] A's parents both had health problems. They did not wish A to live with them in Edinburgh, and he therefore stayed in London.[73] Patient A was afraid that he was causing suffering to his family and might lead to its breakup.[74] Klein continuously tied his concern for the wartime developments with his personal predicaments.

In a session from 11/21/41,[75] for example, Patient A picked up the newspaper but could not read the good news about the Libyan offensive. Klein believed that this in fact represented some improvement in A's sense of the reality of war. While in the past, A used to pick out good news and turn it into a complete and decisive victory, now he avoided seeing the good news because he was too frightened of disappointment, i.e., a more normal way of dealing with it, Klein believed.[76] According to Klein, Patient A's internal reality influenced the way he read the news and his sense of the outside reality.

Klein went back and forth from world events to Patient A's inner world, from the war's battles to internal battles, and from a real destruction to an imagined one in a session from 11/24/41. Patient A again ignored good news about the Libyan offensive and said that the battle was not yet decided there and would never be decided. Klein interpreted this belief as being in fact connected to a battle taking place inside him and to his feeling that in his internal battle he was being destroyed.[77] Patient A looked again at the newspaper and wondered why Japan did not follow Hitler's orders, and commented that it would be so easy for Japan to overturn Asia the way Hitler did Europe. Klein pointed out to A's identification with Japan and interpreted this to mean that A felt like submitting to a master. Patient A, she thought, was so afraid of the "Hitler inside" that he preferred to submit to him, but then he felt disloyal to Britain, and to the good mother and father, and was also afraid of what was happening inside him if Hitler did overrun countries.[78]

On 11/26/41, Patient A argued that the morale of the Germans was low and that unlike the British they ran for shelter and stopped their armament production. Klein interpreted these thoughts as A's guilt and worry about feeling that he was a coward, and less cultured than people who helped to fight. She reminded him of "his fear, openly expressed, that he would do exactly what Herbert Morrison told people not to do in the case of

---

[72] 'Patient A' I, pp. 15, 50, 127–128.   [73] 'Patient A' II, p. 180.
[74] See 'Patient A' I, pp. 30–31, 21–22.   [75] I am using this format: month/day/year.
[76] 'Patient A' I, p. 14.   [77] *Ibid.*, p. 26.   [78] *Ibid.*, p. 37.

invasion – i.e. that he would get panicky, run about, make the whole village panicky, & in his phantasy it spread all over England, stopped communications, directed the enemy and caused the ruin of the whole country." A's statements against the Germans then were seen as related to blame and guilt over things in himself.

Nazi imagery was used for understanding A's selfhood in the meeting of 11/27/41. Patient A mentioned that his brother had behaved badly in the cinema. Klein interpreted this to mean that his brother "must have appeared to him like the bad Nazi and that in his mind he is really the bad A, being a Nazi towards the family, making them unhappy."[79] In the meeting of 11/29/41, Klein suggested that the air raids Patient A mentioned in the meeting were actually taking place inside him, and inside Klein, and were related to A's fear that everything good inside would break down.[80] Similarly, when A spoke in a German accent and imagined that the Gestapo had come into the consulting room during a meeting on 5/15/42, Klein interpreted this to mean that A constantly felt himself to be the Gestapo, both internally and in relations with his parents.[81]

In the meeting of 12/22/41, Patient A was very disturbed about the news from the eastern front and asked Klein if she saw how "Hitler took over command." Patient A was possibly referring to an article in *The Times* with the title "Hitler Takes Personal Command," and to the fact that Hitler had taken over the post of commander-in-chief of the German army.[82] Responding to his words, none of A's concerns about the real situation worried Klein. For her, A's statements meant that "Hitl. [Hitler] took command inside him."[83]

On 12/24/41 Klein thought that A had trouble facing the thought that Hitler was now "almighty inside himself." Due to the external situation of war, this internal situation had worsened.[84] Klein further interpreted this as Patient A feeling hatred and loneliness about having Christmas by himself and that he therefore was feeling much more controlled by the Hitler inside him because he was afraid that he had injured his parents and brothers.[85] The connection between inner and outside reality was a very fluid one, according to Klein. The self's sense of outside reality was built in relation to interior fears. Although it did trigger a psychological reaction, outside reality was almost a random factor, coming and going, in the anxieties and wishes really related to early life.

Patient A came to the session of 3/23/42 "in a very bad state, white in the face, very anxious and full of denial."[86] He was worried about traveling to

[79] *Ibid.*, pp. 55, 57–58.   [80] *Ibid.*, pp. 64–65.   [81] 'Patient A' II, p. 282.
[82] "Hitler Takes Personal Command," *The Times* (22 Dec. 1941), p. 4.
[83] 'Patient A' I, p. 132.   [84] *Ibid.*, p. 140.   [85] *Ibid.*, p. 141.   [86] 'Patient A' II, p. 167.

visit his parents and denied his father's illness. Klein interpreted this as A fearing trouble at home and being terrified of finding his father dead. In reaction to her words, Patient A tried to resist her and lay on the floor with his eyes closed and said "no, no, no." Klein interpreted this as meaning that, besides being worried about what would happen to the family and to himself, he was also worried about "the dead F[ather] as an enemy inside."[87] Even when Klein reacted to A's real worries about the illness of his father, the vocabulary of war, of "enemy," "foe," "life," and "death," entered her interpretations.[88]

In the session of 4/27/42 Patient A was again trying to resist Klein's interpretations, which literally seemed to be torturing him. This was the period of the Nazi Baedeker raids on Britain, in which historic cities with no military importance, such as Bath, were attacked in order to damage civilian morale. Patient A came to the session excited, sat down on the edge of the couch, and did not take off his coat or his gas mask. Klein interpreted this to mean that he was frightened about the recent raid on Bath and that he was ready to run away if a raid on London started. Patient A denied Klein's interpretation and said that the Germans had scarcely any bombs left. He wanted the British to take over Germany and wondered "isn't it what they [the Germans] would do to us [British]?"[89] Klein ignored the war reality that A was referring to and interpreted this as A now replacing the "Hitler inside" with "Germany." Patient A barely listened to her and was in a state of great excitement. He then tried to propose that the British would invade only parts of Germany. For Klein, he therefore tried to separate "a good Germany" from "a bad Germany" and suggested that the goal was that the British should make Germany a real democracy without doing it any harm. A was annoyed with Klein's interpretations and asked her to believe him that he really wanted to take back what he had said earlier. He then wondered aloud about the value of Klein's treatment. Klein replied that he could not stand her mentioning the most terrifying things to him, which in this session was her saying that A was liable to turn into a Hitler and to treat Germany, which stood for an injured mother, in "the Hitler way." Klein said that his greatest fear was "his incapacity to control his murderous and cruel tendencies."[90] Thus, while the real Hitler was violently bombing Britain, in her work Klein was interested in a different kind of aggression, one that was coming from inside the self, i.e., "the Hitler inside." Toward the end of the hour, Klein reported that A seemed a little relieved. He repeatedly asked Klein "why didn't you tell me that [interpretation] straight away?"[91] He then told her,

---

[87] *Ibid.*, p. 168.   [88] *Ibid.*, pp. 180–181.   [89] *Ibid.*, p. 215.   [90] *Ibid.*, p. 217.   [91] *Ibid.*

"if you must tell me those things then just mention it once[;] leave it alone and come back to it[;] some time after I shall be quiet."[92]

When A came to the session of 5/2/42 he looked very depressed. Klein interpreted his belief that Britain could not trust its allies as making him depressed and feel like he could not be trusted to protect his parents or not to attack them. Klein concluded that A's "Hitler inside" was spreading and thereby endangering his good internal parts.[93] Again, the worry that A expressed about reality (as he interpreted it) was seen as an indication of his own instabilities. A's possible concerns about the real war and the real Hitler were not theorized by Klein. At the end of June 1942, however, Klein suggested that, due to the analysis of childhood fears, Patient A had an improved attitude toward external fears related to the war. For example, A was now able to talk about the war in a more objective manner and see the deficiencies on the British side, something that had previously terrified him.[94]

Overall, Dick/Patient A's analysis with Klein began in 1929 and continued until 1946, when he transferred over to Beryle Sandford for three years. Sandford said that, by the time he reached her, Patient A was not the inhibited young "Dick," but a "terrific talker." While his IQ was measured at about 100, he displayed extraordinary memory and a great deal of technical knowledge about music. Klein's biographer, Phyllis Grosskurth, who met A when he was in his fifties, found him to be "extremely friendly in a childlike way, well informed, and capable of holding a job that did not exert undue pressure on him." While he admitted that he was "very fond of Melanie," he also said, "If Melanie were alive today I'd ring her and say [in reference to her analysis] 'Enough is Enough.'" While Klein insisted in her writing that she refrained from physical contact with her child patients, according to Dick/Patient A, she always soothed him when he cried and told him "Life is not all that bad."[95]

Klein and the mid-century self

Placing his own work against Nikolas Rose's Foucauldian narrative mentioned above, historian Mathew Thomson offers a new periodization of "the history of the psychological" in twentieth-century Britain.[96] According to Thomson, the fixation on a narcissistic, individualist-emotionalist

---

[92] Ibid., pp. 217–218.   [93] Ibid., pp. 231–232.   [94] Ibid., pp. 299–300.
[95] Grosskurth, Melanie Klein, pp. 186–188.
[96] See Mathew Thomson, "The Popular, the Practical and the Professional: Psychological Identities in Britain, 1901–1950," in G. C. Bunn, A. D. Lovie and G. D. Richards (eds.), Psychology in Britain: Historical Essay and Personal Reflections (Leicester: BPS Books,

psychological identity is a relatively recent development of the last decades of the twentieth century that actually stands in contrast to much of what preceded it. Quoting from the works of psychoanalysts such as Edward Glover and John Bowlby, Thomson claims that during World War II in particular, psychology had come to the fore as an ethical and social subject and as a discipline for guiding human nature.[97] At that time, he says, the emphasis was on the individual's relation to the social, the spiritual, and the moral, and the focus was on an ideal of "self-overcoming, rather than an inward-looking search for authenticity."[98] It was only after the war, according to Thomson's periodization, that psychology turned inward, and found for itself a new politics, the politics of the personal. Thomson, however, argues that it took another two decades, with the rise of the so-called permissive society, for this vision of individualism to truly capture the public imagination.[99]

How are we to understand Klein's unique theses in relation to historical questions regarding violence and the self in the mid twentieth century? What was Klein's specific historical contribution to the remaking of the self? Kleinian psychoanalysis does not neatly fit Thomson's periodization. While I have emphasized the similarities between Klein's work and that of other analysts throughout this chapter, it is also important to mention that she was unique even among them. Klein did belong at some level to the same category as that of mid-century psychoanalysts and psychologists who concentrated directly on sociopolitical problems. Yet she was also distinct from them and does not fully fall into this category nor does her work resemble the hyperindividualistic scrutiny associated with the last decades of the century. Indeed, Kleinian psychoanalysis plays an overlooked part in the history of modern subjectivity. It viewed self and society in unique ways because it looked at the social and political issues of the time through a very personal perspective of the individual. Klein dealt with the mid-century predicaments of war, violence, bombing, and aggression by looking inside, into the self. The key road to understanding this self, as well as the problem of violence, was by exploration of early childhood ideas about family dynamics. This was also true of other

2001), p. 115. Among other goals, Thomson offers to follow the ways in which "the psychological reached even further into the social fabric to shape and inform everyday life and turn all identity into something which was self-consciously psychological."

[97] As mentioned in the Introduction, Thomson claims that he wants to expand his investigation beyond psychoanalysis, yet many of his references for the mid-century crisis are of psychoanalysts. See Mathew Thomson, *Psychological Subjects: Identity, Culture, and Health in Twentieth-Century Britain* (Oxford University Press, 2006).

[98] *Ibid.*, p. 250.

[99] *Ibid.*, p. 244. While mapping the changes in psychological cultures, Thomson shows continuities between the periods as well as contradictory strands.

analysts, but Klein took it to a new level. In this manner, Klein interpreted her patients' views on Adolf Hitler as only partly related to the real murderous dictator who led Germany to war. For her, he was also something else, or as she called it, a "Hitler inside," a psychological inner image stemming from the patient's internal world. Dealing indirectly in her notes with the world tensions, she emphasized in the mid century a form of distinct individualistic psychological inwardness, one that was overlooked by Thomson. Unlike the individualism of the permissive society, Klein's emphasis on individual psychology was not aimed at freeing the self from social, spiritual, and moral chains.[100] Yet, at the same time, her ideas were also distinct from the social-ethical visions of others of her time and did not connect the individual so tightly to contemporary values.

Klein was not the only one discussing the self in the context of violence and political extremism. As mentioned, Sigmund Freud, of whom she saw herself as a follower, discussed the connection between the individual, violence, and society throughout the 1910s–1930s.[101] Freud's formulations of the "death drive" and "civilization and its discontents" were developed in diverse directions by different kinds of psychoanalysts during the mid century, ranging from Edward Glover to Roger Money-Kyrle to the Freudian-Marxists of the Frankfurt School – Wilhelm Reich, Erich Fromm, and Theodor Adorno. Klein developed Freud's theory on the death drive in her own ways. While other psychoanalysts, mentioned in Chapter 2, also linked inner and outer realities, Klein stands out even among them as a unique thinker who placed the highest value on individual inner psychology and conceptualized, perhaps more than any other theorist of her time, the outside reality of war in relation to an inner conflict.

Indeed Klein was, and still is, frequently accused of offering no place for external reality. Reading her related unexplored war notes, it seems that outside reality for Klein in this period never played a part as its own distinct entity but was always connected to inner reality. Klein's views were therefore a mid-century peak of experimental thought on a particular form of individualistic inwardness. The Kleinian gazing into the self could have been translated to the social. Yet its centrality was on the inside since the outside world was seen as mediated by internal reality. It is the close

100 *Ibid.*, p. 250.
101 Sigmund Freud, "Why War? [1933]," SE/PEP Vol. XXII, pp. 195–216; Sigmund Freud, "Beyond the Pleasure Principle [1920]," SE/PEP Vol. XVIII, pp. 1–64; Sigmund Freud, "Thoughts for the Times on War and Death [1915]," SE/PEP Vol. XIV, pp. 273–300; Sigmund Freud, "Introduction to Psycho-Analysis and the War Neuroses [1919]," SE/PEP Vol. XVII, pp. 205–216; Sigmund Freud, "Civilization and its Discontents [1930]," SE/PEP Vol. XXI, pp. 57–146.

connection that she formed between the "war inside" and the "war outside" that makes her work significant. Julia Kristeva claims, "Although
Klein was moved by the dramatic history of the European continent,
which culminated in the delirium of the Nazis, she did not focus on the
political aspects of madness that tainted the twentieth century." This,
I have showed, is only partly true. While Klein did not write on the war
directly, her archival notes reveal the extent to which she was dealing with
the question of war indirectly and the ways in which her poetics of violence
are symptomatic of the questions of the height of human destruction.[102]
Klein provided a model of selfhood, along with "practicable recipes for
action," that indirectly connected the personal aggression of the family
drama to the wider political and social questions of the time related to war
and peace.[103]

---

[102] Julia Kristeva, *Melanie Klein* (New York: Columbia University Press, 2001), p. 15.
Kristeva too would agree with the last statement.
[103] Nikolas Rose, *Inventing our Selves*, p. 34.

4 Psychoanalysts on the radio in war and peace: from collective to domestic citizenship

While Melanie Klein worked in her clinic and Anna Freud and other psychoanalysts provided psychoanalytic and social help to children and adult civilians of different backgrounds, Donald Winnicott, in addition to working in wartime evacuation hostels, also appealed to the British public through psychoanalytic broadcasts he was invited to deliver on BBC Radio.[1] These broadcasts facilitated a firm relationship between psychoanalysis and the British mass media. They helped the popularization of psychoanalytic ideas on the child, as well as the gendered concepts of the parental responsibilities of the mother and the father. Indeed, child psychoanalysts had a growing public role and a new visibility during and after the war. The presentation of psychoanalytic ideas, we shall see, was influenced by the encounter with the BBC and its staff and the ways in which the BBC audience was imagined and constructed during this period. Specifically, many of Winnicott's ideas were influenced and directed by the BBC's pioneering female producers Isa Benzie and Janet Quigley.[2] In the democratic context that developed during and immediately after the war, Winnicott shaped a particular expert authority and contributed to the ways in which the everyday life of ordinary citizens now fell under psychoanalytic purview. The BBC programs targeting women and children reinforced a broad shift in notions of citizenship in this period. During the war, emphasis was placed on "collective citizenship," that is, on doing one's bit and making sacrifices for the nation. The end of the war and the postwar period, however, saw a new focus on "domestic

---

[1] On his work in the hostels, see Ch. 2. I am grateful to the BBC scholars Paddy Scannell, Jean Seaton, David Hendy, Siân Nicholas, Kristin Skoog, Kate Murphy, and Suzanne Franks for their help. Thanks to Bonnie Smith for her insight and guidance. D. W. Winnicott quotes are reproduced by kind permission of the Winnicott Trust. Permission on behalf of the BBC was granted for quotes related to its work and with the kind help of BBC Written Archives Centre archivist Trish Hayes.

[2] The important work of these producers is little studied. By "popularization" I mean the dissemination of psychoanalytic ideas and the process of making them available in public. My point is to show how at least in the case of Winnicott – though this was also true of many others – theory was made with an eye to its immediate public consumption.

citizenship," i.e., an understanding of citizens' contribution to the nation as related to establishing the correct home and family. Being a good citizen now meant taking care of one's family and the next generation of children.[3] Through radio broadcasting, psychoanalysis reached the hearts and minds of millions of British people and helped to shape domestic citizenship. Analysts linked citizenship, home, and the notion of the child as a future citizen whose stable mental health, "normalcy," and ability to collaborate democratically with others were dependent on good parenthood and family dynamics.[4]

Winncott's radio talks were broadcast in a time when the family across Europe was paradoxically seen as both stable and fragile. From the 1930s, stabilizing new demographic family patterns had emerged: birth and death rates were falling, babies had a higher chance of living to adulthood, and rates of marriage were rising. While family patterns were interrupted by wartime, the underlying trends remained unchanged and were accompanied by a "baby boom" after the war. The middle decades of the century were the golden age of what was celebrated as "the normal family," with a near-universal marriage rate, controlled fertility limiting family size to an average of no more than two children, growing state welfare benefits, and a new cult of motherhood, domesticity, and housekeeping with the help of new technologies. This normal family was envisioned as headed by a male worker whose wife's paid work, if she engaged in any at all, was secondary.[5] Along with this perceived stability, there was also a growing anxiety about the fragility of the family and its members, which was associated with a growing rate of divorce, changing patterns of women's work, and

---

[3] In the 1960s and 1970s, radio would be more connected to individualism and individual listening.

[4] As scholars have written extensively on the early years of the BBC from 1922 to 1939, the war years, and the 1960s and after, yet much less on the immediate postwar period, 1945–1955, this chapter adds to the scarce literature on this period. See Jennifer Doctor, *The BBC and Ultra-Modern Music, 1922–1936: Shaping a Nation's Tastes* (Cambridge University Press, 1999); Paddy Scannell and David Cardiff, *A Social History of British Broadcasting*, Vol. I, *1922–1939: Serving the Nation* (Cambridge, MA: Blackwell, 1991); Siân Nicholas, *The Echo of War: Home Front Propaganda and Wartime BBC, 1939–1945* (Manchester University Press, 1996); Asa Briggs, *The War of Words* (Oxford University Press, 1970); David Hendy, *Life on Air: A History of Radio Four* (Oxford University Press, 2007); Ross McKibbin, *Classes and Cultures: England 1918–1951* (Oxford University Press, 1998), pp. 457–476.

[5] This "normal family life" to which many people aspired and which was promoted in the media and through psychoanalysis after the war was, in fact, a new, rather than traditional, model of the family, although it quickly came to be represented as traditional: Pat Thane, "Family Life and 'Normality' in Postwar Britain," in Richard Bessel and Dirk Schumann (eds.), *Life after Death: Approaches to a Cultural and Social History of Europe during the 1940s and 1950s* (Cambridge University Press, 2003), pp. 193–210.

fears of "war babies" turning into "juvenile delinquents" due to the wartime absence of their fathers or the working hours of their mothers.[6]

After the cataclysmic violence of World War II, the family played an important role in discussions emerging in postwar continental Europe about democratization, welfare, and the keeping of the peace. However, the seemingly universal emphasis on the heterosexual family, proper parenthood, and childhood had specific meanings in different national and ethnic contexts and among diverse social actors.[7] Reeducation for democracy in Britain in particular required a transformation of personal psychology and an imagined "return" to family life that would remedy the wartime "family crisis."[8] This was also true in other countries, but the family took on new meaning in Britain, as psychoanalytic thinking about the self was revised also in relation to the country's reconstruction. Numerically speaking, the scale of death in Britain in World War II was far less than on the continent. On a moral level, for Britons the war did not include many of the murderous experiences and ethical compromises that were the lot of so many of their European neighbors. Nevertheless, as we have seen, the war did bring an unimaginable level of destruction to the British home front. Many in Britain believed that the war had interfered with family and home life and gender relations in alarming ways as men, women, and children were scattered around the country and the world. Concern for gender relations was also heightened as millions of men in the armed services were away during the war and no longer served as bread-winners, while many women "left behind" in Britain itself did essential hard work in war industries and served as heads of their family units. Between the Battle of Britain and the end of 1942 in particular, when civilians endured the primary brunt of enemy blows, a strange inversion of gender roles took place, as it was frequently the male soldier who fretted and waited for news from his wife and children on the home front, rather than the wife and children who worried if the husband who was away was

[6] *Ibid.*

[7] Motherhood meant one thing to Jewish Eastern European women in Displaced Persons Camps for whom giving birth became a way to assign new meaning to their survival, and quite another thing to German women who had been raped by Soviet soldiers: see Atina Grossmann, "Trauma, Memory and Motherhood: Germans and Jewish Displaced Persons in Post-Nazi Germany," in Bessel and Schumann (eds.), *Life after Death*, pp. 93–193. See also Dagmar Herzog, *Sex after Fascism: Memory and Mortality in Twentieth-Century Germany* (Princeton University Press, 2005); Robert Moeller, *Protecting Motherhood: Women and Politics of Postwar West Germany* (Berkeley: University of California Press, 2003); Elizabeth Heinemann, *What Difference Does a Husband Make?: Marital Status in Germany, 1933–1961* (Berkeley: University of California Press, 1999).

[8] Tara Zahra, "Lost Children: Displacement, Family, and Nation in Postwar Europe," *Journal of Modern History* Vol. 81 (March 2009), pp. 45–86.

alive. Peacetime conditions did not bring immediate relief as the demobi-
lization of soldiers took time and was seen to be creating "a crisis at home"
with members of the family needing to adjust to a husband and father who
had been away. Adding to this situation were the housing shortage and the
continuation of austerity.[9] Creating a "happy home" and a "normative"
heterosexual family dynamic (where women of all classes were expected to
embrace full-time domestic life rather than paying jobs) was indeed seen
as a challenge in postwar Britain. Nevertheless, it was on the basis of the
reconstruction of home and family along conservative social norms and
clear gender boundaries that the new society was to be rebuilt, or so
insisted various public officials and experts.[10] This common idea was to
reinforce and extend democracy in the 1940s as the true alternative to
Nazism, fascism, and communism.[11] Psychoanalysis contributed to this
specific historical experience of democracy while reformulating visions of
the self and mental health that tied together patriarchal family life and the
management of aggression. The mother–child bond, as previous chapters
have also showed, became central in the mid century to ensuring normal
family dynamics that would, in their turn, guarantee a tranquil democratic
citizenry for the future.[12] It also served as a symbol for the very possibility
of human relations. Winnicott's radio work was vital in the popularization
of these ideas.[13]

[9] Alan Allport, *Demobbed: Coming Home after the Second World War* (New Haven: Yale
University Press, 2009); Ina Zweiniger-Bargielowska, *Austerity in Britain: Rationing,
Controls, and Consumption, 1939–1955* (Oxford University Press, 2000).

[10] Hoping to reverse the falling birthrate, William Beveridge declared in his famous 1942
report, "In the next thirty years housewives as mothers have vital work to do in ensuring
the adequate continuance of the British race and of British ideals in the world":
William Beveridge, *Social Insurance and Allied Services: A Report by Sir William Beveridge*
(HMSO: London, 1942), p. 53. His conviction that married women should be housewives and that adult women would normally be economically dependent on their husbands "became embodied in the postwar social security legislation which in turn had a
prescriptive effect": Jane Lewis, *Women in Britain since 1945: Women, Family, Work and the
State in the Post-War Years* (Oxford: Blackwell, 1992), p. 21.

[11] Mark Mazower, *Dark Continent: Europe's Twentieth Century* (New York: Vintage, 1998).

[12] See Nikolas Rose, *Governing the Soul: The Shaping of the Private Self* (London: Routledge,
1999, 2nd edn.), pp. 133–134, 155–181.

[13] Other psychoanalysts talked frequently on the BBC. See, for example, BBC Written
Archives Centre (hereafter BBCWAC): Microfilm T659/183: Scripts for Glover's talks
on topics such as "The Dangers of Being Human: A Psychoanalytic Approach to Social
Problems" (22 Oct. 1935), "Inside the Nazi Mind" (3 May 1941), and "Psychology in
Wartime" (12 Nov. 1943). There were more than twenty-five talks broadcast by Glover.
John Bowlby gave a series of talks in 1948 called "Seven to Fourteen" during *Woman's
Hour* that was produced by Isa Benzie. See BBCWAC: Microfilm T659/183: Scripts for
talks on "Children's Fears" (9 Nov. 1948), "Aggression in Children" (16 Nov. 1948),
"The Growth of Self-Control" (25 Nov. 1948), and others. Reprints of some were also
published in *Parents' Review* Vol. 49 (1948). Anna Freud appeared on the radio in the

The BBC in war and peace

If the reading of newspapers and novels in the nineteenth century, as Benedict Anderson argues, helped promote an imagined sense of shared experience that advanced national community, the radio became *the* consolidator of cultural and social unity in the 1930s to 1950s.[14] The BBC's contribution to developing the notion of collective citizenship during World War II cannot be overstated. The war proved to be a time of expansion, popularity, and high domestic esteem for the BBC.[15] It was during the war that it became the "Voice of Britain" and was identified with the nation-in-arms.[16] While the BBC was shaping the "People's War," it was also attentive to its audiences, which included servicemen and -women and workers in war factories, in new and profound ways. When the war ended, this populist tendency was irreversible.[17]

Radio listening increased greatly during the war.[18] By 1945, there were 10.8 million radio licenses in Britain, which represented a large majority of households across social classes.[19] After television transmissions had ceased during the war, they were resumed in 1946 and in the years to come were to threaten the popularity of the radio. In the immediate years after the war, however, the BBC had little interest in television and invested most of its resources in radio. The BBC created a tripartite system of networks with different levels of seriousness: The Light Programme (lowbrow), the Home Service (middlebrow), and the Third Programme (highbrow).[20] The Light Programme was a great success, and had roughly two-thirds of the BBC's listeners tuned in to productions

program "Parents and Children," also produced too by Benzie; see BBCWAC: Microfilm T659/391: Scripts for "Infants Are People" in 1960. Sigmund Freud himself delivered a short message on his life and on psychoanalysis on the BBC on December 7, 1938.

[14] Benedict Anderson, *Imagined Communities: Reflections on the Origin and Spread of Nationalism* (New York: Verso, 1991), pp. 35–36.

[15] Angus Calder, *The People's War: Britain 1939–1945* (New York: Pantheon Books, 1969), pp. 358–359.

[16] *Ibid.*, p. 357; McKibbin, *Classes and Cultures*, p. 468.

[17] Andrew Crisell, *An Introductory History of British Broadcasting* (London: Routledge, 2002), p. 54. See also Siân Nicholas, "From John Bull to John Citizen: Images of National Identity and Citizenship on the Wartime BBC," in Richard Weight and Abigail Beach (eds.), *The Right to Belong: Citizenship and National Identity in Britain, 1930–1960* (London: I. B. Tauris, 1998), pp. 36–58; James Curran and Jean Seaton, *Power without Responsibility: The Press and Broadcasting in Britain* (London: Routledge, 1997), pp. 128–160.

[18] The BBC's 9 a.m. news bulletin, for example, reached an audience of 43 to 50 percent of the population: Crisell, *An Introductory History*, p. 56.

[19] McKibbin, *Classes and Cultures*, p. 457.   [20] Crisell, *An Introductory History*, p. 63.

such as *Woman's Hour, Housewives' Choice, Mrs. Dale's Diary, Children's Hour,* and *Dick Barton, Special Agent.*[21]

These programs marked an important shift in the BBC's assumptions – a transformation that is central to the understanding of Winnicott's radio work. Whereas the direction of wartime programming had been social or collaborative, the tendency of postwar programs was domestic and individual. The latter were designed not for women at war, but for women at home. It was at this time, historian Ross McKibbin argued, that the whole of the Light Programme was "feminized." "The general 'atmosphere' of the Light Programme was middle-classish, feminine, and domestic," he maintained.[22] While radio listening had been a domestic activity since its advent,[23] the war tightened this connection between the private and the public, emphasizing collective citizenship and individual self-sacrifice for the sake of the community at war. The practice of radio listening itself became more collective as the blackout kept people indoors, and communal radio sets in shelters, army camps, and factories served a large public.[24] When the war ended radio reverted to its domestic role.[25] Psychoanalytic experts such as Winnicott played a crucial part in this shift and helped form new connections between the family, citizenship, media, and expertise.

Winnicott's broadcasts were conducted in a period in which the BBC dedicated more attention to children and women as listeners and as important participants in democracy. For example, Derek McCulloch, the director of *Children's Hour,* explained how from 1939 to 1944 the BBC pooled all its resources in an endeavor to project this daily program for younger listeners. *Children's Hour,* which he saw as "a miniature of broadcasting as a whole,"[26] became "a national affair, determined to adopt the slogan 'business as usual.'"[27] The *BBC Yearbook* of 1947 described *Children's Hour* as a program for the "citizens and the license holders of the future."[28] It was broadcast in the afternoon, what was believed to be a

---

[21] Despite their influence and popularity very little has been written on *Children's Hour* and *Woman's Hour.*

[22] McKibbin, *Classes and Cultures,* pp. 471–472.

[23] *Ibid.,* pp. 457–476; Scannell and Cardiff, *A Social History of British Broadcasting,* pp. 14–15.

[24] Angus Calder, *The People's War,* p. 358.

[25] Crisell, *An Introductory History,* pp. 54, 64.

[26] Derek McCulloch, "Children's Hour, 1939 to 1944," in BBC, *BBC Yearbook 1945* (London: BBC, 1945), p. 69.

[27] The aims of the BBC during the war, according to McCulloch, included the wish to give children a sense of stability in a world of chaos, to provide entertainment and encourage the war effort, and to avoid glorifying the war or emphasizing fear: *ibid.,* p. 67.

[28] BBC, *BBC Yearbook 1947* (London: BBC, 1947), p. 57.

peak of domestic time, and the staff of the program believed that it had reached "a vast, real family audience."[29]

The BBC's image of citizenship itself increasingly included women in new and sometimes conflicting ways.[30] By 1951, *Woman's Hour*, which was created in 1946, was described to be "a stable feature in the lives of millions of housewives."[31] It aimed to be "covering every subject of interest to women," and it included personal stories, expert advice, and discussion of listeners' letters.[32] The *BBC Yearbook* of 1958 clarified that *Woman's Hour* was "addressed to one section of listeners, the women at home in the early afternoon, and it includes items that are of immediate practical service to such women in the running of their homes and in caring for the welfare of their families." It added that the program also aimed "to entertain, inform, and refresh women listeners with subjects and people that they may have little opportunity of meeting elsewhere." While the show was mostly aimed at housewives, starting in 1953, *Woman's Hour* was supplemented by the Sunday morning *Home for the Day*, which was addressed primarily to women who worked outside the home and included talks chosen for their particular appeal to business and professional women.[33] Both shows were immensely popular.

Another popular show, this one addressed to both mothers and young children, was titled *Listen with Mother*. According to BBC producer and broadcaster Olive Shapley, the show, which started in the early 1950s, soon "had found its way, like an arrow, straight to the heart of the audience for which it was intended." The BBC received hundreds of enthusiastic letters every week from the audience. Shapley shared the growing postwar concern for children's emotional needs and explained that "there is no doubt that this small and rather special section of the BBC's listeners [children under five] has a right to its own programme, and takes it very seriously." The radio was seen to play an active role in family life, even helping in parenting. Indeed, the 15 minutes of the program "give even quite small children a feeling of being important and cared for, and, as mothers know, they help to give a pattern to even

---

[29] McCulloch, "Children's Hour," p. 67. Public versions of the domestic programs for children during this time were the broadcasts for schools.

[30] Cf. Nicholas, "From John Bull to John Citizen," p. 46. See also Siân Nicholas, "'Sly Demagogues' and Wartime Radio: J. B. Priestley and the BBC," *Twentieth Century British History* Vol. 6 (1995), pp. 247–266.

[31] BBC, *BBC Handbook 1951* (London: BBC, 1951), p. 135.

[32] BBC, *BBC Handbook 1957* (London: BBC, 1957), p. 92; BBC, *BBC Handbook 1959* (London: BBC, 1959), pp. 109–110.

[33] Evidence suggests that both programs were heard by a considerable number of men as well: BBC, *BBC Handbook 1958* (London: BBC, 1958), pp. 103–104.

the most disorganized day. Mother as a story-teller has her limitations; the telephone will probably ring, the kettle boil over, but the friendly, rather grave, quite unsentimental voices of the radio story-tellers bring a feeling of security. Children know they always get through the end."[34] It is in this context of increased attention to the family, women, and children that Winnicott's talks on the BBC developed and popularized psychoanalytic ideas in relation to the needs of a postwar society and the project of domestic citizenship.[35]

Winnicott and the BBC

Donald Winnicott (1896–1971) was born into a middle-class family in Plymouth, England. After studying at Cambridge University, in 1923 he started working as a pediatrician at Paddington Green Children's Hospital in London where he was eventually to be involved in some 60,000 mother–child consultations. In 1923 Winnicott also started psychoanalytic treatment under James Strachey, Sigmund Freud's English translator. Winnicott began training with the British Psycho-Analytical Society in 1927, qualifying as an analyst for adults and children. While Winnicott underwent additional analysis with Melanie Klein's disciple Joan Riviere, he later helped develop the independent, "middle group" in the Society, standing between the Anna Freudians and the Kleinians. After the war, Winnicott continued to work at the Child Department of the Institute of Psychoanalysis and at Paddington Green Children's Hospital. He lectured widely and, in the atmosphere of a growing focus on domestic citizenship, he was called upon by producers Janet Quigley and Isa Benzie to deliver almost sixty broadcasts on BBC Radio from 1943 to 1966 (Illus. 8).[36]

[34] Olive Shapley, "Listen with Mother," in BBC, *BBC Yearbook 1952* (London: BBC, 1952), p. 49.

[35] I use the unexplored archival correspondence between Winnicott and BBC producers and the scripts of Winnicott's talks. Many of the talks are now published but I also cover unpublished ones. I stick to the archival scripts for those talks that have been published, as there are differences between the archival and published versions, with the quotations referring to the war or to listeners usually omitted from the published version. The archival scripts also allow one to follow the immediate context in which the talks were transmitted, to explore the sections that were censored (and that at times made it to the published version), and to study the discussion of listeners' letters.

[36] See BBCWAC: Scripts Index Cards: DW Winnicott; Talk Booking Requisitions in Talks: Winnicott, Donald Woods, File LA, 1943–1959. Some talks were also published as inexpensive popular pamphlets.

Happy Children

The first series Winnicott delivered was titled *Happy Children* and was transmitted on the Home Service Talks on Friday mornings.[37] On his way to the BBC's recording studio in Langham Place in central London, Winnicott often had to drive his car "over the glass and rubble of the previous night's air-raid."[38] Through this series, he developed a close working relationship with Janet Quigley, as Winnicott cultivated his expertise and his views on motherhood and fatherhood before a nation-wide audience.

Janet Quigley (1902–1987), born in Belfast and educated at Oxford, joined the BBC in 1930, where she developed a career spanning thirty years as an imaginative producer and pioneering female broadcaster. She started as an assistant to Isa Benzie in the Foreign Department, becoming an assistant in the Talks Department in 1936.[39] During the war, Quigley made her mark producing groundbreaking radio features for women such as *Calling the Factory Front, The Kitchen Front, The Kitchen in Wartime, Calling All Women, Your Health in Wartime, Talking It Over, Women at War, Wise Housekeeping,* and *Health Magazine.*[40] Indeed, Quigley was appointed MBE for her war work in 1944. Quigley made a major contribution to extending the frontiers of women's broadcasting through her editorship of *Woman's Hour* from 1950 to 1956.[41] Alongside a return to a discussion of what were seen as "traditional" women's issues, she brought to the air topics such as cruelty to children, marriage and divorce, spinsterhood, and homosexuality. Introducing a talk on prostitution, Quigley explained that this would be in accordance with the show's policy of "bringing 'hush-hush' topics into the open, so that the less-educated amongst our listeners may get used to the idea that no subject which concerns them as citizens need be taboo."[42]

---

[37] The Home Service was the main network during the war before the BBC created the three-network system.

[38] Quoted in Brett Kahr, *D. W. Winnicott: A Biographical Portrait* (London: Karnac, 1996), p. 96.

[39] Kate Murphy, "Women in the BBC: A History 1922–2002" (unpublished report used with the kind permission of its author).

[40] *Ibid.*

[41] "Miss Janet Quigley," *The Times* (12 Feb. 1987). In March 1956, Quigley was appointed chief assistant in the Talks Department. In 1957, she became a key developer of the *Today* program and in June 1960 was appointed assistant head of the Talks Department. She retired in October 1962: see Murphy, "Women in the BBC."

[42] Quoted in Paul Donovan, "Quigley, Janet Muriel Alexander (1902–1987)," in *Oxford Dictionary of National Biography* (Oxford University Press, 2004).

On October 12, 1943, Quigley first wrote to Winnicott asking if he would take part in a BBC series in which he would have "a completely free hand" to develop his subjects and "would not be bound by any rigid plan drawn up beforehand." She added, "All we really want is agreement amongst the speakers that we are aiming at the same object in the end, and agreement too on the subjects which should be included."[43] This, however, did not always remain the case as Quigley and Winnicott quickly developed an active dialogue on the content and focus of the talks. For example, as early as November 15, 1943, Quigley asked Winnicott if he wanted to give a talk on "Getting to Know Your Baby." The title and topic of the talk were hers.[44] As a matter of control, Winnicott was to presubmit drafts of his talks for approval. Later that month, Quigley asked Winnicott if he would agree to contribute regularly to the series and mentioned that unless he preferred otherwise it would appear anonymously as being given "by a psychologist."[45] She wrote that she liked his submitted draft but that it was "not factual enough."[46] Her role as producer therefore included a dynamic involvement in the direction of the expert talk. Characteristic of the BBC at the time was the concern not only for educating but also speaking to the audience, significantly here composed of many female listeners (Illus. 9).

In the final script of "Getting to Know Your Baby" on December 12, 1943, on the Home Service from London, Winnicott revealed the ways in which he saw women as mothers by default.[47] His tone shifted from one of general expert observation to direct address of the mothers among the listeners using the second person. Winnicott started by using a universal description of young women's lives according to which every woman

---

[43] BBCWAC, Talks, Winnicott, Donald Woods, File LA, 1943–1959 (hereafter TW): Letter from 12 Oct. 1943.

[44] BBCWAC, TW: Letter from 15 Nov. 1943.

[45] The BBC's careful avoidance of the cult of personality in radio was thrown into confusion by the outbreak of World War II. During the interwar period, the BBC was already fully aware of the power of the radio, a power that was later also symbolized by the microphone as the true authoritative transmitter of truth and diverse realities. The outbreak of the war necessitated a reassessment of an earlier ethos of impartiality and impersonality in delivery of BBC talks. J. B. Priestley's broadcasts during the war offered a new tolerance to a voice of personality and mass appeal. Winnicott delivered his broadcasts not under his full name but under the title "psychologist" or "doctor," but he no doubt became identifiable to some of the listeners, as is apparent from the fan mail that Winnicott received and is discussed later. Indeed, in 1946, Isa Benzie asked Winnicott if he would care to be part of a program on leucotomy and said "the success of the programme is likely to stand or fall by your participation." See BBCWAC, TW: Letter from 13 Sep. 1946; Nicholas, "'Sly Demagogues' and Wartime Radio."

[46] BBCWAC, TW: Letter from (exact date unclear) Nov. 1943.

[47] BBCWAC, Microfilm T659/T660: Script "Happy Children: Getting to Know Your Baby: By a Psychologist" (12 Dec. 1943), p. 6.

would eventually become a mother. Up to a certain point in her life, he said, a woman may have been a person of wide interests. She may have despised the restricted life of a friend with a child or have been repelled by the technical details of the washing and airing of diapers. But, he believed, "sooner or later she herself becomes pregnant." While at first she might resent the interference with her private life, "experience shows" that a change would gradually appear in her feelings and her body once she had conceived. At this point in the broadcast, Winnicott shifted from these generalizations to the second person, addressing an imagined woman/listener directly to say "as you become more and more sure that you'll soon be a mother . . . you begin to take the risk of allowing yourself to be concerned with one object, the little boy or girl human being that will be born." While the mother understands infant care well by the course of her experience, nevertheless, he said to his mother/listener, "you may very well need support from those of us who study your subject, because superstitions and old wives' tales come along and make you doubt your own true feelings."[48] Psychoanalytic expertise was here privileged over the common advice other women – here in the derogatory – could provide the young mother.

Winnicott established his expert authority in a peculiar way. He aimed to communicate directly with mothers, telling them that they were always "the real experts." Throughout the talk, Winnicott emphasized how important it was for the mother to get to know the baby early, something that he believed that the "ordinary healthy-minded mother" knows already. He added, "No-one who comes along to give you [the mother] advice will ever know this as well as you know it yourself." Alternating between asserting his position as an expert and stating that he was only telling mothers what they already knew, Winnicott claimed that, in his view, it was a most alarming thing to be an infant discovering his feelings, but he added "Have you [the mother] ever looked at it that way?" Later, he said, "If no-one has explained all this to you, you may become alarmed too."[49]

Quigley directed Winnicott's next lecture in this series, titled "Why Does Your Baby Cry." Winnicott submitted a draft to her on January 16, 1944. Quigley responded that she read the script with great interest but then suggested that Winnicott should break it into two parts since "apart from the time factor, there is far too much thought in it for any listener to take in at one go." She believed that illustrations and anecdotes would make the script easier listening and suggested that the talk should more

[48] *Ibid.*, pp. 1–2.   [49] *Ibid.*, pp. 4–5.

practically tackle the question of how to deal with crying. "As you know, I am anxious that every talk in this series will give mothers some practical advice that they can easily adapt to their own circumstances," she wrote.[50] Winnicott followed Quigley's instructions and divided his talk into two parts transmitted on February 4 and 11, 1944. In the first part, Winnicott emphasized again the exclusivity of motherhood saying, "no-one can know a baby as well as the mother can, no-one but you can be the right person to help him." Winnicott explained the causes of crying, stemming from pleasure, pain, rage, and grief, demonstrating his sense of authority as stemming from what a mother knows but perhaps does not articulate: "if you have a pencil handy you might want to write down pleasure, pain, rage and grief, so that tomorrow, when you are wondering what on earth the psychologist was saying, you will be able to see that really I was only saying quite obvious things, the sort of thing that every mother of an infant knows naturally, though she hasn't usually tried thinking out how to express what she knows in words." The expert, as Winnicott saw it, then, was only verbalizing in words, systematizing, what the mother already knows. Offering an internal explanation for the crying out of rage and using more psychoanalytic logic than before, Winnicott suggested that "if a baby cries in a state of rage and feels as if he has destroyed anyone and everything, and yet the people round him remain calm and unhurt, this experience greatly strengthens his ability to see that what he feels to be true is not necessarily real, that fantasy and fact, both important, are nevertheless different from each other."[51] These words reflected the psychoanalytic notion of the child – which we have encountered before – as helpless and in need of full-time attention, yet destructive and requiring restraint. Violence was seen to be part of the child (an emerging self) and as something to be contained by good parenting. As is worth emphasizing again, while interwar hygienist and behaviorist literature focused on children's bodies, the importance of habits, and the dangers of excessive parental love, psychoanalysts instead proffered that emotions be understood rather than managed and that the parent–child relationship was central to the planning for stability. The problem of war for psychoanalysts could be solved only by recognition of inner aggressiveness.[52] Accordingly, in his script Winnicott also addressed the

---

[50] BBCWAC, TW: Letter from 16 Jan. 1944.
[51] BBCWAC, Microfilm T659/T660: Script "Why Does Your Baby Cry? (1)" (4 Feb. 1944), p. 1. Winnicott used the third person "he" for baby or child but he meant both sexes, as was usual at the time. I follow him here and throughout for the sake of simplicity.
[52] Cathy Urwin and Elaine Sharland, "From Bodies to Minds in Childcare Literature: Advice to Parents in Inter-War Britain," in Roger Cooter (ed.), *In the Name of the Child: Health and Welfare, 1880–1940* (New York: Routledge, 1992), pp. 174–199.

mother/listener with the following lines that were apparently edited out by Quigley from the broadcast: "You can get a lot of interest out of watching your infant for the first signs that he knows he can hurt you, and that he intends to hurt you."[53] This amendment of statements that were deemed too negative also arises in other talks.

Indeed, in a letter from February 25, 1944, Quigley wrote to Winnicott, "As you say, one has to be very careful in talks of this kind not to alarm people unduly." She also suggested the possibility of a talk on "Where Does Dad Come In?"[54] The title and theme of the talk was again hers.[55] Winnicott agreed and began his draft script for this talk by saying,

Even in peace time men who are working long hours are often away most of the time that their babies are awake; in war time babies often have to do without their fathers altogether. I reckon that there's no way war more seriously affects the coming generation than through depriving babies and small children of the living contact with their fathers. That's one of the reasons why women and children hate war, and long for this one to be over.[56]

Adding a comment that seems to have been too negative for Quigley and was cut out, Winnicott wrote:

Some of you who are listening may be hurt by this war in just this special way, your husband being unavailable, and if this is so I think you may not want to listen to me today, or perhaps father will hear me as he hangs around the canteen between jobs, and I shouldn't think he'd like to hear what I have to say either. I am going to make no bones about it, I think it's very important indeed for children to know their fathers, and that it's a tragedy when they can't. Yet the war isn't over, and whatever we think about it, many people who want to be home can't get home.

Seeing himself as an advisor on family dynamics aiming to prevent harm to the future generation of citizens, Winnicott emphasized the importance of parents sharing responsibility for the child and offered the practice of letter-writing as a partial wartime solution to involve the father in the upbringing of the child.[57]

Quigley was not altogether happy with Winnicott's draft script. She wrote to him that it was very depressing to wives whose husbands are away, and wondered whether Winnicott could give the script a more

---

[53] BBCWAC, Microfilm T659/T660: Script "Why Does Your Baby Cry? (1)" (4 Feb. 1944), pp. 2–7.

[54] BBCWAC, TW: Letter from 25 Feb. 1944.

[55] On March 1, 1944, Quigley thanked Winnicott for sharing with her his fan mail and suggested a talk with another title of hers: "The Importance of Good Mothering," BBCWAC, TW: Letter from 1 Mar. 1944.

[56] BBCWAC, Microfilm T659/T660: Script "Where Does Dad Come In?" (17 Mar. 1944), p. 1.

[57] Ibid.

encouraging slant. She asked him to indicate the different part that fathers play at different ages, mentioning that she thought that most fathers are afraid of babies and feel that they are entirely a woman's business. She also asked Winnicott to give guidance to women whose husbands are at home as to how they ought to draw them into the picture. She wrote, "Many women are apt to feel they should not worry their menfolk. They get the children off to bed before father returns. 'Don't disturb father' becomes a law of the house. They should not, and don't feel that they know him or like him or that he has any place in their life at all. Could you deal with this sort of point rather than stress with story after story the disastrous consequences of father being away?"[58] Her comments reflected the ambiguity of the changing notion of the father at the time, especially among working-class families, from a distant, cold, and vaguely hostile figure within the family to a more active and participatory one.[59]

In his draft script Winnicott described the father in a few ways, none of them requiring full – or equal – participation. First, he saw the father as a separate, important person in the child's life whose main job is to be "a human being representing mother's authority."[60] The father takes over feelings that the infant has already had toward certain properties of the mother, and it is a great relief for the mother that she can make use of the father in this way. The father, for Winnicott (here influenced by the ideas of Melanie Klein on the complex feelings stored in the child's mind), was valuable because the child has a fantasy of the union of the mother and the father, a rock to which he can cling and against which he can kick. The father "doesn't have to be there all the time to do this, but he has to turn up often enough for the child to feel that he is real and alive." Furthermore, "Every now and again the child is going to hate someone, and if father isn't there to tell him where to get off, he'll hate his mother, and this will make him confused because it is his mother that he most fundamentally loves." The father is also needed for the child because of "his positive qualities and the things that distinguish him from other men, and the liveliness of his personality." The father opens up a new world for the children when he gradually discloses the nature of his work or "when he shows the gun that he takes with him into the battle."[61] The father, therefore, signifies

---

[58] BBCWAC, TW: Letter from 13 Mar. 1944.
[59] This active idea of fatherhood had begun to filter down from the middle classes from the interwar period: Allport, *Demobbed*, pp. 70–71.
[60] BBCWAC, Microfilm T659/T660: Script "Where Does Dad Come In?," p. 2.
[61] *Ibid.*, pp. 4–5. Referencing the Oedipus complex without mentioning it by name, Winnicott also said that it was well known that a boy and his father may find themselves at times in a state of rivalry over the mother: *ibid.*, p. 7.

authority and the outside world, he mitigates the child's fantasized negative feelings, and he participates in violence in the name of democracy.

In contrast, a woman's main role in democracy, according to Winnicott, was motherhood. Motherhood and housekeeping, he believed, were sites of freedom, independence, and expression for women. In the talk "Their Standards and Yours," broadcast on May 12, 1944, Winnicott declared, "talk about women coming back from the forces not wanting to be housewives seems to me to be just nonsense, because nowhere else but in her own home is a woman in command; only in her own home is she free, if she has the courage to spread herself, to express herself, to find her whole self."[62] In this rhetorical move, he ignored the possibility of independence for women outside the home (which was feared by some contemporaries, though not nearly to the extent that these issues were debated after World War I), to claim that true independence for women was at home.[63] The newborn child, Winnicott continued, coming into the house with his own need to control a bit of the world can at first seem to threaten the mother's independence. Indeed, in "What Do We Mean by a Normal Child?," a later talk that Quigley and her director made sure would be simplified for the listener,[64] Winnicott tried to explain what would be reasonable to accept from a child, a prime concern in a society experiencing the breakup of families.[65] Winnicott presented theoretical psychoanalytic ideas describing the dynamics of the child's difficulties as existing between the reality of the external world and that of the personal inner world. A normal child was one who "can and does employ every device that nature has provided for avoiding too painful feelings, and for dealing with pain that can't be avoided."[66] The normal child, according to Winnicott's writing at the end of the war, was an aggressive being that could learn to manage its own destructiveness with the help of others. Despite this use of more psychoanalytic language, Winnicott received supportive letters from listeners

[62] BBCWAC, Microfilm T659/T660: Script "Their Standards and Yours" (12 May 1944), p. 2.

[63] Susan Kingsley Kent, *Making Peace: The Reconstruction of Gender in Interwar Britain* (Princeton University Press, 1993); cf. Elizabeth Wilson, *Only Halfway to Paradise: Women in Postwar Britain, 1945–1968* (New York: Tavistock, 1980).

[64] BBCWAC, TW: Letters from 20 and 21 Jun. 1944.

[65] Writing to her director, Quigley introduced Winnicott's script saying, "I believe if you have seen his earlier ones [the scripts] and got used to his approach you would not feel that the ideas he expresses are so unfamiliar and difficult as they strike you when reading this solitary example. I don't think he is really muddled, though he undoubtedly belongs to the Freudian school" (BBCWAC, TW: Letters from 22 Jun. 1944).

[66] BBCWAC, Microfilm T659/T660: Script "What Do We Mean by a Normal Child?" (Jun. 1944), pp. 5–8.

after the talk was broadcast on June 23, 1944. Quigley wrote to Winnicott saying that the letters showed how well his sincerity and sympathy had been conveyed to listeners. She also expressed her wish to do further talks with him.[67]

Difficult Children

This wish was fulfilled in the series *Difficult Children*, broadcast in 1945. On November 8, 1944, Quigley wrote to Winnicott about this new series in which she wanted to concentrate on "the slightly difficult child or perhaps, more accurately, the child where circumstances are difficult," and asked for his help as she "must be guided by the experts."[68] When Quigley suggested this series to the Director of Talks, she explained that this idea arose from a conference at the Ministry of Health which was starting a drive for "better parentcraft."[69] As a transforming editor, Quigley saw radio's role as having to do with "indirect propaganda," as she called it, and with conveying useful social messages.[70] Childrearing and parenthood during this time were the most pressing issues for her as well as for many others. Letters from January 5 and 16, 1945, show that Quigley, rather than Winnicott, was again the one who chose the titles and directed the content of the talks, as she rejected his script about children who were difficult in ways other than those she imagined.[71] Throughout the series, the problem of ensuring stable human relations – both inside the family and later in civic democratic life – was a central one. The solution was envisioned through specific gender roles.

During the transmission of the talk "The Only Child" on February 2, 1945, Winnicott wished to talk about "children who although they live in ordinary good homes have no brothers and sisters."[72] While the fear of a falling birthrate was still in the minds of many during the 1940s, as the postwar "baby boom" had not yet fully materialized, Winnicott's concern was less with demographic growth (although he did specifically encourage

---

[67] BBCWAC, TW: Letter from 11 Jul. 1944.

[68] BBCWAC, TW: Letter from 8 Nov. 1944. Similarly, the popular *Radio Times* described the series saying, "Some 'difficult' [children] are not really difficult if rightly handled, but if they *are* difficult then they need special care." See "Difficult Children in Difficult Times," *Radio Times* (26 Jan. 1945).

[69] Quoted in Donovan, "Quigley."   [70] *Ibid.*

[71] BBCWAC, TW: Letters from 5 and 16 Jan. 1945. See also correspondence between Quigley and Dorothy Bridgman on their unhappiness with some of Winnicott's ideas for the talks, 2 Feb. 1945 and undated. When Winnicott submitted a script titled "Children Who Steal," Quigley decided not to include it in the *Difficult Children* series but suggested instead that it be broadcast on *Woman's Page*; see letter from 26 Mar. 1945.

[72] BBCWAC, Microfilm T659/T660: Script "The Only Child" (2 Feb. 1945), p. 1.

parents not to fear the hardship of having many children). Instead, he concentrated on what he saw as the possible emotional and social toll presented by the only child. The talk focused on the disadvantages of being an only child, among them the lack of playmates and the lack of richness of experience that can result from a child's various relationships. In a big family, Winnicott believed, there is "much more chance for children to play all sorts of different roles in relation to each other and all this prepares them for life in larger groups and eventually in the world." Members of large families are always meeting friends and siblings and have "a good deal of practical experience of human relationships." In contrast, as only children grew older, they would find it difficult to meet others on a casual basis. For Winnicott then, family dynamics were preparing the child for a more social and cooperative life in a democratic society.[73]

The problems of "difficult children" were further discussed in a talk on "The Evacuated Child" delivered by Winnicott on February 16, 1945. Here and in his subsequent talk, "Return of the Evacuated Child," broadcast a week later, the problem of the possibility of harmonious human interaction again resided at the core of the project of democratic life. In these talks, Winnicott reiterated ideas about the danger of evacuation, which he had voiced publicly with others in 1939, claiming that mother–child separation could lead to severe personality development disturbance.[74] In the 1945 BBC talks, Winnicott wrote with more nuances and acknowledged the "tricky relationship" between foster and real parents during evacuation and the problem of double loyalties for the child. Some children might become "difficult" as result of the experience of being unrooted and needed special understanding. The threat of loss of feelings that comes to children who are too long away from all that they love often leads to conflict, Winnicott believed. It was important to realize this in order to deal with different sorts of distress that underline the children's difficulties and symptoms. Without the temporary foster mother's love and understanding, the child would have gone home to the real danger of war or else would have become "disturbed and distorted in his mental development, with a strong likelihood of getting into trouble."[75]

---

[73] *Ibid.*, pp. 6–8. In a later talk in the series on "Twins," transmitted on April 27, 1945, Winnicott dealt with the opposite problem in human relations, that is, the problem of developing a separate personality and handling with jealousy: BBCWAC, Microfilm T659/T660: Script "Twins" (27 Apr. 1945), pp. 1–7.

[74] John Bowlby, Emanuel Miller, and D. W. Winnicott, "Evacuation of Small Children," *British Medical Journal* (16 Dec. 1939), pp. 1202–1203. See Ch. 2.

[75] BBCWAC, Microfilm T659/T660: Script "The Evacuated Child" (16 Feb. 1945), pp. 1–5; BBCWAC, Microfilm T659/T660: Script "Return of the Evacuated Child" (23 Feb. 1945).

The returning child might not remember his or her parents and siblings. Parents could also suffer from a limited ability to keep the child alive in their memory. Winnicott mentioned that those lacking the capacity to recover from "painful separation," at least to some extent, "would be paralysed, unhappy and useless."[76] War and the separation over years, then, endangered family life and emotional life in a significant way. Writing a letter to Winnicott on his submitted script "Return of the Evacuated Child," Dorothy Bridgman of the BBC, assisting Quigley, mentioned with a few editorial comments how very much the BBC staff liked it and said that she was sure it would help many parents.[77] Indeed, Winnicott later shared with her letters that he received from listeners.[78]

Winnicott also broadcast a related talk titled "Home Again" on the *BBC Health Magazine* on June 22, 1945. In this talk he again emphasized the irreplaceable importance of the home to the child's well-being and stated that, although things were often done well in hostels and foster homes, "there are not many who would claim that an ordinary good home can be supplanted . . . a child's home, be it ever so humble, and even when it isn't humble, is more valuable to that boy or girl than any other place to live."[79] Winnicott assigned psychological value to the concept of "home" – already seen as the center of life and of comfort for many middle-class families and, increasingly, more working-class families.[80] On October 3, 1945, Quigley informed Winnicott that she was leaving the BBC and that her manager and close friend Isa Benzie[81] would be looking after the health talks.[82] Benzie (1902–1988) was another

---

[76] BBCWAC, Microfilm T659/T660: Script "The Evacuated Child" (16 Feb. 1945), p. 4.

[77] BBCWAC, TW: Letter from 21 Feb. 1945.

[78] BBCWAC, TW: Letter from 6 Mar. 1945.

[79] BBCWAC, Microfilm T659/T660: Script "Home Again" (22 Jun. 1945), pp. 5–6. When Winnicott and his wife Clare Britton reported to the Government's Care of Children Committee (Curtis Committee) on their work at the wartime evacuation hostels they expressed concern over the aggressivity of the institutional child without a home. See D. W. Winnicott and Clare Britton, "The Problem of Homeless Children," in *Children's Communities: Experiments in Democratic Living* (London: NEF Monograph, 1944), p. 2. See also Ch. 2.

[80] The wartime geographical mobility of many civilians and soldiers further intensified a romance with home life; see Claire Langhamer, "The Meaning of Home in Postwar Britain," *Journal of Contemporary History* (Apr. 2005), pp. 341–362.

[81] Janet Quigley and Isa Benzie enjoyed a close friendship and long professional collaboration. Paul Donovan explained, "They were born in the same year, went to the same Oxford college, and worked for the BBC at the same time. Furthermore, they worked in the same department for the BBC before the Second World War and for the same programmes after it." See Paul Donovan, "Benzie, Isa Donald (1902–1988)," in *Oxford Dictionary of National Biography*.

[82] BBCWAC, TW: Letter from 3 Oct. 1945.

pioneering BBC female broadcaster who worked there for more than thirty years. She joined the BBC in 1927 as secretary to the Foreign Liaison and was appointed Foreign Director in 1934. After resigning from the BBC to marry in 1938, she went to work for the Ministry of Information, but she rejoined the BBC Talks Department as a producer in 1943. She spent twenty years (1943–1964) producing talks on various topics, specializing in health, medical, and psychological issues and discussions about the increasing desire by some women to combine motherhood with career. She became something of a legend at the BBC as she produced programs such as *Taking Stock of Health* and *Is There a Doctor in the House?* and oversaw the health items on programs such as *Woman's Hour*.[83]

How's the Baby

During the months of October and November 1949, Winnicott gave another series of talks on the Home Service, this time produced by Benzie, about babies and young children. This series was titled *How's the Baby*.[84] In the first talk on Wednesday morning, October 5, 1949, Winnicott again placed his expert authority in relation to what he saw as the mother's "natural" role. He started by saying to the mother/listener, as he and the BBC staff imagined it, "You will be relieved to know that I'm not going to be telling you what to do. I'm a man, and I have never been a mother, and so I never really know what it is like to see wrapped up over there in the cot a bit of my own self, a bit of my living an independent life, yet at the same time dependent and gradually becoming a human being. Only a woman can experience this." Winnicott imagined the mother as forever knowing what to do with the baby. He added, "sometimes the urine trickled down your apron or went right through and soaked you as if you yourself had let slip, and you didn't mind it. In fact, by these things you could have known that you were a woman, and what I have ... called an ordinary devoted mother." Explaining his own role, he said, "I can't tell you what to do, but I can talk about what it all means."[85] His position, as he saw it, was therefore as an interpreter of motherhood, shaping it as a social, rather than natural, institution.

[83] In October 1957, she became a senior producer who launched the *Today* program. She retired from the BBC in December 1964: Donovan, "Benzie," and Murphy, "Women in the BBC."

[84] The talks were also published as pamphlets for the price of one shilling. The fact of their publication was mentioned in the *Radio Times*. Winnicott received 15 guineas for each talk. See BBCWAC, TW: Letters from 1 and 2 Feb. 1950.

[85] BBCWAC, Microfilm T659/T660: Script "How's the Baby (1)" (5 Oct. 1949), pp. 1–2.

Winnicott connected the mother's individual childrearing tasks to social life and its benefits in a democratic society. He said, "If human babies are to develop eventually into healthy independent and society-minded adult individuals they absolutely depend on being given a good start; this good start is assured in nature by the experience of the bond between the baby's mother and the baby, the thing called love. So if you love your baby the baby is getting a good start." He further claimed that it is "vitally important that society should get to understand the part played by those who care for the infant so that we can protect the young mother from whatever tends to get between herself and her infant." Yet fathers, as discussed earlier, also had a place in Winnicott's social vision. He saw them as able to be "good mothers" for limited periods of time, and as helping to protect mother and baby from whatever tended to interfere with the mother–child bond, a tie which was "the essence and very nature of child care."[86] In the following talk on October 12, 1949, Winnicott empowered a woman's role as a mother by saying, "You are founding the health of a person who will be a member of our society. This is worth doing." He advised mothers to "Enjoy letting other people look after the world while you are producing a new one of its members . . . Enjoy the way in which your man feels responsible for the welfare of you and your child."[87] In Winnicott's vision of the family – one that went hand in hand with the British model of the welfare state – the father was the breadwinner and protector of the family, while the woman was the main caretaker of the nation's future citizens. Speaking on November 9, 1949, against behaviorist theories that aimed to give mothers recipes for the right behavior, Winnicott said, "No book's rules can take the place of this feeling a mother has for her infant's needs, which enables her to make at times an almost exact adaptation to those needs."[88] His notion contrasted to the behaviorist model of writers such as John Watson who believed that institutions could be ideal environments for children, that love should be done mechanically to avoid invalidism or a "mother's boy syndrome," and that mothers should leave their children alone for a large part of their day.[89]

The mother portrayed in those radio talks did not completely exist as a person in her own right, but rather as *a person for* the baby, giving it individual attention and a setting for its needs as part of a human

[86] *Ibid.*, p. 3.
[87] BBCWAC, Microfilm T659/T660: Script "How's the Baby (2)" (12 Oct. 1949), pp. 2–3.
[88] BBCWAC, Microfilm T659/T660: Script "How's the Baby (6)" (9 Nov. 1949), p. 1.
[89] Urwin and Sharland, "From Bodies to Minds," pp. 179–180.

relationship where the baby was prioritized.[90] In a later talk from January 9, 1952, Winnicott even stressed that "A mother who is enjoying herself is probably a good mother *from the baby's point of view*."[91] Winnicott connected the mother's flexibility toward the child to the development of a civilized adult. He claimed that, if the mother was sensitive to the child, it would soon need less and less to gratify its primitive needs for greediness, messiness, and control, and "civilization would start again inside a new human being." He added, "It's for you to catch on to their [the babies'] primitive morality and to tone it down gradually to the humanity that comes from mutual understanding."[92] This way, the dyadic relationship between mother and child became for Winnicott a relationship on which democratic society was dependent. Women's role in democracy was motherhood, but motherhood in its turn was creating and making democracy. To Sigmund Freud's account of life in society as fraught with frustration and human conflict, Winnicott added the figure of the mother as a mediator of aggression.[93] In a published article, Winnicott explained that democracy is a mature society well adjusted to its healthy individual members. The level of health and maturity of citizens depended on "the ordinary good home" and the early devotion of the mother. Mass interference such as war and evacuation could quickly lessen the democratic potential of society. He believed that psychological research could strengthen democratic tendencies and the healthy emotional development of individuals. "Not ordinary good parents," in his scheme, included those who were psychiatric cases, or were immature, or were anti-social, or unmarried, or in unstable relationships, or bickering, or separated from each other.[94]

Winnicott discussed on the radio the difference between "what the mother has to learn" and "what she knows." He explained that some things about childcare are known naturally to the mother and that she could teach them to the experts. At the same time, Winnicott admitted that there is a great deal that the mother could not know intuitively and about which could benefit from doctors' research. The difficulty of the

---

[90] *Ibid*. BBCWAC, Microfilm T659/T660: Script "How's the Baby (6)" (9 Nov. 1949), pp. 1–6.
[91] BBCWAC, Microfilm T657/T658: Script "The Ordinary Devoted Mother and Her Baby" (9 Jan. 1952), p. 4. Italics are mine.
[92] BBCWAC, Microfilm T659/T660: Script "How's the Baby (8)" (23 Nov. 1949), p. 4.
[93] Sigmund Freud, "Civilization and its Discontents [1930]," SE/PEP Vol. XXI, pp. 57–146.
[94] See D. W. Winnicott, "Some Thoughts on the Meaning of the Word Democracy," *Human Relations* Vol. 3 (1950), pp. 175–186.

talks, he said, was to see how to avoid disturbance of what is natural for mothers while accurately informing them as to the useful facts that emerge from research. Demonstrating how ideas on everyday activities of ordinary individuals were now under scrutiny and management through psychoanalysis, Winnicott connected the trivial tasks of baby care, mental health, and society. He meticulously studied, for example, the way the "wise mother" holds her baby. The naturally devoted mother, who is not anxious and so does not grip the baby too tight and is not afraid of dropping the baby to the floor, can adapt the pressure in her arms to the baby's needs and move slightly or perhaps make sounds and breathe to show that she is alive. He added, "If you do handle your baby well I want you to be able to know that you are doing something of importance. This is part of the way in which you give a good foundation for the mental health of this new member of the community."[95]

Another talk focused on "healthy symptoms" in "ordinary children" and dealt with, among other things, a letter from a mother who described the troubles of her baby during weaning. Winnicott claimed that even if he took for granted the mother's management of the baby to be skilled and consistent, the infant might still have all sorts of symptoms that had to do with the working of instincts, terrifying feelings that belong to them, and the painful conflicts that result from the child's imagination.[96] Winnicott again drew a connection between the inner and external worlds and (unlike behaviorist writers) stressed that the child could be in conflict with the environment. Before this talk was aired, Benzie intervened and required Winnicott to make many changes in his submitted script. In a letter from March 27, 1950, she explained, "I feel myself that if I were a mother . . . I should be more worried than helped by what you have to say – because, I think, I get out of this script a rather strong feeling that (in my imagination) I am to blame about this baby which has had so bad a start; or else I am worried because . . . it sounds as if the baby's illness is something that could never be cured." She also provided a set of comments noting that she would not want to "frighten mothers." Benzie explained, "I believe that what worries me is my suspicion that you do think that they (mothers) are in some way to blame." She asked him to change this impression (which would indeed bother later feminists).[97]

[95] BBCWAC, Microfilm T659/T660: Script "How's the Baby (7)" (22 Mar. 1950), p. 5.
[96] BBCWAC, Microfilm T659/T660: Script "How's the Baby (8)" (29 Mar. 1950), p. 3.
[97] BBCWAC, TW: Letter from 27 Mar. 1950.

The "ordinary devoted mother" and her baby

Winnicott's talks were a great success. In December 1951, Benzie invited Winnicott to rebroadcast live his previous series of talks in a shorter format as part of *Woman's Hour.* "It would be a Christmas present for me," she said, "to hear that you could accept our invitation."[98] She called his earlier broadcasts "notable" and mentioned how they were done "superbly," and greatly "valued – by very many listeners and very many outside interests and connoisseurs."[99] Winnicott rewrote his talks.

Winnicott started by explaining that by talking about the "ordinary devoted mother" he did not mean to expect the mother to be perfect, but to argue that every mother has mixed feelings of love and hate toward the baby. He assumed that, despite possible strain in the first weeks, the mother would usually be able to devote herself to the baby without resentment. He warned his listener/mother, "every bit of experience of your baby affects eventually the personality of a human adult." Winnicott also included a paragraph that seems to have been cut by Benzie, saying that in the first days of life "it is the mother and not the doctors and nurses who knows how to manage the baby."[100]

During the last talk in the series, Winnicott discussed his "fan mail," as he called it, i.e., the letters he received from listeners.[101] Letters were frequently discussed during *Woman's Hour,* a fact that serves as an indication to the responsiveness of the BBC to its listeners. One such letter came from a woman in Liverpool who argued against Winnicott's implication that books on childcare were not worthwhile and claimed instead that she had learned a great deal from them. Winnicott clarified that what he meant was to say "that the management of a baby at the very beginning is something that goes deeper than book-learning, that it comes naturally under suitable conditions just because of the fact of the mother's motherhood." In a section that was crossed out in the script and probably censored by Benzie, Winnicott agreed with a grandmother from Streatham who wrote that breastfeeding was the loveliest thing of her married life. He offered again that the mother, and not doctors and nurses, was the one to know what is right for the baby "since the baby

---

[98] BBCWAC, TW: Letter from 12 Dec. 1951.
[99] BBCWAC, TW: Letter from 5 Feb. 1952.
[100] BBCWAC, Microfilm T657/T658: Script "The Ordinary Devoted Mother and Her Baby (2), The First Weeks: By a Doctor" (16 Jan. 1952), pp. 1–3.
[101] One letter kept in the archive from a Lady Radnor informed Winnicott of how greatly interested she had been in his talks and said that, if he were ever lecturing on a subject she could understand, she would deeply appreciate the privilege of listening to him in person: BBCWAC, TW: Letter from 3 May 1951.

needs exactly what the mother and no one else is shaped for." Yet answering another letter of a mother from Kent who complained about the nursing staff's interference after her delivery, Winnicott said that many mothers should still be grateful for doctors and nurses' tremendous help.[102] On February 28, 1952, Benzie informed Winnicott that more letters from listeners had arrived. One woman wrote, for example, "I listened to your series ... some years ago, and considered it the finest I had ever heard on the subject of motherhood."[103]

The psychoanalytic ideas broadcast on BBC Radio contributed to the shift from a collective wartime citizenship toward a postwar domestic citizenship and to a focus on conservative family relationships in general and the mother–child bond in particular as important to the functioning of a democratic regime. Winnicott's public discussion of psychoanalytic ideas on the child and the parents was not conducted in a vacuum. It was shaped through an active dialogue with BBC staff and with a particular sociopolitical vision of citizenry.[104] Winnicott constructed his expert authority as a psychoanalyst in relation to an audience of mothers that was imagined according to particular gender roles. He believed that he was mostly elucidating the "deep" reasoning behind what mothers were already "naturally" doing with their babies. He was willing to work with the BBC producers and shape his ideas according to their instructions in order to deliver and disseminate his message. Yet while he was willing to use the BBC to increase the public role and visibility of psychoanalysis after the war, the BBC was also utilizing him as an expert and an informal voice of truth for its targeted audience of parents. Through his talks, new behaviors and troubles of "normal ordinary people" – not just those of people labeled mentally ill or disturbed – became topics for expert guidance.

Winnicott was not alone in turning women into symbols of the return to normalcy after the war and calling upon them to return to the home as mothers and housewives. The contribution of his radio talks lay in their claim that full-time motherhood was crucial to the democratic national community in a particular way. Motherhood was women's role in

---

[102] BBCWAC, Microfilm T657/T658: Script "The Ordinary Devoted Mother and Her Baby (5)" (20 Feb. 1952), pp. 1–4. Winnicott gave many more talks on the BBC. He delivered three talks in 1955 and one talk each in 1956 and 1959. He gave thirteen talks in 1960 on *Woman's Hour* and *Parents and Children*. He gave one more talk in 1961, two in 1962, and one in 1966. See BBCWAC: Scripts Index Cards: D. W. Winnicott.

[103] BBCWAC, TW: Letter from 28 Feb. 1952.

[104] Cf. Peter Miller and Nikolas Rose, "The Tavistock Programme: The Government of Subjectivity and Social Life," *Sociology* Vol. 22, No. 2 (May 1988), pp. 171–192.

democracy but, more importantly for Winnicott, good motherhood would ensure the creation of a healthy "mature democracy." Instead of being a haven from the political world, the home here was the very place where democracy was being produced. Childhood was valued as the period of initiation into selfhood and of proto-democratic tendencies. Winnicott envisioned normative family dynamics and adequate parenting that would breed healthy, cooperative, normative, sociable, and non-aggressive children, i.e., the future democratic citizens. He assigned specific gender roles to women and men. Women were seen as mothers by default and natural caregivers whose subjectivity was almost entirely directed toward providing for children's needs so that later aggression on a personal and social level would be diminished. Men, on the other hand, were envisioned as financial providers, and as only partial and secondary, albeit important, caregivers of babies. This vision, which we would now recognize as heterosexist and middle-class, was developed together with the female producers of the BBC talks who were themselves radio pioneers (who helped develop new radio genres specifically targeting women) and are remembered as radicals for their time. Indeed, it is important to note that the ideas that Winnicott presented, now often seen as simplistic, were new and viewed as progressive at the time, as they were set against behaviorist childrearing advice. During the mid century these views were seen as innovations that reassured mothers of their importance and authority as parents. The voices of women producers and listening mothers suggest that many women of the time (despite earlier militant feminist traditions in Britain and in contrast to later feminists) were embracing these ideas.[105] Interestingly, no letters of protest or criticism against Winnicott's ideas were sent to the BBC. Winnicott warned that without the mother's love and care the baby would grow to be a troubled adult yet, following BBC instructions not to upset parents, he spoke mostly in a positive manner, emphasizing the importance of good mothering as something that comes naturally to a woman. Nevertheless, the threat of damage to mental health and the democratic regime was there.

The heritage of World War II in Britain was less tainted than that of countries on the European continent. British women and men did not experience the results of violent occupation, annihilative racism and anti-Semitism, rape, mass deportation, and murder, and did not have to deal with the question of collaboration with or resistance to an enemy. While other countries had to deal with more complex national wartime pasts of either victimizing or being victimized (and sometimes both), Britain's

---

[105] Even different feminist trends focused on the values of childrearing and home in this period of restrained feminist politics: Elizabeth Wilson, *Only Halfway to Paradise*.

legacies of war mostly centered on notions of heroism and the worry for the future stability of its democratic regime. This stability was seen as tied to the promotion and maintenance of mental health. Ideas about mental health, significantly advocated by psychoanalysts, were often described in gendered terms that made full-time motherhood – for better and for worse – a milestone in the process.[106] Evacuated, delinquent, or "democratically immature" children, as psychoanalyst Juliet Mitchell noted, were all seen by psychoanalysts to be "maternally deprived," while bombs, poverty, and absent fathers were a lesser part of this description. The early Freudian triadic relationship of the Oedipus complex and the more radical psychoanalytic debates on femininity from earlier in the century were now replaced by a preoccupation with the mother–child bond, one that fit the political demands of the era.[107]

[106] On the effects of psychological theories on women's lives see Dolly Smith Wilson, "A New Look at the Affluent Worker: The Good Working Mother in Post-War Britain," *Twentieth Century British History* Vol. 17 (2006), pp. 206–229.

[107] Juliet Mitchell, *Psychoanalysis and Feminism* (New York: Basic Books, 2000 [1974]), pp. 228–229.

5   Psychoanalyzing crime: the ISTD, 1931–1945

In the middle decades of the twentieth century, psychoanalysis became key in the field of criminology, and the analytic ideas of the Institute for the Scientific Treatment of Delinquency (ISTD) dominated in the field of understanding crime. While continuing to recover the work of forgotten psychoanalysts, this chapter locates forensic psychoanalysis within the context of wider debates about the meaning of democracy and the ability to tame individual and collective violence. The relevance of psychoanalysis to British society lay in its applicability to various dilemmas of the time. Via psychoanalytic logic and terminology, mental predicaments were taken as serious threats to political stability. Speaking in public forums and on the BBC, psychoanalysts such as Donald Winnicott often concentrated on the everyday problems of "normal" children. But psychoanalysis as a discipline also claimed to be able to account for "abnormality" in order to help promote harmonious democratic society. From the 1930s to the 1960s, British psychoanalysts set the tone in discussions of juvenile delinquency and the rise in crime that were thought to be caused by the upheaval of war. Psychoanalytic accounts of criminality and the work of the ISTD became vital to much of the public and official thinking on the subject at the time. The Institute was willing to develop Sigmund Freud's original view of crime in inventive and far-reaching ways, which had an effect on the lives of law-breakers, the legal and probation systems, the police, and government offices. While Chapter 4 took us to the postwar period, it is important to return to the interwar period in order to understand criminology as yet another area influenced by psychoanalysis. This chapter, then, follows the analytic work of the ISTD throughout the interwar and war years.[1] Chapter 6 will focus on the ISTD's postwar work.

---

[1] As historian David Smith noted, in contrast to World War I, historians have paid little attention to juvenile delinquency during World War II in Britain. Thus in this chapter I contribute to the scholarship filling this gap. See David Smith, "Official Responses to

While in Vienna, Sigmund Freud himself rarely wrote on crime and exercised great caution in applying psychoanalysis to the law. In a 1906 public lecture to future judges, for example, Freud warned against using psychoanalytic methods to discover hidden content in the mind of the criminal. Neurotic criminals who, although innocent, acted as if they were guilty, he believed, might lead judges astray. Freud was concerned as to whether legal practices would succeed in distinguishing self-accusing individuals of this kind from those who are really guilty.[2] In 1916, Freud suggested that many criminals suffered from unconscious guilt that made them seek punishment. This sense of guilt, he believed, was present before the misdeed and "did not arise from it, but conversely – the misdeed arose from the sense of guilt."[3] The origin of this guilt-before-the-deed, he argued, "derived from the Oedipus complex and was a reaction to the two great criminal intentions of killing the father and having sexual relations with the mother." In comparison with these two imagined sins, the crimes committed in order to fix the sense of guilt came as a relief to the sufferers. Yet Freud was again careful of sweeping conclusions. Although he believed that the majority of offenders were "criminals from a sense of guilt," he suggested that further research was needed to decide how many fell into this category. Importantly, for Freud, economic gain was frequently only a superficial reason for criminal behavior. The origins of such action were to be found in childhood.[4]

From the 1920s onward, different analysts provided early developments in forensic psychoanalysis and thinking about juvenile delinquency. All of them stressed that criminals wished to be punished for an offense that felt less offensive than their fantasized one.[5] However, the main – as

Juvenile Delinquency in Scotland during the Second World War," *Twentieth Century British History* Vol. 18, No. 1 (2007), p. 78. See also Edward Smithies, *Crime in Wartime: A Social History of Crime in World War II* (London: Allen & Unwin, 1982); Donald Thomas, *The Enemy Within: Hucksters, Racketeers, Deserters, and Civilians during the Second World War* (New York University Press, 2003).

2 Sigmund Freud, "Psycho-Analysis and the Establishment of Facts in Legal Proceedings [1906]," SE/PEP Vol. IX, pp. 97–114.

3 Sigmund Freud, "Some Character-Types Met with in Psycho-Analytic Work [1916]," SE/ PEP Vol. XIV, p. 332.

4 *Ibid.*, p. 333. See also Sigmund Freud, "The Expert Opinion in the Halsmann Case [1931]," SE/PEP Vol. XXI, p. 252.

5 For the work of the teacher August Aichhorn, Anna Freud's Viennese colleague, see August Aichhorn, *Wayward Youth* (New York: Viking Press, 1935 [1925]). In the Foreword to the book, Sigmund Freud wrote, "The child has become the main object of psychoanalytic research and in this respect has replaced the neurotic with whom the work began." Aichhorn's work was mentioned with praise in the British Parliament: Kurt Eissler (ed.), *Searchlights on Delinquency: New Psychoanalytic Studies Dedicated to Professor August Aichhorn* (New York: International Universities Press, 1949), p. x. See also Melanie Klein, "On Criminality [1934]," in Melanie Klein, *Love, Guilt and Reparation and Other Works 1921–1945* (*The Writings of Melanie Klein*, vol. I), (New York: Free Press, 1975),

yet unexplored – site in which psychoanalytic criminology developed in the twentieth century was the ISTD in Britain.[6] Historians have neglected the pioneering work by its psychoanalytic members.[7] Despite its influence, no studies have ever investigated the work of the ISTD and its prominent role has been largely absent from accounts of this period.[8]

Attention to "juvenile delinquency" as a special category of offense intensified in Britain in the nineteenth century. Crime was a main locus through which different concerns about British national and imperial strengths were expressed in public. Since the mid nineteenth century, a set of legislation and "care proceedings" introduced different treatments for young offenders. These changes in part had to do with a growing concept of childhood as a separate period of life, and with emerging psychological ideas about the best ways for the state and parents to handle children. The first half of the twentieth century saw changes in the legal and social treatment of juvenile delinquents. The 1907 Probation Act formally introduced probation as a means of rehabilitation of criminals; probation gradually became standard for dealing with young offenders. A year later, the Children's Act of 1908 advanced the idea that children deserved "care and protection." The Act formally created a separate system of courts for juvenile delinquents. These courts were convened to be "agencies for the rescue as well as the punishment of children."[9] World War I gave rise to further discussions of juvenile delinquency. The perceived rise in juvenile crime immediately after the war was attributed to the fact that fathers at the battlefront and mothers busy with war work and domestic duties were both unable to take good care of their children (a similar explanation appeared during World War II). The Children and Young Persons Act of 1933 extended the 1908 Act and placed a new emphasis on the welfare of the young person in juvenile courts. The courts were called upon to learn more about the lives of the children brought before them, about their school and

---

pp. 259–261; D. W. Winnicott, "The Antisocial Tendency," in D. W. Winnicott, *Collected Papers: Through Pediatrics to Psycho-Analysis* (New York: Basic Books, 1958), pp. 306–315. On Bowlby's work on delinquency, see Ch. 7.

[6] In 1931 it was first called the Association for the Scientific Treatment of Criminals and then the Association for the Scientific Treatment of Delinquency and Crime. It was later called the Institute for the Scientific Treatment of Delinquency and Crime, and from 1948 the Institute for the Study and Treatment of Delinquency. I am using the acronym ISTD for simplicity.

[7] See Paul Roazen, *Oedipus in Britain: Edward Glover and the Struggle over Klein* (New York: Other Press, 2000).

[8] Except for an internal publication of the ISTD: Eva Saville and David Rumney, "Let Justice Be Done: A History of the ISTD, a Study of Crime and Delinquency from 1931 to 1992" (London: ISTD, 1992). I thank the archival staff of the Centre for Crime and Justice Studies, for their help.

[9] Harry Hendrick, *Child Welfare: Historical Dimensions, Contemporary Debate* (Bristol: Policy Press, 2003), p. 84.

family lives. "Knowing the offender" was crucial for the choice of appropriate treatment. The courts were to help ensure the readjustment of delinquents to the community and to counteract the impact of poverty upon their lives. The majority of children appearing before the courts were boys with working-class backgrounds, and the reformers behind the Acts can be seen to be trying to shape a working-class family based on a middle-class model of "good behavior" and appropriate gender roles. However, with the growth of psychology and the child guidance movement in the 1930s, poverty was only one explanation of juvenile delinquency. Borrowing from the British child study tradition, American psychological medicine, and the Freudian-influenced "New Psychology," the movement gained influence during the interwar period through a set of clinics. Due to its influence, magistrates increasingly referred young offenders for psychological examination. It should be noted, however, that, while some prominent magistrates (such as Basil Henriques) embraced the "reformist" idea that delinquents could and should be rehabilitated, others held a more disciplinary, "reactionary" view and favored corporal punishment. With the passing of the 1948 Children Act, the idea that children and young people who broke the law should be protected and reclaimed as "good citizens" became dominant.[10]

ISTD psychoanalysts played an essential part in this interwar transformation of punishment into "welfare discipline", a process in which the intention was to treat or readjust offenders rather than merely punish them. What they emphasized was distinctive in crucial and powerful ways. Analysts were not the only ones to support an individualized approach in the care of juvenile delinquents; the educational psychologist Cyril Burt, for example, articulated this theme in his 1925 influential book *The Young Delinquent*.[11] Yet while some, like Burt, began incorporating

---

[10] Kate Bradley, "Juvenile Delinquency, the Juvenile Courts and the Settlement Movement 1908–1950: Basil Henriques and Toynbee Hall," *Twentieth Century British History* Vol. 19 (2008), pp. 133–155; Deborah Thom, "The Healthy Citizen of Empire or Juvenile Delinquent?: Beating and Mental Health in the UK," in Marijke Gijswijt-Hofstra and Hilary Marland (eds.), *Cultures of Child Health in Britain and the Netherlands in the Twentieth Century* (Amsterdam: Rodopi, 2003), pp. 189–212; Hendrick, *Child Welfare: Historical*, pp. 99–124; Victor Bailey, *Delinquency and Citizenship: Reclaiming the Young Offender 1914–1948* (Oxford University Press, 1987); Abigail Wills, "Delinquency, Masculinity, and Citizenship in England 1950–1970," *Past and Present* (May 2005), pp. 157–185; Anne Logan, "'A Suitable Person for Suitable Cases': The Gendering of Juvenile Courts in England, c. 1910–1939," *Twentieth Century British History* Vol. 16 (2005), pp. 129–145.

[11] Cyril Burt, *The Young Delinquent* (University of London Press, 1925). See also Cathy Urwin and Elaine Sharland, "From Bodies to Minds in Childcare Literature: Advice to Parents in Inter-War Britain," in Roger Cooter (ed.), *In the Name of the Child: Health and Welfare in England, 1880–1940* (New York: Routledge, 1992), pp. 174–199.

psychology into environmental explanations, and others still underlined poverty and unemployment, ISTD psychoanalysts stressed psycho-internal dynamics as the critical, main cause of crime.[12] Just as analysts turned away from the impact of real violence on British citizens during the Blitz and looked instead at their "inner" emotions, they did the same with crime, in which the environment played a secondary role in analytic explanations. Thus, the ISTD was a unique institution even for this period which saw a growth of emphasis on psychology. It gradually came to predominate the understanding of crime.

The ISTD approach to crime drew both on psychoanalytic theories of delinquency and on an earlier indigenous British tradition of criminology. British criminology did not develop out of the continental Lombrosian theoretical tradition, which searched for an abstract "criminal type." Instead, the homegrown British tradition was closely linked to the daily practical demands of legal authorities, such as providing psychiatric evidence before courts, or assisting prison medical officers with the classification of offenders. In British scientific thinking about crime, most criminals were seen to be generally normal individuals; only a minority required treatment.

After World War I, however, a new emphasis on clinical examination of offenders emerged. M. Hamblin Smith, Britain's first authorized "criminologist," who had a professed interest in psychoanalysis, advocated in 1922 a close psychological study of the individual, despite some official opposition, particularly from psychiatrist W. Norwood East, the medical inspector of prisons.[13] It was the more pronounced criminal psychoanalytic work of Grace Pailthorpe (Smith's co-worker) that ultimately excited some of the interest that led to the emergence of the ISTD. Drawing from a variety of sources of influence, the ISTD had its distinctive brand of criminological theory. On the one hand, the Institute's prioritization of the clinical exploration of individual personality was continuous with previous British ideas. So was its tight collaboration with the legal, probation, and prison systems (at odds with Sigmund Freud's original ideas). The Institute's practical and interdisciplinary type of criminology was also close to earlier ideas formulated by Cyril Burt. On the other hand, the ISTD distinctly supported prevention through the work of its outpatient clinic. It was also unique in its emphasis

---

[12] Hendrick, *Child Welfare: Historical*, pp. 113–117; see also Linda Mahood, *Policing Gender, Class and Family: Britain 1850–1940* (London: UCL Press, 1995).

[13] While Norwood East warned against the dangers of exaggerated psychological claims, he too, it is important to mention, was increasingly an influential proponent of a limited psychological approach to crime.

on psychoanalysis, which was occasionally met with official hostility, but was also welcomed more often than is realized by historians.[14]

The establishment of the ISTD

The ISTD was established in 1931–1932. It was born from a growing expert and public interest in crime, the desire to establish an organization devoted exclusively to its study and, as mentioned, to the psychoanalytic research of Pailthorpe.[15] Pailthorpe, a colorful character, was a front-line surgeon during World War I who had trained in psychoanalysis. She conducted a psychological study of British female criminals in prison and concluded that much crime could be prevented by diagnosis of psychological causes in the individual. Pailthorpe eventually left medicine to become a surrealist artist, yet she is considered the *de jure* founder of the ISTD. It was psychoanalyst Edward Glover, whom we have encountered as an instrumental figure in the debates on total war and anxiety, who was the *de facto* founder of the ISTD after he became its official chairman in 1932.[16]

The Institute's declared goal was to initiate and promote scientific research into the causes and prevention of crime. It hoped to establish observation centers and clinics for the diagnosis and treatment of crime and to consolidate existing scientific work in Britain and abroad. On a more practical level, the members of the ISTD wished to advise the juridical and magisterial bench, as well as hospitals and governmental departments in the investigation and treatment of suitable cases. Beyond the promotion of educational training facilities for students of delinquency, the members of the ISTD also hoped to promote wide discussion of and educate public opinion on these issues. The ISTD's first priority was to organize a clinic for delinquents, which would also serve the courts. Using donations and private funds, on September 18, 1933, the Institute was able to open the "Psychopathic Clinic," and to admit its first patient, an adult woman of violent temper charged with assault on her female employer.[17]

During 1934, work at the ISTD was mainly devoted to the development of the Clinic, to which patients were sent in increasing numbers. Cases referred from police courts by magistrates and probation officers – some of them now keener to learn about the young offenders before them – were

[14] David Garland, "British Criminology before 1935," *British Journal of Criminology* Vol. 28 (1988), pp. 1–17.
[15] See Grace Pailthorpe, *Studies in the Psychology of Delinquency* (London: HMSO, 1932); Saville and Rumney, "Let Justice," p. i; Edward Glover, *The Diagnosis and Treatment of Delinquency* (London: ISTD, 1944), p. 5.
[16] Saville and Rumney, "Let Justice," pp. 1–7.   [17] *Ibid.*, pp. 7–8.

given precedence over those referred for delinquent behavior without a charge. Services were initially offered at no cost so that no one would be barred from the Clinic's services, but donations were accepted from those who could afford them. Magistrates occasionally expressed their satisfaction with reports from the ISTD by making donations from the police court's poor box. During 1934, the Psychopathic Clinic saw 71 new patients;[18] by 1937 this number rose to 167.[19] During these years, the courts referred most patients. Other referrals came from medical practitioners and clinics such as the Tavistock Clinic, local child guidance clinics, and the London Clinic of Psycho-Analysis.[20]

The Clinic first used rooms allocated to it at the West End Hospital for Nervous Diseases in London. This changed in 1937 when the Institute's separate outpatient clinic opened on Portman Street, housing both the Institute and the Clinic under one roof for the first time. The Institute then expanded its activities and had a membership of about 300 individuals coming from different backgrounds. The ISTD was now occupied with the education of public opinion, the provision of training facilities for students, and the organization of other clinical centers. By 1938, the Institute had received wider recognition as a Child Guidance Clinic and as a center for University of London extension courses, and it was invited by the Home Office Committee under A. M. Carr-Saunders to represent its views on juvenile delinquency.[21] That year, the Institute also cooperated with British Paramount News in the making of a newsreel on "Shop-Lifting" to be screened in London's cinemas. Filming the exterior of the ISTD premises and then its interior, the newsreel showed patients being examined physically and psychologically. The ISTD's treasurer, George Wansborough, was filmed saying, "There are two types of shoplifters, the ones with mental disorders and the plain criminals."[22] From its early days, the Institute had been involved in clinical services as well as research and public educational activities. Lectures on different aspects of delinquency, among them psychoanalytic ones, were delivered to the public and to professionals who belonged to bodies such as the Committee of Health Visitors, the Psychiatric Section of the Royal Society of Medicine, and different women's institutes. The lectures were published widely in the press.

[18] Centre for Crime and Justice Studies, ISTD Archive (hereafter ISTDA)/330DDDD: *ISTD Annual Report 1934*.
[19] In 1935, Edward Glover referred to the work of the Institute in a BBC talk: ISTDA/ 330AAAA: *ISTD Annual Reports 1935* and *1937*.
[20] ISTDA/330AAAA and 330DDDD: *ISTD Annual Reports 1934, 1935, 1936, 1937*.
[21] ISTDA/330AAAA: *ISTD Annual Report 1937*, p. 13; A. M. Carr-Saunders et al., *Young Offenders: An Enquiry into Juvenile Delinquency* (Cambridge University Press, 1942).
[22] Saville and Rumney, "Let Justice," pp. 13–14.

Psychoanalytic-psychiatric treatment was the ISTD's original forte and the focus of its work. Nevertheless, the founders of the Institute were determined to have a comprehensive attitude to crime that would also involve mental measurement, psychiatric social work, and physical examination.[23] Indeed, over the years, the ISTD increasingly became a multidisciplinary body, which came to include members of Parliament, magistrates, Home Office officials, lawyers, police and prison staff, probation officers, and social workers.[24] In 1948, the Psychopathic Clinic was taken over by the National Health Service and was renamed the Portman Clinic, while the ISTD continued its educational and research activities with separate funding. Both the Portman Clinic and the ISTD followed a multidisciplinary approach involving the cooperation of psychiatrists, physicians, social workers, sociologists, and statisticians.[25]

The work of the ISTD was therefore not wholly psychoanalytic. When describing the ISTD, Glover preferred to call it "a medico-psychological institute," yet at the same time he acknowledged that the Institute's foundation was largely the work of psychoanalysts, who had played a large part in its direction.[26] The ISTD also attracted therapists with psychoanalytic orientation.[27] Although complete psychoanalysis was rarely carried out, by 1959, an analytic approach was commonly applied in short treatment. Nonetheless, every variety of individual and group psychological treatment was employed in the Clinic.[28]

Psychoanalysis was thus not the sole practice of the ISTD, but it was a central and essential factor in its work. From its early days, psychoanalytical approaches to crime dominated the Institute and were its key inspiration. Sigmund Freud himself was among the vice presidents of the ISTD. Besides Glover and Pailthorpe, analysts Ernest Jones, Carl Jung, Otto Rank, and Alfred Adler were also vice presidents. The Institute's Scientific Committee included the psychoanalysts Denis Carroll, David Eder, and John Rickman. Among the staff were psychoanalysts John Bowlby, Marjorie Franklin, David Matthew, Adrian and

---

[23] Glover, *The Diagnosis*, p. 6.   [24] Saville and Rumney, "Let Justice," p. vii.

[25] Edward Glover, *The Problem of Homosexuality: Being a Memorandum Presented to the Departmental Committee on Homosexual Offences and Prostitution, by a Joint Committee Representing the Institute for the Study and Treatment of Delinquency, and the Portman Clinic* (London: ISTD, 1957), p. 3. See Ch. 6.

[26] Edward Glover, "Outline of the Investigation and Treatment of Delinquency in Great Britain, 1912–1948," in Edward Glover, *The Roots of Crime* (New York: International Universities Press, 1960), p. 51.

[27] Saville and Rumney, "Let Justice," p. 22.

[28] Edward Glover, "The Roots of Crime," in Glover, *The Roots of Crime*, p. 21, n. 1; Edward Glover, "Outline of the Investigation and Treatment of Delinquency in Great Britain, 1956–1959" in Glover, *The Roots of Crime*, pp. 75–76.

Karin Stephen, Melitta Schmideberg, and Barbara Low.[29] Later came psychoanalysts Wilfred Bion, W. H. Gillespie, and the exiled Kate Friedlander, Hedwig Schwarz, and Klara Frank. The Institute regularly published psychoanalytically oriented articles and pamphlets. It is significant that the ISTD did not shy away from publicly identifying itself with psychoanalysis at a time when other child guidance clinics made sure to claim that they had nothing to do with it.[30] For example, on June 25, 1932, the ISTD published in the *Manchester Guardian* a public appeal for financial support with signatures including those of Sigmund Freud, Adler, Glover, Jones, Jung, and Rank.[31]

The leading personalities of the ISTD were the psychoanalysts Edward Glover and Denis Carroll, the psychoanalytic psychiatrist Emanuel Miller, and the German émigré criminologist Hermann Mannheim. In spite of their different backgrounds, an atmosphere of cooperation existed between the psychoanalysts and the non-analysts. A biographical sketch of each of them illustrates their differences and similarities.

Edward Glover, as elucidated in earlier chapters, was an important psychoanalyst in the BPAS. Glover, coming from a medical background, insisted on basing psychoanalysis on research and advocated cooperation with other professionals. His work consisted of original contributions to a wide range of psychoanalytic interests. Yet his central strength was in the work that he did at the ISTD and as the founder and editor of the *British Journal of Delinquency*.[32] Similarly, psychoanalyst and mathematician Denis Carroll's main involvement was in the field of delinquency. Carroll (1901–1956), now a forgotten figure, was a co-director of the Clinic and a leading administrator at the ISTD. He also served as a member of the Home Office Advisory Training Board on Probation, the Home Office Advisory Council on the Treatment of Offenders, the Joint Committee of the British Medical Association, and the Magistrates' Association. He was a prolific speaker and a frequent broadcaster on psychoanalytic criminology. In 1949, he advised the United Nations on

---

[29] ISTDA/330DDDD: *ISTD Annual Report 1934*.

[30] Deborah Thom, "Wishes, Anxieties, Play, and Gestures: Child Guidance in Inter-War England," in Cooter (ed.) *In the Name of the Child*, p. 209.

[31] Saville and Rumney, "Let Justice," p. 7. Others who signed the appeal were Allen Marjory, William Brown, W. J. Brown, Havelock Ellis, H. G. Wells, Edward Mapother, and Emanuel Miller.

[32] Malcolm Pines, "Glover, Edward George (1888–1972)," in *Oxford Dictionary of National Biography* (Oxford University Press, 2004); Clifford Yorke, "Edward Glover, 1888–1972," in *International Dictionary of Psychoanalysis* (Detroit: Macmillan Reference Books, 2005); L. S. Kubie, "Edward Glover: A Biographical Sketch," *Int. J. Psycho-Anal.* Vol. 54 (1973), pp. 85–93; M. N. Walsh, "The Scientific Works of Edward Glover," *Int. J. Psycho-Anal.* Vol. 54 (1973), pp. 95–102. See also Ch. 2, n. 8.

the prevention and treatment of crime. Carroll was a medical consultant to the Q Camp experiment (see below),[33] and chairman of a committee founded to train personnel to deal with the aftereffects of the war on Austrian youth. The whole of Carroll's work was "oriented in a psycho-analytical direction."[34]

Emanuel Miller (1892–1970) was a London psychiatrist of Jewish origin interested in bridging science and the humanities. He was the director of the East London Child Guidance Clinic. Miller believed that work informed by psychoanalysis could help prevent delinquency and neurosis.[35] Miller was also a consultant to the Tavistock Clinic. At the outbreak of World War II, he helped unite several mental-health bodies to form the Campaign for Mental Health.[36] From 1945, he taught psychiatrists at Maudsley Hospital. He founded the *Journal of Child Psychology and Psychiatry* and the Association of Child Psychology and Psychiatry. Miller was involved in the ISTD's work from its establishment and was the joint editor of the *British Journal of Delinquency*. Miller's writing, historian Deborah Thom explains, was "characteristic of the most effective period of British eclecticism in relation to psychoanalytic thinking, where the insights of Freudian and Kleinian analysis could be combined with positivist medicine and enrich each other."[37] In contrast to Miller, Hermann Mannheim (1889–1974) came from quite a different background. Born in Berlin, Mannheim was a pioneer criminologist, a judge, and a prominent law scholar. When the Nazis came to power, he decided in 1934 to move to London. There, he continued his career from the London School of Economics. He combined philosophical thinking with his practical work at the courts, and has often been called "the father of modern British criminology" due to the wide influence of his work.[38] He too was one of the founding editors of the *British Journal of Delinquency*. In addition to his ties with the ISTD, Mannheim was also associated with the Howard League for Penal Reform, another contemporary body

---

[33] During the war, Carroll was a commanding officer at Northfield Military Hospital.

[34] Edward Glover, "Denis Carroll," *Int. J. Psycho-Anal.* Vol. 38 (1957), pp. 277–279; ISTDA/330AAAA: *ISTD Annual Report 1949 & 1950*, p. 4.

[35] Emanuel Miller, *The Generations* (London: Faber & Faber, 1938); Emanuel Miller (ed.), *The Growing Child and its Problems* (London: Kegan Paul, Trench, Trübner & Co., 1937).

[36] See also Emanuel Miller (ed.) *The Neuroses in War* (New York: Macmillan, 1940).

[37] The biographical information is based on Deborah Thom, "Emanuel Miller," in *Oxford Dictionary of National Biography*.

[38] See Hermann Mannheim, *Social Aspects of Crime in England between the Wars* (London: Allen & Unwin, 1940); Hermann Mannheim, *Juvenile Delinquency in an English Middletown* (London: Kegan Paul, Trench, Trübner & Co., 1948); Hermann Mannheim, *Criminal Justice and Social Reconstruction* (London: Kegan Paul, Trench, Trübner & Co., 1946); Terence Morris, "British Criminology: 1935–1948," *British Journal of Criminology* (Spring 1988), pp. 20–34.

advocating changes in the legal system.[39] His name added to the professional prestige of the ISTD.

Psychoanalysts themselves, as shown above, came to this discipline, and to work at the ISTD, from different backgrounds. As another example, this time of women in the Institute, Barbara Low (1877–1955), was a teacher and member of the Fabian Society as well as a founding member of the BPAS before joining the ISTD. Low came from an Anglo-Jewish family of Austrian and Hungarian descent. As one of the first popularizers of psychoanalysis, she was also a frequent public lecturer on criminality.[40] Melitta Schmideberg, Melanie Klein's daughter who is already known to us through her Blitz writings, was another woman working at the ISTD from its early days. Yet she came from a different background than Low, having received her medical and analytic training in Berlin before fleeing to London. As her criticism of Klein grew, Schmideberg eventually withdrew from active participation in the BPAS in 1944 and concentrated on her work with delinquents.[41] Kate Friedlander (1902–1949) was another psychoanalyst with a background in medicine active at the ISTD. She was of Jewish-Austrian decent. Her interest in delinquency started with work in a juvenile court in Berlin. After Hitler's rise to power, she fled to London in 1933 and become a member of the BPAS. She then joined the ISTD, eventually publishing a popular textbook on delinquency. She also set up one of Britain's first child guidance clinics in West Sussex, of which branches were opened in Horsham, Chichester, and Worthing (and which were supported by students who had worked in Anna Freud's Hampstead Nurseries).[42] Coming from diverse circumstances, all of these individuals

---

[39] Leon Radzinowicz, "Hermann Mannheim," in *Oxford Dictionary of National Biography*; John Croft, "Hermann Mannheim: A Biographical Note," in Tadeusz Grygier, H. Jones, and J. C. Spencer (eds.), *Criminology in Transition: Essays in Honour of Hermann Mannheim* (London: Tavistock Publications, 1965); Jack Beatson and Reinhard Zimmermann (eds.), *Jurists Uprooted: German-Speaking Émigré Lawyers in Twentieth-Century Britain* (Oxford University Press, 2004).

[40] Low became a supporter of Anna Freud's ideas. See Pearl King, "Biographical Notes on the Main Participants in the Freud–Klein Controversies in the British Psycho-Analytical Society, 1941–1945," in Pearl King and Riccardo Steiner (eds.), *The Freud–Klein Controversies, 1941–1945* (New York: Routledge, 1991), p. xvii; Marjorie Franklin, "Barbara Low," *Int. J. Psycho-Anal.* Vol. 37 (1956), pp. 473–474; Clifford Yorke, "Barbara Low, 1877–1955," in *International Dictionary of Psychoanalysis*.

[41] See Ch. 2, n. 44; after moving the United States in 1945, Melitta Schmideberg founded the Association for Psychiatric Treatment of Offenders in New York. After the death of her mother in 1960, she decided to return to Europe. See Pearl King, "Melitta Schmideberg," in *International Dictionary of Psychoanalysis*; editorial, *British Journal of Delinquency* Vol. 4, p. 304, and Vol. 7, p. 86. See her many articles in *International Journal of Offender Therapy*.

[42] Clifford Yorke, "Kate Friedländer-Fränkl," *International Dictionary of Psychoanalysis*; Kate Friedlander, *The Psycho-Analytical Approach to Juvenile Delinquency: Theory, Case Studies, Treatment* (London: Kegan Paul, 1947).

Illustration 1: London's East End children made homeless by German air raids, September 1940. Some analysts claimed that children were traumatized not by bombing but by the separation from their mothers.

Illustrations 2–4: Children sheltering from air raids, eating together, and trying out gas masks at Anna Freud and Dorothy Burlingham's Hampstead War Nurseries in London.

Illustrations 2–4: (cont.)

Illustration 2–4: (cont.)

Illustration 5: Child concentration-camp survivors, including the Jewish
orphans from the Bulldogs Bank project, arrive by plane in Britain.

Illustration 6: Melanie Klein, right, with her daughter Melitta Schmideberg-Klein (and one of Melanie Klein's sons).

Illustration 7: A rare image of Melanie Klein (center left) and Anna Freud (center right) together with Ernest Jones on the right.

Illustration 8: Donald Winnicott's talks were broadcast at a time when BBC Radio hoped to appeal to mothers and children.

Illustration 9: Donald Winnicott in analysis with a child.

Illustrations 10–11: Analytic methods influenced work with juvenile delinquents at the Q Camps.

Illustration 10–11: (cont.)

Illustration 12: John Bowlby with a girl in psychoanalysis. Anonymous notes on the reverse of the photograph read: "He realized that her trouble was loneliness. Her father was in the Army, and the mother missed her husband too much to actually pay enough attention to the child."

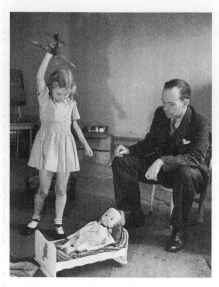

Illustration 13: John Bowlby with a girl in psychoanalysis. Anonymous notes on the reverse of the photograph read: "Mary loves her little sister – and at the same time is jealous of her. In play, she expressed this jealousy by 'buzz bombing' the doll representing her little sister."

Illustration 14: John Bowlby with Richard, a boy in psychoanalysis. Anonymous notes on the reverse of the photograph read: "When Richard has had a good 'smashing session' he feels in a mood to be constructive."

worked together harmoniously at the ISTD during the period between the wars.

The child guidance movement influenced the ISTD, yet it was distinct from it. The early child guidance clinics in Britain followed American models that advanced interdisciplinary scientific teamwork approach, collected case histories from patients, and attached considerable importance to the environment of the child. The first American-style clinic in England was in fact Emanuel Miller's East London Child Guidance Clinic. The British clinics hoped to be a hub for a comprehensive system of child welfare that would embrace the nursery, the home, the school, the playground, and the courts. Referrals were made by parents, teachers, doctors, or probation officers. The clinics advanced the idea that children should be psychologically treated rather than punished. The ISTD shared this vision, and like the clinics, supported the idea of teamwork and collaboration among different agencies, and had also collected case histories from patients. Like the clinics, the ISTD was about teaching citizens self-discipline and communal responsibility in pursuit of democracy. There are therefore similarities between the ISTD and child guidance movement clinics (especially with those clinics that were more psychologically and psychoanalytically leaning such as the Tavistock Clinic and the East London Clinic, as well as Margaret Lowenfeld's Clinic in London). Yet the ISTD was different in the central and consuming role that psychoanalysis played in its work from the interwar period and in its emphasis on inner psychological motives.[43]

Interwar psychoanalytic ideas on crime

Edward Glover described the interwar era as a time when most magistrates were "almost allergic to the idea that any crime could be a manifestation of disorder in human relations."[44] This was something of an exaggeration, since psychological studies of crime were already emerging and gaining influence in this period, yet in 1922, when Glover addressed women magistrates at Oxford on Freud's theories on crime, these ideas were still a novelty.[45] Glover's Oxford lecture presents the core of his analytic views in the years to come and also gives an indication of some responses to such ideas from the audience. Glover's main thesis was that the roots of crime are psychological and originate in early life. Crime is one of the outcomes of unsuccessful domestication of humans, whom he viewed to be naturally savage. The perfectly normal infant, Glover claimed, is almost completely

[43] Hendrick, *Child Welfare: Historical*, 99–113.   [44] Glover, "The Roots of Crime," p. 3.
[45] He claimed that this was the first public lecture to magistrates on forensic psychoanalysis.

egocentric, greedy, dirty, violent in temper, destructive in habit, and pro-foundly sexual in purpose. Glover stated, "judged by adult social standards, the normal baby is for all practical purposes a born criminal."[46] The infantile instincts, Glover believed, could be detected in delinquents who did not fully succeed in mastering their impulses and becoming law-abiding. Glover, therefore, linked experiences of childhood and adult misbehavior in order to foster a new legal attitude to crime. Criminality was a channel through which psychoanalysts like him could discuss childhood in connection with the need for a stable democracy in which aggression would be managed and misconduct avoided.

Glover's ideas were met with some resistance from his listeners. At the end of the lecture, for example, the well-known magistrate Mrs. St. Loe Strachey responded by crying, "But, doctor, the dear babies! How could you say such awful things about them?"[47] It is interesting to note that even Strachey, a leader in the child guidance movement in Britain, saw Glover's ideas as extreme. Likewise, Glover's suggestion that the criminal might suffer from a disordered mental functioning also angered Lord Olivier, a Fabian socialist, who protested, "Never have I listened to such outrageous nonsense regarding the motivation of theft. Quite obviously the motivation of offences against property is economic in nature and the offences will disappear when a reasonable economic organization of soci-ety is established."[48]

Indeed, while attention to class was not something that the British psychoanalysts overlooked, a developed critical analysis of economic differ-ence was largely missing from their accounts. Many psychoanalysts attended children and adults from working-class backgrounds and saw it as part of their vocation. The ISTD, in particular, treated poor young people, and in general analysts advocated better welfare services for working-class people, refugee children, and others. Yet analysts in Britain did not convey a radical class criticism in the spirit that prevailed among some continental socialist analysts in the 1920s and 1930s. What mattered for the second generation of analysts working in Britain after Freud were aggressive internal and family dynamics and their relation to democracy. These were rarely tied directly to an extended critique of class.[49]

So while for his Fabian socialist critic economic factors led to crime, for Glover himself, Freud's work on unconscious guilt alone was "sufficient to

<hr/>

[46] *Ibid.*, p. 8.   [47] *Ibid.*, p. 8, n. 1.   [48] *Ibid.*, p. 12, n. 1.
[49] On class, see also Ch. 7. Earlier in the century such views had enraged leftist analysts such as Wilhelm Reich and Otto Fenichel, who tied social repression, poverty, and desperation to aggression and law-breaking; see George Makari, *Revolution in Mind: The Creation of Psychoanalysis* (New York: HarperCollins, 2008), p. 446.

revolutionize the whole system of penal method."[50] Following Freud, Glover questioned the efficacy of punishment since he believed that many criminals wanted to induce society to punish them. The existence of criminals in the community might serve to strengthen the willingness of "ordinary citizens" to follow the law by providing the latter with scapegoats for their own repressed criminal tendencies, he suggested. Glover emphasized not only the treatment of crime but also its prevention. He stated, "We must see to it that from birth onwards, all measures of upbringing calculated to promote aggressive anti-social responses in later life are reduced to a minimum, that the child is brought up in an atmosphere of security and affection, that its sexual education is sane, candid and realistic and that an example of law-abidingness is shown by its parents in their private domestic lives."[51] In the years to follow, Glover continued to advocate such views to the public and various professional and state officials.

A slightly different interwar psychoanalytic account on the origins of crime came from ISTD member Melitta Schmideberg. Schmideberg maintained that external factors were not the exclusive causes of asocial behavior. Describing patients' histories, Schmideberg limited herself to cases in which asocial reactions were determined by inner conflicts, and not by economic need. She believed, however, that even in the latter type "psychic factors determine the various reactions to frustration and that external need, in addition to possessing the significance of frustration, is apt to reactivate all the earlier conflicts."[52] Among Schmideberg's asocial young patients was a boy named "Willy." Willy "stole everything he could lay hands on, was sexually shameless, and unusually aggressive. To all appearances he was entirely lacking in moral feelings or love."[53] Besides urinating on Schmideberg's couch, Willy liked to arrive too early for his analytic sessions in order to disturb the patient before him. He also stole the contents of the pockets of the coats hanging in her clinic's hall. Stealing, for Willy, meant destruction of real objects that stood for his feared and hated "internal objects" (such as the imagined genitals of his parents), Schmideberg reasoned. By stealing the objects he feared, he could feel that he took possession of and mastery over them, and could use them as weapons against inner and outer assailants.[54] Stealing and asociality emerged out of internal battles.

It is important to acknowledge that the ISTD's psychoanalytic ideas such as these stressing internal emotional dynamics were not reserved for

---

[50] Glover, "The Roots of Crime," p. 17.   [51] *Ibid.*, p. 22.
[52] Melitta Schmideberg, "The Psycho-Analysis of Asocial Children and Adolescents," *Int. J. Psycho-Anal.* Vol. 16 (1935), p. 47, n. 5.
[53] *Ibid.*, p. 22.   [54] *Ibid.*, p. 25.

highbrow psychological circles. While they were reiterated in psychoanalytic and professional journals of neighboring disciplines, during the interwar period and after, they were also presented in more common form in pamphlets, public lectures, and the popular press.[55]

"Delving into the secrets of the criminal's soul": the ISTD in the popular and professional press

Indeed, when the ISTD was established, it received public attention and wide press coverage, often linking it with psychoanalysis. For example, on July 7, 1932, numerous newspapers reported that Sigmund Freud, Carl Jung, and Alfred Adler were among many who gave support and approval to "a serious endeavour to combat crime at its source." The reports further described the ISTD as an association "which is setting out to apply the same skilled diagnosis and scientific treatment to abnormalities of conduct as are now applied to bodily disease."[56] The ISTD and its psychoanalytic approach were identified as offering professional care for a problem that was increasingly seen as requiring expert medical treatment rather than punishment. For example, when the *Birmingham Mail* reported on the work of the ISTD, it emphasized that the treatment of crime was "not a business for amateurs."[57] *Christian World* also described the ISTD's opinion that "the way to arrest the alarming increase of crime [was] to stop the supply of criminals. Punishment does not cure the criminal or reduce crime."[58] Similarly, *Pearson's Weekly* wondered why people commit crime and noted that, while a few years ago the answer was "because they are wicked," modern scientists like those at the ISTD were

---

[55] During the 1930s, the BPAS too offered several lectures on forensic psychoanalysis: Archives of the British Psycho-Analytical Society: The Institute of Psycho-Analysis, Annual Report 1934.

[56] "To Combat Crime: Scientific Plan of Treatment," *Glasgow Evening News* (7 Jul. 1932). Similar reports appeared on the same day: "Scientific Treatment of Crime: Professor Freud Supports New Scheme," *Lincolnshire Echo*; "Scientific Treatment of Crime," *Cambridge Daily News*; "Treatment of Crime," *Western Evening Herald*; "Study of Crime," *Southern Daily Echo*; "'Doctoring' Crime," *Northern Daily Telegraph*; "Fighting Crime by Science," *Birmingham Evening Despatch*; "The Way of Science with Crime: Association to Deal with 'Disease,'" *Daily Echo* (Dorset); "Science as Crime Cure: Experts Support New Scheme; Skilled Diagnosis; Delinquency Treated as a Disease," *Liverpool Echo*; "Scientific Treatment of Crime: Abnormalities of Conduct, Professor Freud Supports New Scheme," *Halifax Daily Courier*, and in many other local newspapers; "To 'Cure' Crime," *Daily Mail* (all 8 July 1932).

[57] "More Crime Study," *Birmingham Mail* (28 Jun. 1932). See also *Cambridge Daily News* (27 Jun. 1932); *Evening Star* (Ipswich) (27 Jun. 1932).

[58] *Christian World* (30 Jun. 1932). Two years later, a correspondent of the *Church Times* deplored the apathy of Christian opinion in the treatment of offenders against the law: *Church Times* (28 Sep. 1934). See also the response of the ISTD in *Church Times* (19 Oct. 1934).

not so sure, and believed instead that there was something wrong with criminals and with the way they were treated. "So, say the scientists, cure instead of punish; set up hospitals instead of prisons."[59]

Articles in the popular press continuously reported on the ISTD's stance that crime was a problem related to individual psychology and to predicaments from childhood, rather than to economic hardship. For example, on July 8, 1932, the *Daily Sketch* described the aim of the ISTD as being "to deal with a criminal as a sick man – sick in mind – and to cure him as the hospital or the doctor cured a patient."[60] In an interview with the *Observer*, E. T. Jensen, the chairman of the Council of the ISTD, who was an early supporter of psychoanalysis, emphasized the importance of early expert intervention and connected treatment with good democratic citizenship. The ISTD's intention, he explained, was primarily to investigate and treat cases of children and young adults who were first-time offenders, since a scientific approach and successful treatment of early cases of anti-social conduct would "check at its source the present constant supply of criminals, a large percentage of whom become habitual ... A great deal of human material would thus be saved from crime to useful citizenship."[61] On these and other occasions, childhood, the family, psychological expertise, the prevention of asocial behavior, and the promotion of good democratic citizenship were woven together.

The ISTD declared in the press that psychological and psychoanalytic intervention rather than punishment was a more appropriate, as well as effective, way to handle crime. Talking to the *Evening Standard*, an ISTD official said that there were many cases in which men were sent to prison when they could be more suitably dealt with at a clinic. The spokesperson said, "The offender could be treated by those who thoroughly understand him and who have formed ideas about what mental state led to the commission of the offence."[62] However, at the *Edinburgh Evening News*, Dr. J. A. Hadfield of the ISTD (who also developed analytic psychology at the Tavistock Clinic) refined such claims, saying, "The Institute is under no illusion that psychotherapy can cure the hardened criminal. But there are cases, like that of the man who had been convicted and sent to prison

---

[59] "Hospital for Naughty Boys," *Pearson's Weekly* (11 Feb. 1933).
[60] "Criminals Are Sick Men: Organisation to Treat them as Such," *Daily Sketch* (8 Jul. 1932).
[61] "Combating Crime at its Source: A New National Effort," *Observer* (10 Jul. 1932). The *Sunday Pictorial*, however, wrote that the establishment of a new ISTD was an admirable move toward suppressing law-breaking at source but thought that "the average man will be forgiven if he regards the new organisation doubtfully": "Crime-Curing," *Sunday Pictorial* (10 Jul. 1932).
[62] "Psychological Treatment of Criminals," *Evening Standard* (1 Dec. 1932).

for slashing a girl's skirt, which are definitely not proper cases for imprisonment but for medical treatment."[63]

The interwar press saw the work of the ISTD as "modern," "scientific," and standing in contrast to previous periods and earlier ways of handling crime. In 1932, the *Birmingham Post* wrote, "This new association is the outcome of the twentieth-century belief that, given timely and proper treatment, the conditions responsible for anti-social conduct may be removed." It continued, "Parents will be encouraged to take children with abnormal tendencies to 'hospital' just as they take them for a broken leg. This should have social value in the gradual emptying of our prisons and in the using of money now spent in tracing, trying and punishing criminals, for constructive purposes."[64] Similarly, the *Manchester Guardian* reported that the ISTD was embarking upon a campaign to "bring into action to prevent wrongdoing all the most recent scientific discoveries regarding psychology and crime."[65] The *Glasgow Herald* linked social change, the post-World War I atmosphere, and the scientific study of crime, saying, "There has been a tendency at times, occasionally with justification, to regard the linking of crime and pathology as a weak relaxation of the sterner methods of another era. But no one who appreciated the period of stress through which the world has passed during and since the war can fail to understand that scientific exploration of the causes of crime, with research into its psychological and social treatment, may produce more lasting benefits than the insistence on punishment as crime's only fit and proper sequel."[66]

Legal and medical magazines also reported on the psychoanalytic work of the ISTD. For example, in an article in the *Police Chronicle*, Jensen wrote that treatment at the ISTD dealt with, among other things, emotional unconscious conflicts and inferiority complexes.[67] Likewise, the *Police Review* recognized the importance of the observations of psychoanalysts into the mentality of criminals.[68] The *Solicitor's Journal* quoted Glover as saying, "a nation of adults could not continue to deal with its

[63] "'Curing' Crime," *Edinburgh Evening News* (27 Jan. 1933).
[64] "The Treatment of Delinquency: A New Association Formed in London," *Birmingham Post* (26 Jul. 1932).
[65] "Scientific Treatment of Crime," *Manchester Guardian* (1 Aug. 1932). See also "Crime Prevention," *Leeds Mercury* (1 Aug. 1932); "Science War on Crime," *Birmingham Gazette* (1 Aug. 1932); "Scientific War on Crime," *Bulletin* (Glasgow) (1 Aug. 1932); *The Times* (2 Aug. 1932).
[66] "The Treatment of Crime," *Herald* (Glasgow) (8 Jul. 1932). See also "Science and Crime," *Evening News* (8 Jul. 1932).
[67] E. T. Jensen, "The Scientific Treatment of Delinquency," *Police Chronicle* (1 Feb. 1935), p. 13.
[68] "The Scientific Treatment of Delinquents," *Police Review* (22 Feb. 1935).

criminological problems by the crude diagnosis and primitive therapy of a two-year-old child ... the first step to the adequate handling of crime was to eliminate hate, anger and anxiety from criminal methods."[69] Democracy, for Glover, demanded psychological maturity from both citizens and state officials.

Indeed, Glover and other ISTD professionals who presented psycho-analytic ideas were regularly quoted in the daily press.[70] The *Nottingham Guardian*, for example, reported on a public lecture given by Miller and meticulously outlined to its readers his psychoanalytic arguments. The article described Miller quoting criminal cases in which "human motives have been probed by doctors peering into the darker recesses of the mind, 'below the threshold of consciousness.'" Miller was reported to deal with neurotics who confessed to crimes they did not commit due to their "deep sense of guilt connected with homicidal thoughts about members of their own family – thoughts which had lain below the surface, influencing health and behaviour in remote and fantastic ways."[71]

Not all were happy with these circulating psychoanalytic assertions. For example, on February 24, 1934, the London magistrate Claud Mullins stated in a lecture to psychologists that he did not believe in "mind-cures" for criminals and preferred to lock them up. Mullins, one of the more progressive magistrats in London, later supported the need for medical and psychological expertise and became a famous advocate of different reforms in domestic hearings. But on that occasion, he was more reserved and wary of experts, perhaps allowing himself to be so more than usual because he was talking to an audience of psychologists. He complained that it was often impossible for the magistrate to consider the individual's interests and that the criminal must in many cases be sacrificed to society. After all, he added, "there is a great deal of reform that can be done behind a 20-foot wall." Mullins expressed sympathy with psychologists' aims, yet

---

[69] "Institute for the Scientific Treatment of Delinquency," *Solicitor's Journal* (10 Dec. 1932). See also "The Scientific Study of Delinquency," *Medical Officer* (23 Mar. 1933); "Publicity and Crime," *Lancet* (16 Mar. 1933); "Crime and the Press," *BMJ* (1 Apr. 1933); "Juvenile Delinquency and the Broken Home," *BMJ* (24 Mar. 1933).

[70] See "Imitative Bandits," *Daily Mail* (19 Oct. 1934); "Punishment and Crime," *The Times* (28 Oct. 1932), p. 8. See also *Medical Press* (11 Jan. 1933); *The Listener* (4 Jan. 1933); *Manchester Guardian* (24 Jan. 1934). For Glover's argument against flogging in jail, see "Jail Flogging Must Stop!: Doctors Join Demand for Inquiry," *Daily Herald* (13 Dec. 1934). On the lively debate on flogging after World War II, see the *Daily Telegraph*'s many reports and articles in December 1952 and January and February 1953.

[71] "Community's 'Sense of Guilt': Deep Recesses of the Mind," *Nottingham Guardian* (1 Apr. 1933). The same was true for "The Modern Treatment of Delinquency," *Birmingham Post* (18 Oct. 1934). See also Edward Glover, "Punishment and Crime," *The Times* (28 Oct. 1932), p. 8; *Medical Press* (11 Jan. 1933); *Listener* (4 Jan. 1933); *Manchester Guardian* (24 Jan. 1934).

said that there were psychologists that made him feel like he must "go on in the good old-fashioned way." Though he was not wholly opposed to the work of psychoanalysis, it is clear that Mullins was referring to psycho-analysts when he mocked them saying, "I read a statement by one psychologist that war debts are due to suppressed sex instincts, and that many of our economic troubles can be traced to the 'Oedipus Complex.' It has been said that walking up and down the stairs has a sexual signifi-cance." He added, "If I want to consider myself sexually normal, I suppose I have to live in a bungalow."[72]

Despite such misgivings, throughout the 1930s, the press reiterated the self-assured words of ISTD staff and provided a favorable public stage for their analytic ideas and work. Glover, for example, was quoted as saying to the *News Chronicle* that "Clinics for criminals will bring about a complete revolution in our attitude towards crime." He said that "Crime has many aspects, including the economic. Hitherto the psychological and medical sides have been the most neglected." Yet he held, "The future for children who have 'never had a chance' is very bright to-day ... These can often be readjusted to life so that they no longer wish to steal, or assault, and so on."[73] Similarly, the *Daily Mail* referred to the work of the ISTD saying, "A new era in crime investigation and the treatment of delinquents is opening in this country."[74] *The Times* published a confident letter by Jensen stating that experience showed that "modern methods," such as those that obtained at the ISTD's Clinic, saved many young people from a life of crime. "Maladjusted instincts, from which these young offenders suffer, are treated in order that their emotional outlook may become sound so that they can become healthy citizens able to live a law-abiding life which they desire."[75]

The "inwardly" oriented psychological and psychoanalytic work of the ISTD's Clinic was described repeatedly in numerous press reports. For example, the *Sunday Dispatch* explained that the patient at the Institute "is induced to talk things over with a kindly man, with shrewd eyes, pleasant voice, and quick brain that analyzes replies without change of look or tone. When the trouble has been located, friendly talks induce the patient to

---

[72] "'Lock Criminals Up,' Says London Magistrate," *Evening Standard* (24 Feb. 1934). See also "Glands and Crime: Popular Scientific Fallacies," *Catholic Herald* (29 Dec. 1934). On Mullins, see "Matrimonial Disputes: Advice of Experts," *The Times* (8 Dec. 1934); S. M. Cretney, "Claud Mullins," in *Oxford Dictionary of National Biography*.

[73] "Clinics to Cure Wrong-Doers: Better Times for Wayward Child," *News Chronicle* (8 Feb. 1934).

[74] "Clinics to Cure Crime: Where Courts May Order Treatment," *Daily Mail* (10 Apr. 1934).

[75] E. T. Jensen, "Scientific Treatment of Young Criminals," *The Times* (4 Dec. 1934).

realize without being actually told that his conduct is out of the ordinary."[76] *People* reported favorably on the ISTD's Clinic saying, "Extraordinary 'cures' of delinquents who would otherwise have found themselves in jail are being effected by a clinic of London doctors who are giving their services voluntarily."[77] Jensen, writing to the *Yorkshire Evening Post*, characterized the staff of the ISTD as "skilled in discovering hidden impulses that cause crime."[78] Indeed, the *Daily Express* described the ISTD's Clinic as "delving into the secrets of the criminal's soul."[79] The *East Anglian Daily Times*, too, used psychoanalytic language to report on the case of a young delinquent boy who underwent what seems to be analytic treatment. As the boy's father was dead and his brother had been killed in the World War I, the boy was viewed as the head of his household. And, thus, the article described the boy had, unknowingly, "formed an exalted opinion of his sex. He saw himself as an elect person who had the right to take what he wanted. Treatment caused him to realise that his unconscious attitude towards life was at the root of his stealing and made him face reality when no amount of punishment would have changed his ways."[80] *Reynold's Illustrated News* also told of the analytic treatment of a young woman accused of theft. In her treatment "it became clear" that her mother expected too much from her and caused her to have "a constant sense of inferiority." Her father, wishing to compensate for the mother's strictness, spoiled the young woman and gave her an exaggerated idea of her own cleverness. The woman therefore stole because her theft made her feel clever. The treatment radically changed this woman's mental attitude toward life. The article concluded that "Heart-to-Heart talks" between delinquents and a specialist in the ISTD bought many cures.[81] Similarly, psychoanalytic ideas about emotional conflicts and fantasies originating in childhood were reported in an article in the

---

[76] "Doctors to 'Cure' Criminals: Send to a Hostel Instead of Prison," *Sunday Dispatch* (15 Jan. 1935). See also "Curing Crime by Science," *Daily Telegraph* (4 Feb. 1935).

[77] "Doctors' Free Service," *People* (17 Feb. 1935). See also "Curing Crime by Science," *Daily Telegraph* (14 Feb. 1935); "Science Treatment for Crime," *Nottingham Evening Post* (14 Feb. 1935).

[78] E. T. Jensen, "Medicine Not Prison for Criminals," *Yorkshire Evening Post* (28 Feb. 1935). See also "Ending Jail for Sex Crimes: Doctors Urge Treatment Centres," *Daily Herald* (16 Mar. 1935); "A New Way with Young Delinquents," *The Times* (4 May 1935).

[79] "15 Men out to Cure Crime: Clinic for Delving into Souls," *Daily Express* (8 Dec. 1933).

[80] "Science Prevents Crime: Curious Causes of Law-Breaking," *East Anglian Daily Times* (11 May 1935). The case was also described by an ISTD member in an article previously mentioned: Jensen, "The Scientific Treatment of Delinquency." See also *Belfast Telegraph* (25 Jul. 1935).

[81] "Talk that Cures Criminals and the Sick; Parsons and Doctors Work Hand-in-Hand; Psycho-Analysis," *Reynold's Illustrated News* (28 July 1935).

Evening Standard that described a case of a man who believed that he was bow-legged and constantly thought someone was laughing at him. Due to this "psychological flaw in his make-up," he started deliberately bumping into perfect strangers in the street, was accused of assault, and was passed to the ISTD for treatment.[82] Besides these reports on successful individual treatments, the ISTD received more attention during the interwar period due to its association with an interesting experiment with maladjusted and anti-social young men that came to be known as Q Camp, which tied the struggle against crime to democracy.

Psychoanalysis at Q Camp: an experiment in democracy

The ISTD became involved in Q Camp during 1936. Opened in that year near Great Bardfield, Essex, the camp operated until 1940 (another Q Camp later carried on, at the same site, from 1944 to 1946).[83] Its aim was to place young people in an open-air community that would offer them scope for physical and mental development and that would improve self-control, social behavior, and physical health.[84] The primary object of the experimental camp, explained Dr. Norman Glaister (a member of the organizing committee) to *The Times*, was to "help young men who might have the makings of useful and happy citizens but were victims of a bad social environment and restricted interests. In this community life in the countryside they would be given every opportunity to develop their specific interests."[85] The goal was therefore to turn asocial young delinquents into well-socialized citizens, and the camp emphasized values important for the maintenance of democracy.

Q Camp drew the attention of the popular press which in its reports also further publicized the ISTD. For example, the *Shields Gazette* (as well as other newspapers) described the ISTD as being among the organizations involved in a "secret camp for 'queer' characters," where "social rebels" would learn how to "live in harmony and happiness with their fellow men." In Q Camp, it explained, youths aged from 7 to 25 would help each other "in the great quest of a higher future." It added, "that is

---

[82] "Underworld Tales of Girl Who Wanted Excitement," *Evening Standard* (24 Jun. 1935). The medical-physical examinations done at the ISTD were described in "Young and Guilty," *News Chronicle* (Jul. 1935).

[83] ISTDA/Pamphlet Collection (hereafter PMC): Marjorie E. Franklin (ed.), "Q Camp: An Experiment in Group Living with Maladjusted and Anti-Social Young Men" (London: Planned Environment Therapy Trust, 1966 [1943]), p. 16, n. 1.

[84] *Ibid.*, p. 15.

[85] "Chance for 'Social Misfits': Experimental Camp for Young Men," *The Times* (7 Aug. 1935).

why it is called the 'Q' camp – the 'Q' stands for quest." The camp was not for the "fellow who is naturally and essentially vicious ... it is for the chap who possibly has been put on probation for a first offence and who, with a little friendliness, discipline, and organised work to do, can be made to feel that he is a member of a community – not a 'lone wolf.'" The goal of Q Camp was to "restore the spirit of self-respect and mutual respect, both of person and [of] property" through "social adjustment and community living."[86] Indeed, individuals referred to Q Camp were seen by the ISTD's Clinic for examination and for determining their suitability for residence at the camp. The ISTD also helped solve problems that arose in connection with the formation of the camp.[87] The Institute waived all fees, both for the examinations and for attendance at its seminars.[88]

Work at Q Camp was not principally psychoanalytic. The camp's organizers emphasized economic factors alongside psychological ones leading to crime. The idea that youth work could instill social order was also not entirely new and had been implemented in different interwar youth clubs aiming to provide organized forms of leisure and protect youngsters from "idleness." Of interest, however, is the way in which through the ISTD, and particularly through one of its important members, the psychoanalyst Marjorie Franklin, who was also an honorary secretary of and a co-psychiatrist at Q Camp, an awareness of psycho-analytic methods and thinking played an important part in the working of the camp.[89] A pamphlet on Q Camp edited by Franklin provides some evidence for this suggestion (Illus. 10–11).

The methods used at the camp, as Franklin described them, placed emphasis on individual personality and on "love" as a motive force of work. The general goal of Q Camp was to place together young malad-justed and anti-social men who, despite what Franklin called their "emotional immaturity and mental conflict," were interested in commun-ity life in simple surroundings. Other principles were shared responsibility between the members of the camp, and living and working together. In addition, Franklin wrote, "Because we valued individuality and because we wished to fit our members to be free citizens of a democratic country,

---

[86] "Secret Camp for 'Queer' Characters," *Shields Gazette* (8 Aug. 1935). See also the reports from the same date in "Human Destinies Remoulded," *Western Evening Herald* and *Evening Post* (Bristol); "'Q' Camp for Social Rebels," *Southern Daily Echo*; "Camp with a Quest," *Evening Citizen* (Glasgow); "New Experiment with 'Social Rebels,'" *Northampton Echo*; "Social Rebels: Q Camp for 'Lone Wolves,'" *Northern Daily Telegraph* (Blackburn). See also "'Social Rebels' to Citizenship," *Yorkshire Herald* (9 Aug. 1935).

[87] ISTDA/330AAAA: *ISTD Annual Report 1936*, p. 9, and *Annual Report 1937*, p. 16.

[88] ISTDA/PMC: Franklin, *Q Camp*, p. 11.

[89] Franklin was also involved for a long time with the Howard League for Penal Reform.

the community was run on democratic lines." Franklin believed that Q Camp could claim distinctiveness in various ways, including "The effort to study and treat anti-social behaviour and mal-adaptation by environmental and educative means with a scientific seriousness comparable to that used for individual methods of psychotherapy."[90] While people in whom "deep-seated psychotic or psycho-neurotic traits dominated the personality" were not admitted, familiarity with psychoanalytic thinking seems to have prevailed in the camp. For example, while the camp's main instruments of treatment were based on "pioneering in open space" and communal work, Franklin also reported that "affection," increasing "feelings of attachment," and "the phenomena of positive transference (and negative transference as well) were appreciated and utilized by the staff."[91] Using psychoanalytic language, she explained how most of the individuals in the camp had in their early years suffered frustration or interference in their emotional relationship to their parents and "had failed to master normally the biological complexities of early family adjustment." Franklin claimed that, at Q Camp, they were enabled to transfer these emotions to members of the staff. The members helped them to become happier and to have a better relationship with society.[92] Invoking Sigmund Freud's ideas indirectly, Franklin wrote further that it was known that an excessive sense of guilt could lead to delinquency. "A delinquent sometimes seeks in an overt act of lawbreaking and its punishment relief from an apparently inexplicable sense of remorse. He does not know the cause of the uneasiness, but it is often connected with unconscious memories, thoughts or phantasies of a sexual or aggressive kind, which the more tolerant and reasonable conscious mind of an adult can accept and understand." Franklin believed that Q Camp gave considerable help in some of these cases, although "usually they need deeper forms of psycho-therapy."[93]

Additional evidence that psychoanalysis had influence in shaping Q Camp could be found in the words of David Wills, the camp chief, and in the summary of data derived from members' case records and after-histories published in a public pamphlet. Wills, a psychiatric social worker working closely with Franklin, casually used psychoanalytic terms, suggesting that "the mechanism of unconscious identification" was a factor in the relationship between staff and members at the camp.[94] Various case descriptions specified that camp members experienced "positive

---

[90] ISTDA/PMC: Franklin, *Q Camp*, p. 14.   [91] *Ibid.*, p. 18.   [92] *Ibid.*, p. 21.
[93] *Ibid.*
[94] *Ibid.*, p. 26, n. 1. See also David Wills, *Hawkspur Experiment* (London: Allen & Unwin, 1967).

transference to Camp Chief," or "turbulent positive and (more often) hostile transference," "much phantasy and some impulsive violence," "sexual phantasies (disguised) in drawing," "inferiority feeling over-compensated by conceit and fabrication," "irrational fears," and "strong emotional stress."[95] As these descriptions were written in the published pamphlet by Wills in collaboration with Franklin, they suggest that this psychoanalytic vocabulary and taxonomy were familiar to the camp's staff. It should also be noted that, while ISTD members mostly made the examinations before entrance to the camp, the responsibility for admission was vested in one or other of the medical members of the Executive Committee, which included Glaister and psychoanalysts Denis Carroll and Franklin herself.[96] In this camp, as in other projects and experiments which psychoanalysts initiated or participated in, social stability was tied to proper childhood and emotional balance. Democratic values such as cooperation, self-governance, and social harmony were emphasized in all of these ventures, especially, as we have seen in previous chapters, during World War II.

The ISTD during World War II

Despite difficulties, the ISTD continued to operate once World War II broke out, and helped maintain a certain vision of democracy that emphasized the importance of psychology in preventing violence and social chaos. Although blackouts and air-raid attacks made evening clinic sessions impossible, overall, the ISTD's work increased during the war years.[97] This process, however, had its ups and downs. From its early days, the majority of cases that reached the ISTD originated in police courts, and this continued to be true for the war years. Other cases were referred by medical practitioners, clinics, and philanthropic societies, and some were recommended by relatives, friends, social workers, employers, and solicitors; a small number of patients referred themselves. Overall, the number of treatments initially decreased with the outbreak of war. While in 1937–1939 the Institute treated an average of 165 patients per year, in 1940 the number dropped to 114 and to 107 patients in 1941. Different circumstances related to the war accounted for variations in the total referrals from 1937 onward. The Munich Crisis, for example, caused a

---

[95] ISTDA/PMC: Franklin, *Q Camp*, pp. 39–49.
[96] *Ibid.*, p. 28. See also ISTDA/PMC: Marjorie Franklin, *An Outline of the Principles & Methods of the Hostel-School* (1948).
[97] ISTDA/330BBBB: *ISTD Annual Report 1946*, p. 7.

decline in referrals for about a month.[98] Yet from January 1939 to the
outbreak of war, there was an increase in the number of patients sent to
treatment. In September 1939, the Clinic closed for a month. For a time,
the members thought that the war would make work impossible, but in
October they decided to reopen.[99] In 1940, during the worst period of the
Blitz, work at the Clinic was almost brought to a halt. A bomb in Portman
Street put the Clinic out of action for several weeks and necessitated
removal in November to new premises on Manchester Street,
London.[100] Other factors that contributed to the drop in numbers were
the call-up of staff to service, civilian evacuation, pressure of work on the
Probation Service, and the temporary closing of most juvenile courts in
the London area. The blackout caused a discontinuation of evening
clinical sessions while the increasing pressure of war work made it difficult
for youths on probation to attend treatment during the day.[101] In June
1942, the Clinic opened for early evening treatment but, due to lack of
attendance, the sessions were discontinued after six months. Owing to
urgent demands for treatment after working hours, late sessions resumed
in August 1943. Numbers remained steady during the winter in spite of
the threat of air raids.[102]

During World War II, Hermann Mannheim of the ISTD published an
influential book in which he claimed that after World War I crime had
increased greatly.[103] Reviewers of his book perceived it as highly relevant
for the present war, and in another publication Mannheim argued that
crime would increase in the future even more than it had after the first
world conflict. He maintained – using a psychoanalytic logic – that during
wartime there was an increase in economic crimes, and a decrease in
crimes of violence, since the war was serving as a substitute for violent
crimes.[104]

And, indeed, what part then did psychoanalytic treatment in specific
play in the ISTD's clinical work during the war? Glover described the
treatment given at the Institute during those years as ranging from techniques of pure suggestion and hypnosis to psychoanalysis. Members
reserved the psychoanalytic method for selected cases. In a great number
of cases, "combined" psychological methods were employed with some
degree of guidance or persuasion.[105] The war conditions and the shortage

[98] ISTDA/330BBBB: *ISTD Annual Report 1938*.
[99] ISTDA/330AAAA: *ISTD Annual Report 1939*, p. 4.
[100] ISTDA/330DDDD: *ISTD Annual Report 1940*; Saville and Rumney, "Let Justice," p. 16.
[101] Glover, *The Diagnosis*, p. 7.   [102] *Ibid.*, p. 23 n.
[103] Mannheim, *Social Aspects of Crime*.
[104] Hermann Mannheim, *War and Crime* (London: Watts & Co., 1941), p. 142.
[105] Glover, *The Diagnosis*, p. 21.

of staff led to a reduction in the duration of treatment and to the increased employment of short-term methods.[106]

However, despite the wartime difficulties that prevented lengthy psychoanalytic work with delinquents, Glover's clinical report for the war years reveals that psychoanalytic language for diagnostic terms, case descriptions, and the causes of crime were continuously a *lingua franca* at the Institute. While it is predictable that Glover as an analyst writing the report would use Freudian terms, the fact that this document was circulated among all members shows that psychoanalytic terminology was a form of speech understood (or used) by all of them, not just by the psychoanalytic members. More importantly, the ISTD chose to publish this report as a public pamphlet for wider circulation, in doing so confirming that the members felt comfortable with this psychoanalytic language representing their work.[107] The report developed, for example, Sigmund Freud's concepts of crime to argue that the wartime disturbance of previously stable family relations or "a history of early maladaptation to family life, due either to internal psychological causes or to unsatisfactory conditions of upbringing," were the two factors responsible for wartime juvenile delinquency in Britain. Glover added that the war conditions acted only as a precipitating factor, providing "a suitable culture medium for the growth of delinquent reactions, the ultimate causes of which are essentially intrinsic."[108] Marginalizing the impact of real violence and instead emphasizing "the war inside" form an interpretation we previously saw other psychoanalysts using during the war. By implication, this argument meant that democratic society should not be concerned with asocial behavior only during wartime, but should view it instead as a general, constant problem of human functionality, to be understood by experts during peacetime as well.

In contrast to expectations, the war did not seriously reduce the public activities and educational efforts of the Institute. For example, on weekends, the ISTD provided classes for students of social studies at the University of London, with high attendance rates even during the worst periods of enemy action. The curriculum included a fourth-year section on "The Freudian Theory of Delinquency." The Institute also organized public seminars for probation officers, policewomen, and welfare workers, in which their day-to-day casework was discussed with a psychiatrist. Among these seminars were some given by analyst Kate Friedlander. These were so successful that probation officers demanded their

---

[106] *Ibid.*, p. 27.   [107] ISTDA/330BBBB: *ISTD Annual Report 1946*, pp. 7–8, 14.
[108] Glover, *The Diagnosis*, pp. 9–10.

continuation, and thus the Institute was invited to take part in the official Home Office probation training course in 1942.[109]

The paper that Melitta Schmideberg gave at a British Social Hygiene Council conference held in London in June 1942 reveals how forensic psychoanalysis was publicly presented at that time and how, in turn, it was also shaped by the war conditions.[110] By then, Schmideberg referred to the question of class more directly than other analysts. Moving away from a still-prevalent Victorian trope linking poverty to idleness and blaming the poor for their own poverty, she emphasized instead that individual psychology could lead to poverty and crime. At the same time, in her talk, she used this particular argument as a call for expert intervention. Schmideberg claimed that most offenders sent to the ISTD – whether they came from poor environmental conditions or were of low intelligence and poor physical health – suffered from psychological difficulties. If a poor man is unable to earn his living owing to a neurotic inhibition at work, for which he cannot receive treatment, he has few alternatives but to obtain money dishonestly. Many criminals, she argued, were psychologically unable to work "not because they are lazy but because of unconscious anxieties, guilt or inferiority reactions."[111] Some of them stole because of unconscious impulses of hate and revenge for an unhappy childhood. Others stole to compensate for the parental love they had missed. Schmideberg argued that such psychological difficulties were aggravated by unsatisfactory social conditions. The circumstances of war were another source of mental stress as "Well-balanced people can endure without lasting ill-effects a surprising amount of strain, but those who are unstable, yet who might manage, with luck, to 'scrape along' in normal times, cannot stand up to the increased strain of wartime conditions."[112] Schmideberg offered interesting links between crime, psychology, democracy, and the struggle to establish a "New Jerusalem" and a better society after the war. Against those who claimed that society should not waste money on criminals, she reminded her audience that the Nazis, when they first came to power, had abolished reforms in the treatment of criminals. For her, the attitude of a society toward the poor, toward children, toward the weak, and toward the maladapted was "a measure of civilization." Unless British democratic society worked to

[109] ISTDA/330BBBB: *ISTD Annual Report 1946*, p. 7. See ISTDA/330AAAA, 330BBBB, and 330DDDD: *ISTD Annual Reports 1938, 1939, 1940*; Kate Friedlander, "Delinquency Research," *New Era* (Jun. 1943).
[110] ISTDA/330AAAA: Melitta Schmideberg, "The Scientific Treatment of Delinquency in Wartime," pp. 1–4.
[111] *Ibid.*, p. 1.   [112] *Ibid.*, p. 2.

understand the social and psychological problems that led to delinquency, all plans for a new world after the war might not lead far.[113]

By 1943, in an article for the popular magazine *The Listener*, Glover too placed delinquency in the context of military struggle as he assigned a social and moral mission to psychology. If Britons wished to reduce the increasing number of unstable and unhappy personalities or the rising toll of juvenile delinquency, he stressed, they must see to it that "the security of family life of any [citizen] is raised to a decent level, mental as well as material." He continued arguing that the civilization of any state can be judged not so much by its education and cultural institutions as by the happiness and psychological security of the families that comprise it. Psychology's greatest service in the future lay in "guiding the development of human society as a whole." Hoping that the secret of civilizing those sprawling, quarrelsome, and destructive infants who make up the aggregate of nations could be found, he expressed optimism that adult wars could be avoided too. "If psychologists can discover the secret anxieties that drive children to behave unreasonably, it is possible that they may be able to locate the secret dreads and superstitions that drive societies into equally childish but infinitely more dangerous tantrums."[114]

The postwar generation of children should have conditions of psychological security in which to create "a truly adult society" where violence is checked, Glover argued. This vision would be more easily materialized if statesmen of all countries abandoned their assumption that societies were run on purely rational lines. Pressure must be put on all individuals of influence to understand that the new postwar order depended "on the degree to which fallible but well-meaning mortals can extend to others the friendly tolerance they are so expert in extending themselves." In this way, Glover generated a call for private citizens and governmental and local institutions to care for the psychological well-being of people in general and children in particular. He crafted a special role for the psychoanalytic expert in preventing future wars and creating a peaceful society. Crime and asocial behavior were positioned as part of this more general political picture of a society between war and peace. They were seen as signs of mental instability that could cause much greater problems, yet could be relieved by psychoanalysts.[115]

The ISTD received more public attention during the war and in its aftermath due to an increased fear of a "crime wave" among juvenile delinquents – a concern to which the ISTD itself significantly

---

[113] *Ibid.*, p. 4.
[114] Edward Glover, "Towards an Adult Society," *Listener* (18 Nov. 1943).   [115] *Ibid.*

contributed. Indeed, official records of delinquency showed that the number of people under seventeen found guilty of indictable offenses rose rapidly between September 1939 and August 1940. This trend had reached a peak in 1941, fell in 1942 and 1943, and had reached a second peak in 1954. For girls, however, there was no decrease in 1942. In addition, there was a 41 percent increase in the number of children under fourteen found guilty of indictable offenses during the first year of the war. The rise in juvenile crime occurred in evacuation, reception, and neutral areas, with cities being particularly affected.[116] It is not entirely clear to what extent the soaring crime rate reflected an increase in actual crime, or more zealous enforcement, or rather a continuation of the rising trend in indictment tied to legal changes introduced by the Children and Young Person Act of 1933. Yet public concern about delinquency remained high and played a continuing role in postwar reconstruction discussions. Like the troubled evacuees, juvenile delinquents remained figures of deep worry. These two figures were often linked in public debates, as it was commonly asserted that evacuated schoolchildren were largely responsible for the rise in juvenile crime. Crime was tied to poverty less than ever before.[117]

The increasingly popular explanation for the rise in juvenile delinquency – influenced in part by psychoanalytic work and dating back to the prewar era – was to highlight the conditions found at home. The war conditions themselves were seen as aggravating the situation by weakening parental guidance, shattering family dynamics, and creating broken homes.[118] For example, Margery Fry, the leading penal reformer and former chair of a London juvenile court (who became influenced by the psychoanalytic writings of John Bowlby) suggested in 1942 that the growth of juvenile delinquency was due to "evacuations, absence of parents in war work, the upset of domestic life by 'shelter nights,' and, perhaps most of all, the general overexcitement, anxiety, and destructiveness of war mentality."[119] In June 1940, *The Times* attributed the rise in

---

[116] Bailey, *Delinquency*, pp. 269–271.
[117] Geoffrey Field, "Perspectives on the Working-Class Family in Wartime Britain, 1939–1945," *International Labor and Working-Class History* Vol. 38 (1990), pp. 12–13.
[118] Bailey, *Delinquency*. See also Hermann Mannheim, "Crime in Wartime England," *Annals* Vol. 271 (Sep. 1941), pp. 129–130; Susan Isaacs, "Cambridge Evacuation Survey," *Fortnightly* Vol. 153 (1940), p. 619; Mannheim, *War and Crime*, p. 142; W. Norwood East, Percy Stocks, and H. T. P. Young, *The Adolescent Criminal: A Medico-Sociological Study of 4,000 Male Adolescents* (London: J. & A. Churchill Ltd., 1942), p. 304.
[119] Margery Fry, "Wartime Juvenile Delinquency in England and Some Notes on English Juvenile Courts," *Journal of Educational Sociology* Vol. 16, No. 2 (Oct. 1942), p. 82. See also Ch. 7.

juvenile delinquency to the effects of war, the lack of parental control, and the favorable conditions for petty pilfering which prevailed during the winter months due to the blackout.[120] In March 1941, *The Times* reported again that child-welfare workers thought that juvenile delinquency was a serious problem with no easy solution. Among the reasons given for it were again the mix of (by now familiar) suggestions of "a lack of discipline, due to absent of fathers and other male relatives, and the closing of schools for long periods; the disappearance of facilities for healthy activity because of the closing of clubs and the use of playing fields for other purposes; emotional strain in some young people and in still more a spirit of adventure and daring; the break up of family life due to calling up, evacuation, and much more time spent in shelters; and the inability of juvenile courts to impose suitable deterrent punishment."[121] There was a variety of opinions on wartime juvenile delinquency but, under the influence of psychoanalysis, attention to home life increasingly dominated as the main cause for this phenomenon.

With an overwhelmed system of remand homes and approved schools, and courts forced to place more children on probation due to accommodation problems in these schools, by March 1941, the Home Office was receiving complaints from all sides about the increase in juvenile delinquency. It was not until mid 1942, however, that the Home Office started outlining postwar penal reform.[122] Indeed, Home Secretary Herbert Morrison urged in September 1942 that work on behalf of juvenile offenders should be regarded as real national service. He stated, "We are fighting this war on behalf of the nation's youth, and we could not ignore the special difficulties of young people who came before the Courts."[123] The ISTD contributed to the spread of such considerations and anxieties and to the particular rhetoric through which they were expressed in public. The continuation of such debates in their turn influenced the flourishing of the work of the ISTD during the postwar years. The home, the family, and inner psychology were increasingly seen

---

[120] "Increased Juvenile Delinquency: Need for Extending Approved Schools," *The Times* (22 Jun. 1940), p. 3.

[121] "Increased Juvenile Delinquency: No Easy Solution to a Serious Problem," *The Times* (8 Mar. 1941), p. 2. Cf. "Increased Juvenile Delinquency: Educational System to Blame," *The Times* (2 Apr. 1941), p. 2. See also "Fun Fairs," *The Times* (13 Mar. 1942), p. 5; "Causes of Juvenile Delinquency: The Task of Religious Education," *The Times* (7 Apr. 1942), p. 2.

[122] "Increased Juvenile Delinquency: Need for Healthy Activities," *The Times* (16 Jun. 1941), p. 2; Bailey, *Delinquency*, pp. 271–273.

[123] "Juvenile Delinquency," *The Times* (15 Sep. 1942), p. 2. See also "Juvenile Delinquency," *The Times* (24 Mar. 1944).

as central to the understanding of ways to prevent problems in a social democratic society and secure the peace.[124]

The uncovering of the ISTD psychoanalytic work throughout the interwar and war years challenges the view that psychoanalysis was an exclusive science whose work was limited to private clinical practice. Like other spheres of psychoanalytic activity, the work at the ISTD reveals that what characterized psychoanalysis during the middle decades of the twentieth century in Britain was its applied nature as a discipline intertwined not only with questions of individual psychology, but also with larger political questions of the age of mass violence and with the general concern for democracy and for creating collaborative law-abiding citizens. Rather than acting as though they belonged to a selective sect, psychoanalysts from the ISTD saw themselves as pioneering reformers, albeit of a particular kind. They saw their discipline as having a unique social and moral role.

While not exclusively a psychoanalytic institute, but rather a multi-disciplinary one, the ISTD as a whole was psychoanalytically oriented, and psychoanalysis influenced its non-analytic work also. Many of the ISTD's founders and leading members were psychoanalysts. As shown, Sigmund Freud himself was among the ISTD's vice presidents, and in the reports of the popular press the Institute was frequently linked to psychoanalysis. The 1930s were years of increasing work for the ISTD and a time when it received extensive public attention. It was able to continue its work during World War II despite blackouts and air raids. Psychoanalytic criminology proliferated during the interwar and war periods in popular, expert, and official circles. The ISTD, as a leading contemporary reform organization, claimed with confidence that crime could, and should, be understood scientifically.

A shift toward psychological explanation of crime and a new emphasis on family life had already emerged before the war. The more deterministic attention to the socioeconomic environment of young offenders was modified during the interwar period, when further consideration was given to psychological explanatory models. The call for reform that came from organizations such as the ISTD (and the Howard League for Penal Reform) was connected to the emergence of juvenile courts and the more frequent use of probation services during this time. This led to the growing acceptance of the idea that authorities should concern themselves with treating rather than punishing delinquency, and should learn about children and their home life. The war, others have suggested too, escalated the interwar developments and deeply underscored the

---

[124] Cf. Sarah Fishman, *The Battle for Children: World War II, Youth Crime, and Juvenile Justice in Twentieth-Century France* (Cambridge, MA: Harvard University Press, 2002).

connections frequently drawn by psychoanalysts between criminality, family breakdown, and democracy.[125]

It was during the postwar period, the focus of Chapter 6, that the ISTD reached an even higher position of influence. At the end of the 1940s and throughout the 1950s, the Institute treated a growing number of patients, reaching a caseload of more than 900 patients in the late 1950s.[126] It gave numerous expert testimonies to government committees, which often emphasized psychoanalytic views. The ISTD aimed to collaborate with magistrates, probation officers, state officials, and other mental-health professionals. In working closely with authorities, the ISTD participated in an established British criminology tradition of serving the needs of the legal and prison systems. Yet the ISTD professionals did so while simultaneously critiquing existing systems and developing psychoanalytic ideas whose origins were, at least in part, in continental Europe. During the postwar years, the ISTD spread its message regularly and, starting in 1950, it published the leading *British Journal of Delinquency* (from 1960 the *British Journal of Criminology*), which quickly reached 700 subscriptions and which, at times, served as a stage for analytic ideas.[127] Furthermore, from the time of its establishment, but during the postwar period in particular, the ISTD delivered numerous popular psychoanalytic public lectures and courses. Instead of functioning as distant clinicians – as frequently characterized today – the analytic experts at the Institute were actively involved in the lives of those who fell into the group of "criminals." Psychoanalysts frequently questioned the existing categories of criminology and the treatment of those considered criminals, but they also offered their own explanations and forms of classification for making sense of behaviors deemed problematic at the time. Changes in the perception of delinquency were promoted through psychoanalytic work and ideas. Chapter 6 will focus on the postwar forensic psychoanalytic work of the Institute and its contribution to the development of a democratic "therapeutic state."

---

[125] Field, "Perspectives," pp. 13–14.   [126] Glover, "The Roots of Crime," p. 21, n. 1.
[127] Saville and Rumney, "Let Justice," p. 48.

6 Toward the therapeutic state: the ISTD during the postwar years, c. 1945–1960

After World War II, the activities of the ISTD increased substantially.[1] In the postwar era, the ISTD was frequently called on by state committees to provide expert testimony on topics ranging from corporal punishment to homosexuality and prostitution. The problems of children and young people continued to capture public attention in the wake of the war, as did the question of rehabilitating delinquents into good citizens.[2] This chapter examines the Institute's postwar psychoanalytic work and explores some of its expert testimony to the government. Like Chapter 5, it shows how ISTD psychoanalysts saw themselves as a certain type of "reformers" involved in the political dilemmas of the creation of a democratic citizenry. Psychoanalysts at this time had an active, and at times interventionist, role in the lives of patients who broke the law. The ISTD reshaped concepts of criminality and the division between notions of normal and abnormal in this transitional era of efforts to build a new future for Britain. As in the debates over air-raid anxiety or those on the evacuation process, the psychoanalytic perspective on crime emphasized ways of educating society for democracy. Total war did not push psychoanalysts – unlike others writing at the time – toward a humanist Enlightenment perspective. Instead, in envisioning the success of democracy, psychoanalysts retained the idea that anxiety, aggression, guilt, and other negative emotions were the ones leading psychological and, importantly, social activity.[3]

While the question of how to best mold non-violent and non-delinquent citizens had already emerged in the interwar era, it took on greater urgency

---

[1] See Eva Saville and David Rumney "Let Justice Be Done: A History of the ISTD, A Study of Crime and Delinquency from 1931 to 1992" (London: ISTD, 1992), pp. 19–20 (internal publication of the ISTD).

[2] Cf. Richard Jobs, *Riding the New Wave: Youth and the Rejuvenation of France after the Second World War* (Stanford University Press, 2007).

[3] See Eli Zaretsky, *Secrets of the Soul: A Social and Cultural History of Psychoanalysis* (New York: Knopf, 2004); George Makari, *Revolution in Mind: The Creation of Psychoanalysis* (New York: HarperCollins, 2008).

during the postwar period, as the British welfare state developed first under the new socialist Labour government from 1945 to 1951, and later under different Conservative governments from 1951 to 1964.[4] It is important to note that many of the anti-fascist and anti-totalitarian theories on the nature of violence and aggression – psychoanalysis included – had already been articulated by the 1930s and in fact pre-dated the actual acts of mass murder on the European continent. There is indeed an intellectual continuity of ideas about Nazism (and Stalinism to a lesser extent) and about the nature of violence from the interwar through war periods. Yet the postwar realization of the extent of the evils of Nazism in particular, along with the actual war experience in Britain, made the need to reinterpret democracy and to tame aggression and "asociality" an even more pressing task than before. Thus, despite a continuity of many of the ideas on violence from the interwar all the way through the postwar period, they overall earned new currency.

In this postwar context, juvenile delinquency was seen as an even more threatening problem of maladjusted citizenship in a welfare state that aimed to address social ills and that developed in part as a political alternative to a Nazi model of society. British ideas on the "humane" treatment of juvenile delinquency were frequently contrasted with "authoritarian" German ones. For example, witnessing the high postwar increase in juvenile delinquency in the British zone of occupied Germany, British officials tried to impose British methods on the Germans and criticized German institutions for being too harsh in their treatment of youth. British administrators pledged to the Germans to establish a separate and "enlightened" system for treating juvenile delinquents in which rehabilitation would take precedence over punishment. The nourishment of progressive psychological attitudes toward crime, the British believed, would be an important means of reeducating German youth toward democracy and of eradicating Nazism. This wish mirrored the mid-century British methods (themselves contested at times) of treating delinquents and reclaiming them for citizenship. Such methods stressed rehabilitation over retribution and insisted that prison should be the last resort for young people. British officials hoped that their welfarist policies would eventually educate German experts in the psychological theories that had become more commonplace in Britain. The British way of dealing with juvenile offenders, British officials claimed, was democratic,

---

[4] Victor Bailey, *Delinquency and Citizenship: Reclaiming the Young Offender 1914–1948* (Oxford University Press, 1987). Cf. Harry Hendrick, *Images of Youth: Age, Class and the Male Youth Problem 1880–1920* (Oxford University Press, 1990); Geoffrey Pearson, *Hooligan: A History of Respectable Fears* (New York: Palgrave, 1983).

standing in stark contrast to German ideas, some of which were based on Nazi legislation which preferred authoritarian punishment and the frequent use of imprisonment. The British authorities in Germany pushed for psychological treatment of crime (with emphasis on child guidance methods) and wished to cultivate youth to be self-disciplined and self-reliant rather than submissive in the face of authority.[5] Similar views about the proper handling of crime befitting a democracy were constantly advocated in Britain itself by the ISTD, which led this trend.[6]

The intellectual concerns of criminology at the end of the 1940s were largely dominated by psychoanalysis to an extent that is hard to comprehend today. For at least a decade, psychoanalytic principles were at the heart of the training of social workers and probation officers.[7] At the ISTD, the main body disseminating forensic psychoanalysis, the immediate postwar years were full of activity. The year 1946 was marked by a return to normal working conditions. Staff returning to civil life made it possible for the ISTD's Psychopathic Clinic to carry a heavier caseload. The Institute and the Clinic moved back to Bourdon Street in Mayfair, London, enabling their expansion in clinical and educational activities. For example, the educational work of the Institute included student seminars given by psychoanalyst Kate Friedlander and a study group on "Some Aspects of Freudian Theory Specially Relevant to Human Maladjustment," conducted by psychoanalyst Barbara Low. The Home Office furthered its close connection with the ISTD by asking for the Institute's collaboration in arranging courses for trainee probation officers and, as a result, the ISTD continually arranged lectures and case conferences for them.[8] When the Ministry of Health expressed its wish to place the ISTD under the National Health Service Act of 1948, some members of the Institute feared that its identity would be diffused and lost. Eventually, the members decided that the Clinic would fall within the scope of the National Health Service, but that the non-clinical work done at the ISTD would not.[9]

---

[5] David Smith, "Juvenile Delinquency in the British Zone of Germany, 1945–1951," *German History* Vol. 12 (1994), pp. 39–63. For the shift away from the welfarist approach during the 1960s and 1970s, see David Garland, *The Culture of Control: Crime and Social Order in Contemporary Society* (University of Chicago Press, 2001).

[6] Indeed, the Beveridge Report imagined a welfare state that would free citizens from the evils of want, squalor, ignorance, and disease but also from idleness.

[7] J. P. Martin, "The Development of Criminology in Britain 1948–1960," *British Journal of Criminology* (Spring 1988), pp. 38–39. For competing psychological theories, see D. J. West, "Psychological Contribution to Criminology," *British Journal of Criminology* (Spring 1988), pp. 77–91.

[8] Centre for Crime and Justice Studies, ISTD Archive (hereafter ISTDA)/330BBBB: *ISTD Annual Report 1946*, p. 13.

[9] The Clinic then became the financial responsibility of the Paddington Group Management Committee of the North West Metropolitan Regional Hospital Board.

In this year, the Institute changed its name to the Institute for the Study and Treatment of Delinquency, and the Clinic to the Portman Clinic.[10] The caseload for that year rose to 400 new patients.[11] Additionally, in 1949, the ISTD's psychoanalyst Edward Glover was appointed Honorary Adviser in Criminal Psychiatry to a group of seven experts (including ISTD analyst Denis Carroll) convened by the United Nations to consider the study of crime on an international basis.

During the postwar period, as in its early days, the Institute delivered lectures to both members and outsiders. It conducted teaching seminars for magistrates and prison officers, and conferences, courses, and case demonstrations for small groups of experts and students.[12] Among these postwar activities, for example, were psychoanalytic lectures to university students by Low on "Difficult and Delinquent Personalities – the Freudian Approach," and lectures on the "Psychopathic Personality" to lawyers and magistrates by Glover. Following a previous conference called by the home secretary and the minister of education to discuss the increase in juvenile delinquency, a follow-up conference was convened by different organizations, including the ISTD, to discuss the scientific implications of the problem.[13] Indeed, by 1950, the ISTD had reached roughly 400 active members.[14] The years 1949 to 1950 had been the most productive in the whole history of the Institute.[15]

In July 1950, the ISTD published the first issue of the *British Journal of Delinquency*. An additional development took place in 1953 when the Scientific Committee of the ISTD formed a 150-member Scientific Group for the Discussion of Delinquency Problems. The group flourished (although at times it was critical of psychoanalysis), and in 1961 it became the British Society of Criminology. Among its members were several Home Office officials.[16] The postwar years, as all these activities indicate, were a time of growth, extramural dialogue, and intensified

---

[10] See Ch. 5, n. 6. In the 1970s, the Portman Clinic had moved to northwest London and the Institute moved to Croydon, Surrey: Saville and Rumney, "Let Justice," p. 23.

[11] *Ibid.*, p. 18. See ISTDA/330BBBB: *ISTD Annual Report 1947*. In its early years, the Clinic treated an average of 144 criminal offenders annually. Following the war, the numbers rose to 170 in 1946, 272 in 1947, and 488 in 1949. Most of the cases were sent directly by magistrates. The three largest groups of offenses were larceny, sexual offenses, and, in the case of juveniles, "behaviour problems" or "being out-of-control." See *Minutes of Evidence: Memorandum Submitted on behalf of the ISTD by Dr. Edward Glover, Royal Committee on Capital Punishment* (London: HMSO, 1950), p. 491.

[12] The ISTD continued to collaborate with the University of London Extension Lectures and gave courses with high enrollments: Saville and Rumney "Let Justice," p. 32.

[13] ISTDA/330AAAA: *ISTD Annual Report 1949–1950*, p. 6.

[14] *Minutes of Evidence: Capital Punishment*, p. 498.

[15] ISTDA: *ISTD Annual Report 1949–1950*, p. 3.

[16] Saville and Rumney, "Let Justice," p. 19.

influence for the ISTD. The Institute also constantly called upon the state to extend its responsibilities toward citizens, to protect and regulate the lives of delinquents, and to intervene in family dynamics and in education. The ISTD influentially contributed to the new reimagination of parenthood not only as a natural capacity but also as a social responsibility.

Interdisciplinary team work, social reform, and active involvement: psychoanalysis at the postwar ISTD

The main contributions of forensic psychoanalysis after the war, Glover (and other analysts before him) believed, were in its application to the fields of diagnosis, prevention, and the practical handling of delinquents, rather than in long-term treatment.[17] As the leading figure in the ISTD, Glover, as we have seen, emphasized cooperation among different experts. Yet he believed that psychoanalysis could add a crucial perspective that would create a rearrangement of data on delinquency across disciplines. Using psychoanalysis in team research, he argued, would transform many social factors contributing to delinquency into emotional factors. Even poverty "would be rated as an external emotional stimulus exerting its maximum force on constitutional sensitivities with a history of early instinctual frustration."[18]

The cases of Dorothy and Josephine

While she did not refer to team research directly, the treatment work of ISTD member and refugee analyst Hedwig Schwarz with a juvenile delinquent she named "Dorothy" reveals a psychoanalyst at work who is in close communication with magistrates and probation officers, and who is playing a very active role in her patient's life. This treatment serves as a testimony to the hardships of war and the postwar period and to the flexibility and pliability of psychoanalytic work with delinquents. It is therefore worth looking at in detail.[19]

Schwarz described the case of a nineteen-year-old girl whom she treated from March 1945 until April 1946. "Dorothy," as Schwarz called her, was on probation, and special permission was obtained for her to come once a

---

[17] Edward Glover, "Recent Advances in the Psycho-Analytical Study of Delinquency," in Edward Glover, *The Roots of Crime* (New York: International Universities Press, 1960), pp. 292–310. Cf. Kate Friedlander, "Delinquency Research," *New Era* (Jun. 1943).

[18] Edward Glover, "Team Research?," in Glover, *The Roots of Crime*, p. 179.

[19] Hedwig Schwarz, "Dorothy: The Psycho-Analysis of a Case of Stealing," *British Journal of Delinquency* Vol. 1 (1950–1951), pp. 29–47. Hedwig Schwarz was also a member of the Institute of Psycho-Analysis, London.

week for treatment, at first accompanied by a probation officer. Dorothy was charged with a long list of offenses involving stealing, the first of which was when she stole a bottle of milk at age twelve. She was evacuated during the war to a foster family on the order of the court under the assumption that the poverty of her family was responsible for her stealing. Dorothy continued to steal and was put in a hostel for difficult children. At the age of fourteen, she insisted on going back home. After Dorothy's brother was killed in an air raid, both she and her mother were evacuated to the country. There, Dorothy stole again and was put back in a hostel. Dorothy's father had been wounded in World War I and had become what Schwarz called a "permanent invalid." He died on Dorothy's seventeenth birthday.

At the beginning of Dorothy's treatment, Schwarz intervened in her patient's life to an extent well beyond that recommended by classic Freudianism.[20] Schwarz, for example, tried to make Dorothy feel that she was on her side and provided her with paints and knitting wool to counteract her boredom in the hostel. Dorothy's wish to return home and support her mother and youngest brother, while her two elder brothers were in the services, was used by Schwarz, who offered to persuade the probation officer to let Dorothy go home on condition that she agreed to psychoanalytic treatment. Schwarz also convinced the probation officer to find Dorothy a job in the vicinity of the consulting room. Schwarz explained that she chose to act more as a psychoanalyst proceeding in the introductory phase of child analysis, when there is a need to establish a positive relationship and to make the child aware of its problems, and when the practical arrangements are made by the parents.[21] According to Schwarz, adult delinquents, who have a personality structure not unlike that of a child, cannot be expected to behave responsibly. She explained, "very often, I think, we have to resort to unorthodox methods, e.g., bringing the delinquent into coming [to the Clinic], or threatening him with possible consequences if he refuses, or again using both methods alternately so that we get a chance to begin treatment and to make the patient dependent enough on us to accept our help." She believed that probation offered an excellent basis of agreement between patient and analyst, especially when treatment was made a condition of probation.[22]

---

[20] Though it should be noted that, in practice, Sigmund Freud himself and other analysts of his generation were themselves often "unorthodox" with their patients.

[21] This approach was influenced by the work of Anna Freud.

[22] Schwarz, "Dorothy," p. 31. Glover believed that, next to social workers and educational psychologists, probation officers provided some of the stronger supporters of institutions like the ISTD: Edward Glover, "Outline of the Investigation and Treatment of Delinquency in Great Britain, 1912–1948," in Glover, *The Roots of Crime*, p. 44.

After pressing Dorothy to undergo psychoanalytic treatment, Schwarz was able to see her four times a week. Schwarz insisted, like other analysts before her, that Dorothy's stealing had to do with her childhood family dynamics, her rivalry with and envy of her mother, and aggression toward and envy of her siblings, followed by guilt and a desire for punishment. Dorothy's stealing served the purposes of gratifying such a desire. She was therefore "a criminal from a sense of guilt," the term Sigmund Freud had introduced earlier in the century.[23] This guilt was also expressed by the fact that Dorothy was always caught and succeeded in making people call the police.

When Schwarz shifted into a more "orthodox" analysis, Dorothy's "resistance" to it grew and she began seeing her analyst as a person forcing her to come to treatment.[24] When Dorothy inquired whether she would need to come for the whole duration of the probation, Schwarz urged Dorothy to see the treatment as an opportunity to understand her own behavior so that she could finish her probation without a relapse. Schwarz also decided to intervene again and secure Dorothy's release from regular visits to the probation officer.[25] However, Schwarz was not yet aware that during that time Dorothy was already relapsing to crime by stealing copies of the *Picture Post* magazine[26] from her analyst's waiting room. Dorothy also made a train-ticket collector stop her for traveling without a ticket on the eve of VJ Day when the whole town was celebrating. This latter impressed Schwarz again that Dorothy had a strong wish to be punished.

Shortly after, Dorothy went to northern England to visit the mother of the man she was dating. Instead of coming back to her work and to her analysis, Dorothy decided, unexpectedly, to stay there. Schwarz's reaction was again unusually interventionist. Discussing the matter with the probation officer, Schwarz decided to go visit Dorothy and persuade her to finish her probation. During the visit, Schwarz asked to meet Dorothy's boyfriend to make sure that he intended to marry her. Schwarz was able to come to an agreement with the probation officer that Dorothy would write regularly to her and would report to the Probation Service. Unfortunately, Dorothy again found herself in jail after stealing in her new area. Schwarz tried to help her by sending a report to the local judiciary, explaining the "psychological aspect" of Dorothy's thefts and the promised marriage.

---

[23] See Ch. 5.

[24] Denis Carroll claimed that willingess of patients to attend treatment was connected to the fact that the therapy was identified with court-assigned punishment. See Denis Carroll, W. H. de B. Hubert, J. R. Rees, and O. H. Woodcock, "Symposium on 'The Unwilling Patient,'" *British Journal of Medical Psychology* Vol. 17 (1937), pp. 54–77.

[25] Schwarz, "Dorothy," p. 36.

[26] A popular photojournalistic magazine that was anti-fascist and supported the welfare state.

Despite this only partial success of the treatment, Schwarz believed that it was of some help to Dorothy as it made her conscious of certain "emotional conflicts." Schwarz also believed that the analysis of Dorothy's childhood would make this young woman a better mother to her own future children.[27] Thus, perhaps more than demonstrating the effectiveness of analytic treatment, this reported case was a testimony to the extent to which psychoanalysts in the ISTD had an active influence on penal issues and worked in close alliance with the legal and probation system. The case shows that analysts such as Schwarz were willing to go a long way in influencing the life of patients who were in economically inferior and vulnerable positions. As this report was published in the *British Journal of Delinquency* without noted reservations from readers, it seems safe to assume that this case was not entirely exceptional.

An ISTD public pamphlet written for the mass consumption of non-specialists presents the same spirit of involvement. In this publication, ISTD member Ethel Perry described the psychoanalytic treatment of a delinquent she named "Josephine." As with Dorothy, unorthodox methods were also used in Josephine's case, revealing direct involvement in the analytic dealing with delinquents.[28]

Josephine was in psychoanalysis during the time she was on probation for attempted burglary. Previously, she had also been shoplifting. Before coming to treatment with Perry, Josephine was briefly examined by different experts. A welfare officer meeting Josephine reported that she never could hold a job and claimed, "she revolted from any ordered life and just could not fit into the group." Her psychiatrist believed that she had "no affective roots" since she was an illegitimate child abandoned in an orphanage, and that beneath her façade of confidence and alertness were anxiety and apprehension.[29] Perry seemed to agree with this description. When the analysis started, Perry argued that Josephine wanted to take revenge against authority and had aggressive and cruel traits resulting from intolerable feelings of unimportance. Perry suggested that the purpose of her delinquency was to keep her stimulated so that she would have no time to feel her anxious loneliness. Josephine's treatment had then to uncover unpleasant memories that delinquency had been utilized to repress.

Using unorthodox psychoanalytic methods, Perry encouraged Josephine to talk about her life and then attempted to give her

---

[27] *Ibid.*, pp. 43–44.

[28] ISTDA/Pamphlet Collection (hereafter PMC)/330DDDD: Ethel Perry, "The Psycho-Analysis of a Delinquent: Interplay between Phantasy and Reality in the Life of a Law Breaker" (London: Psychological and Social Series, 1947).

[29] *Ibid.*, pp. 4–6. This conceptualization was influenced by the work of John Bowlby, to be explored in Ch. 7.

interpretations when she was least suspecting it. Josephine was able to tell more about herself when outside the clinic, so Perry wandered with her in the park. Perry described, "sometimes I manage to offer what I hope were words of wisdom between movements of a concerto at a lunch-hour concert or between mouthfuls of Argentine beef at a British restaurant."[30] Perry believed that this "peculiar form of therapy" was helping Josephine and made herself available to her patient even during the weekend, becoming a friend and a substitute mother to her.

Josephine's problems were many and the descriptions that Perry offered of them are moving, providing some testimony to the troubles of young people through poverty and war. Josephine needed to hide the fact that she lived in a hostel and did not have a real home like her work colleagues. In addition, she was terrified of feeling that she was alone in the world and without a family. Along with her fear of isolation, she also dreaded having an emotional relationship with others as well as the possibility of mental disease. Josephine had a sense of injustice when she compared her life with that of those she served in her work. At one point, Perry described how Josephine witnessed a discussion of the Beveridge Report, the key document for envisioning a new form of social democracy in which the postwar welfare state would take care of all citizens "from the cradle to the grave."[31] Josephine "had to wait at a meeting where the Beveridge proposals for Social Security were discussed. There she had to listen to people who had never earned their living denounce these as 'unjust,' and had been unable to say anything."[32] During treatment, Josephine explored how routine at her childhood orphanage was deadening to her and "made her mad." Later in her life, she was put in a home for delinquents whose purpose, in her words, was, "to make a good honest citizen out of me working my guts out." She added, "I didn't agree so I made a little exit from there … then I got in with the crooks and learned how to dodge authorities." She objected to what she saw as the "normality" of her analyst, i.e., the fact that Perry was holding a job and adjusting to a life with no change. This, Josephine thought, was "unbearable" and "limiting," and she said, "I'd rather die than be normal if it means doing the same things at the same time every day."[33] Indeed, Josephine's own adjustment to reality was tested when a V2 bomb fell near the hostel where she was staying, almost wounding her and reawaking her fear of mental disease.

---

[30] *Ibid.*, p. 9.

[31] While promising greater equality to all and a new state commitment to citizens, the Report prescribed different gender roles for men and women. See Susan Pedersen, *Family, Dependence, and the Origins of the Welfare State: Britain and France, 1914–1945* (Cambridge University Press, 1993).

[32] Perry, "The Psycho-Analysis," p. 13.   [33] *Ibid.*, p. 14.

In her analysis, she told Perry that she hated her body and pleaded, "if only my spirit could get away from it. I just can't escape from my body. It had to be fed and clothed and worked for at horrible jobs."[34] Despite these difficulties and Josephine's direct and poignant criticism of the treatment, of her analyst, and of welfare policies on delinquency, Perry believed that psychoanalysis, here in its unorthodox forms, helped Josephine, since she had better insight into her condition and better adjustment to outside workaday reality. Perry hoped to help Josephine adjust further to reality by affording her the happiness that good social relationships could provide.[35] Both Perry's and Schwarz's work resonated with the prevailing public postwar wish to contain asocial behavior in juvenile delinquents. This desire was connected to wartime anxieties about a wave of crime stemming from the breaking-up of family unities and concern for the strengthening of a democratic citizenry.[36] Their analytic work was also written in the context of changes in childcare policy, significantly with the new 1944 Education Act and the new 1948 Children Act.[37]

Is the criminal amoral?

ISTD member Kate Friedlander explored connections between childhood experiences, crime, and life in a democratic society during a time of war and peace in a different manner in an influential book titled *The Psycho-Analytic Approach to Juvenile Delinquency*. The book developed a popular version of the quintessential Freudian stance in relation to crime, while also calling for reform and the integration of psychoanalytic knowledge of ways of handling the problem.[38] Friedlander started by claiming, "delinquency is a disease of society, just as cancer, for instance, is a disease of the individual."[39] She called for further modifications of criminal law and changes in public opinion by advancing "modern scientific methods" of dealing with delinquency and by exchanging punishment for the reeducation and rehabilitation of offenders by the extension of probation and the provision of hostels, remand homes, and centers of observation.[40]

---

[34] *Ibid.*, p. 15.   [35] *Ibid.*, p. 16.

[36] See Ch. 5. Indeed, pressure to behave well was high in the immediate postwar years. See ISTDA/PMC/330DDDD: Joan Warburg, "Play Therapy" (London: Psychological and Social Series, 1946), pp. 1, 16. See also Melitta Schmideberg, *Children in Need* (London: Allen & Unwin, 1948); ISTDA/PMC/330DDDD: Melitta Schmideberg, "Folklore of Parenthood" (London: Psychological and Social Series, 1947).

[37] Harry Hendrick, *Child Welfare: Historical Dimensions, Contemporary Debates* (Bristol: Policy Press, 2003).

[38] Kate Friedlander, *The Psycho-Analytic Approach to Juvenile Delinquency: Theory, Case Studies, Treatment* (London: Kegan Paul, 1947).

[39] *Ibid.*, p. vii.   [40] *Ibid.*

Sociological research emphasizing the ways in which the environment contributed to the development of delinquency, Friedlander argued, was unable to answer why some people become delinquent while others from the same place do not.[41] In order to answer such questions, one must turn to psychoanalysis. Criminals, she like other analysts claimed, are human beings who have failed to achieve social adaptation in their childhood and have been frustrated in their human relationships, especially their relationship with their mothers.[42]

Yet delinquency was more than just a social nuisance for Friedlander. Significantly, it had to do with the possibility of collaborative living in democracy. She said, "Our civilization is built upon the assumption that people are able to set their relationship to their fellow human beings above the gratification of their instinctive desires ... [However,] One feature which all delinquents have in common is their inability to postpone desires because they cannot form good relationships with the people in their surroundings, and this results in their excessive self-love."[43] Friedlander ended her book by warning that delinquency rates were rising due to the war. She said, "Let us meet this threat to our community by helping these young boys and girls to become useful citizens in the post-war world: they have suffered, through no fault of their own, in their emotional development by the insecurity of family life and a world at war. They are victims as much as the wounded soldier or the bombed-out citizen."[44] Friedlander linked the concern for children's mental care and stable democratic citizenship, saying, "By realizing the emotional need of these boys and girls and by working out plans for their re-education on scientific lines, we shall not only prevent an increase in criminal careers but also increase the numbers of happy, socially adapted and, therefore, useful citizens."[45]

Similar ideas led ISTD analyst Melitta Schmideberg to question from a psychoanalytic perspective whether criminals were in fact amoral.[46] While criminals commit actions from which "respectable" people refrain, it was erroneous to claim that they commit them without hesitation, anxiety, guilt, or regret, she argued.[47] As in her other writings, Schmideberg placed her analytic ideas in social context. The phenomenon of criminals forgetting their feelings of anxiety after the offense, she said, was similar to that of civilians during the Blitz who after the bombing forgot how scared

---

[41] *Ibid.*, pp. 7–10.   [42] *Ibid.*, p. 49.   [43] *Ibid.*, p. 70.   [44] *Ibid.*, pp. 286–287.
[45] *Ibid.*, p. 287.
[46] Melitta Schmideberg, "Is the Criminal Amoral?," *British Journal of Delinquency* Vol. 4 (1953–1954), pp. 272–281.
[47] *Ibid.*, p. 272. Schmideberg wrote, "we must study criminals, as anthropologists have studied the aborigines, against their own background, watching the sum total of their lives and reactions without being shocked by the actions we condemn."

they had been. In treatment, Schmideberg found that criminals could be excellent husbands or loyal to their fellow criminals, and that the only difference between them and law-abiding citizens was that "respectable society is their enemy, and they fight it as the underground French fought the Nazis, taking similar pride in their exploits."[48]

Schmideberg offered the counterintuitive idea that there is in fact also a moral drive behind crime. Many individuals, she explained, have difficulty tolerating praise or even the good opinion of others. Delinquents try to make it impossible for others to have a good opinion of them with their criminal behavior. Paradoxically, she argued, moral impulses could sometimes make the criminal act amorally. For example, one patient, who felt guilty of rising above his parents, could not act in a respectable way and instead searched for "bad company."[49]

ISTD psychoanalysts such as Schmideberg, Friedlander, Glover, and others were then willing to see themselves as social educators of public opinion advocating certain reformist views in relation to crime. During the postwar period, the handling of delinquency and asocial behavior was more urgently linked to concern about the successful maintenance of democratic citizenry. The years of total war had focused attention on problems of managing the lives of citizens in new ways. Ensuring their mental health, happiness, and healthy social and collaborative human relations with their fellow citizens became a pressing pursuit of government. In the process of the "return to normality" after the war, asocial behavior in the national community held a special place in the debates of the time.

"The enemy within": fear of a crime wave after the war

Some in Britain expected juvenile delinquency to decline as postwar society returned to normal home life. Yet, according to official statistics, after a short calm period, crime began climbing again in the mid 1950s and continued to do so until the mid 1960s.[50] Debates about juvenile delinquency had already intensified in 1948–1949. In a lengthy correspondence in *The Times*, different contributors linked the behavior of youth to the upheaval of war; they expressed fears about asocial and uncivil behavior, and envisioned new types of intervention for the welfare state. Psychoanalytic work thrived in the context of the postwar renewal of such debates. Those who participated in the debates expressed various,

---

[48] *Ibid.*, p. 274.   [49] *Ibid.*, p. 280.
[50] Hendrick, *Child Welfare: Historical*, p. 147. See also "Juvenile Delinquency: Return to Pre-War Level in London," *The Times* (21 Feb. 1946), p. 2; H. D. Willcock, *Report on Juvenile Delinquency by Mass Observation* (London: Faber & Faber, 1949).

conflicting ideas. Yet they all testified to the continuous growing importance of the family, home life, and other non-materialistic factors in explaining juvenile delinquency. The ISTD, as we saw earlier, contributed to such an emphasis over explanations stressing the role of poverty and the material environment in the manifestation of crime. As in wartime, in the postwar period the ISTD was also instrumental in advocating the need to transform delinquents into contributing citizens (rather than punish them), and was vocal in the new emphasis on the responsibility of adults and the state to reform the behavior of young people.

Writing on November 26, 1948, to *The Times*, Rowntree Clifford of Marnham House Settlement echoed the anxiety expressed at the time in the House of Lords about juvenile delinquency. The problem of crime, Clifford claimed, must be tackled at its source, which in most cases lay in bad home conditions.[51] Four days later, psychiatrist Alan Maberly and magistrate John A. F. Watson argued against the Lord Chancellor, who put the sole responsibility for crime on parents. Instead, Maberly and Watson believed that new factors had undermined parental authority and made the increase in juvenile delinquency inevitable. Among these factors were the evacuation of town children and their separation from their parents during the war. "Parents, for the most part, were serving their country in the forces or elsewhere. It is manifestly unfair to blame such parents for failing to 'instill the right sort of instincts into the children' under these conditions," they argued. Among the other factors undermining parental authority was the state's encroachment upon fields that formerly were the sole province of the parents, like the provision of food, clothing, and shelter. The solution, Maberly and Watson suggested, was to help parents reestablish their authority. Ewen E. S. Montagu, Chairman of the Pioneer Health Centre in Peckham (known as the "Peckham Experiment"), also pointed to changes in society. Nowadays, he claimed, almost all factors of life militate against what he saw as the foundations of Britain's "national greatness," namely, the spirit of family unity, responsibility, mutual dependency and support, and interest between parents and children. Social factors such as pressure of work and separate leisure activities for different ages had divided the two generations.[52] However, Marjory Allen of Hurtwood, a key promoter of and active leader in child welfare who was instrumental in setting up the government's Care of Children Committee (the Curtis Committee 1946), argued against the opinion of Maberly and Watson who believed that state encroachment into the province of the parent caused an increase in

---

[51] "Juvenile Delinquency," *The Times* (26 Nov. 1948), p. 5.
[52] "Combating Child Delinquency," *The Times* (30 Nov. 1948), p. 5. See also "Juvenile Delinquency," *The Times* (16 Dec. 1948), p. 5.

delinquency. She claimed instead that moral exhortation without material assistance from the state would not help solve the problem of delinquency.[53] Headmaster C. A. Joyce wrote too, arguing that juvenile delinquents were "nothing but unhappy children" who grew up in homes where there had been an absence of discipline.[54] James Whitehead of the Methodist Church Youth Department, however, thought that one of the main reasons for the high rate of juvenile delinquency was the "fall in the spiritual and moral standards of the community as a whole."[55] In contrast, other correspondences in *The Times* – including a letter from the ISTD – emphasized the need for a scientific and psychological study of the problem of juvenile delinquency.[56]

The debates continued. When asked in 1950 about the apparent greater destructiveness of some children compared with those of earlier generations, the magistrate Basil Henriques suggested that a possible cause was the extreme modernization in education that included no repression or punishments and "no restraints on impulses to throw stones through windows." Some children in need of care and protection, he suggested, came from "vile and horrible homes." Other children "bore no bruises but were made to feel unwanted and unloved and became drudges." Henriques expressed his concerns in gendered ways characteristic of the time. He associated boys' delinquency with violence and girls' delinquency with permissive sexuality. He complained about the existence of girls in moral danger who became young prostitutes attracted by "American dollars" during the war, that is, by American GIs stationed in Britain who would pay them for sex. Films had bad effects on girls, he believed, since in cinemas they learned that divorce did not matter and that fidelity was of little value. The effect on the future mothers of England "could be awful." Henriques also emphasized the effect of broken homes on maladjustment and mental sickness among children. He included among these homes the ones in which mothers went to work "at times when they were needed by their children."[57] His letter manifested many of

---

[53] "Juvenile Delinquency," *The Times* (6 Dec. 1948), p. 5. On Marjory Allen, see John Welshman, "Evacuation, Hygiene, and Social Policy: The Our Towns Report of 1943," *Historical Journal* Vol. 42, no. 3 (1999), pp. 781–807.

[54] "Juvenile Delinquency," *The Times* (9 Dec. 1948), p. 5.

[55] "Juvenile Delinquency," *The Times* (29 Dec. 1948), p. 5.

[56] "Juvenile Delinquency," *The Times* (16 Aug. 1949), p. 5; "Juvenile Delinquency: A Scientific Study," *The Times* (23 Sep. 1949), p. 7; "Causes of Juvenile Delinquency: Large-Scale Research Recommended," *The Times* (3 Oct. 1949), p. 2. For further discussions, see also "Juvenile Delinquency," *The Times* (10 Oct. 1949), p. 5; (12 Oct. 1949), p. 2; (13 Oct. 1949), p. 5; (28 Oct. 1949), p. 5; (5 Nov. 1949), p. 5.

[57] "Effects of Films on Girls," *The Times* (30 Dec. 1950), p. 2. See also "Is This the Time to Put Thugs on the Screen?," *Evening Standard* (3 Feb. 1953).

the anxieties of the time of "boys going wild" and young women becoming "good-time girls."[58]

Later, in January 1953, the *Daily Telegraph* published a series of articles on child crime. The first investigated the causes of child crime and moved away from listing poverty as the main cause of "social evils." The article found it disturbing that there was still an increase in crime among young children who had grown up under the new welfare state. Youthful delinquency across Europe had increased sharply as the result of the war, it stated. For a child, the common factor in all the calamities of war is a plunge into insecurity. Echoing the words of analysts such as Anna Freud (and therefore demonstrating their dissemination), it said: "The mere removal from the familiar surroundings and routine of home may be, emotionally, as devastating as a bomb. The child criminal is, in the widest sense, a 'displaced person' – displaced either from physical amenities which his development needs, or from parental affection."[59] In the following article, the newspaper supported the view that in many cases one ought to think rather of "delinquent parents" than of "delinquent children." It also mentioned the fact that "more and more frequently magistrates now ask also for a psychologist's report. His findings give further insight into the personality with which the court has to deal."[60] This, as we have seen, was true in cases such as that of Dorothy and many others treated at the ISTD.

Reinforcing all the links made in these debates between the prevention of crime, the success of democracy, and the maintenance of peaceful society after the war was an ISTD article titled "The Enemy Within." Published in *The Times* as part of a funding appeal for the Institute, the article said, "nations spent money on military defence, or for economic welfare, but they did not seem to spend enough on the study and correction of the enemy within. If they could not correct the enemies who were part of their own flesh and blood, it would seem to stand to reason that

---

[58] Sonya Rose, *Which People's War?: National Identity and Citizenship in Wartime Britain 1939–1945* (Oxford University Press, 2003); Abigail Wills, "Delinquency, Masculinity, and Citizenship in England 1950–1970," *Past and Present* (May 2005), pp. 157–185; Anne Logan, "'A Suitable Person for Suitable Cases': The Gendering of Juvenile Courts in England, c. 1910–1939," *Twentieth Century British History* Vol. 16 (2005), pp. 129–145; Pamela Cox, *Gender, Justice and Welfare: Bad Girls in Britain* (New York: Palgrave, 2003), p. 15.

[59] Martin Moore, "Crime and the Child: A Study of Causes and Remedies," *Daily Telegraph* (20 Jan. 1953). The article added, "It is the happy home, even if housed in a slum, the united family, even if cramped into two rooms, which give a child a sense of security, of 'belonging'; and it is the lack of this feeling which most often lies at the root of delinquency." See also "Head Defends the Modern Boy," *Sunday Times* (8 Feb. 1953).

[60] Martin Moore, "Crime and the Child II: The Courts in the Parents' Shoes," *Daily Telegraph* (21 Jan. 1953). See also "Letter to the Editor: Crime and the Child," *Daily Telegraph*. (29 Jan. 1953); "Schools for Wives," *Daily Telegraph* (2 Feb. 1953).

they would be remiss in their efforts to deal with matters outside their own boundaries."[61] In the context of such heated debates and the general shift to psychology generated by the ISTD, psychoanalysts from the Institute were called upon by the state to serve as expert witnesses in government committees on different aspects of what was regarded as "criminal" and "asocial" after the war. The ISTD's stance broadened in this context to different social realms, as we shall see next.

The ISTD's psychoanalysts in postwar state committees

From its early days, one of the ISTD's goals was to influence both public opinion and state policy.[62] In the postwar years, the ISTD was regularly invited to give evidence to official bodies and state committees. Among these were: Royal Commission on Capital Punishment (1950); Departmental Committee on Maladjusted Children (1952);[63] Royal Commission on the Law relating to Mental Illness and Mental Deficiency (1954–1955); Departmental Committee on Homosexual Offences and Prostitution (the Wolfenden Committee, 1955–1957); Inter-Departmental Committee on the Business of the Criminal Courts (the Streatfeild Committee, 1958); Departmental Committee on the Probation Service (1960); Home Office Advisory Council on the Treatment of Offenders (1960, evidence on corporal punishment); Home Office Advisory Council Sub-Committee on Non-Residential Treatment (1961); Labour Party Study Group on Penal Reform (1964); Royal Committee on the Penal System (1965, evidence on young offenders); and the Committee on Mentally Abnormal Offenders (the Butler Committee, 1974).[64] I concentrate in this section on psychoanalytic evidence and expert testimonies of the ISTD to the Royal Commission on Capital Punishment and to the Departmental Committee on Homosexual Offences and Prostitution to show how the ISTD members linked early childhood and family dynamics to postwar legal and penal questions.

---

[61] "The Enemy Within," *The Times* (6 Mar. 1956).
[62] See ISTDA/PMC/330DDDD: Edward Glover, "The Psycho-Pathology of Flogging: A Study in the Motivation of Penal Method," in George Benson and Edward Glover, *Corporal Punishment: An Indictment* (London: Howard League for Penal Reform, 1931), pp. 15–29.
[63] National Archives/ED50/333: ISTD memorandum by John D. W. Pearce and Peter D. Scott in Memoranda submitted by Witnesses to the Committee on Maladjusted Children (Underwood Committee). See also *Report of the Committee of Maladjusted Children* [Underwood Report] (London: HMSO, 1955), and Adrian Wooldridge, *Measuring the Mind: Education and Psychology in England, c. 1860–1990* (Cambridge University Press, 1994), p. 315.
[64] Saville and Rumney, "Let Justice," pp. 105–107.

ISTD's psychoanalysts on capital punishment

With more than 500 offenders having been executed in Britain in the first half of the twentieth century, Clement Attlee's Labour government established the Royal Commission on Capital Punishment in 1949 to decide whether capital punishment for murder should be limited or modified.[65] On May 4, 1950, the Commission questioned Glover as an expert witness after he had submitted a memorandum on behalf of the ISTD.[66] Both the memorandum and the testimony reveal how psychoanalytic ways of thinking on criminal violence and murder were represented to state officials. Glover started his memorandum by warning the Commission that an unknown number of psychopaths must have already been executed by the state despite their gravely disordered mental state.[67] Early treatment rather than capital punishment, he repeatedly argued, was the best deterrent for capital offenses. The memorandum challenged the view that corporal punishment would rationally deter criminals. While this might be true of offenders of "normal" mentality, it stressed, this was not the case for psychopathic offenders.[68] In a number of cases, instead of being a deterrent, punishment actually produced the opposite effect, that is, of acting as an incentive to further criminal acts. This was particularly true of the psychiatric group and of all cases where "negativistic" responses (i.e., tendencies to perform acts in opposition to those suggested) existed. The memorandum mentioned that occasionally, when the press reported on executions, delinquent patients at the ISTD became more "negativistic" about treatment and therefore prone to relapse.[69]

Punishment, retribution, and deterrence could not be understood without examination of their unconscious roots, the ISTD memorandum declared. While psychoanalysis was not a statistical science, it claimed, the most illuminating discoveries as to the nature of mental disorder had been made by the close analysis of individual cases.[70] The unconscious processes of normal persons, it added, could offer important information on the murderous tendencies "inherent in the human race and of the deeper motivations which lead individuals and societies both to inflict

---

[65] *Royal Commission on Capital Punishment* (London: HMSO, 1953). Of 3,130 persons committed for trial at assizes on charges of murder, 1,275 were deemed insane under the test of responsibility established by the M'Naghten Rules of 1843.

[66] *Minutes of Evidence: Capital Punishment*, pp. 490–507.   [67] *Ibid.*, p. 492.

[68] *Ibid.*, p. 493. Glover defined as a psychopath "a person who manifests, and has manifested from childhood, chronic disorders of his instinctual life, of the emotions, of thought processes (including absence of moral senses, feeling or thought) and of behaviour (including outbreaks of violence or sexual perversion, or both)" (*ibid.*, p. 492).

[69] *Ibid.*, p. 493.   [70] *Ibid.*

and to endure punishment. Such phenomena as unconscious hate, death wishes, murder dreams, sadism, masochism, unconscious phantasies of violence, atonement, scapegoat relations … provide a necessary complement to the study of abnormal mental function and of actual cases of pathological violence."[71]

Based on these psychoanalytic ideas, the memorandum boldly stated that if it could be proven that even *one* psychopathic murderer could be prevented from committing further crimes under appropriate treatment, it would be necessary to revise the view that capital punishment was essential for public safety. It would be unethical to recommend execution for offenders for actions committed as the result of mental disorder. The problems of murder and capital punishment, the ISTD memorandum claimed, had not yet been subjected to a satisfactory scientific examination, and many pathological offenders could be dealt with along medico-psychological and social lines. Early recognition and treatment of tendencies toward pathological crime could in many cases arrest this pathological process in childhood.[72]

When Glover appeared as an expert witness in front of the Royal Commission, he called for an increase in the legal role of mental-health professionals.[73] Present at the discussion were Ernest Gowers as chair, A. C. Cameron, N. R. Fox-Andrews, Florence Hancock, William Jones, Horace Macdonald, John Mann, Alexander Maxwell, G. A. Montgomery, Earl Peel, Leon Radzinowicz, and Eliot Slater. Asked whether he would agree that it was right for the law to assume that everyone was responsible for his actions unless otherwise shown, Glover answered that he believed in a broader view of the law. If the law has the authority to say what was wrong, he replied, it should also accept responsibility for trying to establish – with the help of experts of disorders of the mind – whether the offender was normal or abnormal. "In other words," Glover insisted, "the state should accept the duty of protecting the individual from himself."[74] Glover thought it ideal that every case of murder be examined, and expert information be put at the disposal of authorities so that it could affect the verdict.[75]

When asked by the Commission about his suggestions that many pathological cases liable to commit murder could be detected by experts during early childhood, Glover answered that he believed a practical way should

---

[71] *Ibid.*, p. 493 n.   [72] *Ibid.*, p. 494.
[73] However, when asked directly whether he thought psychoanalysis was necessary to cure psychopathic personalities, Glover's answer was negative. He noted that psychopaths respond very well to simple psycho-therapeutic care and that the ISTD's Clinic rarely analyzed psychopaths. He remained true, therefore, to his suggestion elsewhere that psychoanalysis's main contribution was in research rather than treatment: *ibid.*, p. 506.
[74] *Ibid.*, p. 500.   [75] *Ibid.*, pp. 500–501.

be further developed to do so. He advocated the creation of an extensive organization of psychological medicine and psychiatry, including the establishment of numerous child guidance centers. He also claimed that, using techniques like the Rorschach inkblot test, it was possible to take a child who was by all appearances merely inhibited and discover that he was potentially violent. When questioned by the Commission whether he thought he could distinguish between early childhood abnormalities that would lead to murder and those that would not, Glover's answer was in the affirmative.[76] When asked if he thought there was a case for punishment at all, Glover replied with a question, asking whether the nature of punishment had ever been investigated. "Punishment is not a social practice derived from purely rational considerations advanced by civilised scientists trying to cope with a social problem, but [one that] originated among primitive tribal organizations who lived in prehistoric times almost before religion existed," he proposed.[77] The Commission did not accept the ISTD's psychoanalytic call for the abolishment of capital punishment (indeed, the Commission did not have the mandate to do so). Yet the Commission did end up recommending compulsory psychiatric examination of all murder offenders.[78] It also urged the immediate establishment of an institution for the detention and treatment of psychopaths and other prisoners who were mentally abnormal though not insane, as well as research into the problems of psychopathic personality.[79] Similar psychoanalytic views advocating treatment instead of punishment were presented to the Departmental Committee on Homosexual Offences and Prostitution, known as the Wolfenden Committee, in 1957. Also repeated there were the ISTD's claims about the origins of criminality and asociality in childhood and the role of mental-health professionals. In both committees, psychoanalytic views contributed to a call for legal reform.

The ISTD at the Wolfenden Committee: homosexuality as a mental disorder with origins in childhood

Questions of crime were tied to other major areas of debate in the 1940s welfare state, including population policies, family life, and sexual unorthodoxy.[80] Given the national concern generated by war, reconstruction,

---

[76] *Ibid.*, p. 501.   [77] *Ibid.*, p. 503.

[78] The ISTD was not the only one advocating this; see "Capital Punishment for Murder: The Royal Commission's Report," *BMJ* (3 Oct. 1953), pp. 775–776. The Commission recommended that the offender should be examined by two doctors, at least one of whom should be a psychiatrist who was not a member of the prison service.

[79] "The Death Sentence," *Lancet* (1 Aug. 1953).

[80] The summary in the next two paragraphs is based on Jeffrey Weeks, *Sex, Politics and Society: The Regulation of Sexuality since 1800* (New York: Longman, 1989), pp. 232–248.

and the onset of the Cold War, there was a refocusing on the question of population and the stability of society and the family. Family life, "which was curiously seen both as 'natural' and permanent and as fragile and threatened," was constantly imagined in this period via rigid gender roles for men and women. The postwar years saw a continuing official worry about the future of the family, which was demonstrated in different commissions and reports. Besides the Beveridge Report in 1942, there were also the Curtis Committee on the Care of Children in 1946, the Population Commission in 1949, the Morton Commission on Divorce in 1955, the Wolfenden Committee on Homosexual Offences and Prostitution in 1957, and the Ingleby Committee on Children and Young Persons in 1960. Modified psychoanalysis overwhelmingly influenced the expanding field of social work in the community, and as a theory it became a dominant element during the 1950s. It should also be remembered that though familial stress was high at this time, it was accompanied by an official rejection of an ideology of the authoritarian, patriarchal family which was now associated with German ways of upbringing and family life.

Such preoccupations led the Wolfenden Committee to concern itself with a conceived "loosening of formal moral standards" and the "weakening of the family," and with the questions of homosexuality and prostitution. By the time the Committee met, there were important signs of change and calls for reform of attitudes to homosexuality that were reflected in and advanced by the psychoanalytic literature coming from the ISTD, among other channels. As important as the Kinsey Reports on the sexual behavior of males and females in this atmosphere of change was the acceptance of a psychoanalytically influenced model of homosexuality both in the medical profession and in the long-established public-morality bodies. Societies as diverse as the Public Morality Council, the National Vigilance Association, and the Moral Welfare Council of the Church of England called for legal reform, and many, in different ways, utilized the analytic idea that homosexuality was a mental illness, not a criminal act. What led the Wolfenden Report itself was a tradition of "legal utilitarianism" that stressed that the only justification for legal intervention in private life was the prevention of harm to others. The Committee viewed the purpose of the criminal law as preserving public order and decency and protecting the weak from exploitation. The Committee wished to refrain from imposing a particular pattern of moral behavior on individuals. Yet the Report also concerned itself with the nature of homosexuality and prostitution and showed a readiness to explore their psychological

See *Report of the Departmental Committee on Homosexual Offences and Prostitution* [Wolfenden Report] (London: HMSO, 1957); Matt Houlbrook, *Queer London: Perils and Pleasures in the Sexual Metropolis, 1918–1957* (University of Chicago Press, 2005).

elements. It rejected the idea that homosexuality was a disease, but it did accept the psychologization of homosexuality and prostitution. It was antagonistic about "treatment" and "cure," though it did not reject them out of hand and in fact urged further research.

In 1957, Glover drafted the ISTD memorandum to the Wolfenden Committee.[81] Both Glover and Carroll later orally presented the results to the Committee. The memorandum first noted that the problem of homosexuality was "an acutely controversial one."[82] Indeed, vice – identified in the 1950s with prostitution and male homosexuality – was seen as a divisive "peace-time problem, the product of a society no longer engaged in the fight for survival." This stood in contrast to the war period; while London and other cities had not been free from "immorality," the struggle was exclusively represented as one with the enemy.[83] The advances of psychiatry during the war led many different advocates of psychoanalysis (both practicing analysts and others) to insist on a role for themselves "in the pantheon of experts called upon in 1945 to build the New Jerusalem."[84] Thus, psychoanalysis offered to identify the cause of personal disorders (at times seen as connected to disorders of the social body) and to provide remedies for them.[85] While psychoanalytic models of psychosexual development were contested forms of knowledge during the late 1940s and the 1950s, Freudian understandings of homosexuality as a "disorder of mind" influenced in part both the scientific studies of those such as Gordon Westwood and D. J. West and the narratives of self-understanding of homosexual identity of individuals such as the journalist Peter Wildeblood.[86]

[81] ISTDA/PMC/330DDDD: Edward Glover (ed.), "The Problem of Homosexuality: Being a Memorandum Presented to the Departmental Committee on Homosexual Offences and Prostitution, by a Joint Committee Representing the Institute for the Study and Treatment of Delinquency, and the Portman Clinic" (London: ISTD, 1957).
[82] Ibid., p. 2.
[83] Frank Mort, "Mapping Sexual London: The Wolfenden Committee on Homosexual Offences and Prostitution 1954–1957," Sexual Geographies: New Formations No. 37 (1999), p. 93.
[84] Chris Waters, "Disorders of the Mind, Disorders of the Body Social: Peter Wildeblood and the Making of the Modern Homosexual," in Becky Conekin, Frank Mort, and Chris Waters (eds.), Moments of Modernity: Reconstructing Britain 1945–1964 (New York University Press, 1999), p. 141.
[85] Ibid., p. 143. Waters mentions the existence of at least three commonly held views of homosexuality at the time, i.e., ones that drew from Kinsey, Ellis and Magnus Hirschfeld, and Freud. Waters emphasizes that during the postwar period no single explanatory system in relation to homosexuality triumphed, and demonstrates that psychoanalysis had an important direct and indirect role in relation to the making of modern homosexuality.
[86] Ibid. See Gordon Westwood, Society and the Homosexual (London: Gollancz, 1952); D. J. West, Homosexuality (London: Duckworth, 1955). In his testimony to the

The understanding of homosexuality via psychoanalysis as a form of "arrested development" of sexuality during childhood was very much a postwar phenomenon, historian Chris Waters argues. In the early interwar years, homosexual selfhood (at least as it was narrated by well-educated writers) was not usually cast in Freudian terms; rather it borrowed from models of ancient Greek male friendship, ideas of a third sex, or the notion of "anomaly" advanced by sexologist Havelock Ellis. The public and official turn to psychoanalysis after the war was therefore not an obvious one. Indeed, the status of psychoanalysis in official discourses of homosexuality in the 1950s owed much to the early efforts of Sigmund Freud himself and his followers to discredit Ellis' research, and to the work of 1930s criminologists who adopted quasi-psychoanalytic thinking in their own campaign for penal reform.[87] The ISTD itself made a major contribution to the subject; Glover, who presented psychoanalytic ideas to state officials and the general public, advocated its stance. Glover advanced and popularized Sigmund Freud's basic ideas about homosexuality. Despite the fact that Freud saw homosexuality as an inhibition of "normal" psychosexual progress, he did not believe it to be a special category of personhood, or an innate inversion in the way sexologists such as Ellis saw it. Freud believed in the radical idea that every person could make a homosexual object choice and he was wary of attempts to alter and treat homosexuals with a firmly established object choice.[88] While other British psychoanalysts such as Ernest Jones (or writers such as Thomas Ross) were more open to direct therapeutic interventions than Freud himself, Glover remained closer to Freud's nuanced ideas. Nevertheless, Glover was less cautious than Freud when it came to applying psychoanalysis to legal issues and in his greater willingness to be in active dialogue with the state. During the 1950s, psychoanalytic accounts of homosexuality had dominated a great deal of official thinking on the subject, and discussions were increasingly – though not solely – couched in analytic terms.[89] These terms were popularized by Glover in particular.

In 1945, Glover was already calling in a public pamphlet for penal reform and social change in regard to sexual offenses. He used Freud's theories to suggest that "perversions" were derived from infantile sexuality and were regressions to earlier stages of development. Every sexual

Wolfenden Committee, for example, Wildeblood's self-representation as a homosexual mixed previous notions from sexology with elements derived from psychoanalysis: Mort, "Mapping," p. 110.

[87] Chris Waters, "Havelock Ellis, Sigmund Freud and the State: Discourses of Homosexual Identity in Interwar Britain," in Lucy Bland and Laura Doan (eds.), *Sexology in Culture: Labelling Bodies and Desires* (University of Chicago Press, 1999), pp. 165–167.

[88] Waters, "Disorders," p. 168.   [89] Waters, "Havelock Ellis."

offender, he believed, should be psychologically examined and given the opportunity to receive treatment.[90] In advocating psychological observation of offenders, Glover was not unique. He can be seen here as part of a broader, existing call for reform that had emerged since the interwar period. William Norwood East, chief medical inspector of prisons for England and Wales, and W. H. de B. Hubert, a prison psychotherapist, for example, advocated psychological views in relation to homosexuality and other offenses in the influential 1939 *Report on the Psychological Treatment of Crime.* Their resolutely Freudian report (which also borrowed from Ellis) did not see therapeutic intervention as the "solution" to homosexuality, yet it recommended psychiatric investigation for determining which offenders could be mapped according to a Freudian grid, so experts could focus their therapeutic energies accordingly. Doctors, magistrates, and barristers using new interwar work on the psychological treatment of crime also influenced the Home Office to draft legislation that permitted courts the option of sentencing individuals for psychiatric treatment. Calls for reform were indebted to Freud insofar as they drew from him the view that homosexuality was a mental disorder that arose from a stage in individual sexual development that could require therapy. It was Glover's careful arguments emphasizing that tolerance, and not treatment, was the main solution to homosexuality, rather than those of Ross or East, that had greater (though contested) influence on the members of the Wolfenden Committee.[91]

The call for reform in regard to homosexuality along psychoanalytic lines was not a simple move in a Whiggish progression from "intolerance" to "full social acceptance." Rather, it was a multifaceted development with contradictory claims. Glover's memorandum to the Wolfenden Committee had a dual agenda of calling for reform while shaping a special place for the expert. It can be read as a form of psychoanalytic political manifesto that presented complex, and at times opposing and paradoxical, views on homosexuality. Its fundamental argument was that homosexuality *per se* should not be treated as a crime, yet concurrently it was willing to label some cases of homosexuality as a mental disorder. It suggested that psychological treatment was not the "answer" for homosexuality, but it simultaneously recommended

[90] ISTDA/PMC/330DDDD: Edward Glover, "The Social and Legal Aspects of Sexual Abnormality" (London: ISTD, undated), p. 7.
[91] Waters, "Havelock Ellis," pp. 152–154; William Norwood East and W. H. de B. Hubert, *Report on the Psychological Treatment of Crime* (London: HMSO, 1939). W. Rees-Thomas, Maurice Hamblin Smith, Grace Pailthorpe, and H. E. Field had already advocated different forms of psychoanalytic criminology in the 1920s.

psychological intervention for specified cases that were considered appropriate.[92]

The law in regard to homosexuality, the ISTD's memorandum stated, fostered a sharp distinction between the normal and abnormal. By implication, the law suggested that the only "normal" act is that of heterosexual genital intercourse between adults. This, the memorandum declared, "is far from being the case." Furthermore, homosexuality between women was not legally treated as a sexual offense, "a fact which disposes to a large extent of the argument that legal objections to homosexuality are based on a biological fear of sterility of the race."[93] In contrast to the law, the memorandum boldly argued, *"the problem of homosexuality raises no question of criminality unless the sexual deviation is associated with acts of violence, assault or seduction of minors."* Glover believed that in many instances homosexuality was a natural form of sexual deviation, which could not be described as a "disease." Yet in many other cases, he claimed, homosexuality is "a sign of mental disorder."[94]

Glover's memorandum used Freud's ideas to inform state officials that, contrary to both legal and popular opinion, sexuality did not start at puberty, but rather existed from birth. During childhood, the memorandum preached Freudian gospel, sexuality manifested itself in polymorphous ways. A state of homosexuality occurred when impulses remain directed toward an object of the same sex. Glover's approach contrasted with the general view that homosexuality was an isolated, adult manifestation of a perverse and criminal nature. The memorandum offered its own taxonomy of homosexuality. It described homosexuality as varying from extremes of "active masculine" to "passive feminine" types. It argued that, in the latter group, constitutional factors played a more important role, while "pathological types" are more frequently found in the active group.[95] Against this background, the memorandum then shifted to a more explicit call for reform.

Public opinion and law, the ISTD maintained, were influenced by "profound emotional prejudices which are neither moral nor rational in nature."[96] The source of prejudice lay in conscious and unconscious

---

[92] Glover, "The Problem of Homosexuality." Cf. ISTDA: British Medical Association, *Homosexuality and Prostitution: A Memorandum of Evidence for the Departmental Committee on Homosexual Offences and Prostitution* (London: BMA, 1955).

[93] Glover, "The Problem of Homosexuality," p. 5. See also Rebecca Jennings, "'The Most Uninhibited Party They'd Ever Been To': The Postwar Encounter between Psychiatry and the British Lesbian, 1945–1971," *Journal of British Studies* Vol. 47 (Oct. 2008), pp. 883–904.

[94] Glover, "The Problem of Homosexuality," p. 6. The italics are in the original text.

[95] *Ibid.*, p. 7.   [96] *Ibid.*, p. 10.

reactions, established in childhood, against any form of sexuality. Since every individual had to cope with bisexuality, it was characteristic of people who were not manifestly homosexuals, but whose own defenses against homosexuality were not securely established, to disapprove of homosexual practices in others.[97] The memorandum argued against the view that the law should reflect public opinion. This would "run counter to modern opinion, both humane and scientific."[98]

While preparing the memorandum, the ISTD circulated a question-naire regarding homosexuality among thirty-four members of its staff. Their answers reveal that the possible recommendations for legal reform were diverse. These included the following suggestions: that homosex-uality between consenting adults should not be regarded as an offense; that homosexual acts, whether of adults or minors, should be regarded as offenses only if they involved a breach of public decency, violence or rape, or seduction; that homosexual acts between adults and minors should be regarded as offenses on the part of the adult if the minor was below the age of consent; that homosexual acts between consenting minors should not be regarded as offenses unless they included breaches of public decency, seduction, or violence; and finally that the laws should be modified to govern heterosexual and homosexual acts equally.[99] The ISTD statistics suggested that there was no change in about half of the clinical cases as the result of treatment, and thus the members emphasized the importance of patients' cooperation in treatment.[100]

The memorandum then stated that only tentative and provisional con-clusions could be made. Treatment at the ISTD and the Portman Clinic for homosexuality included psychological, social, and organic (i.e., treat-ment by hormones) methods or some combination of the three. Psychotherapy was used most frequently while hormone treatment was infrequent. The variety of psychological treatments ranged from psycho-analysis, to psychological analysis, suggestion or hypnosis, to simple psychological investigation or advice. Psychotherapy was used mainly for cases complicated by neurosis, while other treatments were used for cases "complicated by low intelligence."[101] Many members of the ISTD believed that special mental institutions or centers could serve as an alternative to prison for cases "requiring institutional control."[102]

Refusing to a view homosexuality as a crime, the conclusions of the memorandum maintained that psychological treatment should *not* be looked on as the answer to the problem of homosexuality. This was because *"there is no answer to homosexuality save tolerance on the part of the intolerant*

---

[97] *Ibid.*, p. 11.   [98] *Ibid.*   [99] *Ibid.*, pp. 12–13.   [100] *Ibid.*, pp. 15–16.
[101] *Ibid.*, p. 18.   [102] *Ibid.*, p. 22.

anti-homosexual groups in the community." Psychological treatment was appropriate only for "cases of pathological homosexuality, cases in which owing to age, seduction, temptation, and other factors, a person who might otherwise have developed in a heterosexual direction has become temporarily homosexual or has developed a homosexual organization, and cases in which the homosexual urge leads to criminal conduct of a pathological type (violence, rape, seduction)."[103] The memorandum then both called for reform and disputed that fact that homosexuality as such required treatment; at the same time it advocated expert intervention in special cases. It emphasized the place of childhood and a developmental view of sexuality. It also specified that sex-education measures starting in childhood could reduce the number of adult pathological sexual deviations.[104]

The figure of the homosexual generated excitement in the Wolfenden Committee not matched in debates about the prostitute.[105] Indeed, Glover's memorandum to the Committee concentrated on homosexuality rather than prostitution. Yet Glover also wrote on prostitution in a 1945 public pamphlet, whose exploration adds another layer to the understanding of the work of the ISTD. Glover used child psychoanalysis to mobilize a political agenda regarding prostitution. Although the prostitute seemed to have broken away from family life, Glover argued, a closer look would reveal that she had a strong fixation on the Oedipus phase from childhood. Her psychology was affected by a childhood disappointment with the father and hostility toward the mother. The psychology of the prostitute's male client also had its origins in childhood. The client's mother was split into a good and a bad image in the child's mind, and the bad-mother image would be later equated with that of the prostitute. In turn, for the prostitute, the client is the deteriorated image of the father. She also registers her violently jealous disapproval of her mother's marriage by "debasing her own feminine currency."[106] As in relation to other crimes, economic factors here came second in explaining prostitution.[107]

These concerns about asocial behavior were continually connected to anxieties about rebuilding a peaceful democratic society. Glover's views on prostitution led him to call for legal reform and advocating the expansion of what was called the "therapeutic state."[108] Since Glover saw

---

[103] *Ibid.*, pp. 20–21. The italics are in the original text.   [104] *Ibid.*, p. 22.

[105] Mort, "Mapping," p. 99.

[106] ISTDA/PMC/330DDDD: Edward Glover, *The Psycho-Pathology of Prostitution* (London: ISTD, 1945), pp. 5–6.

[107] *Ibid.*, p. 12.

[108] Waters, "Disorders," p. 151. Waters defines it as "based on the belief that experts, with their 'modern knowledge,' could assist in the eradication of any number of social maladies."

prostitution as a sign of psychological backwardness and of mental stress in a society transitioning to peace, he believed that "it [was] incumbent on the State to use every device, psychological, and sociological, to remedy the defect. No small-scale and haphazard efforts of voluntary societies [could] hope to deal with defects that develop in society as a whole, and [were] a reaction to forces inherent in the human race."[109] Yet Glover also believed that state measures would not strike at the root of the problem, since this was determined in childhood. Hence, he suggested that a solution to the problem of prostitution would depend on the extent to which childhood patterns could be modified. He called for a radical change in the system of upbringing of children in order to promote normal sexual adaptation in later life. Glover stressed, "Parents and educators alike must grasp the fact that if we deny children the amount of love that is necessary for their normal development, we cannot expect them to love in normal ways."[110] For active prostitutes, he offered various forms of psychotherapy.[111] Psychoanalytic ways of thinking, then, influenced the manner in which homosexuality and prostitution were discussed in the postwar period with Glover and the ISTD research taking prominence.

The previous chapter and the current one together follow the history of the ISTD from the interwar through the postwar periods. The Institute, they both show, was a thriving, influential hothouse for psychoanalytic ideas and practical work on delinquency in the mid century, which gained professional, public, and official recognition. Instead of viewing "criminals" and "law-abiding citizens" as belonging to two opposing and mutually exclusive categories, psychoanalysts placed them in a spectrum, wondering if criminals were indeed always amoral. All psychoanalysts working at the ISTD emphasized the importance of unconscious inner dynamics, early childhood experiences and feelings of anxiety, the drama of the Oedipus complex, and the effects of good or bad parenting in the causing of crime. By doing so, they were willing to go far with their patients and with their suggestions for social and legal reform. To influence patients to look "inside themselves" in order to find the reasons for their delinquent behavior, analysts diverged from classic psychoanalysis and became involved in the lives of their patients, to a point of crude intervention. Called by the state for numerous expert testimonies after the war, psychoanalysts were willing to present their transformative ideas using psychological rather than economic explanations for crime. They contributed to the development of the origins of the "therapeutic state."

---

[109] ISTDA/PMC/330DDDD: Glover, "The Psycho-Pathology of Prostitution," p. 13.
[110] Ibid., p. 15.   [111] Ibid.

Psychoanalytic expert testimony on capital punishment urged government officials to rethink the morality and efficacy of executing criminals
rather than treating them. Similarly, innovative ideas on homosexuality
were presented to the Wolfenden Committee. While analysts no longer
saw those labeled homosexuals as criminals, they did consider some of
them to be suffering mental disorders, needing treatment.

Psychoanalysis in this period played a crucial part in conceptualizing
social reconstruction. It helped define both the optimism and the pessi-
mism of social democracy and of the era in general. On one hand, it
continued to describe crime as a threat. On the other hand, it drew new
solutions to this problem. It referred both to the human forces of iration-
ality and social disorder and to the ability to address them in "modern"
and "scientific" ways.[112]

Psychoanalysts worked in close collaboration with magistrates, probation officers, and other human and social-sciences professionals. The very
nature of psychoanalysis in this era followed this hybrid form of an applied
science in the making, with active experts hailing from very diverse backgrounds. Throughout this period, psychoanalytic ideas on crime were
increasingly popularized and were frequently reported on in popular and
professional newspapers and magazines. Delinquency and the wartime
and postwar "crime waves," which worried many contemporaries, were
seen by analysts as more than just temporary nuisances. Their correct
treatment had to do with the very possibility of living harmoniously in a
society of equal, happy, mentally stable, and useful citizens. These concerns also appeared in debates on child hospitalization and motherhood,
which are at the center of Chapter 7. This was a time of reconstruction of
the notion of motherhood through psychoanalysis (as previous chapters
have also indicated). While psychoanalytic views of motherhood would
themselves later become a critical focus for feminists, they were also, at
some level, an influential liberal force in the 1950s.[113]

---

[112] Cf. Daniel Beer, *Renovating Russia: The Human Sciences and the Fate of Liberal Modernity
1880–1930* (Ithaca: Cornell University Press, 2008).
[113] Weeks, *Sex, Politics and Society*, p. 236; Elizabeth Wilson, *Only Halfway to Paradise:
Women in Postwar Britain, 1945–1968* (New York: Tavistock, 1980).

7   Hospitalized children, separation anxiety, and motherly love: psychoanalysis in postwar Britain

In 1951, a two-and-a-half-year-old girl, given the scientific pseudonym "Laura," was admitted for surgery at a hospital in Britain. Laura was the only child of working-class parents. She would soon become the protagonist of a psychoanalytic, documentary direct-observation film aiming to demonstrate that children were highly distressed when left alone in the hospital without their parents.[1] In this chapter, I examine how the idea, often taken for granted today, that young children need their parents, especially their mothers, with them constantly in times of illness or pain is in fact a constructed sensitivity whose shifting history can be traced to the crisis of the mid twentieth century.[2]

Prior to the 1940s sick young children were admitted to hospitals without their parents. Hospital visiting hours were either non-existent or limited to thirty minutes, yet the fact that children stayed in the hospital by themselves, under the care of doctors and nurses, without real contact with their parents had raised no special public concern. Quite the contrary, according to the prevailing medical wisdom of the early twentieth century it was best for children to not meet with their parents or to see very little of them during their hospital stay, sometimes for weeks or even months. The common belief was that after a short period of distress the young child would "settle" into the ward, rapidly forget the parents, and soon be content. Frequent visits were, then, seen as unhealthy for the child. Each new meeting with the parents, it was claimed, would cause a renewal of the child's anguish, which would cast the ward into chaos. Visits would create a vicious cycle of repeated distress after adjustment to

---

[1] See James Roberston and Joyce Robertson, *Separation and the Very Young* (London: Free Association Books, 1989), p. 26.

[2] This idea of full-time motherhood of course had its roots in early periods, in the late nineteenth century in particular. Yet it reached a peak of interest, and was only elaborately conceptualized, in the middle of the twentieth century. See Jane Lewis, *The Politics of Motherhood: Child and Maternal Welfare in England, 1900–1939* (London: Croom Helm, 1980); Ellen Ross, *Love and Toil: Motherhood in Outcast London, 1870–1918* (Oxford University Press, 1993).

the ward had been achieved. Visits could also help spread disease to the community. Reports from this period show that medical staff perceived the requests of mothers who wanted to stay near the beds of their sick children as eccentric.

This very logic regarding the advantages of leaving the child alone during hospitalization – which nowadays might seem odd, if not cruel – was about to change after World War II. During the second half of the 1940s and throughout the 1950s, an intense public debate about the care of hospitalized children in general, and hospital visits in particular, developed among parents, government officials, medical professionals, and psychoanalytic experts. This debate helped shift ideas about the needs of children, the nature of parenthood, and the role of medical staff. It is yet another example of a sphere of influence on which psychoanalysis had a decisive influence.

In contrast to established medical beliefs about child hospitalization, new ways of thinking that developed in the 1940s and the 1950s emphasized the strong ties of the child to the parents and the possible psychological damage that separation from them, especially from the mother, might cause. What was earlier seen as the temporary distress of the hospitalized child left alone now appeared as dangerous and uncontained feelings of anxiety, protest, despair, withdrawal, and detachment. Even a short-term separation was seen as something that might lead to a severe psychological disorder that could influence the child for life. Mothers were called to visit frequently or preferably to stay with their children in the hospital and to be part of the care of their children's physical and, more importantly, emotional needs. This new logic also helped to shape a shift in the authority of medical professionals and influenced a change in the role of the hospital in the community. Prior to the 1940s, doctors and nurses were considered the best experts in taking care of the child, but now mothers were seen as the most knowledgeable about what was best for their anxious children; motherly love was seen as irreplaceable. Indeed, nurses and doctors were asked to cooperate with parents. The hospital itself underwent a change in the mid century from being an institution still viewed – in a nineteenth-century way – as serving the needs of the poor to being a body under the National Health Service (NHS) in the service of the general community. The discussion of child hospitalization helped to change the hospital from being a site of high authority and knowledge to being a facility that was called upon to put on a friendly face and be responsive to citizens.

Child psychoanalytic work, as it was most famously generated through the writings, observations, and films of John Bowlby, James Robertson, and their colleagues at the Tavistock Institute, made a key contribution to the shift in thinking about child hospitalization and to the historical making of the relationship between mother and child. This chapter uncovers questions neglected by historians related to the history of children in hospitals, the notion of the sick child, and the hospital as a place for expert debate.[3] As previous chapters have revealed, the middle decades of the twentieth century saw a new problematization of the feelings of anxiety and aggression due to the experience of war. Both the hospital and the family became sites for expert discussion and social intervention in innovative ways. As we have already seen, during the evacuation process and through aerial bombardments, in war clinics, hostels, and juvenile courts the question of defining, understanding, and managing civilians' uncontained emotions had become a goal of government in a democratic society, with a growing view of the child as an object of care and a "citizen in the making."[4] In the case of hospitalization, the anxiety of children, parents, and medical staff, as well as the threat of violence posed by separated children, moved to the center of examination. This chapter first focuses on the new psychological understandings of the child that were advocated by Bowlby and his Tavistock colleagues, the techniques of management that followed from their "attachment theory," and the relationships formed through them between mental health, citizenship, and democracy.[5] It then explores how ideas and practices similar to those offered by attachment-theory experts in relation to hospital childcare appeared in the language of social-policy makers, of the medical and popular press, and of private citizens in this period. They were reiterated continually, ultimately becoming a dominant mode of thinking.[6]

---

[3] Roger Cooter, "In the Name of the Child and Beyond," in Marijke Gijswijt-Hofstra and Hilary Marland (eds.), *Cultures of Child Health in Britain and the Netherlands in the Twentieth Century* (Amsterdam: Rodopi, 2003), p. 290.

[4] Hilary Marland and Marijke Gijswijt-Hofstra, "Introduction," in Gijswijt-Hofstra and Marland (eds.), *Cultures of Child Health*, p. 9.

[5] These relationships have been explored in other chapters from different angles.

[6] See Nikolas Rose, *The Psychological Complex: Psychology, Politics and Society in England, 1869–1939* (London: Routledge and Kegan Paul, 1985), pp. 1–10; Nikolas Rose, *Governing the Soul: The Shaping of the Private Self* (London: Routledge, 1999, 2nd edn.), p. 155; Harry Hendrick, "Children's Emotional Well-Being and Mental Health in Early Post-Second World War Britain: The Case of Unrestricted Hospital Visiting," in Gijswijt-Hofstra and Marland (eds.), *Cultures of Child Health*, pp. 213–242. This chapter reaches conclusions similar to Hendrick's work. It adds to his investigation by focusing on psychoanalysis, investigating Bowlby's work in detail, and following the popularization of his ideas and the dissemination of psychoanalytic language in the words of citizens and state officials.

The shift in thought regarding child hospitalization must be understood in the light of new sensitivities about care for the emotional needs of children that emerged throughout the interwar period, and even more so during World War II.[7] Professional literature on institutional care and the damaging effects of a child's stay in the hospital had already started to appear in the 1930s.[8] But it was World War II and the experience of mass evacuation from cities due to Nazi air raids, as previous chapters have shown, that provided new prominence to the mental troubles of children, to the importance of understanding infantile anxiety and violent behavior, and the dangers of taking children away from their mothers. What is important for the examination of child hospitalization is that the literature on the evacuation process helped construct a perception of the fragility of the emotional life of "normal" children. Unlike previous psychological studies that concentrated on "abnormal" children who either came from "broken families" or were already under institutional care, evacuated children suffered due to the war conditions alone and came from all segments of the population.[9] The answers that psychoanalysts offered to the problems of children in distress during the war on the home front helped create new ways of thinking about the child and the self that emphasized their irrationality, anxiety, potential for aggressiveness, and easily disrupted mental health. These ideas and the warnings against mother–child separations were circulated during the war and became conventional in its aftermath, among other loci in the debate on child hospitalization in the developing welfare state.

Psychoanalytic ideas about the dangers of child evacuation and child hospitalization were of a similar logic. Just as analysts claimed that the real dangers to children during evacuation were not the air raids but being apart from their mothers, they also suggested that separation from the mother during hospitalization was again more upsetting to the child than medical examination, illness, or pain. Internal reality played a greater role than the external reality of war or hospital surgery. Anxiety and aggression were the main factors in accounts provided of the events of evacuation and hospitalization. In both cases, the danger of

[7] As we have seen, it was mainly after World War I that a new focus beyond the child's physical well-being emerged. Alongside a continuing interest in the body, more attention began to be paid to the child's psyche and mental health. This was an end product of a trend that had started in the late nineteenth century and peaked in the middle of the twentieth: Harry Hendrick, *Child Welfare: Historical Dimensions, Contemporary Debate* (Bristol: Policy, 2003), pp. 99–131. For early child psychology, see Denise Riley, *War in the Nursery: Theories of the Child and Mother* (London: Virago, 1983), pp. 42–80.
[8] See, for example, H. M. Skeels, "Mental Development of Children in Foster Homes," *Journal of Consulting Psychology* Vol. 2 (1938), pp. 33–43.
[9] As suggested in Nikolas Rose, *Governing the Soul*, pp. 163–164.

being subjected to uncontained nervousness and violence called for special expertise.

The increased focus on children as psychological individuals can also be traced in official government records of the immediate postwar era. The Curtis Committee, 1946, appointed by the government to investigate ways of providing for children "deprived of a normal home life," viewed children as emotional beings who could be damaged by the lack of individualized care and affection.[10] Psychoanalysts John Bowlby, Susan Isaacs, Donald Winnicott, and Clare Britton all gave expert testimony to the Committee and told of their experiences with evacuated children.[11] The recommendations of the Curtis Committee were implanted in the Children Act of 1948, and were also used as a source for interpreting the meaning of childcare, child welfare, and hospitalization in the years to come.[12]

The mental health of both the individual and the community became a central issue in the years after the war. The experience of the rise of dictatorships, the weaknesses of democracies, social instability, and the breaking-up of families due to war, as well as the years of unprecedented violence that demonstrated the ability of a variety of individuals to commit brutalities, made the search for a stable citizenship, well fitted to demo- cratic life, an urgent one.[13] In this context, the emotional lives of children as future citizens became a matter for public and official concern and an issue that required expert knowledge and guidance. Since the 1940s, psychoanalysts had increasingly provided the terms in which the troubles of children, the tasks of parents, and the standards for judging the normal- ity of child development and family life were conceived. The work of John Bowlby, James Robertson, and their colleagues in the Tavistock's Separation Research Unit educated the public about the inner forces of family love and their role in promoting a balanced subjectivity in children that would be suitable to the needs of a society recovering from war.[14] Their unique analytic contribution and attachment theory in the hospital is therefore at the center of this chapter, complementing earlier

[10] *Report of the Care of Children Committee* [Curtis Report] (London: HMSO, 1946), p. 5.
[11] National Archives files MH/102/1451/B69; MH/102/1451/B96; MH/102/1451/A22; MH/102/1451/A33.
[12] On the Curtis Committee and the Children Act 1948, see Hendrick, *Child Welfare: Historical*, pp. 133–140; Pat Thane, *Foundations of the Welfare State* (London: Longman, 1982); Jean Packman, *The Child's Generation: Child Care Policy from Curtis to Houghton* (Oxford: Blackwell, 1975).
[13] Mathew Thomson, "Before Anti-Psychiatry: 'Mental Health' in Wartime Britain," in Marijke Gijswijt-Hofstra and Roy Porter (eds.), *Cultures of Psychiatry and Mental Health Care in Postwar Britain and the Netherlands* (Amsterdam: Rodopi, 1998), pp. 43–59.
[14] Nikolas Rose, *Governing the Soul*, pp. 133–134, 159–160, 162.

investigations on the nature of childhood, democracy, mental health, and analytic expertise.

The development of attachment theory and research

John Bowlby was one of the founders of attachment theory and was its greatest popularizer.[15] His attachment theory advocated new ways of looking at the relationship between mother and child and the consequences of an interruption in this relationship. Such a disruption, Bowlby argued, might result in harsh feelings in the child of anxiety, anger, and grief, as well as long-term problems of development, mental-health disorders, juvenile delinquency, and difficulties establishing future relationships and providing good future parenting to the next generation of the nation's children. The belief that the experiences of early life could influence the child's development and have long-lasting mental-health consequences was at the center of attachment theory.[16] Anna Freud, working with wartime children, and Donald Winnicott, speaking on the BBC, also emphasized the importance of full-time motherhood and the relationship with the child. Yet it was Bowlby who developed the idea of attachment into an overarching theory. We encountered some of his work in earlier chapters; in this chapter I will undertake to explore it systematically in its historical context.

Influenced by Darwinism and biological research on the strong bond of certain animals with a mother-figure around the intermediary of food, Bowlby developed his own version of the mother–child relationship that went beyond the one that Sigmund Freud introduced. Bowlby proposed that "the human infant comes into the world genetically biased to develop a set of behavioral patterns that, given an appropriate environment, will result in his keeping more or less close proximity to whomever cares for him."[17] While Sigmund Freud saw the mother as an accidental instinct-gratifying object that provides food, Bowlby argued that the child's attachment to another person was biological and not merely derived from the mother's satisfying actions. For Bowlby, the mother was important in and of herself, not just as a food provider, and the child was seen as seeking relationships with others as an end in itself, rather than as a mere means for stimuli reduction. In this way, Bowlby explained the issue of

---

[15] Peter Fonagy, *Attachment Theory and Psychoanalysis* (New York: Other Press, 2001).
[16] See John Bowlby, *Attachment and Loss*, 3 vols. (New York: Basic Books, 1969, 1973, 1980).
[17] John Bowlby, "Psychoanalysis as a Natural Science," *Int. R. Psycho-Anal.* Vol. 8 (1981), pp. 245–246.

"separation anxiety" as something that happened when the child experienced fear of being removed from the "secure base" that the mother provided.[18]

Indeed, at the core of Bowlby's theories was the notion of "separation anxiety," perhaps the idea most associated with him.[19] Putting sexuality to the side, Bowlby placed "attachment" at the center of his explanation of emotional life. He explained all anxieties as connected to the struggles and separations of the early attachment to the mother.[20] Bowlby believed that mother–child attachment and separation anxiety should be studied using scientific tools taken from the natural sciences. There were, therefore, indeed tensions between psychoanalysis and attachment theory. At the same time, as the Introduction suggested, there were some core ideas that psychoanalytic strands shared across the various traditions and that were reflected in postwar culture and social policy.

Like Bowlby, others in this period were also interested in exploring scientifically the child's special relationship with the mother beyond the mere satisfaction of physical needs. For example, René Spitz (1887–1974), a Hungarian psychoanalyst who had fled the Nazis and settled in the United States, published a groundbreaking article titled "Hospitalism," which was based on statistics, films, and direct observations.[21] The article followed the tragic fate of infants under one year of age left in a foundling home. The physical needs of the children, such as food

---

[18] Stephen A. Mitchell and Margaret J. Black, *Freud and Beyond* (New York: Basic Books, 1995), pp. 136–137. See also Mathew Thomson, "'Savage Civilization': Race, Culture, and Mind in Britain: 1898–1939," in Waltraud Ernst and Bernard Harris (eds.), *Race, Science and Medicine* (London: Routledge, 1999), pp. 238–258.

[19] His notion of anxiety differed from that of Sigmund Freud. For Freud's initial concept of anxiety, see Sigmund Freud, "Three Essays on the Theory of Sexuality [1905]," SE/PEP Vol. VII, p. 224. Freud presented a new theory of anxiety in 1926, more in connection with the mind. While Freud claimed in his initial presentation that repression caused anxiety, in his second formulation he declared that in fact it was anxiety that caused repression: see Sigmund Freud, "Inhibition, Symptoms and Anxiety [1926]," SE/PEP Vol. XX, pp. 75–174. See Jean-Michel Quinodoz, *Reading Freud: A Chronological Exploration of Freud's Writings* (London: Routledge, 2005), pp. 215–226; Jean Lalanche and J. B. Pontalis, *The Language of Psycho-Analysis* (New York: Norton, 1974), pp. 48, 184, 379, 422, 37–40.

[20] Jay R. Greenberg and Stephen A. Mitchell, *Object Relations in Psychoanalytic Theory* (Cambridge, MA: Harvard University Press, 1983), pp. 184–187. See John Bowlby, "Separation Anxiety," *Int. J. Psycho-Anal.* Vol. 41 (1960), pp. 89–113.

[21] R. A. Spitz, "Hospitalism – An Inquiry into the Genesis of Psychiatric Conditions in Early Childhood," *Psychoanal. St. Child* Vol. 1 (1945), pp. 53–54, and R. A. Spitz, "Hospitalism – A Follow-Up Report on Investigation Described in Volume 1, 1945," *Psychoanal. St. Child* Vol. 2 (1946), pp. 113–117. On p. 53 of the article's first part, Spitz explained that the term hospitalism "designated a vitiated condition of the body due to long confinement in a hospital, or the morbid condition of the atmosphere of a hospital." Hospitalism should not be confused with hospitalization, the temporary stay of a sick

and medical care, were adequately fulfilled, but they were deprived of "maternal care" and "maternal love."[22] The small number of personnel in the foundling home allowed only limited individualized care. Consequently, the babies of this institution lacked all human contact for most of the day. The effects of this deprivation were horrendous and most of the children became sick, Spitz argued. Perhaps his most shocking finding was that by the age of two and a half, a third of the children had died. The surviving children developed severe retardation of speech, perceptual, motor, and mental functions. Up to the time they could stand up in their cots, they lay in solitary confinement. They thus remained motionless on their backs for many months until a hollow was worn into their mattresses.[23] Based on such findings, Spitz argued that meeting physical needs was not enough in itself and that, in the absence of loving motherly care, children would suffer severe damage.[24]

Bowlby was therefore not the only one to collect data on the mother–child emotional connection and the consequences of its disruption, and his work can be read in the context of trans-Atlantic interest in children's mental health in the mid century.[25] Nevertheless, it is important to note that Bowlby was the one who constructed an all-embracing theory integrating this data and who conducted large-scale research.[26] Bowlby had an ability to extend the implications of research from abnormal to normal children with ease. It was Bowlby's conceptualization that became the most popular one in Britain. He had a genuine capacity to discuss psychoanalytic concepts in a very accessible and clear manner. This ability, in the context of both the evacuation process and the particular sociopolitical and cultural situation in Britain at that time, made him a public persona – the "British Dr. Spock." His name became associated with the concepts of "attachment" and "separation anxiety" in public discussions of the time.[27] Bowlby's attachment theory was frequently seen as a theoretical development on his part that emerged from his work with evacuated

---

person in a hospital. It is interesting to note that the first volume of the *Psychoanalytic Study of the Child*, published in 1945, dedicated articles to both the evacuation process and hospitals.

22 Spitz, "Hospitalism – A Follow-Up Report," p. 115.
23 Spitz, "Hospitalism – An Inquiry," pp. 59, 63.
24 Mitchell and Black, *Freud and Beyond*, pp. 38–43. For Spitz's reservations on Bowlby's work, see R. A. Spitz, "Discussion of Dr. Bowlby's Paper," *Psychoanal. St. Child* Vol. 15 (1960), pp. 85–94.
25 See Benjamin Spock, *The Common Sense Book of Baby and Child Care* (New York: Duell, Sloan, and Pearce, 1946).
26 As noted by Susan van Dijken, *John Bowlby: His Early Life, A Biographical Journey into the Roots of Attachment Theory* (New York: Free Association Books, 1998), p. 4.
27 Cf. Riley, *War in the Nursery*.

children during World War II. Yet, his interest in separation and its consequences had already begun before the war.[28] Separation seems to have been a lifelong interest for Bowlby, who has been described as a "man with a mission," single-minded in his work and his attempts to spread his ideas to the public of what he perceived to be the dangers of separation between mother and child.[29]

Bowlby's interest in the mother–child bond emerged during his work at the Freudian-oriented Priory Gate School for Maladjusted Children in 1928. A year later, Bowlby began psychoanalytic training with Joan Riviere, a follower of Melanie Klein. His interest in separation and attachment and his emphasis on the importance of real-life experiences developed as he worked throughout the 1930s at the London Child Guidance Clinic, Maudsley Hospital, and the ISTD, and during his doctoral studies under Cyril Burt. The work done at the Clinic from 1936 to 1939 provided the research base for his 1944 article "Forty-Four Juvenile Thieves: Their Characters and Home Life." In this very influential article, which earned him the nickname "Ali Bowlby and his forty thieves,"[30] he famously suggested that the mother's attitude toward the child and separations during the first decade of life were crucial in explaining the origin of the delinquent character. Earlier in 1937, Bowlby also started his training in child analysis under the supervision of Melanie Klein, another intellectual source of inspiration. Klein's emphasis on the infant's capacity to form relationships and the stress she put on loss, mourning, and depression influenced Bowlby. Yet his thinking eventually (though not initially) differed from hers on the question of the relative importance of environmental factors. Bowlby focused more on the question of the

---

[28] Van Dijken, *John Bowlby*, p. 2; Riley, *War in the Nursery*, p. 97.

[29] Susan van Dijken speculated that Bowlby's interest in separation research had to do with his own personal experience as a boy who underwent several parental separations in his early life, among them a four-year separation from his father, who served in the army during World War I. See van Dijken, *John Bowlby*, pp. 153–154. On the sources of his intellectual ideas and his work at different institutions, see Susan van Dijken *et al.*, "Bowlby before Bowlby: The Sources of an Intellectual Departure in Psychoanalysis and Psychology," *Journal of the History of the Behavioural Sciences* Vol. 34 (1998), pp. 247–269. Cf. Nora Newcombe and Jeffrey Lerner, "Britain between the Wars: The Historical Context of Bowlby's Theory of Attachment," *Psychiatry* Vol. 45 (1982), pp. 1–12.

[30] John Bowlby, "Forty-Four Juvenile Thieves: Their Characters and Home Life," *Int. J. Psycho-Anal.* Vol. 25 (1944), pp. 19–53, 107–128; van Dijken, *John Bowlby*, p. 118. See also John Bowlby, "The Influence of Early Environment in the Development of Neurosis and Neurotic Character," *Int. J. Psycho-Anal.* Vol. 21 (1940), pp. 154–178; John Bowlby, *Personality and Mental Illness* (London: Kegan Paul, Trench, Trübner & Co., 1940).

impact of actions of the "real mother" than Klein, who was primarily concerned with internal relationships.[31]

Bowlby based his research on interviews and data collected about children and their caregivers, and his published article on juvenile thieves included case histories and statistics. Bowlby focused on children whom he termed "affectionless characters" (a label that became widely used by others). He described them as lacking affection for anyone and responding neither to kindness nor to punishment. These children, he believed, suffered from depression of an early origin, and they had usually experienced a complete emotional loss of their mothers or foster mothers. Bowlby considered the study of affectionless characters as critical since they formed the "real hard core of recidivism."[32] He concluded, "*prolonged separation of a child from his mother (or mother-substitute) during the first five years of life stands foremost among the causes of delinquent character development and persistent misbehaviour.*"[33]

His explanation of the correlation between separation and juvenile delinquency was a psychoanalytic one. A child separated from the mother comes to crave her love, and this craving, if unsatisfied, later presents itself as stealing. The act of stealing was also an act of aggression. "If one has suffered great deprivation oneself, one will feel inclined to inflict equal suffering on someone else," he reasoned. However, if the mother–child bond was uninterrupted, the child would learn to control the aggressive and libidinal impulses.[34]

In this article, Bowlby presented important themes related to separation and its possible mental and social costs. He reiterated and developed these themes in relation to child evacuation and hospitalization. While this article focused on "abnormal" children, Bowlby's future work would increasingly deal with the problems of "normal" children. In so doing, Bowlby turned the possible threat that separation's ill effects posed into an opportunity to call for public intervention. Love, for him, had a natural potentiality within children that could serve wider social ends.[35] By implication, the family was the answer for preserving democracy.

---

[31] Van Dijken, *John Bowlby*. When Bowlby read Klein's work in 1935 he noted at the margins "Role of environment = zero," but it took him some time to realize that his position was not compatible with hers: van Dijken *et al.*, "Bowlby before Bowlby," p. 259.

[32] Bowlby, "Forty-Four Juvenile Thieves," p. 39. See also a popular version of his emerging ideas: John Bowlby, "The Abnormally Aggressive Child," *New Era* Vol. 19 (1938), pp. 230–234; John Bowlby, "Jealous and Spiteful Children," *Home and School* (1939), pp. 83–85.

[33] Bowlby, "Forty-Four Juvenile Thieves," p. 113. The italics are in the original text.

[34] *Ibid.*, pp. 121–122.

[35] Nikolas Rose, *Governing the Soul*, p. 168; Ben Mayhew, "Between Love and Aggression: The Politics of John Bowlby," *History of the Human Sciences* Vol. 19 (2006), pp. 19–35.

The makeup of democratic socialism was at the forefront of Bowlby's mind when he conceived his theories and participated in political activities. Like other psychoanalysts during the interwar period, Bowlby showed great concern about violence and looked for ways of understanding and preventing it. Shifting his affiliation from Tory to Labour in 1926–1927, Bowlby befriended Labour politician and economist Evan Durbin and the future Labour Party leader Hugh Gaitskell. Bowlby and Durbin both became members of the New Fabian Research Bureau, which (influenced by G. D. H. Cole) advocated collectivist socialism and expert involvement in government affairs. Durbin believed that a psychology that fostered peace was necessary for economic expansion. This belief was central to his collaboration with Bowlby. In their work, psychology was seen as necessary for the maintenance of peace and for active cooperation among citizens that would in turn also enable the creation of an affluent society.[36]

Bowlby and Durbin published essays together in 1938 under the title "Personal Aggression and War" for a symposium on "War and Democracy," organized by Labour economists alarmed by the possibility of another world conflict.[37] The main thesis that Bowlby and Durbin advocated was that "war is due to the expression in and through group life of the transformed aggressiveness of individuals."[38] Influenced by evolutionary psychology theories concerning fighting between baboons in the London Zoo and struggles between "primitive people," Bowlby deduced statements about Western children, seeing them as halfway between the animal mind and that of the adult human. In ways similar to the baboons and "primitives," he thought, children were also in a

---

[36] Mayhew, "Between Love." Cf. "Professor Durbin Quarrels with Professor Keynes," *Labour* (April 1936), p. 188.

[37] Evan Durbin and John Bowlby, "Personal Aggression and War," in Evan Durbin and George Catlin (eds.), *War and Democracy: Essays on the Causes and Prevention of War* (London: Kegan Paul, Trench, Trübner, & Co., 1938), pp. 3–150. The organizers of the symposium included Ivor Thomas, Douglass Jay, Richard Crossman, Robert Fraser, George Catlin, Durbin, and Bowlby. On Labour politicians between appeasement and rearmament, see van Dijken, *John Bowlby*, pp. 104–105; Douglass Jay, *Change and Fortune: A Political Record* (London: Hutchinson, 1980). In the 1930s, Durbin's interest in psychoanalysis deepened due to his friendship with Bowlby. Durbin used psychoanalysis in order to rethink political questions and group relations. Employing psychoanalytic ideas, he wished to understand tensions between rationality and irrationality as well as those between conflict and cooperation in human society. With his psychological vision, Durbin was a key figure in establishing Clement Attlee's party economic outlook. See Stephen Brooke, "Evan Durbin: Reassessing a Labour 'Revisionist,'" *Twentieth Century British History* Vol. 7 (1996), pp. 37–39; Stephen Brooke, "Problems of 'Socialist Planning': Evan Durbin and the Labour Government of 1945," *Historical Journal* Vol. 34 (1991), pp. 687–702.

[38] Durbin and Bowlby, "Personal Aggression," p. 41.

frequent state of rivalry over "possession of goods or affection and frustration after failure or punishment." Deprivation or the threat of deprivation of the above, Bowlby warned, should be seen as one of the chief sources of hatred and aggression in childhood. Bowlby stressed the importance of parental love for the human child and warned, "any frustration of the desire to possess ... the love and approval of others leads to outbursts of anger and aggression."[39] These hazardous feelings of aggression could last into adulthood, endangering democracy. They could be projected onto random scapegoats and lead to the seeking of ways to punish them by making war.[40] By implication, Bowlby argued that the ability to modify early psychological bonding was a solution to domestic and international problems of his time. His collaboration with Durbin was underpinned by a belief that social responsibility was an evolved psychological potentiality that could be actualized in the mother–child relationship. This belief reflected and reinforced their democratic socialist vision and their wish to use psychological expertise in state affairs. They called for greater state involvement in psychological development and family life and in helping to regulate and convert natural violent tendencies in young members of society to altruistic feelings of cooperation.[41]

The implied threat to civil democratic society that children deprived of their emotional needs might pose also appeared in Bowlby's discussion of child evacuation.[42] In a report to the Fabian Society, he called for a more informed state policy that would take psychology into consideration in order to minimize children's anxieties and the social troubles and disorders stemming from mother–child separation.[43] Bowlby complained to his wife at that time, "people think I'm making a fuss about nothing."[44] This, as we shall see, was about to change after the war. As previous chapters have also showed, the evacuation process in Britain, and the new psychological knowledge generated through this experience, focused attention on the emotional needs of children and the importance of family

---

[39] *Ibid.*, p. 67.

[40] Van Dijken, *John Bowlby*, pp. 105–107. Bowlby and Durbin's work was widely reviewed. Most reviews found value in the work, but some also questioned whether their conceptualization was the best way to study aggression. See, for example, "The Urge to Fight," *Manchester Guardian* (23 May 1939); *Friend* (12 May 1939); *Lancet* (17 Jun. 1938); *Listener* (16 Mar. 1939); *New Leader* (19 Aug. 1938). More negative reviews included: *Tribune* (31 Mar. 1939); *Nineteenth Century & After* (Oct. 1939).

[41] Mayhew, "Between Love."

[42] John Bowlby, Emanuel Miller, and D. W. Winnicott, "Evacuation of Small Children," *BMJ* (16 Dec. 1939), p. 1202. See Ch. 2.

[43] John Bowlby, "Psychological Aspects," in R. Padley and M. Cole (eds.), *Evacuation Survey: A Report to the Fabian Society* (London: Routledge, 1940), pp. 186–196.

[44] Quoted in van Dijken, *John Bowlby*, p. 108.

life to their development. As a result, an image of the child as both helpless and at risk became more widespread. Such psychological ideas become important to social-welfare policy after 1945.

After the war, Bowlby was involved in the reorganization of the Tavistock Clinic, and became the head of its Children's Department in 1946.[45] He recruited staff and developed training programs for mental-health professionals. He combined clinical services with training and research in the Tavistock's spirit of "No research without therapy; and no therapy without research."[46] Indeed, following the recommendations of the Curtis Report, there was an increased need for training in child guidance in Britain that the program at the Tavistock helped to remedy. Bowlby shared the widespread postwar concern over civilians' mental health and helped advocate the declared goal of the Tavistock, which was "the promotion of mental health and the prevention of mental disorders both in childhood and in later adult life."[47] Work at the Tavistock can be seen as part of a general atmosphere of optimism in the immediate postwar period about the ability of the NHS to solve social problems. This optimism was coupled with worry about the mental health of citizens.[48]

The connections between democracy, mental health, psychology, and family life after the war can be found in an article Bowlby published with Robert Tod in 1947 titled "Families under World Tensions." The article's maxim was that "the best method of safeguarding community morale in the face of danger lies in the preservation of family ties."[49] The article linked the presence of peace or aggression within the family to the situation in the outside world. The importance of peaceful and stable family dynamics could not be overestimated since the family was the whole world to the small child. However threatening the international situation, the child was mainly affected by what was transmitted through the parents. The article made an explicit link between peaceful family life and democratic social cooperation in school and later in the workplace.

---

[45] Henry V. Dicks, *Fifty Years of the Tavistock Clinic* (London: Routledge & Kegan Paul, 1970), pp. 121–172, 176. During the war, Bowlby was enlisted as an army psychiatrist for the emergency medical services and helped in the process of officer selection. He made valuable connections with psychiatrists such as John D. Sutherland and Eric Trist who after the war might have helped in his appointment as the head of the Tavistock Children's Department. See van Dijken, *John Bowlby*, p. 131.

[46] Van Dijken, *John Bowlby*, pp. 131–132; Dicks, *Fifty Years*, p. 142.

[47] Van Dijken, *John Bowlby*, pp. 132–133.

[48] Hendrick, "Children's Emotional Well-Being," pp. 221–224.

[49] Tavistock Archive (hereafter TA), Pamphlet Collection (hereafter PMC)/IMC K Acc. No. X0975: John Bowlby and Robert Tod, "Families under World Tensions," *Child Study* (Fall 1951), p. 29.

The child from the happy home, it claimed, met teachers and schoolmates with trust and confidence, and therefore got along well at school. The adult with an experience of warm relationships in childhood would manage more easily both with superiors and with subordinate workers. In contrast, "any prevailing unrest or anxiety has the most unsettling impact upon the adult for whom it is a repetition of childhood disturbances." Anxiety, in specific, connected inner and outer worlds: "In the present world atmosphere of apprehension and anxiety, psychological factors are closely intermingled with reality," the article argued. Parents swept away by the prevailing winds of anxiety and aggression could expect their children to absorb some of their own feelings.[50]

Starting in 1948, the Tavistock Clinic received funding under the NHS and, with the help of additional fellowships, Bowlby was able to form a Separation Research Unit in the Children's Department.[51] Before looking closely at the research done at the Separation Research Unit, it is worth discussing the work that Bowlby did for the United Nations' World Health Organization (WHO) after the war. This work represented a condensed statement of his views in this period and was a source for the research done at the Unit.[52]

In 1948, the Social Commission of the United Nations passed a decision to study the needs of homeless children.[53] At the end of 1949, Ronald Hargreaves, chief of the Mental Health Section of the WHO, asked Bowlby to write a report on the psychiatric aspects of homeless children. Bowlby agreed, and began traveling through the UK, France, the Netherlands, Sweden, and Switzerland, to meet with professionals working with children. In March 1951, Bowlby published his WHO final report under the title *Maternal Care and Mental Health*.[54] Two years later, it was also made available in an abridged Penguin version called *Child Care and the Growth of Love* that was immensely popular and sold

---

[50] *Ibid.*, p. 26.

[51] Besides believing that separation could have serious ill effects, Bowlby decided to concentrate on its study also because he thought that there could be no scientific dispute about whether the event of separation occurred or not. He also believed that in this field preventive measures were possible: John Bowlby, "Psychoanalysis as Art and Science," *Int. R. Psycho-Anal.* Vol. 6 (1979), pp. 5–6. Interestingly, he also stated: "I was stimulated by the sheer incredulity with which my views were met by some, though by no means all, of my colleagues when I first advanced them just before the war": Bowlby, "Psychoanalysis as a Natural Science," p. 244.

[52] Cf. other work done for the UN after the war, for example, Claude Lévi-Strauss' report on racism for UNESCO: Claude Lévi-Strauss, *Race and History* (Paris: UNESCO, 1952).

[53] John Bowlby, *Maternal Care and Mental Health* (Geneva: World Health Organization, 1951), p. 6.

[54] *Ibid.*; van Dijken, *John Bowlby*, pp. 6, 147.

more than 400,000 copies in the English edition, and was translated into fourteen additional languages.[55]

Bowlby's report was very well received and widely reviewed. National newspapers such as *The Times* praised the report.[56] *The Times* repeated Bowlby's message that "maternal care in early life is as essential for mental health as is correct feeding for physical well-being." The newspaper noted that this theme "is not new but it is too easily forgotten and far too often neglected." It supported Bowlby's call to pay more attention to mental health while declaring, "Physical cruelty, for which parents are sent to prison, may in the long run be less important than mental cruelty, ignorantly caused by well-meaning officials as well as by parents themselves."[57] Local newspapers, like the *Southern Daily Echo*, recommended the abridged report to all parents, teachers, children's nurses, social workers, and local government administrators.[58] The *Portsmouth Evening News* declared, "One of the big achievements of the United Nations Social Commission has been to initiate research into a report on the relations of children to their parents under the impact of modern world catastrophes."[59] The *Evening Telegraph* said that the abridged report was "an exceptionally sane exposition on the subject of children and a particular aspect of their upbringing." It added, "Bowlby goes to the heart of the matter and expresses himself with the minimum of psycho-jargon."[60] The *Catholic Times* reviewed the abridged report positively but with some reserve. The report, it said, summarized "in a simple form many important conclusions on a fundamental sociological need." Yet the newspaper complained that in dealing with the problems of children the report did not refer to the "help which religion can bring, or to the fact that love of the child is born of the love of God."[61]

Bowlby's main thesis in the report was that "what is believed to be essential for mental health is that the infant and young child should experience a warm, intimate, and continuous relationship with his mother (or permanent mother-substitute) in which both find satisfaction and

---

[55] John Bowlby, *Child Care and the Growth of Love* (Harmondsworth: Penguin, 1953); Hendrick, "Children's Emotional Well-Being," p. 226. See also Nicholas Joicey, "A Paperback Guide to Progress: Penguin Books 1935–c. 1951," *Twentieth Century British History* Vol. 4 (1993), pp. 25–56.

[56] "Care of Children," *The Times* (15 May 1951), p. 5. (Cf. about twenty years later, "Exploring the Medical Myths of Maternal Deprivation," *The Times* (17 Jan. 1975), p. 11.)

[57] "Care of Children," *The Times* (15 May 1951), p. 5.

[58] "Mother Love," *Southern Daily Echo* (27 Apr. 1953).

[59] *Portsmouth Evening News* (6 May 1953).

[60] "Mother Love," *Evening Telegraph* (2 May 1953).

[61] "Just Lacks One Essential," *Catholic Times* (26 Jun. 1953).

enjoyment. Given this relationship, the emotions of anxiety and guilt, which in excess characterize mental ill-health, will develop in a moderate and organized way." He used the term "maternal deprivation" to describe a situation in which the child does not have this kind of relationship.[62]

Maternal deprivation could cause diverse ill effects, Bowlby argued. He supplied a long list of possible outcomes that when read today seems excessive, even absurd. Partial deprivation, he said, could cause "acute anxiety, excessive need for love, powerful feelings of revenge, and, arising from these last, guilt and depression." These might lead to neurosis and instability of character. Complete deprivation was seen as having even more far-reaching effects that might "entirely cripple the capacity to make relationships."[63] Children who were maternally deprived could also suffer from "diminished interest and reactivity; reduced integration of total behaviour . . . ; general retardation; blandness of facial expression; impoverished initiative . . . ; [and] ineptness in new social situations."[64] The immediate aftereffects of separation, "although not always evident to the untrained observer, are also frequently very disquieting to the psychiatrist." Among them were a hostile reaction to the mother on her return, a cheerful but shallow attachment to any adult, and "an apathetic withdrawal from all emotional entanglements, combined with monotonous rocking of the body and sometimes head banging." In sum, maternal deprivation could cause serious consequences to both mind and body. In the WHO report, Bowlby discussed hospitalization briefly. He suggested that a substitute mother could remedy the distress caused by separation from the mother and declared that "the advent of a mother-substitute may change a group of apathetic or amiably undiscriminating children into possessive and tempestuous little savages."[65]

A key theme in the report, like in Bowlby's other writings, was the connection between separation's harm and its possible influence on society. The proper care of children deprived of a normal home life should not be seen merely as an act of common humanity, but as an essential step in protecting the mental and social welfare of a democratic community. Deprived children, he argued, "are a source of social infection as real and serious as are carriers of diphtheria and typhoid." As a solution to this problem, Bowlby emphasized the benefits of psychoanalysis. He finished the report with a call for change saying "Let it be hoped, then, that all over the world men and women in public life will recognize the relation of mental health to maternal care, and will seize their opportunities for promoting courageous and far-reaching reforms."[66]

---

[62] Bowlby, *Maternal Care*, pp. 11–12.   [63] *Ibid.*, p. 12.   [64] *Ibid.*, p. 17.
[65] *Ibid.*, p. 25.   [66] *Ibid.*, pp. 157–158.

The discussion of Bowlby's different works during the mid twentieth century therefore shows how he was able to connect democracy, the tasks of government, mental health, psychoanalysis, and the study of the child.[67] These issues were refined and reworked in the research on hospitalized children performed by the Tavistock's Separation Research Unit with the help of Bowlby's assistant James Robertson (Illus. 12–14).[68]

Hospital direct observations by the Separation Research Unit

Born in 1911 to a working-class family in Glasgow, James Robertson was a Quaker and a conscientious objector during World War II. Before working with Bowlby, Robertson served as the social worker in Anna Freud's and Dorothy Burlingham's Hampstead War Nurseries, where he worked with his wife Joyce, herself later a pioneer in child research.[69] Under Bowlby's direction, Robertson conducted research on separated children in residential nurseries, sanatoriums, and hospitals.[70] Robertson soon became a prominent figure in his own right in the study of separation in general, and hospitalized children in particular. Robertson eventually had his differences with Bowlby and viewed some of Bowlby's statements about mother–child separation to be sweeping generalizations that did not pay enough attention to circumstantial variations. But in the public discussions of the time, the work of the two experts (Bowlby the psychoanalyst and Robertson the social worker influenced by psychoanalysis and later a psychoanalyst himself) was paired together.[71]

Hospitalization was quite a common experience for children in Britain and, as has been mentioned, early in the twentieth century hospitals did

---

[67] Nikolas Rose, *Governing the Soul*, pp. 167–168.

[68] Bowlby, "Psychoanalysis as Art," pp. 5–6.

[69] Joyce Robertson returned to work at the Anna Freud Centre in 1957 and joined James Robertson at the Tavistock Clinic in 1965 to do further research: Robertson and Robertson, *Separation and the Very Young*, pp. xiii–xiv.

[70] Robertson was part of a Tavistock research team that included Mary Ainsworth, Christoph Heinicke, Rudolph Schaffer, Mary Boston, Dina Rosenbluth, Colin Murray Parkes, and Tony Ambrose. Bowlby and the members published most of the team's findings, although some were assembled in an unpublished manuscript; see Archives and Manuscripts Collection, The Wellcome Library (hereafter WAMC)/PP/BOW/D.3/1–44.

[71] Throughout the years Robertson and Bowlby developed several theoretical disagreements that almost led to a public debate in the early 1970s. See WAMC/PP/BOW/B.3/25/2 and PP/BOW/D.3/1/7.

not welcome parents visiting their children.[72] Robertson described how, when he began his research, conflicting public views on hospitals existed. On the one hand, hospitals were held in awe and were respected as places where those who treated illness "were endowed with almost magical expectation of skill leading to recovery." But hospitals also evoked feelings of anxiety because when child patients were admitted "they were immediately shut off from contact with their parents, absorbed into a highly authoritarian structure in which doctors and nurses knew best what was good for patients. Relatives were excluded as likely carriers of infection and as potential disturber of the smoothness of long-established ward routine."[73]

A 1951 Ministry of Health inquiry revealed how limited the visits were, finding that "out of the 1,300 hospitals in Britain which admitted children only 300 allowed daily visiting (usually limited to thirty minutes) and 150 prohibited visiting altogether."[74] In 1949 in London's principal hospitals, visits at Guy's, for example, were only allowed once a week for two hours, while at St. Bartholomew's they were restricted to 30 minutes once a week. In London Hospital, children under three years old had no visiting time, yet parents could see their children through partitions. Children in those days sometimes stayed in the hospital for long periods. For example, in Harefield Hospital in Middlesex, children with pulmonary tuberculosis, common in 1948, sometimes stayed for three to four years.[75]

Throughout the 1940s, a sporadic interest in the issue of children's emotional distress during hospitalization appeared in professional journals, but did not amount to the live public debate soon to transpire at the end of this decade and throughout the 1950s. Infrequent discussion in the popular press, Parliament, and the Ministry of Health did not generate a call for change. Robertson complained that doctors and nurses at that

---

[72] According to a census from 1951 "there were in hospital in England and Wales 36,856 children between the ages of 4 weeks and 14 years, 20,621 of them boys and 16,235 girls. This represents 0.387 per cent of the child population (0–15 years). Figures obtained from the sample analysis of in-patients in 1955 suggested that some 685,000 children under 15 were admitted to non-mental hospital in that year, compared with a total of 3.5 million of persons of all ages." In addition, "Nearly one child in three has his tonsils out before the age of 13, and nearly 200,000 operations for removal of tonsils and adenoids are performed each year in England and Wales – largely in the 5–8 group." See *Report of the Committee on the Welfare of Children in Hospital* [Platt Report] (London: HMSO, 1959), pp. 1, 32.

[73] Robertson and Robertson, *Separation and the Very Young*, p. 7.

[74] *Ibid.* See also "Effects on Personality," *Nursing Times* (11 Apr. 1953), p. 355.

[75] Robertson and Robertson, *Separation and the Very Young*, pp. 8–14. For the full survey of London's hospitals, see H. G. Munro-Davies, "Visits to Children in Hospitals," *Spectator* (18 Mar. 1949).

time had "no insight into a concept of distress and psychological dam-age."[76] This was the arena Robertson entered when he started to conduct direct observations of hospitalized children.

It was in London's Central Middlesex Hospital that Robertson first believed he had detected the hidden realities of children's anxieties due to separation from their mothers. In contrast to commonplace medical thought that the child would be upset only for a short period and then would settle into the ward and be content, Robertson claimed to notice buried anxieties and a dangerous, concealed mental process. Against this myth of the "happy children's ward," Robertson claimed that children were actually upset and in deep distress. The quiet, settled child was to him an illusion of masked anxiety. Following Bowlby, he explained that the child's attachment to the mother was "fiercely possessive, selfish, utterly intolerant of frustration." A child taken from the mother's care would suffer distress and eventually grief that was not dissimilar to the one suffered by bereaved adults.[77]

Robertson argued that children moved through three phases of response to hospitalization without their mothers that he called Protest, Despair, and Denial (or Detachment).[78] During the Protest phase, the child would cry constantly for the mother, and would scream when the parents left. During the succeeding Despair phase, the child would feel an increasing sense of hopelessness and would be more withdrawn and apathetic. This is the state, according to Robertson, that is sometimes mistaken for thinking that the child is "settling in." The next phase is Denial or Detachment. In this stage, the young patient shows more interest in the environment and appears happier. For Robertson, how-ever, this was a "danger signal." Robertson explained, "because the child cannot tolerate the intensity of the distress, he begins to make the best of his situation by repressing his longing for the mother who has failed to meet his needs, particularly his need of her as a person to love and be loved by." If this phase continues, the child might end up denying the need not only for the mother but for mothering at all. Robertson was of the opinion that even short-term hospital separations "could leave a scar that might be

---

[76] Robertson and Robertson, *Separation and the Very Young*, p. 9.

[77] WAMC/PP/BOW/J.6/12/13: James Robertson, "Some Responses of Young Children to Loss of Maternal Care"; also printed in *Nursing Times* (18 Apr. 1953), p. 382.

[78] *Ibid.*, pp. 382–386. See also John Bowlby, James Robertson, and Dina Rosenbluth, "A Two-Year-Old Goes to Hospital," *Psychoanal. St. Child* Vol. 7 (1952), pp. 82–94. For a comparison of these phases in French children, see TA/PMC/IMMUCQ Acc. No. X1129: M. David, *et al.*, "Responses of Young Children to Separation from their Mothers – Part I," *Courrier de la Centre Internationale de l'Enfance* Vol. 2, No. 2 (1952), pp. 66–78.

known only to the individual as a nub of anxiety which could be activated by trivial happenings."[79]

Anxiety was a prime component in Robertson's explanation of the dynamics of child hospitalization. Yet separated children were not the only ones suffering from it. Robertson's explanation for the fact that the nurses did not notice the children's distress – so obvious to him – was that nurses needed to repress their own anxieties in order to grow accustomed to the children's misery and perform their work. In a later lecture called "The Problem of Professional Anxiety," James and Joyce Robertson explained that the staff developed immunity and become habituated to the distress of children and that their sensitivity was blunted due to a process of "repressing anxieties." Accordingly, children were treated "with little awareness of their individuality and less of their extended individual experience." The Robertsons called for the restoration of a sufficient degree of anxiety in the nurses so that it could be put to constructive use.[80]

Another Tavistock psychoanalytic paper, written by Isabel E. P. Menzies, discussed the problems of anxiety among nurses as related to the structure of their jobs, and later in his work James Robertson used Menzies' insights.[81] Influenced by Melanie Klein, Menzies explored the diverse anxieties of nurses. Menzies explained, "Unconsciously, the nurse associates the patient's and relative's distress with that experienced by the people in her phantasy-world, which increase her own anxiety and difficulty in handling it."[82] Menzies explored the ways in which the nature of the profession put the nurse at risk of being flooded by intense and unmanageable anxiety. She discussed the techniques used in the nursing service to contain and modify anxiety. Among the methods used that were most relevant to cases of child hospitalization were the eradication of a personal relationship between patients and individual nurses, depersonalization of and denial of the significance of the individual, and detachment and denial

---

[79] Robertson and Robertson, *Separation and the Very Young*, pp. 16–19.

[80] *Ibid.*, pp. 3–4.

[81] James Robertson, *Hospital and Children: A Parent's-Eye View. A Review of Letters from Parents to the Observer and the BBC* (New York: International Universities Press, 1962), p. 137.

[82] Isabel E. P. Menzies, "A Case-Study in the Functioning of Social Systems as a Defence against Anxiety," *Human Relations* Vol. 13, No. 2 (1960), p. 99; published also as a pamphlet, Isabel E. P. Menzies, "The Functioning of Social Systems as a Defence against Anxiety: A Study of the Nursing System of a General Hospital" (London: Tavistock Publications, 1960), and in a more popular format as "Nurses under Stress," *Nursing Times* Vol. 57 (1961), pp. 5–7. I thank Denise Riley for telling me about Menzies' work.

of feelings – all of these aimed to avoid the experience of anxiety, guilt, and doubt, but actually caused a great deal of secondary anxiety.[83]

When Robertson expressed his concerns about children's distress to the medical staff, they dismissed them as those of "a sentimental psychologist."[84] In order to tackle their resistance to the idea that children need their mothers beside them and suffer from separation anxiety, Robertson decided to make a direct-observation film that would document the emotional reactions of one child alone in a hospital. In order to ensure the film's objectivity, the staff agreed that Robertson would film main events as well as time samples of the child's behavior each day.[85]

Shooting in 1951 on a 16 mm camera Robertson chose to make a film in order to "capture actuality with a minimum of distortion," as he explained in an article titled "Nothing but the Truth."[86] "The visual presentation goes deep and commands attention in a way that the spoken or written word does not," he thought.[87] In order to ensure the natural behavior of the participants, Robertson tried to make himself invisible in the ward by spending time there before the shooting started. This was because direct observation meant that "There could be no rehearsals, no acting, no direction, and no re-take. It was up to the cameraman [Robertson himself] to make the best possible job of following but not influencing events – keeping inside the situations but out of the way of subjects."[88] The film's

[83] Menzies, "A Case-Study," p. 110.
[84] Robertson and Robertson, *Separation and the Very Young*, p. 13.   [85] *Ibid.*, p. 25.
[86] T A, Box 21: James Robertson, "Nothing but the Truth"; also published in *Film User*, Vol. 14 (March 1960), p. 161. Indeed, the middle decades of the century were a time of high realism with film practices aspiring to deliver a sense of reality via documentaries and wartime newsreels. This is also the time when Italian neo-realism developed a documentary-like style that had a powerful influence in presenting film as having the capacity to capture unedited reality. In the 1940s, traumatic memories were recovered in many research films and military medical training films through "flashbacks" that brought with them a return of the original experience. Robertson's film, in contrast, aimed to show trauma as it was occurring. Interestingly, Sigmund Freud himself dismissed the idea that film could be used to convey analytic ideas. See Alison Winter, "Film and the Construction of Memory in Psychoanalysis, 1940–1960," *Science in Context* Vol. 19 (2006), pp. 111–136. See also Paul Ries, "Popularise and/or be Damned: Psychoanalysis and Film at the Crossroads in 1925," *Int. J. Psycho-Anal.* Vol. 76 (1995), pp. 759–791.
[87] WAMC/PP/BOW/J.6/12/22: James Robertson, "On Making Two Mental Health Films," also printed in *The International Catalogue of Mental Health Films*. Other films recording deprived children made in this era are: René Spitz, *Grief – A Peril in Infancy* (United States: The Researchproject, 1946); W. Hoffer, *Feeding Processes*, made in the Hampstead War Nurseries. In later years, more hospital films were created. Among them are: Stephen Ramsey, *Please Don't Leave Me* (New York: Australian Information Service, 1980); Edward A. Mason, *We Won't Leave You* (Boston: Documentaries for Learning, 1975); Gary Schlosser, *A Mother's Worry* (Los Angeles: Little Red Filmhouse, 1979); H. Lowenstein and D. MacCarthy, *Film: Separations and Reunions* (Aylesbury: Stoke Mandeville Hospital, 1968).
[88] TA, Box 21: James Robertson, "Nothing but the Truth."

goal was to provide an objective visible record, which "permits the viewer to make his own judgment on the meaning of the material presented."[89]

Titled *A Two-Year-Old Goes to Hospital*, Robertson's completed film followed the eight-day hospitalization of Laura, the child presented in this chapter's introduction.[90] Laura was chosen randomly from a waiting list for an umbilical hernia surgery.[91] Her mother was pregnant with a second child at the time of Laura's operation. Laura's parents, Robertson described, "applied pressure for good behaviour; she was a 'little madam' who talked well, was very well behaved and had unusual control over the expression of feeling; a child discouraged from crying or making a fuss."[92] Yet the film Robertson made was successful in purportedly showing that Laura was anxious and distressed when left alone, a behavior that was typical of all children, according to Robertson's account. The film implied that Laura had started to go through the different emotional phases of separation (in her case Protest and Despair and, had she stayed longer in the hospital, Denial or Detachment).

The film showed how at first Laura burst into tears despite her general ability to restrain herself and repeatedly said "I want my Mummy." Increasingly, Laura became quiet but broke down every time a friendly person approached her. The film showed how on the third day of her stay, she seemed to have settled and made no demands, but when approached she broke out crying bitterly for her mother. She displayed, according to Robertson, "a cycle of withdrawal, breakdown, and resumed control." Gradually, the film presented Laura showing more unfriendly reactions toward her mother during the visits. Yet she seemed not to forget her mother, and had bursts of crying even on the sixth day. When Laura left the hospital, on the eighth day, she looked happy to leave. Yet the film showed that when she was outside the hospital she chose to walk apart from her mother.[93]

Laura's misery continued after the hospitalization. For the two days after her stay, Robertson reported, she was "unusually anxious and irritable. Her voice took on a higher pitch. She slept badly. She soiled herself several times. She became distressed if mother was even momentarily out of sight."[94] Six months later when accidentally seeing a sequence from the

---

[89] TA/PMC/IMM TW Acc. No. XII3: James Robertson, *A Guide to the Film: A Two-Year-Old Goes to Hospital* (London: Tavistock Publications, 1965 [1953]), p. 2.

[90] James Robertson, *A Two-Year-Old Goes to Hospital* (London: Tavistock Child Development Research Unit, 1952); WAMC/PP/BOW/J.6/12/22: Robertson, "On Making Two Mental Health Films."

[91] TA, Box 21, Robertson, "Nothing but the Truth."

[92] Robertson and Robertson, *Separation and the Very Young*, p. 26.

[93] Robertson, *A Guide to the Film: A Two-Year-Old Goes to Hospital*, pp. 4–6.   [94] *Ibid.*, p. 6.

film when it was presented to her parents, Laura became very agitated and said angrily to her mother, "'Where was you all the time, Mummy? Where was you?' Then she burst into loud crying and turned to her father for comfort."[95] Robertson therefore declared that the film "showed clearly that Laura . . . was under severe emotional stress throughout her stay in hospital, even when she quieted down and 'settled,' and that the main factor [in this distress] was not illness or pain but the separation from her mother."[96]

Robertson's views and the film itself were received as controversial in the medical community. At the film's premiere screening at the Royal Society of Medicine in 1952, according to the *Lancet*, reactions varied from criticism and disbelief to anger and calls for the withdrawal of the film.[97] The report of the *British Medical Journal* was sympathetic but raised critical questions, wondering whether the experiences of hospitalization were permanently damaging to children and whether they occurred commonly enough to be part of the recognized effects of admission to hospital.[98] In another review, Anna Freud argued that the film constituted a major attack on the beliefs which are ingrained in the professional attitudes of hospital workers. She complained about the age-old beliefs that illnesses of the body have to be attended to before the child's emotional upsets can be considered and that skilled nursing care can give more relief to the illness than the clumsy attention of an untrained young mother. At the time of her review, the film was touring in the United States under the auspices of the Children's Bureau in Washington and the World Health Organization. Following the reception of the film in England, she predicted "that majority of paediatricians will find it difficult to believe that a simple hernia operation with the minimal pain attached to it can be more than a minor passing incident in a child's life."[99] Indeed, due to the negative responses of medical professionals, it was decided not to distribute the film widely until they had time to come to terms with it. The film did not go on general release until 1959 in order to prevent resistance to reform in child hospitalization.[100]

---

[95] *Ibid.*, p. 7. Robertson also described how fourteen years later, when Laura saw the film again at age sixteen, she took hold of her father's tie as she had done when she was in the hospital: Robertson and Robertson, *Separation and the Very Young*, p. 42.

[96] Robertson, "On Making Two Mental Health Films."

[97] "'A Young Child in the Hospital': Report of Film Premiere at Royal Society of Medicine," *Lancet* (2 Dec. 1952).

[98] "Young Children in Hospital," *BMJ* (6 Dec. 1952), pp. 1249–1250.

[99] Anna Freud, "Review: James Robertson's A Two-Year-Old Goes to Hospital: A Scientific Film by James Robertson," in Anna Freud, *The Writings of Anna Freud*, 8 vols. (New York: International Universities Press, 1967–1981), vol. IV, pp. 280–292. See also "Effects on Personality," *Nursing Times* (11 Apr. 1953), p. 355.

[100] Robertson and Robertson, *Separation and the Very Young*, p. 45, and WAMC: PP/BOW/ A.5/2: Transcripts of Interviews with Alice Smuts and Milton Senn, October 1977, pp. 27–28.

The reaction of the psychoanalytic community to the film was also a mixed one. Analyst Wilfred Bion, for example, seemed to claim that Laura's distress was nothing to do with the separation from her mother but was entirely due to the fact that her mother was pregnant with another child. Bowlby recalled that, when the film was shown at the British Psycho-Analytical Society (BPAS), "the Kleinians challenged the observation and also the theory."[101] From a Kleinian perspective, the film neglected the child's internal phantasies raised by the physical experience of operation or pain. For example, invasive physical treatment could have been seen by the child as a deliberate attack on her body aimed to punish her.[102] Yet, others, like Anna Freud, saw benefits in the film and viewed the records of direct observations as "illustrating, extending or confirming analytic findings."[103]

Indeed, this immanent critique voiced by psychoanalytic colleagues – about what Robertson and Bowlby saw as scientific truths – represented differences of opinions about the nature of psychoanalysis in the BPAS. This question also had a gendered dimension. Almost all male psycho-analysts in the Society had a formal university education and had received doctoral medical degrees. This was true, for example, of Edward Glover, Ernest Jones, John Rickman, Donald Winnicott, and John Bowlby. Most women in the Society, on the other hand, came from a lay background and either had training in the humanities and social sciences or were self-taught and trained in the craft of psychoanalysis. Among them, for example, were Anna Freud and Melanie Klein – whose theories dominated the Society – and others like Joan Riviere and Ella Freeman Sharpe.[104] Bowlby's work was an extreme model for those who wished to see psychoanalysis as a natural science, an option that was exceptional even among the medical men at the Society. Bowlby wanted to base psychoanalytic research on scientific methods aimed at seeking truths and establishing facts. He believed that psychoanalysis should be open to the most advanced scientific developments from other academic

---

[101] John Bowlby, Karl Figlio, and Robert M. Young, "An Interview with John Bowlby on the Origins and Reception of his Work," *Free Associations* Vol. 6 (1986), p. 48.

[102] Anna Freud, "Review," pp. 285–286. See also Anna Freud, "The Role of Bodily Illness in the Mental Life of Children," in Anna Freud, *Writings*, vol. IV, pp. 260–279.

[103] Anna Freud, "Review," p. 286. See also the critical discussion of Bowlby's work: Anna Freud, M. Schur, and R. A. Spitz, "Discussion of Dr. Bowlby's Paper," *Psychoanal. St. Child* Vol. 15 (1960), pp. 53–62, 63–84, 85–94.

[104] The Society also had women members who were doctors, among them Marjorie Brierley, Kate Friedlander, and Sylvia Payne. James Strachey is a male example of a member who did not have a medical doctoral degree. See also Pearl King, "Biographical Notes on the Main Participants in the Freud–Klein Controversies in the British Psycho-Analytical Society," in Pearl King and Riccardo Steiner (eds.), *The Freud–Klein Controversies, 1941–1945* (New York: Routledge, 1991), pp. ix–xxv.

fields. Since one of the things for which psychoanalysis had been criticized was its failure to adhere sufficiently to classic observation and hypothetico-deductive methods, he hoped to address this problem through his research. In so doing, Bowlby also positioned himself as a male scientist acting in a Society under the influence of the theories of laywomen analysts. As he put it, "unfortunately some of the leading people in psychoanalysis have had no scientific training. Neither Melanie Klein nor Anna Freud knew the first thing about scientific method. They were totally ignorant."[105] He further complained that Klein "didn't know what science was about."[106]

Controversial as *A Two-Year-Old Goes to Hospital* and the underlying questions of psychoanalytic scientific research were, the film eventually drew numerous positive responses. It was widely discussed by both professionals and the public. The British Film Institute thought the film was "of national and historical importance," and preserved it in its archives.[107] And the WHO bought copies of the film for use in Africa and India and provided funding for its distribution.[108] In 1959, Winnicott declared in a review of the film, "One seldom meets a nurse or a social worker who has not had an opportunity to see it, and its influence has been very great."[109] *Nursery World* declared that the film was "one of the most valuable documents we could have on the subject." It believed the film to state a problem clearly and without prejudice. "We know for certain, that the problem [of hospitalization alone] was not solved when Laura walked out with her mother – rather that it would need many more years to be completely resolved." *Nursery World* did not see the film as critical of the nursing profession. Rather, it said, "The kindness, patience and humanity of the nursing side of the problem is

[105] Bowlby, Figlio, and Young, "An Interview," p. 45. See Bowlby, "Psychoanalysis as Art," pp. 3–14. In the debate on the nature of psychoanalysis between hermeneutics and science, Bowlby was closer to the latter. See Paul Ricoeur, *Freud and Philosophy: An Essay in Interpretation* (New Haven: Yale University Press, 1970). Relying on Freud's views from 1895, Bowlby saw psychoanalysis as a natural science; see Sigmund Freud, "Project for a Scientific Psychology [1895]," SE/PEP Vol. I, pp. 283–397.

[106] Bowlby, Figlio, and Young, "An Interview," p. 57. Despite the fact that Bowlby saw psychoanalysis as a natural science, he also viewed it as a therapeutic art. He explained, "The treatment of a patient is not scientific. The treatment of the patient is, to some extent, applied science, but very largely intuitive, and is a unique relationship between therapist and patient: this is not what science is about. But in so far as we are concerned with aetiology, personality development, and anything in the way of preventive work, that should be as scientific as we can make it": *Ibid.*, p. 49.

[107] Robertson, *A Guide to the Film: A Two-Year-Old Goes to Hospital*, p. iii.

[108] Robertson and Robertson, *Separation and the Very Young*, p. 47.

[109] D. W. Winnicott, "Going to Hospital with Mother," *Int. J. Psycho-Anal.* Vol. 40 (1959), p. 62.

not called into question. But the magnitude of the ordeal for a small child is only too evident, and it clamours loudly for our reply."[110] The *Daily Telegraph* reported that Robertson's film was applauded after it was shown to a captivated audience of 700 scientists, doctors, and social workers attending the Sixth International Scientific Film Congress.[111]

In addition, Robertson was invited to present this film, as well as another one he made called *Going to Hospital with Mother*, in many places in the UK and around the world.[112] When the government appointed the Committee for the Welfare of Children in Hospital under the chairmanship of Harry Platt (the Platt Committee) in 1956, Robertson, representing the Tavistock, submitted his film and a memorandum. A summary of this memorandum was later published as a book that was translated into nine languages.[113]

Robertson's memorandum to the government's Committee presented the same rationale as the one laid out by Bowlby in the WHO report. The memorandum claimed that the family was a microcosm of the larger society in which the child would one day be an adult, and that the child's development was dependent on the nature of care and love in early life. If the child felt secure, "it is likely that in later years he will face life with confidence and with a capacity for good social relationships that are an extension of his early experience."[114] Yet if the child were admitted to hospital and separated from his mother, he would feel anxiety and insecurity; an experience that might badly affect the child later in life.[115] In view of this, Robertson's main advice was that mothers should be admitted with children. The objections usually raised against this practice were that "the mothers would obstruct the work of the ward by their presence and by anxious and unreliable behaviour."[116] In contrast, Robertson

[110] WAMC/PP/BOW/A.4/1: *Nursery World* (12 Feb. 1953), p. 228.
[111] *Daily Telegraph* (30 Sep. 1952).
[112] Robertson and Robertson, *Separation and the Very Young*, pp. 43–51; James Robertson, *Going to Hospital with Mother* (London: Tavistock Child Development Research Unit, 1958); TA/PMC/HXO EMU GRS: James Robertson, *A Guide to the Film: Going to Hospital with Mother* (London: Tavistock Publications, 1958); also in WAMC/PP/BOW/J.6/1/6. Robertson was appointed as a temporary mental-health consultant to the WHO and was sent with the film on a six-week tour of universities, hospitals, and learned societies in the United States.
[113] James Robertson, *Young Children in Hospital* (London, 1970 [1958]); Hendrick, "Children's Emotional Well-Being," p. 231.
[114] Robertson, *Young Children in Hospital*, p. 4.
[115] See also D. G. Prugh *et al.*, "A Study of the Emotional Reactions of Children and Families to Hospitalization and Illness," *American Journal of Orthopsychiatry* Vol. 23 (1948), pp. 70–106; G. F. Vaughan, "Children in Hospital," *Lancet* (1 Jun. 1957), pp. 1117–1120.
[116] Robertson, *Young Children in Hospital*, p. 38.

argued, depriving mothers of the ability to see their children might cause them to behave in a frustrated or anxious way. He concluded that "the presence of even an 'anxious' mother is infinitely better for the young child than she should be absent."[117] Indeed, Robertson's film *Going to Hospital with Mother* showed that a child who was accompanied by the mother was in a better state emotionally. Robertson also recommended no restriction on visiting times for parents. He even went as far as calling for visits to be allowed in infectious-diseases hospitals, preferring care for the minds of children to the possibility of putting other civilians' bodies in danger.[118]

Mental-health considerations and the prevention of anxiety were also to influence the organization of hospital staff's work. Robertson offered to rearrange the system of nursing from "work-assignment," in which many nurses worked to provide the physical needs of the children, to "case-assignment," in which each nurse would be given a group of children to be attached to her as a substitute mother.[119] Robertson also called for an integration of mental-health concepts into medical and nursing training and for close collaboration with mental-health professionals, among them psychoanalysts.[120]

In his memorandum to the Platt Committee, Robertson also resorted to the principles advocated by the previous childcare Curtis Committee (itself influenced by psychoanalytic ways of thinking). He used them as a source for his arguments. Indeed, the Curtis Report of 1946 recommended that "children who 'for any cause whatever' are deprived of a normal home life with their parents or relatives should be cared for in small family groups so that they could experience the stable relationships and the rich emotional life that the more fortunate child finds in the family."[121] While the Curtis Report did not discuss the care of sick children, Robertson called for the extension of its recommendations to the field of child hospitalization at stake in the Platt Committee.

Psychoanalysis and public policy: the Platt Committee for the Welfare of Children in Hospital

In essence, the Committee for the Welfare of Children in Hospital accepted all of the Tavistock memorandum recommendations. Psychoanalytic vocabularies and modes of interpretation of the mother–child relationship appeared throughout the Committee's Report. The Platt Report represented

---

[117] *Ibid.*, p. 41. See also Joyce Robertson, "A Mother's Observations on the Tonsillectomy of her Four-Year-Old Daughter," *Psychoanal. St. Child* Vol. 11 (1956), pp. 410–427.
[118] Robertson, *Young Children in Hospital*, pp. 56–57.   [119] *Ibid.*, pp. 59–63.
[120] *Ibid.*, pp. 84–85.   [121] Quoted *ibid.*, p. 67.

and contributed to the growing sensitivities to children's emotional care beyond the body. It also served as a testimony to the deep concern after the war for the child's mental health and to the shifting views about the place of the hospital in democratic society. The Report demonstrates how far and with what great precision the state was now willing to involve itself in the lives of children and parents. It is therefore worth exploring in detail.

In June 1956, the Platt Committee was appointed at a meeting of the Central Health Services Council.[122] Its goal was to study the arrangements made in hospitals for the welfare of ill children beyond their medical and nursing treatment, and to make suggestions to hospital authorities.[123] The Committee met twenty times and received expert witnesses from different organizations, both voluntary and state-sponsored, who dealt with issues such as hospital administration, child welfare, education, and women's and mothers' interests.[124] The resulting Platt Report recognized the work that the Tavistock had done to "inform public opinion" about the experience of children in hospitals.[125] The Report started by acknowledging that in postwar Britain "general attention needs to be paid to the emotional and mental needs of the child in hospital, against the background of changes in attitudes towards children, in the hospital's place in the community, and in medical and surgical practice." It added, "The authority and responsibility of parents, the individuality of the child, and the importance of mitigating the effects of the break with home should all be more fully recognized."[126] The Report therefore placed itself at a juncture of sociocultural changes that it wished to promote further in new ways.[127]

---

[122] Members of the Committee were Harry Platt, Wilfrid Sheldon, P. H. Constable, F. M. Rose, Norman B. Capon, Charles Gledhill, E. Hollis, Margaret W. Janes, Marjorie E. John, C. A. McPherson, and Elizabeth Tylden.

[123] *Report of the Committee on the Welfare of Children in Hospital*, p. 1.

[124] The organizations included: Association of Children's Officers; Association of Hospital Administrators; Association of Hospital Matrons; Association of Occupational Therapists; Association of Psychiatric Social Workers; British Medical Association; British Orthopaedic Association; British Paediatric Association; British Paediatric Nurses Association; Central Council for the Care of Cripples; Central Council for Health Education; College of General Practitioners; Institute of Almoners; Institute of Hospital Administrators; Ministry of Education; National Association for Maternal and Child Welfare; National Institute for the Deaf; National Federation of Women's Institutes; National Union of Townswomen's Guilds; Nuffield Foundation; Mothers Union; Royal College of Nursing; Royal College of Physicians; Royal College of Surgeons; Royal Medico-Psychological Association; Royal National Institute for the Blind; Society of Medical Officers of Health; Women Public Health Officers' Association; and the Tavistock Institute for Human Relations. See *ibid.*, p. 42.

[125] *Ibid.* p. 1.   [126] *Ibid.*, p. 37.

[127] Earlier attempts had been made to deal with child welfare in the hospital. The Central Health Services Council had disseminated memoranda and reports to hospitals in 1949, 1953, and 1956, asking to allow daily visits for children.

Since the beginning of the century, the Report noted, there have been transformations in the perception of childhood and a profound change in the lives of children. The "child today" was better housed, better clothed, and better nourished than at any earlier time, "his individuality is recognized and appreciated both at home and in school and there is a growing readiness to understand and care for his emotional needs." Furthermore, "Parents are adopting a much more liberal and sensitive attitude than in the past, and since 1948 they have had available to them a wide range of domiciliary health services, including the services of a family doctor."[128] These transformations were seen by the Committee as positive rather than negative ones.

Changes in the relationship between the hospital and the community were also noted, partly in connection to questions of class and the development of the welfare state. According to the Report, when most hospitals were built, their purpose was mainly in serving the sick who came from a background of poverty, bad housing, or malnutrition, while children of better-off families were nursed at home or in private nursing homes. After ten years of a National Health Service, which removed financial barriers to medical care, the hospital's sphere had widened to cover all citizens. The Report suggested that, as a consequence, new attitudes to patients of all ages were demanded.[129] It thus made a link between the right to welfare and the right to individualized care.

At first, it seems that the Committee was trying to find a middle ground between hospitals and their critics. It acknowledged the existence of critical views of the hospital as an environment in which discipline was more severe than the home, leaving the child separated from the parents when they were most needed. The Committee used cautiously moderate language, accepting that there was some substance in such opinions. But, in fairness to those responsible for the management of hospitals, it argued, it was essential that a sense of proportion be maintained in assessing the criticisms. It would certainly be wrong to assume that medical and nursing staff in hospital were generally unsympathetic. However, it was this declared "sense of proportion" that was almost immediately set aside in the Report in favor of more psychological views in line with those

---

[128] *Ibid.* p. 2.
[129] *Ibid.* This was a more nuanced historical development, yet the important sentiment expressed here was about the extended responsibility of the welfare state. See M. Gorsky, J. Mohan, and T. Willis, "Hospital Contributory Schemes and the NHS Debates 1937–1946: The Rejection of Social Insurance in the British Welfare State?," *Twentieth Century British History* Vol. 16 (2005), pp. 170–192; Alysa Levene, "Between Less Eligibility and the NHS: The Changing Place of Poor Law Hospitals in England and Wales, 1929–1939," *Twentieth Century British History* Vol. 20 (2009), pp. 322–345.

advanced by the Tavistock. In contrast to its moderate initial words, the Committee seemed to end up adopting the vocabulary and the logic behind the psychoanalytic idea of separation anxiety. It eventually concluded: "We are unanimous in our opinion that the emotional needs of a child in hospital require constant consideration. Changes of environment and separation from familiar people are upsetting, and frequently lead to emotional disturbances which vary in degree."[130]

The Report called for a new attitude of mutual understanding between hospital staff and parents. It saw parents in the postwar welfare society as responsible for bringing up children and claimed that, so long as the child was educated and not neglected or physically ill treated, the absolute authority of the parents should not be challenged. Consequently, it demanded that hospitals recognize and respect the authority of parents. Medical staff attitudes, it said, should coincide with the great advantages in childcare which had been made over the past 20 years or so. "Their attitudes to parents should take into account the general rise in the standard of living and the influence of health education on the mind of the public."[131] In effect, the Report advocated a more democratic relationship between parents and medical authorities.

It was the belief of the Committee that the new sensitivities to the mental needs of the child and the growing power of parents entailed specific changes in the hospital's purpose, mandate, organization, design, and staff training. The Committee's recommendations again show a resemblance to psychoanalytic thought. During the time of the Report, children were treated either in children's wards inside hospitals, children's units in a specialized department, or in adult wards. The Report newly recommended that children should not be admitted to the hospital unless necessary, and instead should be cared for at home. It also advised that children should not be cared for in the adult wards due to the special attention they needed. It argued that nurses should treat as few children as possible in order to take care of their individual needs.[132]

A new place for the hospital was crafted. The Report suggested that informal contacts between a hospital and the community could do much to increase the confidence of parents and children in the hospital's ability to look after children. The Report's view, reflecting psychoanalytic concerns and the language of psychoanalysis, was that "Many parents have anxieties and fears about hospital life and about their child's illness, and worry is very easily communicated to the child."[133] In order to prevent parents' and children's anxieties, a cooperative system between experts,

[130] *Report*, pp. 2–3.   [131] *Ibid.*   [132] *Ibid.*, pp. 5, 11.   [133] *Ibid.*, p. 12.

such as the family doctor and staff of the local clinic, was to develop to help explain the place of the hospital in the community.[134] In order to calm the child, who might be "naturally fearful" of strange surroundings and parting from his parents, the hospital's environment and the Sister Nurse should be welcoming. The hospital should resemble the home, and the Sister Nurse should show interest in the child's individuality and "should find out about the child's personal habits, his likes and dislikes, including for instance his name for the toilet, and any other essential private vocabulary."[135]

This level of state interest and involvement in personal behavior was new. Another example of this tendency was revealed when the Report declared that, if the child was admitted at bedtime, the mother should be allowed to stay and help with feeding and putting to bed. "It is a comfort both to the mother and the child if she is able to stay with him for this short period."[136] In this manner the Report also advised that hospital clothes should be attractive to the child and should fit well, that meals should be full of flavour, and that the child should be able to bring special beloved toys. The Report specified in a meticulous way that "The choice of what to bring must be the child's, and neither parent not hospital should stop him bringing something he loves on the ground that it is not clean or respectable enough to take into hospital."[137] In addition, the Committee recommended that nurses and doctors obtain more training on the psychological needs of the child beyond the study of disease.[138] "The children's nurse needs to know all that she can learn about the functions and difficulties of parenthood and the significance of family life," it stressed.[139] In sum, similar to psychoanalytic views, the hospital was no longer seen as a place taking care only of the physical problems of ill children. Care for their mental needs was seen as an integral part of their hospitalization.

The Committee decided to welcome the admission of the mother with the child, and in words very comparable to those of Robertson it claimed that this was of great benefit to the child, and that if the mother were allowed to play a full part in his or her care she could be a help rather than a hindrance to the hospital staff.[140] The mother's stay would "obviate the harm of a sharp separation and demonstrate mutual trust between parent and hospital staff."[141] The Committee rejected the idea that the mother's admission would increase cross-infection and claimed that the child would probably suffer less emotional disturbance on returning home if the mother were admitted. Like Robertson, the Report recognized the

---

[134] *Ibid.*, p. 38.   [135] *Ibid.*, pp. 4–5, 14.   [136] *Ibid.*, p. 15.   [137] *Ibid.*, p. 26.
[138] *Ibid.*, p. 41.   [139] *Ibid.*, p. 36.   [140] *Ibid.*, p. 38.   [141] *Ibid.*, p. 17.

possible emotional disturbances in children after being discharged from the hospital, among them regressive behavior "due to stress" and aggressive conduct, which was seen as "the natural response to being hurt or the memory of being hurt." The Report explained that it was not possible for the child in hospital to be allowed to act out his own aggression when he was hurt or frightened as he would in the playground or at home. "Hence aggression is stored up and released at home."[142]

Similarly to psychoanalytic lines of reasoning, the Report also stated that parental visiting should be allowed and described children as needing a close emotional contact with familiar adults.[143] The Committee concluded that it was desirable for the majority of children to be visited daily and recommended that as few restrictions as possible should be made on visiting.[144] The Report argued, it was much better for a child to be visited daily, even if he was upset at the end of visiting time, than for him to have no visitors and become quiet and withdrawn.[145] Influenced by Robertson, then, the Report pointed out that, while the child who was left alone might look like he was "settled" in the ward, "the reverse is true; while his surroundings are new and strange he needs the support of someone he knows and trusts."[146] As all of the above quotes demonstrate, the main concern of the Platt Committee was with the child's emotional needs and mental health – both of which were conceptualized in ways similar to those of Robertson and Bowlby.

Bowlbyisms in the popular and medical press and in private lives

Numerous articles in postwar medical and popular newspapers and magazines as diverse as the *News Chronicle*, *Daily Telegraph*, *Northern Echo*, *Star*, *Housewife*, *Daily Mail*, and *The Times*, as well as the *Church of England Newspaper* and the *Catholic Times*, show the extent to which language similar to that of psychoanalysis was to be found not only in official circles, but also in public forums and discussions about the child–mother relationship. Bowlby himself was quoted regularly in newspapers and magazines, and his views were widely popularized. In addition to reports on child hospitalization, Bowlby's ideas were also cited in relation to other issues concerning childcare and mental health, such as the question of

---

[142] *Ibid.*, p. 34.   [143] *Ibid.*, p. 16.
[144] The length of visiting time in different hospitals in Britain was usually half an hour to two hours a day. *Ibid.*, p. 18.
[145] *Ibid.*, pp. 18–19.   [146] *Ibid.*, p. 20.

foster homes,[147] adoption, residential nurseries,[148] and divorce.[149] Both he and Robertson were frequently invited to publish their ideas and transmit them on BBC Radio.[150]

For example, in April 1952 the *Daily Mail* asked, "What Makes a Child Grow Up 'Good' or 'Bad'?" Its answer was "It's Mother Who Counts." The newspaper reported that the child starved of mother-love will often suffer for the rest of his life. "The effect may show in a warped personality – spanning the gamut of anti-social tendencies from failure as a citizen to delinquency, and sometimes extending to the acutest forms of mental disorder." Referring specifically to the ideas of Bowlby, it asked, "Why should separation from his mother leave a child with an emotional 'scar'? The experts' explanation is simple: Mother-love is to the budding personality what sunshine is to a flower; it yields the vitamins vital to mental health."[151]

The *Daily Mail*'s article went on reiterating Bowlby's views while taking them to their logical extreme. When a separation from the mother occurred, it stressed, a man's personality would stay undeveloped or would develop along the wrong lines. In such a case, he would be impulsive and lacking self-control; he would not be able to plan ahead nor learn from his experience. Because he would have no feelings for anyone, or anything, he would often be beyond cure. This, according to the *Daily Mail*, was "a personality picture of the criminal type, who is released from one jail sentence only to qualify for another." The newspaper mentioned that separation during a short hospital stay could cause such an effect.

---

[147] See for example: "Foster Children: Child Care Conference," *The Times* (6 May 1952); "Doctor's 'Homes Fit for Children' Call," *Northern Echo* (5 May 1952); "Women Tackle Child Cruelty," *Daily Dispatch* (5 May 1952); "Comment," *Daily Graphic* (5 May 1952).

[148] See for example: "Causes of Social Ill 'to Be Found in Early Childhood': Adoption Law Reform Urged," *Manchester Guardian* (18 Apr. 1953); "Adoption Delays Worry Doctor," *Yorkshire Evening Post* (18 Apr. 1953); "Child Adoption 'Too Slow': But There Are Underground Ways," *News Chronicle* (18 Apr. 1953); "Make Adoptions Easier," *Daily Herald* (18 Apr. 1953). See also "Adoption Trends in England and Wales," *Nursing Times* (21 Mar. 1953) and "Child Adoption in the Modern World," *Listener* (12 Jun. 1952). Bowlby was also quoted on the issue of illegitimacy: see "Illegitimacy: Call for Inquiry into Existing Law," *Manchester Guardian* (3 Oct. 1952); "When to Keep a Child," *Daily Herald* (3 Oct. 1952); "For the Illegitimate Child," *Nursing Times* (1 Oct. 1952).

[149] "When Parents Part . . . ," *Daily Herald* (4 Aug. 1952); "Divorce Hurts Children, Not Their Parents," *Church of England* (27 Jun. 1952).

[150] See Ch. 4.

[151] *Daily Mail* (8 Apr. 1952). The article referred to Bowlby, saying, "A child needs his mother. That seems pretty obvious; but very few people know why that exists, how strong it is, nor how grave can be the effects if it is left unsatisfied. Among the knowledgeable few are Dr John Bowlby, MD, and the team of five research workers at his Child Guidance Department of the Tavistock Clinic in London – hardy pioneers in what till recently was unexplored territory."

Returning home, it claimed, "at first the child is emotionally frozen, then thaw brings tears, hysteria, and often that heart-rending plea for comfort and renewed security: 'Mummy why did you send me away?'" The child is convinced that he was sent to hospital as a punishment and is consumed with guilt. As consequence, he "may resign himself to facing a life with anti-social apathy, and all the unpredictable risks which that involves."[152]

In another article in the popular *Family Doctor* titled "They Need their Mothers," and subtitled "At last science has to admit that mother-love is all-important to young people," Bowlby preached to the mothers among the readers, saying:

Never feel guilty about giving your toddler the continuous reassurance of your presence. On the contrary, if you do respect the child's real need for you – as you should – then you will also be respecting one of the most important rules of mental health. It is a rule quite as important as the familiar rules about orange juice and cod-liver oil.[153]

Similarly, the *Bulletin* published an article titled "Mother Right, Says Expert." The article declared, "medical science now has to admit that mother is right when she refuses to be parted from her baby." It reported that Bowlby "advises mothers to 'snap their fingers' at those who say that they are spoiling their children by refusing to leave them for the first few years of their lives." Bowlby "urges that no child under three should be sent away to hospital unless it is absolutely necessary, because the emotional shock is too great. If he has to go every effort should be made to visit him daily." The article also stated, "Dr. Bowlby admits that mothers need a break sometimes but advises them never to leave the child too long and to leave him with someone he knows."[154] The *Weekly Scotsman* published an article titled "Chats with Doctors: When a Child Is 'Upset.'" Basing the article on Bowlby's work, the newspaper described:

It is only in recent years that we have been proving, scientifically and by experiment, that separation from his mother for long periods may damage a child's mind so much that he never recovers. This statement may sound too dramatic but it is not so. It applied to children generally below the age of seven, but most particularly to those who are too young to talk. A child who has been particularly attached to his mother (that is, at that age a normal child) will be more affected than one whose mother is cold towards him.[155]

---

[152] *Ibid.*
[153] "They Need their Mothers," *Family Doctor: The Popular Health Magazine of the British Medical Association* Vol. 7 (Jul. 1952), p. 350.
[154] "Mother Right, Says Expert," *Bulletin* (Glasgow) (28 Jun. 1952).
[155] "Chats with Doctors: When a Child Is 'Upset,'" *Weekly Scotsman* (31 Jul. 1952).

In October 1952, the women's magazine *Good Housekeeping* ran a forum on hospital visiting and presented the spectrum of opinions of parents and medical staff. Significantly, vocabulary similar to that of psychoanalytic theories appeared in arguments both for and against hospital visiting.[156] A doctor from Surrey, for example, exhibited what Bowlby and Robertson would have labeled "a traditional view." This doctor believed that children under four years old have short memories and on the whole rapidly forget their mothers. Curiously, despite this "traditional" stance she also referred to the issue of the importance of attachment, claiming that after a day or two of fretting the children "settle down well, form an attachment to a nurse and are quite happy.'" She believed that the mother tended to fret more than the child and contended that the "most satisfactory solution was to allow the mother to visit two or three times a week and watch the child without being seen." This opinion, by this time seen as old-fashioned, was in the minority. The editor of the magazine's forum argued against this view, using Bowlby's WHO report to prove that children's quiet behavior was actually a sign of deep distress. Likewise, one reader from Fife claimed at the forum: "Surely ... it is better for a child to be temporarily upset [at the end of a visit] than to get quite out of touch with its parents, the only link to normal life to which the child will have to return. Lack of tears in a small child may merely be the signs of complete bewilderment, not of an active state of happiness." A number of other readers responded with examples from their own children's stays in hospital. One of them, a woman from Ipswich, described how she asked her son on his return if he would rather not have seen her than have had to say good-bye each time. The son replied quickly, "'Oh, see you, Mummy, every time!'" Another letter to the magazine's forum came from a woman from Hertford, who recounted her own memories from being in the hospital when she was a young child. She remembered: "although visiting was allowed for one and a half hours on Sunday afternoons, the eternity in between was an agony I have not yet forgotten. I cried myself sick."[157]

Nursery World reported that readers of the magazine had occasionally expressed concern over the effects of a child's stay in hospital. Again, the readers' worries were analogous to those of psychoanalytic experts. Many readers described how the child might have changed during hospitalization, and "though cured of his physical illness he might ... [return] home bad-tempered, nervy, fretful, whiny, clinging, anxious and so on." *Nursery World* added, "The first thing that might strike us about evidence of this kind is that the writers [of the letters] are all agreed on this subject at

---

[156] *Good Housekeeping* (Oct. 1952), pp. 86–87, 142, 145.   [157] *Ibid.*

least!" Revealing the spread of psychoanalytic views, the magazine even reported that mothers talked more about the problem of the child's anxiety and distress than about the child's illness.[158] *Nursery World* stressed its support of the views of Bowlby's and Robertson's work on the ill effects of separation and called for more changes in the field of child hospitalization.[159] In a similar manner, the *Nursing Times* supported reform because, it explained, Bowlby and other authorities showed that the consequences of hospitalization are "seriously significant not only to the individual but [also] for the community."[160]

Readers' letters to the *News Chronicle* also talked in "Bowlbyisms" against leaving the child alone in the hospital. One letter said, "Thank goodness our bureaucrats are satisfied at last that the 'dangers' of parents visiting their children in hospital have been 'over-emphasised in the past.'" The writer, a father, described:

I shall carry to my grave the memory of my younger son's spell in hospital for the removal of his tonsils at the age of four. When I left him at the hospital his cries pushed me into the street, and when I fetched him five days later he was reduced to despairing apathy. Now he is nine, and we still have to fight his terror of doctors and hospitals.[161]

Another letter-writer who quoted Bowlby's work said "The capacity for human relationships, on which good citizenship depends, starts in the trusting reliance on the mother. That trust once broken (the child is not to know through whose fault) this all-important capacity may be crippled. This is a heavy price to pay for a quiet ward."[162] And novelist Elizabeth Taylor wrote, "No mother should be excluded at this time [during the hospital stay]. It is no occasion for unknown voices and unfamiliar faces. However kind, strangers can only add to bewilderment." Taylor decided to admit her child to a private ward and said, "My daughter was reassured when I promised her that I should be with her when she awoke, and I am sorry that this should be a promise which not every mother is able to make."[163] Her words point to the fact that the expert prescriptions of Bowlby had different implications for mothers from different classes.

In an article titled "'Mothers Told: Revolt on Hospital Ban," the *News Chronicle* reported on the idea of a parents' revolt against the restriction on their staying in the hospital along with their children. Edith Honor Earl, the portrait-painter niece of Somerset Maugham, put the revolt idea

---

[158] *Nursery World* (12 Feb. 1953), p. 212.   [159] *Ibid.*, pp. 228, 232.
[160] "The Child – as a Person in Hospital," *Nursing Times* (14 Nov. 1953), pp. 1153–1154.
[161] "Children in Hospital," *News Chronicle* (12 Mar. 1953).
[162] "Children in Hospital," *News Chronicle* (16 Mar. 1953).
[163] "Children in Hospital," *News Chronicle* (18 Mar. 1953).

forward. She said, "If my boys ... had to be in hospital when they were young, nobody could have kept me away. I have seen much evidence on the terrible effects of separation." She told how her friend, a politician's wife, hired an ambulance and took her child to be nursed at home when she found out she could not stay with him at the hospital, an option that obviously was not available to women of all economic backgrounds.[164] In another report on the same issue by the *Manchester Guardian*, Bowlby was quoted as saying, "no more children's hospitals or extensions should be built until there has been a thorough exploration of the possibility of caring for sick children in their homes ... Where, because of housing or other difficulties, this [is] not possible we need to evolve some kind of hostel-hospital which would enable mothers and children to remain close together."[165] The words of the private citizen (Honor Earl) and the expert (Bowlby) complement one another.

An article in the magazine *Housewife* shows how the popularization of psychoanalytic ideas about the importance of the emotional lives of children had influenced changes in the attitudes of medical staff. The writer of the article described how as a young nurse she supported the mother's stay in the hospital with the child as well as parental visits. She reported that she was haunted by the memory of a child who died from the "shock" of the separation from the mother.[166] *Housewife* then interviewed members of medical and nursing staff about the issue of hospital visits. Its conclusion was that in "more up-to-date hospitals" the staff acknowledged their debt to the research work of their psychiatric colleagues and admitted that, despite difficulties, regular visits were important. The article added,

It is a mother's duty as well as her right to be with any one of her children if and when the child needs her. And, *If she is the right kind of mother*, she will realise that, because he quickly ceases to fret openly ... if she stays away, it does not mean that he is not being hurt inside ... So let us be thankful that those whose good work it is to heal children's bodies no longer wish to hurt their minds in the process.[167]

The article quoted a children's physician who, referring to Bowlby's work, said that if the proper growth of the relationship with the mother is interfered with by separation, "it may well be that the normal development of his potentialities as good citizen and husband will be impaired."[168] The

---

[164] "Mothers Told: Revolt on Hospital Ban," *News Chronicle* (16 Mar. 1953).
[165] "Causes of Social Ill 'to be Found in Early Childhood': Adoption Law Reform Urged," *Manchester Guardian* (18 Apr. 1953). See also a letter supporting the admission of the mother to the hospital, "Admit the Mothers," *Birmingham Gazette* (20 Mar. 1953).
[166] "Mummy Where Are You?," *Housewife* (5 Mar. 1953), p. 40. See also "Teaching Student Nurses," *Nursing Times* (11 Apr. 1953), p. 363.
[167] "Mummy Where Are You?," p. 41. The italics are in the original text.
[168] *Ibid.*, pp. 41–42.

article also quoted the matron of a hospital that allowed daily visits saying, "we find that the visits of intelligent and co-operative parents help both us and the child. The parents without common sense, on the other hand, do make things very difficult for all of us." She also mentioned that the idea of "parent–nurse co-operation, is new to many ward-sisters, but we at least are gradually making a success of it."[169]

Letters by parents of hospitalized children written in a response to Robertson's articles in the *Observer*, and the presentation of his hospital films *A Two-Year-Old Goes to Hospital* and *Going to Hospital with Mother* on BBC Television, revealed ways of thinking equal to those of psychoanalytic ones among other private citizens. Thinking psychologically and searching for hidden anxieties and inner realities became a dominant mode in which individuals made sense of their experiences. Letters from parents of children under five years old demonstrated the new ideas about the mother's role, the care of children, and the dangers of separation.[170]

The Platt Report recommendations were not mandatory and so changes were not immediate. As late as 1983 only about 50% of children's wards offered accommodations for parents and about 50% had unrestricted visiting.[171] In their efforts to influence hospital regulations or enact the Platt Report recommendations, some parents recounted how they made use of different state policy papers, the Platt Report included, as well as of Robertson's research material.[172] A mother from Sussex described how before her daughter's second operation she successfully used Robertson's articles to insist on accompanying the girl.[173]

Protest against restricted hospital visiting continued in the post-Platt era and took the form of a grassroots parents' movement. In Scotland in 1959–1960, a group of fifty mothers organized to fight the practice of restricted visits using the Platt Report and circular SHM 56/68 of 1956 in which the Secretary of State for Scotland urged the removal of restrictions on the visiting of children in isolation hospitals. In 1961, a group of mothers, who were also advised by the Tavistock Clinic, formed the charity organization Mother Care for Children in Hospital, later called the National Association for the Welfare of Children in Hospital (NAWCH), in order to persuade hospitals that the Platt Report recommendations could work.[174] In

---

[169] *Ibid.*, p. 43.   [170] James Robertson, *Hospital*, p. 73, Letter 51.
[171] Rosemary Thornes, "Parental Access and Family Facilities in Children's Wards in England," *BMJ* Vol. 287 (6386) (16 Jul. 1983), pp. 190–192.
[172] Robertson, *Hospital*, p. 125, Letter 110.   [173] *Ibid.*, p. 106, Letter 88.
[174] Robertson and Robertson, *Separation and the Very Young*, pp. 68–72. The organization still exists today and since 1991 has been called Action for Sick Children. Its goal is to improve health services for children and young people. See www.actionforsickchildren.org/abouthistory.html.

addition, once they retired from the Tavistock Institute, Joyce and James Robertson established the Robertson Centre in order to promote understanding of the emotional needs of young children.[175]

Ideas about caring for the emotional lives of children shifted through the debates on child hospitalization in mid-twentieth-century Britain. Psychoanalytic experts held crucial positions in this shift. The vocabularies and concepts that they formulated allowed for new ideas, as well as far-reaching practical changes, to take hold in relation to childcare, parenthood, the authority of medical staff, and the hospital's place in the community as well as its design, organization, and purpose. Terms and modes of thought similar to those of psychoanalysis were to be found among public officials and private citizens, in the popular and medical press, and in grassroots protest movements. Their overall declared interest was the care of children and their mental health – notions whose very meanings were in the making in this period. Another goal cut across the different contemporary discussions: the understanding and prevention of anxiety and aggression as distinct components of human relationships and communal life. This was linked to a general worry about the uncontained emotions of citizens and to a quest for citizenship fitted to a democratic order in a world that had undergone horrendous catastrophes. The debate on child hospitalization was part of new connections between democracy, citizenship, mental health, and expertise formed in Britain at this time. Psychoanalysis, this chapter and all previous ones have indicated, had a key role in their creation.

One conclusion that a study of the change in the care of hospitalized children yields is that the young child's bond with the mother, and the misery the separation from her would supposedly cause – ideas that now often seem commonsensical, even instinctual or natural – are constructed sensitivities. History tells us that these concepts became knowable in the mid twentieth century. In fact, to those who cared for children prior to this period, the infants' supposedly traumatic emotional experiences were not visible at all. Robertson, as this chapter demonstrates, needed to make films of children in hospital cots in order to convince the public and the medical community of his belief in the pure suffering and acute anxiety experienced by the children during separation from the mother.

As have all previous chapters, this chapter also concludes with a call for the need to revise the ways in which the psychoanalytic movement is usually perceived. Rather than being only immersed in high theoretical debates or the problems of wealthy patients, British psychoanalysis was an

---

[175] Robertson and Robertson, *Separation and the Very Young*, p. 199. See also www.robertsonfilms.info/.

immensely influential political discipline committed to reform, according to a certain set of ideas that tied together mental health, balanced self-hood, and the preservation of democracy. Yet this new view is not meant to imply that the psychoanalytic discourse was of a liberating nature. Besides creating new domains for investigation and making new realms of experience evident and exposed to management,[176] the constitutive reality-making role of these experts' knowledge also had gender-specific elements. Psychoanalysis contributed to the gendered perception of "motherhood" and "fatherhood" in war and postwar society when concern arose over the need to rejuvenate the family and ensure its ability to emotionally attend to children in order to ensure social tranquility. In a period when many women also worked outside the home, psychoanalysis emphasized that around-the-clock mothering was important to the health of the future generation and to the solidity of society. Through psycho-analytic discourse, the mother's presence or absence became a prime issue in the wartime and postwar climate with diverse consequences for women's lives that deserve further investigation.[177] As mentioned in the Introduction to this book, while paying attention to these concerns, my work has tried to look beyond more current feminist debates that label analysts simply as anti-feminists, and to explore how gendered notions were perceived and discussed at the time.[178]

It is important to note that the focus of parts of this chapter on the work of John Bowlby is not an obvious one, as his place in the psychoanalytic community was an ambivalent one. Despite the fact that Bowlby's thought was embedded in analytic theory, and that he himself was an active member of the BPAS,[179] who also went through supervision with

---

[176] See Peter Miller and Nikolas Rose, "The Tavistock Programme: The Government of Subjectivity and Social Life," *Sociology* Vol. 22, No. 2 (May 1988), p. 174.

[177] Jane Lewis, *Women in Britain since 1945: Women, Family, Work and the State in the Post-War Years* (Oxford: Blackwell, 1992), pp. 1–26; Dolly Smith Wilson, "A New Look at the Affluent Worker: The Good Working Mother in Post-War Britain," *Twentieth Century British History* Vol. 17 (2006), pp. 206–229; Juliet Mitchell, *Psychoanalysis and Feminism* (New York: Basic Books, 2000 [1974]).

[178] Mitchell, *Psychoanalysis and Feminism*. Riley, *War in the Nursery*. Riley shows that the link, frequently made by feminists, between Bowlby's ideas and the cancellation of daytime war nurseries for working mothers is a false one, demonstrating that Bowlby's theories had less effect on social policy than is commonly believed. This chapter shows how Riley's proposal should be rethought in relation to the case of child hospitalization. Her suggestions regarding the war nurseries, it seems, could not be extended to other realms. See also Jane Lewis, *Women in Britain since 1945*, pp. 1–26.

[179] Bowlby served in different research and administrative roles, among them the secretary of the Medical Committee, training secretary of the Deputy President of the Society, and chairman of the Board of the Institute of Psycho-Analysis. See Pearl King and Eric Rayner, "Obituary: John Bowlby (1907–1990)," *Int. J. Psycho-Anal.* Vol. 64 (1983), pp. 1823–1828.

Melanie Klein as part of his training as a child analyst, many psycho-analysts, especially from the 1950s, did not fully consider him to be one of their own. In a Society that emphasized the importance of the uncon-scious, fantasy, and internal conflicts, the integration that Bowlby pro-posed between psychoanalysis and sociobiological and evolutionary ideas was in dispute. Bowlby, for his part, was dissatisfied with the fact that most psychoanalysts did not base their views on scientific tools, such as stat-istical data and direct observational experiments.[180] He remained, there-fore, "unclassified" in the British analytic community.[181] Yet true to the methodology I presented in the Introduction of this book of examining psychoanalytic statements in accordance with what they have in common and the channels by which they are diffused, I view Bowlby as part of a unified psychoanalytic discourse of the time that had mutual features beyond its contemporary intellectual disagreements and schisms. Bowlby was part of a strand of psychoanalysis that advanced and empha-sized both the vulnerability of selfhood and the importance of early familial relationships (whether real or imaginary) in mitigating this volatility. Despite their differences, all British psychoanalysts – Bowlby included – saw the child to be helpless and demanding attention and yet living with ferocious angst and aggressive desires that needed to be eased and handled. By making healthy childhood important to the future safeguarding of personal mental health and social interactions, he and other experts, drawing from different analytic methods, created a social place for experts and helped in the remaking of democracy and modern Britain.

---

[180]   Bowlby, Figlio and Young, "An Interview," pp. 45, 57.
[181]   King and Rayner, "Obituary: John Bowlby (1907–1990)," p. 1828; Fonagy, *Attachment Theory*, p. 1. In 1979, Bowlby described: "When I qualified in psychoanalysis in 1937, members of the British Society were occupied in exploring the fantasy worlds of adults and children, and it was regarded as almost outside the proper interest of an analyst to give systematic attention to a person's real experience ... Almost by definition it was assumed that anyone interested in the external world could not be interested in the internal world, indeed was almost certainly running away from it" (Bowlby, "Psychoanalysis as Art," p. 5).

Bibliography

Abbreviations:

BMJ	*British Medical Journal*
Int. J. Psycho-Anal.	*International Journal of Psycho-Analysis*
Int. R. Psycho-Anal.	*International Review of Psycho-Analysis*
Psychoanal. St. Child	*Psychoanalytic Study of the Child*
SE/PEP	Standard Edition of the Complete Psychological Works of Sigmund Freud, Psychoanalytic Electronic Publishing website and digital archive, www.p-e-p.org.

ARCHIVAL COLLECTIONS

BBC Written Archives Centre, Caversham Park, Reading, UK
    BBC Administrative and Programme Files
    BBC Radio Scripts Index Cards
    BBC Radio Talk Scripts

Archives of the British Psycho-Analytical Society, London, UK
    Annual Reports
    Book Collection
    Document Collection

Centre for Crime and Justice Studies, ISTD Archive, London, UK
    Annual Reports and Bulletins
    Book Collection
    Document Collection
    Pamphlet Collection
    Press-cutting Collection

Freud Museum Archive, London, UK
    Anna Freud and Dorothy Burlingham Collection

Institute of Education Archive, University of London, London, UK
    Susan Isaacs Collection
    Newspaper and Journal Collection

National Archives (formally Public Record Office), Kew, London, UK
     Cabinet Office Files (CAB)
     Foreign Office Files (FO)
     Home Office Files (HO)
     Ministry of Education Files (ED)
     Ministry of Health Files (MH)
     Ministry of Information Files (INF)
     War Office Files (WO)

The Archive of the Tavistock Institute for Human Relations, London, UK
     Document Collection
     Film Collection
     Pamphlet Collection

Archives and Manuscripts Collection, The Wellcome Library, London, UK
     John Bowlby Collection
     Melanie Klein Collection
     Donald Winnicott Collection

Wiener Library for Contemporary History, London, UK
     Dann Family Collection

NEWSPAPERS
     Birmingham Evening Despatch
     Birmingham Gazette
     Birmingham Mail
     Birmingham Post
     Bulletin
     Bulletin (Glasgow)
     Cambridge Daily News
     Catholic Herald
     Catholic Times
     Christian World
     Church Times
     Daily Dispatch
     Daily Echo (Dorset)
     Daily Express
     Daily Graphic
     Daily Herald
     Daily Mail
     Daily Mirror
     Daily Telegraph
     Daily Sketch
     East Anglian Daily Times
     Edinburgh Evening News
     Evening Citizen (Glasgow)

Evening News
Evening Post (Bristol)
Evening Standard
Evening Star (Ipswich)
Evening Telegraph
Glasgow Evening News
Good Housekeeping
Halifax Daily Courier
Herald (Glasgow)
Housewife
Leeds Mercury
Listener
Manchester Guardian
Medical Officer
Medical Press
New Era in Home and School
New Leader
News Chronicle
Northampton Echo
Northern Daily Telegraph (Blackburn)
Northern Echo
Nottingham Evening Post
Nottingham Guardian
Nursery World
Nursing Times
Observer
Pearson's Weekly
People
Police Chronicle
Police Review
Portsmouth Evening News
Radio Times
Reynold's Illustrated News
Shields Gazette
Southern Daily Echo
Spectator
Sunday Dispatch
Sunday Pictorial
The Times
Times Literary Supplement
Tribune
Weekly Scotsman
Western Evening Herald
Yorkshire Evening News
Yorkshire Evening Post
Yorkshire Herald

PRINTED PRIMARY SOURCES

Ahrenfeldt, Robert. *Psychiatry in the British Army.* London: Routledge, 1958.

Aichhorn, August. "Some Remarks on the Psychic Structure and Social Care of a Certain Type of Female Juvenile Delinquents." *Psychoanal. St. Child* Vol. 4 (1949), pp. 439–448.

Wayward Youth. New York: Viking Press, 1935 [1925].

Alcock, A. T. "War Strain in Children." *BMJ* Vol. 1 (25 Jan. 1941), p. 124.

Alexander, Frank and Healy, William. *Roots of Crime: Psychoanalytic Studies.* New York: Knopf, 1935.

Alexander, Frank and Staub, Hugo. *The Criminal, the Judge, and the Public: A Psychological Analysis.* Glencoe, IL: Free Press, 1956.

Allen, Clifford. "Obscure Nervous Effects of Air Raids." *BMJ* Vol. 1 (10 May 1941), p. 727.

Auden, W. H. "In Memoriam Sigmund Freud." *Another Time: Poems.* London: Faber & Faber, 1940, p. 118.

Bathurst, M. E. "Juvenile Delinquency in Britain during the War." *Journal of Criminal Law and Criminology* Vol. 34, No. 5 (Jan.–Feb. 1944), pp. 291–302.

Beveridge, William. *Social Insurance and Allied Services.* London: HMSO, 1942.

Bion, Wilfred. "Psychiatry at a Time of Crisis." *British Journal of Medical Psychology* Vol. 21 (1948), pp. 281–289.

"'The 'War of Nerves': Civilian Reaction, Morale, and Prophylaxis." In E. Miller (ed.) *The Neuroses in War.* London: Macmillan, 1940, pp. 180–200.

Blacker, C. P. *Neurosis and the Mental Health Services.* London: Oxford University Press, 1946.

Bowlby, John. "The Abnormally Aggressive Child." *New Era in Home and School* Vol. 19 (1938), pp. 230–234.

Attachment and Loss, 3 vols. New York: Basic Books, 1969, 1973, 1980.

Child Care and the Growth of Love. Harmondsworth: Penguin, 1953.

"Forty-Four Juvenile Thieves: Their Characters and Home Life." *Int. J. Psycho-Anal.* Vol. 25 (1944), pp. 19–53, 107–128.

Forty-Four Juvenile Thieves: Their Character and Home-Life. London: Baillière, Tindall & Cox, 1946.

"Grief and Mourning in Infancy and Early Childhood." *Psychoanal. St. Child* Vol. 15 (1960), pp. 9–52.

"The Influence of Early Environment in the Development of Neurosis and Neurotic Character." *Int. J. Psycho-Anal.* Vol. 21 (1940), pp. 154–178.

"Jealous and Spiteful Children." *Home and School* (1939), pp. 83–85.

Maternal Care and Mental Health. Geneva: World Health Organization, 1951.

Personality and Mental Illness. London: Kegan Paul, Trench, Trübner, & Co., 1940.

"The Problem of the Young Child." *New Era in Home and School* Vol. 21, No. 3 (Mar. 1940), pp. 59–60.

"Psychoanalysis as a Natural Science." *Int. R. Psycho-Anal.* Vol. 8 (1981), pp. 243–256.

"Psychoanalysis as Art and Science." *Int. R. Psycho-Anal.* Vol. 6 (1979), pp. 3–14.

"Psychological Aspects." In R. Padley and M. Cole (eds.) *Evacuation Survey: A Report to the Fabian Society.* London: Routledge, 1940, pp. 186–196.

"Separation Anxiety." *Int. J. Psycho-Anal*. Vol. 41 (1960), pp. 89–113.

Bowlby, John and Durbin, Evan. *Personal Aggression and War*. London: Routledge and Kegan Paul, 1939.

Bowlby, John, Miller, Emanuel and Winnicott, D. W. "Evacuation of Small Children." *BMJ* (16 Dec. 1939), pp. 1202–1203.

Bowlby, John, Robertson, James and Rosenbluth, Dina. "A Two-Year-Old Goes to Hospital." *Psychoanal. St. Child* Vol. 7 (1952), pp. 82–94.

Bowlby, John and Soddy, Kenneth. "Treatment of War Neurosis – Letter." *Lancet* Vol. 236 (14 Sep. 1940), pp. 343–344.

Bowlby, John and Tod, Robert. "Families under World Tensions." *Child Study* (Fall 1951), pp. 6–8, 28–29.

BBC (British Broadcasting Corporation). *BBC Yearbooks 1945–1960*. London: British Broadcasting Corporation, 1944–1960.

Brock, A. J. "Boredom on the Home Front." *BMJ* Vol. 1 (30 Mar. 1940), p. 547.

Brown, Felix. "Civilian Psychiatric Air-Raid Casualties." *Lancet* (31 May 1941), pp. 686–691.

Brown, William. *War and Peace: Essay in Psychological Analysis*. London: A. & C. Black, 1939.

Burlingham, Dorothy and Freud, Anna. *Young Children in War Time in a Residential War Nursery*. London: Allen & Unwin, 1942.

Burt, Cyril. "The Incidence of Neurotic Symptoms among Evacuated School Children." *British Journal of Educational Psychology* Vol. 10, Part 1 (Feb. 1940), pp. 8–15.

The Young Delinquent. University of London Press, 1925.

Calder, Ritchie. *The Lesson of London*. Plymouth: Mayflower Press, 1941.

"Capital Punishment for Murder: The Royal Commission's Report." *BMJ* (3 Oct. 1953), pp. 775–776.

Carroll, Denis. "Review: The Psycho-Analytic Approach to Juvenile Delinquency." *Int. J. Psycho-Anal*. Vol. 30 (1949), pp. 138–139.

"Some Observations on the Treatment of Delinquents." *Mental Welfare* Vol. 16, No. 2 (1935), p. 35.

Carroll, Denis, Hubert, W. H. de B., Rees, J. R. and Woodcock, O. H. "Symposium on 'The Unwilling Patient.'" *British Journal of Medical Psychology* Vol. 17 (1937), pp. 54–77.

Carr-Saunders, A. M. *et al. Young Offenders: An Enquiry into Juvenile Delinquency*. Cambridge University Press, 1943.

Carver, A. E. "Conditioned to Bangs." *Lancet* (14 Mar. 1942), pp. 330–331.

The Children Act, 1948 and The Nurseries and Child-Minders Regulation Act, 1948. London: Butterworth & Co., 1948.

Crichton-Miller, H. "Obscure Nervous Effects of Air Raids." *BMJ* Vol. 1 (26 Apr. 1941), pp. 574, 647, 906.

Croft, John. "Hermann Mannheim: A Biographical Note." In Tadeusz Grygier, H. Jones and J. C. Spencer (eds.) *Criminology in Transition: Essays in Honour of Hermann Mannheim*. London: Tavistock Publications, 1965.

Dann, Sophie and Freud, Anna. "An Experiment in Group Upbringing." *Psychoanal. St. Child* Vol. 6 (1951), pp. 127–168.

David, M. *et al.* "Responses of Young Children to Separation from Their Mothers – Part I." *Courrier de la Centre Internationale de l'Enfance* Vol. 2, No. 2 (1952), pp. 66–78; Vol. 2, No. 3, pp. 131–142.

Davidson, M. A. and Slade, I. M. "Result of a Survey of Senior School Evacuees." *British Journal of Educational Psychology* Vol. 10, Part 3 (Nov. 1940), pp. 179–195.

Dicks, H. V. "In Search of our Proper Ethics." *British Journal of Medical Psychology* Vol. 21 (1948), pp. 1–14.

Dunner, L. R. *Report of the Inquiry into the Accident at Bethnal Green Tube Station Shelter on 2 March 1943.* London: HMSO, 1945.

Durbin, Evan. *The Politics of Democratic Socialism.* London: Routledge, 1940.

Durbin, Evan and Bowlby, John. "Personal Aggression and War." In Evan Durbin and George Catlin (eds.) *War and Democracy: Essays on the Causes and Prevention of War.* London: Kegan Paul, Trench, Trübner & Co., 1938, pp. 3–150.

East, W. Norwood. "Review: Social Aspects of Crime in England between the Wars," *Journal of the Royal Statistical Society* Vol. 104, No. 3 (1941), pp. 292–293.

East, W. Norwood and Hubert, W. H. de B. *Report on the Psychological Treatment of Crime.* London: HMSO, 1939.

East, W. Norwood, Stocks, Percy and Young, H. T. P. *The Adolescent Criminal: A Medico-Sociological Study of 4,000 Male Adolescents.* London: J. & A. Churchill Ltd., 1942.

Edelston, Harry. "Anxiety in Young Children: Study of Hospital Cases." *General Psychological Monographs* Vol. 28 (1943), pp. 2–95.

Eder, David M. *War Shock.* London: Heinemann, 1917.

Eissler, Kurt (ed.). *Searchlights on Delinquency: New Psychoanalytic Studies Dedicated to Professor August Aichhorn.* New York: International Universities Press, 1949.

Fleischmann, Otto, Kramer, Paul and Ross, Helen (eds.). *Delinquency and Child Guidance: Selected Papers of August Aichhorn.* New York: International Universities Press, 1964.

Fluger, J. C. *Man, Morals and Society: A Psycho-Analytical Study.* New York: International Universities Press, 1945.

Franklin, Marjorie. "Barbara Low." *Int. J. Psycho-Anal.* Vol. 37 (1956), pp. 473–474.

(ed.). "Q Camp: An Experiment in Group Living with Maladjusted and Anti-Social Young Men." *London: Planned Environment Therapy Trust*, 1966 [1943]. *The Use and Misuse of Planned Environmental Therapy.* London: Psychological and Social Series, 1945.

Freud, Anna. "August Aichhorn, July 27, 1878–October 17, 1949." In Anna Freud, *Writings*, vol. IV, pp. 625–638.

"Four Lectures on Child Analysis (1927) [1926]." In Anna Freud, *Writings*, vol. I, pp. 3–69.

"Discussion of Dr. Bowlby's Paper." In Anna Freud, *Writings*, vol. V, pp. 167–186.

"Review: James Robertson's A Two-Year-Old Goes to Hospital – A Scientific Film by James Robertson." In Anna Freud, *Writings*, vol. IV, pp. 280–292.

"The Role of Bodily Illness in the Mental Life of Children." In Anna Freud, *Writings*, vol. IV, pp. 260–279.

The Writings of Anna Freud, Vols. I–VIII. New York: International Universities Press, 1967–1981.

Friedlander, Kate. "Formation of the Antisocial Character." *Psychoanal. St. Child* Vol. 1 (1945), pp. 189–203.

The Psycho-Analytical Approach to Juvenile Delinquency: Theory, Case Studies, Treatment. London: Kegan Paul, 1947.

"Psychoanalytic Orientation in Child Guidance Work in Great Britain." *Psychoanal. St. Child* Vol. 2 (1946), pp. 343–357.

Fromm, Erich. *Escape from Freedom*. New York: Reinhart, 1941.

Fry, Margery. "Wartime Juvenile Delinquency in England and Some Notes on English Juvenile Courts." *Journal of Educational Sociology* Vol. 16, No. 2 (Oct. 1942), pp. 82–85.

Glover, Edward. "The Birth of Social Psychiatry." *Lancet* (24 Aug. 1940), p. 239.

"Denis Carroll." *Int. J. Psycho-Anal*. Vol. 38 (1957), pp. 277–279.

The Diagnosis and Treatment of Delinquency: Being the Clinical Report on the World of the Institute during the Five Years 1937–1941. London: ISTD Publications, 1944.

"Eder as a Psychoanalyst." In Joseph Burton Hobman (ed.) *David Eder: Memoirs of a Modern Pioneer*. London: Victor Gollancz, 1945, pp. 88–116.

Freud or Jung. London: Allen & Unwin, 1950.

"Notes on the Psychological Effects of War Conditions on the Civilian Population." *Int. J. Psycho-Anal*. Vol. 22 (1941), pp. 132–146.

"Notes on the Psychological Effects of War Conditions on the Civilian Population." *Int. J. Psycho-Anal*. Vol. 23 (1942), pp. 17–37.

On the Early Development of Mind: Selected Papers. London: Imago Publishing, 1956.

"The Problem of Homosexuality: Being a Memorandum Presented to the Departmental Committee on Homosexual Offences and Prostitution by a Joint Committee Representing the Institute for the Study and Treatment of Delinquency and the Portman Clinic." London: ISTD, 1957.

The Psychology of Fear and Courage. Harmondsworth: Penguin, 1940.

"The Psycho-Pathology of Flogging: A Study in the Motivation of Penal Method." In George Benson and Edward Glover, *Corporal Punishment: An Indictment*. London: Howard League for Penal Reform, 1931, pp. 15–29.

The Psycho-Pathology of Prostitution. London: ISTD, 1945.

The Roots of Crime. New York: International Universities Press, 1960.

"The Social and Legal Aspects of Sexual Abnormality." London: ISTD, undated.

The Technique of Psycho-Analysis. London: Baillière, Tindall, and Cox, 1955.

War, Sadism and Pacifism. London: Allen & Unwin, 1933.

War, Sadism and Pacifism: Further Essays on Group Psychology and War. Edinburgh: Hugh Paton, 1947.

Graves, Robert and Hodge, Alan. *The Long Weekend: A Social History of Great Britain 1918–1939*. London: Faber & Faber, 1940.

Greenwood, W. "Panic in Wartime." *BMJ* Vol. 1 (16 Mar. 1940), p. 448.

Haldane, J. B. S. *ARP*. London: Victor Gollancz, 1938.

Harrisson, Tom. *Living through the Blitz*. New York: Schocken Books, 1976.

"Obscure Nervous Effects of Air Raids." *BMJ* Vol. 1 (12 Apr. 1941), pp. 573–574.

Hurst, Arthur. "Air-Raid Noises in Psychotherapy." *BMJ* Vol. 2 (6 Sep. 1941), p. 354.

Hutchison, Robert and Winnicott, D. W. "Enuresis," *Public Health* Vol. 51 (Oct. 1937–Sep. 1938), pp. 340–341.

Isaacs, Susan. "Cambridge Evacuation Survey." *Fortnightly* Vol. 153 (1940), pp. 619–630.

(ed.). *The Cambridge Evacuation Survey: A Wartime Study in Social Welfare and Education.* London: Methuen & Co., 1941.

(ed.). *Concerning Children: Ten Pamphlets.* University of London Institute of Education and Home and School Council of Great Britain, 1937.

Intellectual Growth of Young Children. London: Routledge, 1930.

"The Nature and Function of Phantasy." In King and Steiner (eds.) *The Freud–Klein Controversies*, pp. 264–321.

The Nursery Years: The Mind of the Child from Birth to Six Years. London: Routledge, 1929.

Social Development in Young Children. London: Routledge, 1933.

"The Uprooted Child." *New Era in Home and School* Vol. 21, No. 3 (Mar. 1940), p. 54.

Jay, Douglass. *Change and Fortune: A Political Record.* London: Hutchinson, 1980.

Jersild, Arthur T. "Mental Health of Children and Families in Wartime." *Review of Educational Research* Vol. 13, No. 5 (Dec. 1943), pp. 468–477.

John, E. M. "A Study of the Effects of Evacuation and Air Raids on Children of Pre-School Age." *British Journal of Educational Psychology* Vol. 11, Part 3 (Nov. 1941), pp. 173–182.

Jones, Ernest. *Essays in Applied Psycho-Analysis.* London: Hogarth Press, 1951.

Free Associations: Memories of a Psycho-Analyst. New York: Basic Books, 1959.

"How Can Civilization Be Saved?" *Int. J. Psycho-Anal.* Vol. 24 (1942), pp. 1–7.

Papers on Psychoanalysis. London: Ballière, Tyndall and Cox, 1923.

"The Psychology of Quislingism." *Int. J. Psycho-Anal.* Vol. 22 (1941), pp. 1–12.

"Reminiscent Notes on the Early History of Psychoanalysis in English Speaking Countries." *Int. J. Psycho-Anal.* Vol. 26 (1945), pp. 8–11.

"Sigmund Freud 1865–1939." *Int. J. Psycho-Anal.* Vol. 21 (1940), pp. 2–26.

"War Shock and Freud's Theory of the Neuroses [1918]." In Sándor Ferenczi *et al.* (eds.) *Psychoanalysis and the War Neuroses.* London: International Psychoanalytic Library, 1921, pp. 44–59.

Klein, Melanie. "A Contribution to the Psychogenesis of Manic-Depressive States [1935]." In Klein, *Love, Guilt and Reparation and Other Works*, pp. 262–289.

"Criminal Tendencies in Normal Children [1927]." In Klein, *Love, Guilt and Reparation and Other Works*, pp. 170–185.

Envy and Gratitude and Other Works, 1946–1963 (The Writings of Melanie Klein, vol. III). New York: Free Press, 1975.

"The Importance of Symbol-Formation in the Development of the Ego [1930]." In Klein, *Love, Guilt and Reparation and Other Works*, pp. 219–232.

Love, Guilt and Reparation and Other Works 1921–1945 (The Writings of Melanie Klein, vol. I). New York: Free Press, 1975.

"Mourning and its Relation to Manic-Depressive States [1940]." In Klein, *Love, Guilt and Reparation and Other Works*, pp. 344–369.

Narrative of a Child Analysis: The Conduct of the Psycho-Analysis of Children as Seen in the Treatment of a Ten-Year-Old Boy (*The Writings of Melanie Klein*, vol. IV). New York: Free Press, 1961.

"The Oedipus Complex in the Light of Early Anxieties [1945]." In Klein, *Love, Guilt and Reparation and Other Works*, pp. 370–419.

"On Criminality [1934]." In Klein, *Love, Guilt and Reparation and Other Works*, pp. 259–261.

The Psycho-Analysis of Children (*The Writings of Melanie Klein*, vol. II). New York: Free Press, 1982.

"Some Psychological Considerations." In Hal Waddington Conrad *et al.* (eds.) *Science and Ethics*. London: Allen & Unwin, 1942.

Klein, Melanie, Riviere, Joan, Searl, M. N., Sharpe, Ella F., Glover, Edward and Jones, Ernest. "Symposium on Child-Analysis." *Int. J. Psycho-Anal.* Vol. 8 (1927), pp. 339–391.

Langdon-Davies, John. *Air Raid*. London: Routledge, 1938.

Lévi-Strauss, Claude. *Race and History*. Paris: UNESCO, 1952.

Lewis, Aubrey. "Incidence of Neurosis in England under War Conditions." *Lancet* (15 Aug. 1942), pp. 176–178.

Low, Barbara. *Psycho-Analysis: A Brief Account of the Freudian Theory*. London: Allen & Unwin, 1920.

McCulloch, Derek. "Children's Hour, 1939 to 1944." In *BBC Yearbook 1945*. London: British Broadcasting Corporation, 1945.

Mackwood, J. C. "Air-Raid Noises in Psychotherapy." *BMJ* Vol. 2 (23 Aug. 1941), pp. 279–280.

McLaughlin, F. L. and Millar, W. M. "Employment of Air-Raid Noises in Psychotherapy." *BMJ* Vol. 2 (2 Aug. 1941), p. 157.

Mannheim, Hermann. "Crime in Wartime England," *Annals* Vol. 271 (Sep. 1941), pp. 129–130.

Criminal Justice and Social Reconstruction. London: Kegan Paul, Trench, Trübner & Co., 1946.

Juvenile Delinquency in an English Middletown. London: Kegan Paul, Trench, Trübner & Co., 1948.

Social Aspects of Crime in England between the Wars. London: Allen & Unwin, 1940.

War and Crime, London: Watts & Co., 1941.

Martin, W. E. and Stendler, C. B. (eds.). *Reading in Child Development*. New York: Harcourt, 1954.

Menzies, Isabel E. P. "A Case-Study in the Functioning of Social Systems as a Defence against Anxiety." *Human Relations* Vol. 13, No. 2 (1960), pp. 95–121.

The Functioning of Social Systems as a Defence against Anxiety: A Study of the Nursing System of a General Hospital. London: Tavistock Publications, 1960.

"Nurses under Stress." *Nursing Times*, Vol. 57 (1961), pp. 5–7.

Miller, Emanuel. *The Generations*. London: Faber & Faber, 1938.

(ed.). *The Growing Child and its Problems*. London: Kegan Paul, Trench, Trübner & Co., 1937.

(ed.). *The Neuroses in War*. New York: Macmillan, 1940.

Minski, Louis. "Mental Disorder associated with the Recent Crisis." *BMJ* Vol. 2 (28 Jan. 1939), p. 163.

Minutes of Evidence: Memorandum Submitted on behalf of the ISTD by Dr Edward Glover, Royal Committee on Capital Punishment. London: HMSO, 1950.

Mira, Emilio. "Psychiatric Experience in the Spanish War." *BMJ* Vol. 1 (7 Jun. 1939), pp. 1217–1220.

Money-Kyrle, Roger. *Psychoanalysis and Politics: A Contribution to the Psychology of Politics and Morals.* London: Duckworth, 1951.

   Superstition and Society. London: Hogarth Press and Institute of Psycho-Analysis, 1939.

   "Towards a Common Aim: Psychoanalytic Contribution to Ethics." *British Journal of Medical Psychology* Vol. 20 (1944), pp. 105–117.

"Neuroses in War Time: Memorandum for the Medical Profession." *BMJ* Vol. 2 (16 Dec. 1939), pp. 1199–1200.

Orwell, George. "War-time Diary 28 May 1940–28 August 1941." In George Orwell, *The Collected Essays, Journalism and Letters of George Orwell,* Vol. II, *My Country Right or Left 1940–1943.* Boston: Nonpareil Books, 2000, pp. 339–409.

Pailthorpe, Grace. *Studies in the Psychology of Delinquency.* London: HMSO, 1932.

   What We Put in Prison. London: Williams and Norgate, 1932.

Pegge, George. "Notes on Psychiatric Casualties of the First Days of War." *BMJ* Vol. 2 (14 Oct. 1939), pp. 764–765.

   "Psychiatric Casualties in London, September 1940." *BMJ* Vol. 2 (26 Oct. 1940), pp. 553–555.

Perry, Ethel. "The Psycho-Analysis of a Delinquent: Interplay between Phantasy and Reality in the Life of a Law Breaker." London: Psychological and Social Series, 1946.

Pickworth, F. A. "Obscure Nervous Effects of Air Raids." *BMJ* Vol. 1 (24 May 1941), p. 790.

"Problems of War Casualties." *BMJ* Vol. 1 (29 Mar. 1941), p. 490.

"Professor Durbin Quarrels with Professor Keynes." *Labour* (Apr. 1936), p. 188.

Prugh, D. G. *et al.* "A Study of the Emotional Reactions of Children and Families to Hospitalization and Illness." *American Journal of Orthopsychiatry* Vol. 23 (1948), pp. 70–106.

"Publicity and Crime." *Lancet* (16 Mar. 1933), p. 704.

Rees, John R. *The Shaping of Psychiatry by War.* New York: Norton, 1945.

Reich, Wilhelm. *The Mass Psychology of Fascism.* New York: Orgone Institute Press, 1946.

Reik, Theodor. *The Compulsion to Confess: On the Psychoanalysis of Crime and Punishment.* New York: Farrar, Straus and Cudahy, 1945.

Reith, John. *Broadcast over Britain.* London: Hodder and Stoughton, 1924.

"Report of Psycho-Analysis Committee." *Supplement to the British Medical Journal* (29 Jun. 1929), pp. 262–270.

Report of Royal Committee on Capital Punishment. London: HMSO, 1953.

Report of the Care of Children Committee [Curtis Report]. London: HMSO, 1946.

Report of the Committee on Maladjusted Children [Underwood Report]. London: HMSO, 1955.

Report of the Committee on the Welfare of Children in Hospital [Platt Report]. London: HMSO, 1959.

Report of the Departmental Committee on Homosexual Offences and Prostitution [Wolfenden Report]. London: HMSO, 1957.

Report of the War Office Committee on Enquiry into "Shell-Shock." London: HMSO, 1922.

Rickman, John. "Government and ARP." *The Times* (1 Jun. 1939).

   "Letter: Evacuation and the Child's Mind." *Lancet* (2 Dec. 1939), p. 1192.

   "Panic and Air Raid Precautions." *Lancet* (4 Jun. 1938), pp. 1291–1295.

   "War Wounds and Air-Raid Casualties: The Mental Aspects of ARP." *BMJ* (26 Aug. 1939), pp. 457–458.

Rivers, W. H. R. "Freud's Psychology of the Unconscious." *Lancet* Vol. 189 (16 Jun. 1917), pp. 912–914.

Robertson, James. *A Guide to the Film: A Two-Year-Old Goes to Hospital.* London: Tavistock Publications, 1965 [1953].

   A Guide to the Film: Going to Hospital with Mother. London: Tavistock Publications, 1958.

   Hospital and Children: A Parent's-Eye View. A Review of Letters from Parents to the Observer and the BBC. New York: International Universities Press, 1962.

   "Nothing but the Truth." *Film User* Vol. 14 (Mar. 1960), p. 161.

   "Some Responses of Young Children to Loss of Maternal Care." *Nursing Times* (18 Apr. 1953), pp. 382–386.

   Young Children in Hospital. London: Tavistock Publications, 1970 [1958].

Robertson, James and Robertson, Joyce. *Separation and the Very Young.* London: Free Association Books, 1989.

Robertson, Joyce. "A Mother's Observations on the Tonsillectomy of her Four-Year-Old Daughter." *Psychoanal. St. Child* Vol. 11 (1956), pp. 410–427.

Ross, T. A. *Lectures on War Neuroses.* London: Edward Arnold, 1941.

Royal Commission on Capital Punishment. London: HMSO, 1953.

Schmideberg, Melitta. *Children in Need.* London: Allen & Unwin, 1948.

   "Folklore of Parenthood. " London: Psychological and Social Series, 1947.

   "Is the Criminal Amoral?" *British Journal of Delinquency* Vol. 4 (1953–1954), pp. 272–281.

   Knowledge, Thinking and Intuition. London: Psychological and Social Series, 1946.

   "The Psycho-Analysis of Asocial Children and Adolescents." *Int. J. Psycho-Anal.* Vol. 16 (1935), pp. 22–48.

   "Some Observations on Individual Reactions to Air Raids." *Int. J. Psycho-Anal.* Vol. 23 (1942), pp. 146–176.

Schur, M. "Discussion of Dr. Bowlby's Paper." *Psychoanal. St. Child* Vol. 15 (1960), pp. 63–84.

Schwarz, Hedwig. "Dorothy: The Psycho-Analysis of a Case of Stealing." *British Journal of Delinquency* Vol. 1 (1950–1951), pp. 29–47.

Skeels, H. M. "Mental Development of Children in Foster Homes." *Journal of Consulting Psychology* Vol. 2 (1938), pp. 33–43.

Spitz, R. A. "Anxiety in Infancy: A Study of its Manifestations in the First Year of Life." *Int. J. Psycho-Anal.* Vol. 31 (1950), pp. 138–143.

"Discussion of Dr. Bowlby's Paper." *Psychoanal. St. Child* Vol. 15 (1960), pp. 85–94.

"Hospitalism – A Follow-Up Report on Investigation Described in Volume 1, 1945." *Psychoanal. St. Child* Vol. 2 (1946), pp. 113–117.

"Hospitalism – An Inquiry into the Genesis of Psychiatric Conditions in Early Childhood." *Psychoanal. St. Child* Vol. 1 (1945), pp. 53–54.

Spitz, R. A. and Wolf, K. M. "Anaclitic Depression: An Inquiry into the Genesis of Psychiatric Conditions in Early Childhood." *Psychoanal. St. Child* Vol. 2 (1946), pp. 313–342.

Spock, Benjamin. *The Common Sense Book of Baby and Child Care.* New York: Duell, Sloan, and Pearce, 1946.

Stalker, Harry. "Panic States in Civilians." *BMJ* Vol. 1 (1 Jun. 1940), pp. 877–888.

Stone, J. J. "Some Problems of Filming Children's Behaviour." *Child Development* Vol. 23 (1952), pp. 227–233.

Struthers, A. M. "Juvenile Delinquency in Scotland." *American Sociological Review* Vol. 10, No. 5 (Oct. 1945), pp. 658–662.

Telfer, A. C. D. "Group Psychology." *BMJ* Vol. 1 (28 Feb. 1942), pp. 309–310.

"Psychological Treatment Centres." *BMJ* Vol. 2 (7 Oct. 1939), p. 744.

Titmuss, Richard. *Problems of Social Policy.* London: HMSO, 1950.

"Treatment of Neurosis in the Emergency Medical Service." *BMJ* Vol. 2 (3 Dec. 1939), p. 1242.

Vaughan, G. F. "Children in Hospital." *Lancet* (1 Jun. 1957), pp. 1117–1120.

"War Neuroses." *BMJ* Vol. 2 (5 July 1941), p. 21.

Warburg, Joan. "Play Therapy." London: Psychological and Social Series, 1946.

Watson, John A. F. *The Child and the Magistrate.* London: Jonathan Cape, 1942.

"The War and the Young Offender." *Fortnightly* Vol. 157 (Feb. 1942), pp. 90–94.

West, D. J. *Homosexuality.* London: Duckworth, 1955.

Westwood, Gordon. *Society and the Homosexual.* London: Gollancz, 1952.

Whiles, W. H. "Psychiatric Casualties of War." *BMJ* Vol. 2 (28 Oct. 1939), p. 881.

Willcock, H. D. *Report on Juvenile Delinquency by Mass Observation.* London: Faber & Faber, 1949.

Wills, David. *Hawkspur Experiment.* London: Allen & Unwin, 1967.

Wilson, Henry. "Mental Reactions to Air-Raids." *Lancet* (7 Mar. 1942), pp. 284–287.

Winnicott, D. W. *The Child, the Family, and the Outside World.* Harmondsworth: Penguin Books, 1964.

Collected Papers: Through Paediatrics to Psycho-Analysis. New York: Basic Books, 1958.

Deprivation and Delinquency. London: Tavistock Publications, 1984.

"The Deprived Mother." *New Era in Home and School* Vol. 21 (Mar. 1940), pp. 63–73.

The Family and Individual Development. London: Tavistock Publications, 1965.

Getting to Know Your Baby. London: Wm. Heinemann Medical Books, 1945.

"Going to Hospital with Mother." *Int. J. Psycho-Anal.* Vol. 40 (1959), pp. 62–63.

Home Is Where We Start From: Essays by a Psychoanalyst. New York: W. W. Norton, 1986.

"The Ordinary Devoted Mother and her Baby: Nine Broadcast Talks." London: privately distributed, 1949.

"Oscar Friedmann, 1903–1958." *Int. J. Psycho-Anal.* Vol. 40 (1959), pp. 247–248.

Playing and Reality. London: Routledge, 1982.

"Some Thoughts on the Meaning of the Word Democracy." *Human Relations* Vol. 3 (1950), pp. 175–186.

Talking to Parents. Workingham and Cambridge, MA: Addison-Wesley, 1993.

Thinking about Children. London: Karnac Books, 1996.

"Visiting Children in Hospital." *New Era Home and School* Vol. 33, No. 6 (Jun. 1952).

Winnicott on the Child. Cambridge, MA: Perseus, 2002.

Winnicott, D. W. and Britton, Clare. "The Problem of Homeless Children." In *Children's Communities: Experiments in Democratic Living.* London: NEF Monograph, 1944.

Wolf, M. Katharine. "Evacuation of Children in Wartime." *Psychoanal. St. Child* Vol. 1 (1945), pp. 389–404.

Wright, Maurice B. "Psychological Emergencies in War Time." *BMJ* Vol. 2 (9 Sep. 1939), pp. 576–578.

"Young Children in Hospital." *BMJ* (6 Dec. 1952), pp. 1249–1250.

Zetzel, E. R. "The Concept of Anxiety in Relation to the Development of Psychoanalysis." *Journal of the American Psychoanalytic Association* Vol. 3 (1955), pp. 369–388.

Zilboorg, Gregory. "The Contribution of Psycho-Analysis to Forensic Psychiatry." *Int. J. Psycho-Anal.* Vol. 37 (1956), pp. 318–324.

Zulliger, Hans. "Unconscious Motives for Theft." *British Journal of Delinquency* Vol. 1 (1950–1951), pp. 198–204.

SECONDARY SOURCES

Addison, Paul. *No Turning Back: The Peacetime Revolutions of Post-War Britain.* Oxford University Press, 2010.

The Road to 1945: British Politics and the Second World War. London: Cape, 1975.

Alexander, Sally. "Psychoanalysis in Britain in the Early Twentieth Century: An Introductory Note." *History Workshop Journal* Vol. 45 (Spring 1998), pp. 135–143.

Allen, Ann Taylor. *Feminism and Motherhood in Western Europe, 1890–1970: The Maternal Dilemma.* New York: Palgrave, 2005.

Allport, Alan. *Demobbed: Coming Home after the Second World War.* New Haven: Yale University Press, 2009.

Anderson, Benedict. *Imagined Communities: Reflections on the Origin and Spread of Nationalism.* New York: Verso, 1991.

Anzieu, Didier. "Beckett and Bion." *Int. J. Psycho-Anal.* Vol. 16 (1989), pp. 163–169.

Appignanesi, Lisa and Forrester, John. *Freud's Women.* New York: Basic Books, 1993.

Ariès, Philippe. *Centuries of Childhood: A Social History of Family Life.* New York: Vintage Books, 1962.

Ash, M. "Central European Émigré Psychologists and Psychoanalysts in the United Kingdom." In J. Carlebach *et al.* (eds.) *Second Chance: Two Centuries of German-Speaking Jews in the United Kingdom.* Tübingen: Mohr, 1991, pp. 101–120.

Audoin-Rouzeau, Stephane and Becker, Annette. *14–18: Understanding the Great War.* New York: Hill & Wang, 2003.

Avery, Todd. *Radio Modernism: Literature, Ethics, and the BBC, 1922–1938.* Burlington, VT: Ashgate, 2006.

Bailey, Victor. *Delinquency and Citizenship: Reclaiming the Young Offender 1914–1948.* Oxford University Press, 1987.

Barham, Peter. *Forgotten Lunatics of the Great War.* New Haven: Yale University Press, 2004.

Beatson, Jack and Zimmermann, Reinhard (eds.). *Jurists Uprooted: German-Speaking Émigré Lawyers in Twentieth-Century Britain.* Oxford University Press, 2004.

Beer, Daniel. *Renovating Russia: The Human Sciences and the Fate of Liberal Modernity 1880–1930.* Ithaca: Cornell University Press, 2008.

Bell, Amy. "Landscapes of Fear: Wartime London, 1939–1945." *Journal of British Studies* Vol. 48 (2009), pp. 153–175.

Berezin, Mabel. *Making the Fascist Self: The Political Culture of Interwar Italy.* Ithaca: Cornell University Press, 2007.

Berrios, G. E. and Freeman, H. (eds). *150 Years of British Psychiatry, 1841–1991.* London: Athlon Press, Vol. I 1991; Vol. II 1996.

Binneveld, H. *From Shellshock to Combat Stress: A Comparative History of Military Psychiatry.* Amsterdam University Press, 1990.

Bock, Gisela and Thane, Pat (eds.). *Maternity and Gender Policies: Women and the Rise of the European Welfare States, 1880–1950s.* London: Routledge, 1991.

Bogacz, Ted. "War Neurosis and Cultural Change in England 1914–1922: The Work of the War Office Committee of Enquiry into 'Shell-Shock.'" *Journal of Contemporary History* Vol. 24 (1989), pp. 227–256.

Bourke, Joanna. "Disciplining the Emotions: Fear, Psychiatry and the Second World War." In Roger Cooter, Mark Harrison and Steve Sturdy (eds.) *War, Medicine and Modernity.* Stroud: Sutton Publishing, 1998, pp. 225–238.

Dismembering the Male: Men's Bodies, Britain, and the Great War. University of Chicago Press, 1996.

Fear: A Cultural History. Emeryville, CA: Shoemaker Hoard, 2006.

"Fear and Anxiety: Writing about Emotion in Modern History." *History Workshop Journal* Vol. 55 (2003), pp. 111–133.

Bowlby, John, Figlio, Karl and Young, Robert M. "An Interview with John Bowlby on the Origins and Reception of his Work." *Free Associations* Vol. 6 (1986), pp. 36–64.

Boyden, Jo and De Berry, Joanna. *Children and Youth on the Front Line.* New York: Berghahn Books, 2004.

Bradley, Kate. "Juvenile Delinquency, the Juvenile Courts and the Settlement Movement 1908–1950: Basil Henriques and Toynbee Hall." *Twentieth Century British History* Vol. 19 (2008), pp. 133–155.

Braybon, Gail and Summerfield, Penny. *Out of the Cage: Women's Experiences in Two World Wars.* London: Pandora, 1987.

Briggs, Asa. *The War of Words*. Oxford University Press, 1970.

Brooke, Stephen. "Evan Durbin: Reassessing a Labour 'Revisionist.'" *Twentieth Century British History* Vol. 7 (1996), pp. 27–52.

 Labour's War. Oxford University Press, 1992.

 "Problems of 'Socialist Planning': Evan Durbin and the Labour Government of 1945." *Historical Journal* Vol. 34 (1991), pp. 687–702.

Caine, Barbara. "The Stracheys and Psychoanalysis." *History Workshop Journal* Vol. 45 (1998), pp. 145–169.

Calder, Angus. *The Myth of the Blitz*. London: Pimlico, 1991.

 The People's War: Britain 1939–1945. New York: Pantheon Books, 1969.

Cameron, Laura and Forrester, John. "Tansley's Psychoanalytic Network: An Episode out of the Early History of Psychoanalysis in England." *Psychoanalysis & History* Vol. 2 (2000), pp. 189–256.

Carpenter, Humphrey. *The Envy of the World: Fifty Years of the BBC Third Programme and Radio 3, 1946–1996*. London: Weidenfeld & Nicolson, 1996.

Caruth, Cathy. *Unclaimed Experience: Trauma, Narrative and History*. Baltimore: Johns Hopkins University Press, 1996.

Ceadel, Martin. *Pacifism in Britain 1914–1945: The Defining of a Fight*. New York: Oxford University Press, 1980.

 Semi-Detached Idealists: The British Peace Movement and International Relations, 1854–1945. Oxford University Press, 2000.

Chodorow, Nancy. *The Reproduction of Mothering: Psychoanalysis and the Sociology of Gender*. Berkeley: University of California Press, 1978.

Clark, M. J. "The Rejection of Psychological Approaches to Mental Disorders in Late Nineteenth-Century British Psychiatry." In Andrew Scull (ed.) *Madhouses, Mad-Doctors and Madmen: The Social History of Psychiatry in the Victorian Era*. Philadelphia: University of Pennsylvania Press, 1981, pp. 271–312.

Clarke, Peter. *Hope and Glory: Britain 1900–1990*. London: Penguin, 1996.

Cocks, Geoffrey. *Psychotherapy in the Third Reich: The Goering Institute*. Oxford University Press, 1985.

Cohen, Deborah. *The War Comes Home: Disabled Veterans in Britain and Germany, 1914–1939*. Berkeley: University of California Press, 2001.

Cooter, Roger. "In the Name of the Child and Beyond." In Gijswijt-Hofstra and Marland (eds.) *Cultures of Child Health*, pp. 287–296.

Cox, Pamela. *Gender, Justice and Welfare: Bad Girls in Britain*. New York: Palgrave, 2003.

Crisell, Andrew. *An Introductory History of British Broadcasting*. London: Routledge, 2002.

Crosby, Travis, *The Impact of Civilian Evacuation in the Second World War*. London: Croom Helm, 1986.

Cunningham, Hugh. *Children and Childhood in Western Society since 1500*. New York: Longman, 1995.

Curran, James and Seaton, Jean. *Power without Responsibility: The Press and Broadcasting in Britain*. London: Routledge, 1997.

Damousi, Joy and Ben Plotkin, Mariano (eds.). *Psychoanalysis and Politics: Histories of Psychoanalysis under Conditions of Restricted Political Freedom*. Oxford University Press, 2012.

Danto, Elizabeth Ann. *Freud's Free Clinics: Psychoanalysis and Social Justice, 1918–1938*. New York: Columbia University Press, 2007.

Danziger, Kurt. *Constructing the Subject: Historical Origins of Psychological Research*. Cambridge University Press, 1990.

Dicks, Henry V. *Fifty Years of the Tavistock Clinic*. London: Routledge & Kegan Paul, 1970.

Doctor, Jennifer. *The BBC and Ultra-Modern Music, 1922–1936: Shaping a Nation's Tastes*. Cambridge University Press, 1999.

Donzelo, Jacques. *The Policing of Families*. New York: Pantheon Books, 1979.

Downs, Laura Lee. *Childhood in the Promised Land: Working-Class Movements and the Colonies de Vacances in France, 1880–1960*. Durham: Duke University Press, 2002.

Dwork, Deborah. *Children with a Star*. New Haven: Yale University Press, 1991.
War Is Good for Babies and Other Young Children: A History of the Infant and Child Welfare Movement in England, 1898–1918. New York: Tavistock Publications, 1987.

Dyer, Raymond. *Her Father's Daughter: The Work of Anna Freud*. New York: J. Aronson, 1983.

Eissler, K. R. *Freud as an Expert Witness: The Discussion of War Neurosis between Freud and Wagner-Jauregg*. Madison, CT: International Universities Press, 1986.

Elias, Norbert. *The Civilizing Process*, 2 vols. Oxford: Blackwell, 1978, 1982.

Ellesley, Sandra. "Psychoanalysis in Early Twentieth Century: A Study in the Popularisation of Ideas." Unpublished Ph.D. thesis, University of Essex, 1995.

Fass, Paula (ed.). *Encyclopedia of Children and Childhood: In History and Society*, 3 vols. New York: Macmillan Reference, 2004.

Felman, Shoshana and Laub, Dori. *Testimony: Crises of Witnessing in Literature, Psychoanalysis and History*. New York: Routledge, 1991.

Field, Geoffrey. *Blood, Sweat, and Toil: Remaking the British Working Class, 1939–1945*. Oxford University Press, 2012.
"Perspectives on the Working-Class Family in Wartime Britain, 1939–1945." *International Labor and Working-Class History* Vol. 38 (1990), pp. 3–28.

Fishman, Sarah. *The Battle for Children: World War II, Youth Crime and Juvenile Justice in Twentieth-Century France*. Cambridge, MA: Harvard University Press, 2002.

Fitzpatrick, John J. "Psychoanalysis and Crime: A Critical Survey of Salient Trends in the Literature." *Annals of the American Academy of Political and Social Science* Vol. 423 (Jan. 1976), pp. 67–74.

Fleay, C. and Sanders, M. L. "Looking into the Abyss: George Orwell at the BBC." *Journal of Contemporary History* Vol. 24, No. 3 (Jul. 1989), pp. 503–518.

Fonagy, Peter. *Attachment Theory and Psychoanalysis*. New York: Other Press, 2001.

Forrester, John. "'A Whole Climate of Opinion': Rewriting the History of Psychoanalysis." In Mark Micale and Roy Porter (eds.) *Discovering the History of Psychiatry*. New York: Oxford University Press, 1994, pp. 174–190.

Foucault, Michel. *The Archeology of Knowledge*. New York: Routledge, 1972.
The Birth of the Clinic: An Archeology of Medical Perception. New York, 1973.
Discipline and Punish: The Birth of the Prison. New York: Vintage Books, 1979.

Francis, Martin. *The Flyer: British Culture and the Royal Air Force, 1939–1945*. Oxford University Press, 2008.

Frosh, Steven. *Hate and the "Jewish Science": Anti-Semitism, Nazism and Psychoanalysis*. London: Palgrave, 2005.

Fussell, Paul. *The Great War and Modern Memory*. New York: Oxford University Press, 1975.

Gardiner, Juliet. *Wartime: Britain 1939–1945*. London: Headline, 2004.

Garland, David. "British Criminology before 1935." *British Journal of Criminology* Vol. 28 (1988), pp. 1–17.

   The Culture of Control: Crime and Social Order in Contemporary Society. University of Chicago Press, 2001.

Gay, Peter. *The Bourgeois Experience: From Victoria to Freud*, 5 vols. New York: W. W. Norton, 1999.

   Freud: A Life for our Time. New York: Norton, 1988.

Geissmann, Claudine and Geissmann, Pierre. *A History of Child Psychoanalysis*. New York: Routledge, 1998.

Gijswijt-Hofstra, Marijke and Marland, Hilary (eds.). *Cultures of Child Health in Britain and the Netherlands in the Twentieth Century*. Amsterdam: Rodopi, 2003.

Gilbert, Martin. *The Boys: The Story of 732 Young Concentration Camp Survivors*. London: Holt, 1998.

Gilman, Sander. *The Case of Sigmund Freud: Medicine and Identity at the Fin de Siècle*. Baltimore: Johns Hopkins University Press, 1993.

Gorsky, M., Mohan, J. and Willis, T. "Hospital Contributory Schemes and the NHS Debates 1937–1946: The Rejection of Social Insurance in the British Welfare State?" *Twentieth Century British History* Vol. 16 (2005), pp. 170–192.

Grayzel, Susan R. *At Home and Under Fire: Air Raids and Culture in Britain from the Great War to the Blitz*. Cambridge University Press, 2012.

   Women's Identities at War: Gender, Motherhood, and Politics in Britain and France during the First World War. Chapel Hill: University of North Carolina Press, 1999.

Greenberg, Jay R. and Mitchell, Stephen A. *Object Relations in Psychoanalytic Theory*. Cambridge, MA: Harvard University Press, 1983.

Grosskurth, Phyllis. *Melanie Klein: Her World and her Work*. New York: Knopf, 1986.

Grossmann, Atina. "Trauma, Memory and Motherhood: Germans and Jewish Displaced Persons in Post-Nazi Germany." In Richard Bessel and Dirk Schumann (eds.) *Life after Death: Approaches to a Cultural and Social History of Europe during the 1940s and 1950s*. Cambridge University Press, 2003, pp. 93–193.

Grosz, Elizabeth. *Volatile Bodies: Toward a Corporeal Feminism*. Bloomington: Indiana University Press, 1994.

Gullace, Nicoletta. *"The Blood of Our Sons": Men, Women and the Renegotiation of British Citizenship during the Great War*. New York: Palgrave, 2002.

Hacking, Ian. *Rewriting the Soul: Multiple Personality and the Sciences of Memory*. Princeton University Press, 1995.

Hale, Nathan G. *Freud and the Americans*, Vol. I, *The Beginnings of Psychoanalysis in the United States, 1876–1917*. New York: Oxford University Press, 1971.
  Freud and the Americans, Vol. II, *The Rise and Crisis of Psychoanalysis in the United States, 1917–1985*. New York: Oxford University Press, 1995.
Halfin, Igal. *From Darkness to Light: Class, Consciousness, and Salvation in Revolutionary Russia*. University of Pittsburgh Press, 2000.
  Terror in My Soul: Communist Autobiographies on Trial. Cambridge, MA: Harvard University Press, 2003.
Hardyment, Christina. *Dream Babies: Child Care from Locke to Spock*. London: Cape, 1983.
Harris, Jose. *Private Lives, Public Spirit: A Social History of Britain*. Oxford University Press, 1993.
  "War and Social Change: Britain and the Home Front during the Second World War." *Contemporary European History* Vol. 6, No. 1 (1992), pp. 17–35.
Harrison, Tom. *Bion, Rickman, Foulkes and the Northfield Experiments: Advancing on a Different Front*. London: Jessica Kingsley, 2000.
Haynal, André. "Central European Psychoanalysis and its Move Westwards in the Twenties and Thirties." In H. Ehleers and J. Lidi (eds.) *The Trauma of the Past: Remembering and Working Through*. London: Goethe-Institut, 1994, pp. 101–116.
Hearnshaw, Leslie S. *A Short History of British Psychology, 1840–1940*. London: Methuen and Co., 1964.
Heinemann, Elizabeth. *What Difference Does a Husband Make?: Marital Status in Germany, 1933–1961*. Berkeley: University of California Press, 1999.
Hellbeck, Jochen. *Revolution on My Mind: Writing a Diary under Stalin*. Cambridge, MA: Harvard University Press, 2009.
Hellman, Ilse. *From War Babies to Grandmothers: Forty-Eight Years in Psychoanalysis*. London: Karnac, 1990.
Hendrick, Harry. *Child Welfare: England 1872–1989*. New York: Routledge, 1994.
  Child Welfare: Historical Dimensions, Contemporary Debate. Bristol: Policy Press, 2003.
  "Children's Emotional Well-Being and Mental Health in Early Post-Second World War Britain: The Case of Unrestricted Hospital Visiting." In Gijswijt-Hofstra and Marland (eds.) *Cultures of Child Health*, pp. 213–242.
  Images of Youth: Age, Class and the Male Youth Problem 1880–1920. Oxford University Press, 1990.
Hendy, David. "Bad Language and BBC Radio Four in the 1960s and 1970s." *Twentieth Century British History* Vol. 17, No. 1 (2006), pp. 74–102.
  Life on Air: A History of Radio Four. Oxford University Press, 2007.
  Radio in the Global Age. Cambridge: Polity Press, 2000.
Hennessy, Peter. *Having It So Good: Britain in the Fifties*. London: Penguin Press, 2007.
  Never Again: Britain, 1945–1951. London: Cape, 1992.
Herzog, Dagmar. *Sex after Fascism: Memory and Mortality in Twentieth-Century Germany*. Princeton University Press, 2005.
Heywood, Colin. *A History of Childhood: Children and Childhood in the West from Medieval to Modern Times*. Cambridge: Polity Press, 2001.

Hilmes, Michele. "Front Line Family: 'Women's Culture' Comes to the BBC." *Media, Culture & Society* Vol. 29, No. 1 (2007), pp. 5–29.

Hinshelwood, R. D. "Psychoanalysis in Britain: Points of Cultural Access, 1893–1918." *Int. J. Psycho-Anal.* Vol. 76 (1995), pp. 135–151.

Hinton, James. *Nine Wartime Lives: Mass Observation and the Making of the Modern Self.* Oxford University Press, 2010.

Hoffman, Louise E. "War, Revolution and Psychoanalysis: Freudian Thought Begins to Grapple with Social Reality." *Journal of the History of Behavioral Sciences* Vol. 17 (1981), pp. 251–269.

Houlbrook, Matt. *Queer London: Perils and Pleasures in the Sexual Metropolis, 1918–1957.* University of Chicago Press, 2005.

Hunt, Lynn. *The Family Romance of the French Revolution.* Berkeley: University of California Press, 1992.

Hynes, Samuel. *A War Imagined: The First World War and English Culture.* New York: Atheneum, 1991.

Inglis, Ruth. *The Children's War: Evacuation, 1939–1945.* London: Collins, 1989.

Jay, Martin. *The Dialectical Imagination: A History of the Frankfurt School and the Institute of Social Research, 1923–1950.* Berkeley: University of California Press, 1996, new edn.

Jennings, Rebecca. "'The Most Uninhibited Party They'd Ever Been To': The Postwar Encounter between Psychiatry and the British Lesbian, 1945–1971." *Journal of British Studies* Vol. 47 (Oct. 2008), pp. 883–904.

Jobs, Richard. *Riding the New Wave: Youth and the Rejuvenation of France after the Second World War.* Stanford University Press, 2007.

Joicey, Nicholas. "A Paperback Guide to Progress: Penguin Books 1935–c. 1951." *Twentieth Century British History* Vol. 4 (1993), pp. 25–56.

Jones, Edgar. "Aubrey Lewis, Edward Mapother and the Maudsley." *Medical Journal* Vol. 22 (2003), pp. 3–38.

Jones, Edgar *et al.* "Civilian Morale during the Second World War: Responses to Air Raids Re-examined." *Social History of Medicine* Vol. 17, No. 3 (2004), pp. 463–479.

Jones, Ernest. *Sigmund Freud: Life and Work*, 3 vols. New York: Basic Books, 1953–1957.

Jones, Helen. *British Civilians in the Front Line: Air Raids, Productivity and Wartime Culture, 1939–1945.* Manchester University Press, 2006.

Joyce, Patrick. *Democratic Subjects: The Self and the Social in Nineteenth Century England.* Cambridge University Press, 1994.

Kahr, Brett. *D. W. Winnicott: A Biographical Portrait.* London: Karnac, 1996.

Kanter, Joel (ed.). *Face to Face with Children: The Life and Work of Clare Winnicott.* London: Karnac, 2004.

Kent, Susan Kingsley. *Aftershocks: The Politics of Trauma in Britain, 1918–1931.* New York: Palgrave Macmillan, 2009.

  Making Peace: The Reconstruction of Gender in Interwar Britain. Princeton University Press, 1993.

King, Pearl. "Activities of British Psychoanalysts during the Second World War and the Influence of their Inter-Disciplinary Collaboration on the

Development of Psychoanalysis in Great Britain." *Int. J. Psycho-Anal.* Vol. 16 (1989), pp. 15–32.

"The Evolution of Controversial Issues." *Int. J. Psycho-Anal.* Vol. 75 (1994), pp. 335–342.

"The Life and Work of Melanie Klein in the British Psycho-Analytical Society." *Int. J. Psycho-Anal.* Vol. 64 (1983), pp. 251–260.

King, Pearl and Rayner, Eric. "Obituary: John Bowlby (1907–1990)." *Int. J. Psycho-Anal.* Vol. 74 (1993), pp. 1823–1828.

King, Pearl and Steiner, Riccardo (eds.). *The Freud–Klein Controversies 1941–1945.* New York: Routledge, 1991.

Kohon, Gregorio (ed.). *The British School of Psychoanalysis: The Independent Tradition.* New Haven: Yale University Press, 1986.

Koonz, Claudia. *The Nazi Conscience.* Cambridge, MA: Harvard University Press, 2003.

Koven, Seth. "Borderlands: Women, Voluntary Action, and Child Welfare in Britain, 1840–1914." In Seth Koven and Sonya Michel (eds.) *Mothers of a New World: Maternalist Politics and the Origins of Welfare States.* New York: Routledge, 1993, pp. 94–127.

Kristeva, Julia. *Melanie Klein.* New York: Columbia University Press, 2001.

Kubie, L. S. "Edward Glover: A Biographical Sketch." *Int. J. Psycho-Anal.* Vol. 54 (1973), pp. 85–93.

Kurzweil, Edith. *The Freudians: A Comparative Perspective.* New Haven: Yale University Press, 1989.

LaCapra, Dominick. *Representing the Holocaust: History, Theory, Trauma.* Ithaca: Cornell University Press, 1994.

Langhamer, Claire. "The Meaning of Home in Postwar Britain." *Journal of Contemporary History* (Apr. 2005), pp. 341–362.

Laplanche, Jean and Pontalis, J.-B. *The Language of Psycho-Analysis.* New York: Norton, 1974.

Latour, Bruno. *Science in Action: How to Follow Scientists and Engineers through Society.* Cambridge, MA: Harvard University Press, 1987.

Lawrence, Jon. "Forging a Peaceable Kingdom: War, Violence, and Fear of Brutalization in Post-First World War Britain." *Journal of Modern History* Vol. 75 (Sep. 2004), pp. 557–589.

Leed, Eric J. *No Man's Land: Combat and Identity in World War I.* Cambridge University Press, 1979.

Leese, Peter. *Shell Shock: Traumatic Neurosis and the British Soldiers of the First World War.* New York: Palgrave, 2002.

LeMahieu, D. L. *A Culture for Democracy: Mass Communication and the Cultivated Mind in Britain between the Wars.* Oxford University Press, 1988.

"The Gramophone: Recorded Music and the Cultivated Mind in Britain between the Wars." *Technology and Culture* Vol. 23, No. 3 (Jul. 1982), pp. 372–391.

Lerner, Paul. *Hysterical Men: War, Psychiatry, and the Politics of Trauma in Germany, 1890–1930.* Ithaca: Cornell University Press, 2003.

Lerner, Paul and Micale, Marc S. (eds.). *Traumatic Pasts: History, Psychiatry, and Trauma in the Modern Age, 1870–1930.* Cambridge University Press, 2001.

Levene, Alysa. "Between Less Eligibility and the NHS: The Changing Place of Poor Law Hospitals in England and Wales, 1929–1939." *Twentieth Century British History* Vol. 20 (2009), pp. 322–345.

Lewis, Jane. *The Politics of Motherhood: Child and Maternal Welfare in England, 1900–1939*. London: Croom Helm, 1980.
  Women in Britain since 1945: Women, Family, Work, and the State in the Post-War Years. Oxford: Blackwell, 1992.

Leys, Ruth. *Trauma: A Genealogy*. University of Chicago Press, 2000.

Light, Alison. *Forever England: Femininity, Literature and Conservatism between the Wars*. London: Routledge, 1991.

Likierman, Meira. *Melanie Klein: Her Work in Context*. London: Continuum, 2002.

Limentani, Adam. "The Psychoanalytic Movement during the Years of the War (1939–1945) According to the Archives of the IPA." *Int. R. Psycho-Anal.* Vol. 16 (1989), pp. 3–13.

Logan, Anne. "'A Suitable Person for Suitable Cases': The Gendering of Juvenile Courts in England, c. 1910–1939." *Twentieth Century British History* Vol. 16 (2005), pp. 129–145.

London, Louise. *Whitehall and the Jews, 1933–1948: British Immigration Policy, Jewish Refugees and the Holocaust*. Cambridge University Press, 2003.

Lowe, Rodney. "The Second World War, Consensus and the Foundation of the Welfare State." *Twentieth Century British History* Vol. 1 (1990), pp. 152–182.

McClay, Wilfred M. *The Masterless: Self and Society in Modern America*. Chapel Hill: University of North Carolina Press, 1994.

Mackay, Robert. *Half the Battle: Civilian Morale in Britain during the Second World War*. Manchester University Press, 2002.

McKibbin, Ross. *Classes and Cultures, England 1918–1951*. Oxford University Press, 1998.
  Parties and People: England, 1914–1951. Oxford University Press, 2010.

Macnicol, John. "The Evacuation of Children." In Harold Smith (ed.) *War and Social Change: British Society in the Second World War*. Manchester University Press, 1986, pp. 3–31.

Maddox, Brenda. *Freud's Wizard: Ernest Jones and the Transformation of Psychoanalysis*. London: Perseus, 2007.

Mahood, Linda. *Policing Gender, Class and Family: Britain 1850–1940*. London: UCL Press, 1995.

Makari, George. *Revolution in Mind: The Creation of Psychoanalysis*. New York: HarperCollins, 2008.

Mandler, Peter. *Return from the Natives: How Margaret Mead Won the Second World War and Lost the Cold War*. New Haven: Yale University Press, 2012.

Marland, Hilary and Gijswijt-Hofstra, Marijke. "Introduction." In Gijswijt-Hofstra and Marland (eds.) *Cultures of Child Health*, pp. 7–30.

Marquis, Alice Goldfarb. "Written in the Wind: The Impact of Radio during the 1930s." *Journal of Contemporary History* Vol. 19 (1984), pp. 385–415.

Martin, J. P. "The Development of Criminology in Britain 1948–1960." *British Journal of Criminology* (Spring 1988), pp. 38–39.

Marwick, Arthur. *The Home Front: The British and the Second World War*. London: Thames and Hudson, 1976.

Mayhew, Ben. "Between Love and Aggression: The Politics of John Bowlby." *History of the Human Sciences* Vol. 19 (2006), pp. 19–35.

Mazower, Mark. *Dark Continent: Europe's Twentieth Century*. New York: Vintage, 1998.

Meisel, Perry and Kendrick, Walter (eds.). *Bloomsbury/Freud: The Letters of James and Alix Strachey, 1924–1925*. New York: Basic Books, 1985.

Melman, Billie. *Borderlines: Genders and Identities in War and Peace 1870–1930*. New York: Routledge, 1998.

Menzies, Isabel E. P. *Containing Anxiety in Institutions: Selected Essays*. London: Free Association Books, 1992.

Meyer, Jessica. "Separating Men from Boys: Masculinity and Maturity in Understandings of Shell Shock in Britain." *Twentieth Century British History* Vol. 20, No. 1 (2008), pp. 1–22.

Micale, Marc. *Approaching Hysteria: Disease and its Interpretations*. Princeton University Press, 1995.

Micale, Marc and Lerner, Paul (eds.). *Traumatic Pasts: History, Psychiatry, and Trauma in the Modern Age, 1870–1930*. Cambridge University Press, 2001.

Miller, Martin. *Freud and the Bolsheviks: Psychoanalysis in Imperial Russia and the Soviet Union*. New Haven: Yale University Press, 1998.

Miller, Peter and Rose, Nikolas (eds.). *The Power of Psychiatry*. New York: Blackwell, 1986.

"The Tavistock Programme: The Government of Subjectivity and Social Life." *Sociology* Vol. 22, No. 2 (May 1988), pp. 171–192.

Mitchell, Juliet. *Psychoanalysis and Feminism*. New York: Basic Books, 2000 [1974].

Mitchell, Stephen A. and Black, Margaret J. *Freud and Beyond*. New York: Basic Books, 1995.

Moeller, Robert G. "On the History of Man-Made Destruction: Loss, Death, Memory, and Germany in the Bombing War." *History Workshop Journal* Vol. 61 (2006), pp. 103–134.

Protecting Motherhood: Women and Politics of Postwar West Germany. Berkeley: University of California Press, 2003.

Morgan, Kenneth O. *The People's Peace: British History 1945–1989*. Oxford University Press, 1990.

Morris, Terence. "British Criminology: 1935–1948." *British Journal of Criminology* (Spring 1988), pp. 20–34.

Mort, Frank. "Mapping Sexual London: The Wolfenden Committee on Homosexual Offences and Prostitution 1954–1957." *Sexual Geographies: New Formations* No. 37 (1999), pp. 92–113.

"Social and Symbolic Fathers and Sons in Postwar Britain." *Journal of British Studies* Vol. 38, No. 3 (1999), pp. 353–384.

Moskovitz, Sarah. "Longitudinal Follow-Up of Child Survivors of the Holocaust." *Journal of the American Academy of Child Psychiatry* Vol. 24, No. 4 (1985), pp. 401–407.

Love despite Hate: Child Survivors of the Holocaust and their Adult Lives. New York: Schocken Books, 1983.

Mowat, Charles. *Britain between the Wars 1918–1940*. London: University of Chicago Press, 1955.

Murphy, Kate. "Women in the BBC: A History 1922–2002." Unpublished paper.

Newcombe, Nora and Lerner, Jeffrey. "Britain between the Wars: The Historical Context of Bowlby's Theory of Attachment." *Psychiatry* Vol. 45 (1982), pp. 1–12.

Nicholas, Siân. *The Echo of War: Home Front Propaganda and the Wartime BBC, 1939–1945*. Manchester University Press, 1996.

"From John Bull to John Citizen: Images of National Identity and Citizenship on the Wartime BBC." In Richard Weight and Abigail Beach (eds.) *The Right to Belong: Citizenship and National Identity in Britain, 1930–1960*. London: I. B. Tauris, 1998, pp. 36–58.

"'Sly Demagogues' and Wartime Radio: J. B. Priestley and the BBC." *Twentieth Century British History* Vol. 6 (1995), pp. 247–266.

Nolan, Mary. "Germans as Victims during the Second World War." *Central European History* Vol. 38, No. 1 (2005), pp. 7–40.

Oppenheim, Janet. *"Shattered Nerves": Doctors, Patients, and Depression in Victorian England*. New York: Oxford University Press, 1991.

Overy, Richard. *The Air War: 1939–1945*. London: Potomac, 1980.

The Morbid Age: Britain between the Wars. London: Penguin, 2009.

Owen, Alex. *The Place of Enchantment: British Occultism and the Culture of the Modern*. University of Chicago Press, 2004.

Packman, Jean. *The Child's Generation: Child Care Policy from Curtis to Houghton*. Oxford: Blackwell, 1975.

Paskauskas, R. Andrew (ed.). *The Complete Correspondence of Sigmund Freud and Ernest Jones, 1908–1939*. Cambridge, MA: Harvard University Press, 1993.

Pearson, Geoffrey. *Hooligan: A History of Respectable Fears*. New York: Palgrave, 1983.

Pedersen, Susan. *Family, Dependence and the Origins of the Welfare State: Britain and France, 1914–1945*. Cambridge University Press, 1993.

Pegg, Mark. *Broadcasting and Society, 1918–1939*. London: Routledge, 1983.

Peters, Uwe Henrik. *Anna Freud: A Life Dedicated to Children*. New York: Schocken Books, 1985.

Phillips, Adam. "Bombs Away." *History Workshop Journal* Vol. 45 (1998), pp. 183–198.

Winnicott. Cambridge, MA: Harvard University Press, 1989.

Pick, Daniel. *The Pursuit of the Nazi Mind: Hitler, Hess, and the Analysts*. Oxford University Press, 2012.

Pick, Daniel and Milton, Jane. "Interview with Betty Joseph." www.melanie-klein-trust.org.uk/downloads.

Ponting, Clive. *1940: Myth and Reality*. Chicago: I. R. Dee, 1991.

Porter, Roy (ed). *Rewriting the Self: Histories from the Renaissance to the Present*. London: Routledge, 1997.

Pronay, Nicholas and Taylor, Philip M. "'An Improper Use of Broadcasting...': The British Government and Clandestine Radio Propaganda Operations against Germany during the Munich Crisis and after." *Journal of Contemporary History* Vol. 19, No. 3 (Jul. 1984), pp. 357–384.

Quinodoz, Jean-Michel. *Reading Freud: A Chronological Exploration of Freud's Writings*. London: Routledge, 2005.

Rabinbach, Anson. *The Human Motor: Energy, Fatigue and the Origins of Modernity*. New York: Basic Books, 1990.

Raitt, Suzanne. "Early British Psychoanalysis and the Medico-Psychological Clinic." *History Workshop Journal* Vol. 58 (2004), pp. 63–85.

Rapp, Dean. "The Early Discovery of Freud by the British General Educated Public, 1912–1919." *Social History of Medicine* Vol. 3, No. 2 (1990), pp. 217–243.

"The Reception of Freud by the British Press: General Interest and Literary Magazines, 1920–1925." *Journal of the History of the Behavioral Sciences* Vol. 24 (1988), pp. 191–201.

Richards, Graham. "Britain on the Couch: The Popularization of Psychoanalysis in Britain, 1918–1940." *Science in Context* Vol. 13 (2000), pp. 183–230.

Ricoeur, Paul. *Freud and Philosophy: An Essay in Interpretation*. New Haven: Yale University Press, 1970.

Rieff, Philip. *The Triumph of the Therapeutic: Uses of Faith after Freud*. University of Chicago Press, 1987.

Ries, Paul. "Popularise and/or be Damned: Psychoanalysis and Film at the Crossroads in 1925." *Int. J. Psycho-Anal.* Vol. 76 (1995), pp. 759–791.

Riley, Denise. "Some Peculiarities of Social Policy Concerning Woman in Wartime and Postwar Britain." In Margaret Higonnet *et al.* (eds.) *Behind the Lines: Gender and the Two World Wars*. New Haven: Yale University Press, pp. 260–271.

War in the Nursery: Theories of the Child and Mother. London: Virago, 1983.

Roazen, Paul. *Oedipus in Britain: Edward Glover and the Struggle over Klein*. New York: Other Press, 2000.

Rodman, Robert. *Winnicott: Life and Work*. Cambridge, MA: Da Capo Press, 2003.

Rolnik, Eran J. "Between Ideology and Identity: Psychoanalysis in Jewish Palestine (1918–1948)." *Psychoanalysis and History* Vol. 4 (2002), pp. 203–224.

Osei Nefashot: Im Freud le'Eretz Yisrael 1918–1948. Tel Aviv: Am Oved, 2007 [in Hebrew].

Roper, Lyndal. *Oedipus and the Devil: Witchcraft, Sexuality and Religion in Early Modern Europe*. London: Routledge, 1994.

Roper, Michael. "Between Manliness and Masculinity: The 'War Generation' and the Psychology of Fear in Britain, 1914–1950." *Journal of British Studies* Vol. 44 (Apr. 2005), pp. 343–362.

Rose, Jacqueline. *Why War?: Psychoanalysis, Politics, and the Return to Melanie Klein*. Cambridge, MA: Blackwell, 1993.

Rose, Nikolas. *Governing the Soul: The Shaping of the Private Self*. London: Routledge, 1999, 2nd edn.

Inventing our Selves: Psychology, Power, and Personality. Cambridge University Press, 1998.

The Psychological Complex: Psychology, Politics and Society in England, 1869–1939. London: Routledge and Kegan Paul, 1985.

Rose, Sonya. *Which People's War?: National Identity and Citizenship in Britain 1939–1945.* Oxford University Press, 2003.

Ross, Ellen. *Love and Toil: Motherhood in Outcast London, 1870–1918.* Oxford University Press, 1993.

Roudinesco, Élisabeth. *Jacques Lacan & Co.: A History of Psychoanalysis in France, 1925–1985.* University of Chicago Press, 1990.

Saville, Eva and Rumney, David. *"Let Justice Be Done: A History of the ISTD, A Study of Crime and Delinquency from 1931 to 1992."* London: ISTD, 1992.

Scannell, Paddy and Cardiff, David. *A Social History of British Broadcasting,* Vol. I, *1922–1939: Serving the Nation.* Cambridge, MA: Blackwell, 1991.

Scarfone, Dominique. "'Controversial Discussions': The Issue of Differences in Method." *Int. J. Psycho-Anal.* Vol. 83 (2002), pp. 453–456.

Schafer, Sylvia. *Children in Moral Danger and the Problem of Government in Third Republic France.* Princeton University Press, 1997.

Schivelbusch, W. *The Railway Journey: The Industrialization of Time and Space in the Nineteenth Century.* Berkeley: University of California Press, 1986.

Schorske, Carl. *Fin-de-Siècle Vienna: Politics and Culture.* New York: Vintage, 1980.

Scull, Andrew. *The Most Solitary of Afflictions: Madness and Society in Britain, 1700–1980.* New Haven: Yale University Press, 1993.

Segal, Hanna. *Introduction to the Work of Melanie Klein.* New York: Basic Books, 1980 [1964].

Seigel, Jerrold. *The Idea of the Self: Thought and Experience in Western Europe since the Seventeenth Century.* Cambridge University Press, 2005.

Shephard, Ben. "'Pitiless Psychology': The Role of Prevention in British Military Psychiatry in the Second World War." *History of Psychiatry* Vol. 10 (1999), pp. 491–524.

 A War of Nerves: Soldiers and Psychiatrists in the Twentieth Century. Cambridge, MA: Harvard University Press, 2001.

Sherry, Norman. *The Life of Graham Greene,* Vol. I, *1904–1939.* New York: Penguin, 1989.

Showalter, Elaine. *The Female Malady: Women, Madness and English Culture, 1830–1980.* London: Virago, 1987.

Smith, Bonnie G. *The Gender of History.* Cambridge, MA: Harvard University Press, 1998.

Smith, David. "Juvenile Delinquency in Britain in the First World War." *Criminal Justice History* Vol. 11 (1990), pp. 119–145.

 "Juvenile Delinquency in the British Zone of Germany, 1945–1951." *German History* Vol. 12 (1994), pp. 39–63.

 "Official Responses to Juvenile Delinquency in Scotland during the Second World War." *Twentieth Century British History* Vol. 18, No. 1 (2007), pp. 78–105.

Smith, Harold. *Britain and 1940: History, Myth and Popular Memory.* London: Routledge, 2000.

Smithies, Edward. *Crime in Wartime: A Social History of Crime in World War II.* London: Allen & Unwin, 1982.

Snodgrass, David. "The Debate over a Style for Serious Radio Talks on the BBC: 1946–1957." *Journal of Radio Studies* Vol. 10, No. 1 (2003), pp. 104–119.

Spillius, Elizabeth. "Developments in Kleinian Thought: Overview and Personal View." *Psychoanalytic Inquiry* Vol. 14 (1994), pp. 324–364.

"Freud and Klein on the Concept of Phantasy." *Int. J. Psycho-Anal.* Vol. 82 (2001), pp. 361–373.

"Melanie Klein Revisited: Her Unpublished Thoughts on Technique." In Elizabeth Spillius, *Encounters with Melanie Klein: Selected Papers of Elizabeth Spillius.* New York: Routledge, 2007, pp. 67–86.

Melanie Klein Today: Developments in Theory and Practice. London: Routledge, 1988.

Springhall, J. *Coming of Age: Adolescence in Britain, 1860–1960.* Dublin: Gill & Macmillan, 1986.

Stargardt, Nicholas. *Witnesses of War: Children's Lives under the Nazis.* London: Jonathan Cape, 2005.

Steedman, Carolyn. *Landscape for a Good Woman: A Story of Two Lives.* New Brunswick, NJ: Rutgers University Press, 1987.

Strange Dislocations: Childhood and the Idea of Human Interiority, 1780–1930. Cambridge, MA: Harvard University Press, 1995.

Steiner, Riccardo. "It Is a New Kind of Diaspora." *Int. R. Psycho-Anal.* Vol. 16 (1989), pp. 35–72.

"It Is a New Kind of Diaspora": Explorations in the Sociopolitical and Cultural Context of Psychoanalysis. London: Karnac Books, 2000.

Tradition, Change, Creativity: Repercussions of the New Diaspora on Aspects of British Psychoanalysis. London: Karnac Books, 2000.

Stenton, Michael. *Radio London and Resistance in Occupied Europe: British Political Warfare, 1939–1943.* Oxford University Press, 2000.

Stone, Dan. *Responses to Nazism in Britain, 1933–1939.* New York: Palgrave, 2003.

Stone, Martin. "Shellshock and the Psychologists." In W. F. Bynum, Roy Porter and Michael Shepherd (eds.) *The Anatomy of Madness*, Vol. II. London: Tavistock Publications, 1985, pp. 242–271.

Stonebridge, Lyndsey. "Anxiety at a Time of Crisis." *History Workshop Journal* Vol. 45 (1998), pp. 171–182.

The Destructive Element: British Psychoanalysis and Modernism. New York: Routledge, 1998.

Sulloway, Frank. *Freud, Biologist of the Mind.* New York: Basic Books, 1979.

Tanaka, Yuki and Young, B. Marilyn (eds.). *Bombing Civilians: A Twentieth-Century History.* New York: New Press, 2009.

Taylor, Charles. *Sources of the Self: The Making of Modern Identity.* Cambridge University Press, 1989.

Thane, Pat. "Family Life and 'Normality' in Postwar Britain." In Richard Bessel and Dirk Schumann (eds.) *Life after Death: Approaches to Cultural and Social History of Europe during the 1940s and 1950s.* Cambridge University Press, 2003, pp. 193–210.

Foundations of the Welfare State. London: Longman, 1982.

Thom, Deborah. "The Healthy Citizen of Empire or Juvenile Delinquent?: Beating and Mental Health in the UK." In Gijswijt-Hofstra and Marland (eds.) *Cultures of Child Health*, pp. 189–212.

"Wishes, Anxieties, Play, and Gestures: Child Guidance in Inter-War England." In Roger Cooter (ed.) *In the Name of the Child: Health and Welfare, 1880–1940*. London: Routledge, 1992, pp. 200–219.

Thomas, Donald. *The Enemy Within: Hucksters, Racketeers, Deserters and Civilians during the Second World War*. New York University Press, 2003.

Thomson, Mathew. "Before Anti-Psychiatry: 'Mental Health' in Wartime Britain." In Marijke Gijswijt-Hofstra and Roy Porter (eds.) *Cultures of Psychiatry and Mental Health Care in Postwar Britain and the Netherlands*. Amsterdam: Rodopi, 1998, pp. 43–59.

"The Popular, the Practical and the Professional: Psychological Identities in Britain, 1901–1950." In G. C. Bunn, A. D. Lovie and G. D. Richards (eds.) *Psychology in Britain: Historical Essay and Personal Reflections*. Leicester: BPS Books, 2001, pp. 115–131.

Psychological Subjects: Identity, Culture, and Health in Twentieth-Century Britain. Oxford University Press, 2006.

"Psychology and the 'Consciousness of Modernity' in Early Twentieth-Century Britain." In Martin Dauton and Bernard Rieger (eds.) *Meanings of Modernity: Britain from the Late-Victorian Era to World War II*. Oxford: Berg, 2001.

"'Savage Civilization': Race, Culture, and Mind in Britain: 1898–1939." In Waltraud Ernst and Bernard Harris (eds.) *Race, Science and Medicine*. London: Routledge, 1999, pp. 238–258.

Thornes, Rosemary. "Parental Access and Family Facilities in Children's Wards in England." *BMJ* Vol. 287 (6386) (16 Jul. 1983), pp. 190–192.

Timms, Edward and Segal, Naomi (eds.). *Freud in Exile: Psychoanalysis and its Vicissitudes*. New Haven: Yale University Press, 1988.

Todd, Selina. *Women, Work, and Family in England 1918–1950*. Oxford University Press, 2005.

Trist, Eric and Murray, Hugh, "Historical Overview: The Foundation and Development of the Tavistock Institute to 1989." In Eric Trist and Hugh Murray (eds.) *The Social Engagement of Social Science: A Tavistock Anthology*. Philadelphia: University of Pennsylvania Press, 1997, pp. 1–46.

Tuttle, William. "Daddy's Gone to War": *The Second World War in the Lives of America's Children*. Oxford University Press, 1995.

Urwin, Cathy and Sharland, Elaine. "From Bodies to Minds in Childcare Literature: Advice to Parents in Inter-War Britain." In Roger Cooter (ed.) *In the Name of the Child: Health and Welfare, 1880–1940*. New York: Routledge, 1992, pp. 174–199.

Valiér, Claire. "Psychoanalysis and Crime in Britain during the Inter-War Years." In Jon Vagg and Tim Newburn (eds.) *British Criminology Conferences: Selected Proceedings* Vol. 1 (Sep. 1998).

van Dijken, Susan. *John Bowlby: His Early Life, A Biographical Journey into the Roots of Attachment Theory*. London: Free Association Books, 1998.

van Dijken, Susan *et al.* "Bowlby before Bowlby: The Sources of an Intellectual Departure in Psychoanalysis and Psychology." *Journal of the History of the Behavioural Sciences* Vol. 34 (1998), pp. 247–269.

Vernon, James. "The Ethics of Hunger and the Assembly of Society: The Techno-Politics of the School Meal in Modern Britain." *American Historical Review* Vol. 110, No. 3 (Jun. 2005), pp. 693–725.

Viner, Russell. "Melanie Klein and Anna Freud: The Discourse of the Early Dispute." *Journal of the History of the Behavioral Sciences* Vol. 32 (1996), pp. 4–15.

Wahrman, Dror. *The Making of the Modern Self: Identity and Culture in Eighteenth-Century England*. New Haven: Yale University Press, 2004.

Walsh, M. N. "The Scientific Works of Edward Glover." *Int. J. Psycho-Anal.* Vol. 54 (1973), pp. 95–102.

Waters, Chris. "Disorders of the Mind, Disorders of the Body Social: Peter Wildeblood and the Making of the Modern Homosexual." In Becky Conekin, Frank Mort and Chris Waters (eds.) *Moments of Modernity: Reconstructing Britain 1945–1964*. New York University Press, 1999, pp. 134–151.

"Havelock Ellis, Sigmund Freud and the State: Discourses of Homosexual Identity in Interwar Britain." In Lucy Bland and Laura Doan (eds.) *Sexology in Culture: Labelling Bodies and Desires*. University of Chicago Press, 1999, pp. 165–179.

Weeks, Jeffery. *Sex, Politics and Society: The Regulation of Sexuality since 1800*. New York: Longman, 1989.

Welshman, John. *Churchill's Children: The Evacuee Experience in Wartime Britain*. Oxford University Press, 2010.

"Evacuation and Social Policy during the Second World War: Myth and Reality." *Twentieth Century British History* Vol. 9, No. 1 (1998), pp. 28–53.

"Evacuation, Hygiene, and Social Policy: The Our Towns Report of 1943." *Historical Journal* Vol. 42, No. 3 (1999), pp. 781–807.

West, D. J. "Psychological Contribution to Criminology." *British Journal of Criminology* (Spring 1988), pp. 77–91.

Whitehead, Kate. *The Third Programme: A Literary History*. Oxford University Press, 1989.

Wills, Abigail. "Delinquency, Masculinity, and Citizenship in England 1950–1970." *Past and Present* (May 2005), pp. 157–185.

Wilson, Dolly Smith. "A New Look at the Affluent Worker: The Good Working Mother in Post-War Britain." *Twentieth Century British History* Vol. 17 (2006), pp. 206–229.

Wilson, Elizabeth. *Only Halfway to Paradise: Women in Postwar Britain, 1945–1968*. New York: Tavistock, 1980.

Winslow, Edward. "Keynes and Freud: Psychoanalysis and Keynes' Account of the 'Animal Spirits of Capitalism.'" *Social Research* Vol. 53 (1986), pp. 549–578.

Winter, Alison. "Film and the Construction of Memory in Psychoanalysis, 1940–1960." *Science in Context* Vol. 19 (2006), pp. 111–136.

Mesmerized: Powers of Mind in Victorian Britain. University of Chicago Press, 1998.

Wooldridge, Adrian. *Measuring the Mind: Education and Psychology in England, c. 1860–1990*. Cambridge University Press, 1994.

Wright, Martin. "Twenty Years of the British Journal of Delinquency/ Criminology." *British Journal of Criminology* Vol. 10 (1970), pp. 372–382.

Young-Bruehl, Elisabeth. *Anna Freud: A Biography*. New York: Norton, 1988.

Zahra, Tara. "Lost Children: Displacement, Family, and Nation in Postwar Europe." *Journal of Modern History* Vol. 81 (March 2009), pp. 45–86.

  The Lost Children: Reconstructing Europe's Families after World War II. Cambridge, MA: Harvard University Press, 2011.

  "'The Psychological Marshall Plan': Displacement, Gender, and Human Rights after World War II." *Central European History* Vol. 44 (Mar. 2011), pp. 37–62.

Zaretsky, Eli, *Secrets of the Soul: A Social and Cultural History of Psychoanalysis*. New York: Knopf, 2004.

Ziegler, Philip. *London at War 1939–1945*. New York: Knopf, 1995.

Zweiniger-Bargielowska, Ina. *Austerity in Britain: Rationing, Controls, and Consumption, 1939–1955*. Oxford University Press, 2000.

FILMS

Jennings, Humphrey and Watt, Harry. *London Can Take It!* London: GPO Film Unit, 1940.

Lowenstein, H. and MacCarthy, D. *Separations and Reunions*. Aylesbury: Stoke Mandeville Hospital, 1968.

Mason, Edward A. *We Won't Leave You*. Boston, MA: Documentaries for Learning, 1975.

Ramsey, Stephen. *Please Don't Leave Me*. New York: Australian Information Service, 1980.

Robertson, James. *Going to Hospital with Mother*. London: Tavistock Child Development Research Unit, 1958.

  A Two-Year-Old Goes to Hospital. London: Tavistock Child Development Research Unit, 1952.

Schlosser, Gary. *A Mother's Worry*. Los Angeles: Little Red Filmhouse, 1979.

Spitz, René. *Grief – A Peril in Infancy*. United States: The Researchproject, 1946.

DATABASES

Mass Observation Online: www.massobservation.amdigital.co.uk.

Psychoanalytic Electronic Publishing website and digital archive: The Standard Edition of the Complete Psychological Works of Sigmund Freud, www.p-e-p. org/ (SE/PEP).

The Times Digital Archive, 1785–1985: www.galeuk.com/times/.

Index

Abraham, Karl, 90
Adler, Alfred, 145
Adorno, Theodor, 110
Advisory Council on the Treatment of
    Offenders (1960), 185
Advisory Council Sub-Committee
    on Non-Residential Treatment
    (1961), 185
Aichhorn, August, 139
Ainsworth, Mary, 214
air raids, 24–47, 48–77, 86, 87–111, 178,
    180; sirens, 26, 39, 44, 45, 57, 73, 74
Allen, Lady Marjory of Hurtwood, 182
Ambrose, Tony, 214
Anderson, Benedict, 116
Anschluss, 88, 92–96
anti-Semitism, 3, 11, 14, 77–83, 90
appeasement, 96
Ariès, Philippe, 6
Attlee, Clement, 186
Auden, W. H., 10

Baldwin, Stanley, 32
BBC, 16, 22, 39, 56, 112–137, 230
behaviorism, 64–65, 123, 131, 133
Benzie, Isa, 112, 119, 129–135
Bernays, Minna, 69
Beveridge, William, 115, 178
Bibring, Edward, 13
Bibring, Grete, 13
Bion, Wilfred, 146, 221
Bloomsbury Group, 8
Boston, Mary, 214
Bowlby, John, 1, 13, 15, 16, 22, 55, 60, 62,
    104, 145, 166, 198–238
BPAS, 7, 8, 9, 11, 13, 14, 19–21, 48,
    49–52, 56, 72, 88, 90–92, 102, 104,
    148, 221, 237
Brierley, Marjorie, 221
British Film Institute, 222
British Journal of Criminology, 169, 173

British Journal of Delinquency, 146, 147, 169,
    173, 177
British Society for Psychical Research, 7
Britton, Clare, 63–64, 202
Brown, Felix, 40–41
Brown, William, 29
Bulldogs Bank, 16, 77–83
Burlingham, Dorothy, 66, 82, 214
Burt, Cyril, 141, 142, 206

Calder, Angus, 25
Calder, Ritchie, 45–46
Cambridge Evacuation Survey, 16
Cameron, A. C., 187
Care of Children Commitee (Curtis
    Committee), 1946, 64, 182, 189, 202,
    210, 224
Carroll, Denis, 145, 146, 161
Carr-Saunders, A. M., 144
Central Middlesex Hospital, 216
Chamberlain, Neville, 55, 96, 97
Child Care and the Growth of Love, 211
child guidance clinics, 42, 144, 146, 148, 149
child guidance movement, 65, 141, 149,
    150, 172
childhood, 1–23, 26–27, 30, 32, 36,
    38, 47, 49, 54–86, 89–90, 92–94,
    97, 102–104, 112–137, 139–141,
    147–151, 153, 157, 161, 164–165,
    168, 170, 175–177, 179, 180,
    182–184, 187, 188, 191, 193, 195,
    196, 198–238
Children Act, 1908, 140
Children Act, 1948, 141, 202
Children and Young Persons Act, 140, 166
Children's Hour, 117
Churchill, Winston, 33, 55, 101
citizenship, 49, 63, 66, 71, 76, 112–115,
    118–119, 124, 131, 141, 153, 158–161,
    165, 170–174, 180, 182, 200, 202,
    230, 233, 236

268

272   Index